A Long Way East of Eden

Could God Explain the Mess We're In?

Pete Lowman

PATERNOSTER PRESS

First published in 2002 by Paternoster Press

08 07 06 05 04 03 02   7 6 5 4 3 2 1

Paternoster Press is an imprint of Authentic Media,
PO Box 300, Carlisle, Cumbria, CA3 0QS, UK
and
PO. Box 1047, Waynesboro, GA 30830-2047
www.paternoster-publishing.com

British Library Cataloguing in Publication Data
A catalogue record for this book is available from the British Library

ISBN 1-84227-108-3

Cover Design by Compudava, Moldova
Typeset by WestKey Ltd, Falmouth, Cornwall
Printed in Great Britain by Cox and Wyman, Reading, Berkshire

contents

acknowledgements

Special thanks to friends who have helped during this project with encouragement and good counsel, particularly Chua Wee Hian, Lindsay Brown, Emma Carswell, Tony Graham, Tara Smith, Jonathan Francis, Anne Norrie, John Allan, Suzanne Valentine, Andy Draycott, Michael Ramsden, Ada Lum, James Catford, Vanessa Bronnert, Andy Bathgate, Nigel Pollock, John Ayrton and Paul Hine. Obviously this commits none of them to agreement with anything it contains!

Thanks also to the following authors, publishers, copyright holders and others for granting permission to use excerpts from the following works:

Excerpts from 'Choruses from the Rock', 'Burnt Norton', 'East Coker', 'Gerontion', 'Portrait of a Lady' and 'The Hollow Men' from T.S.Eliot's *Collected Poems 1909–62* are reprinted by permission of Faber and Faber Ltd. Excerpts from 'Choruses from the Rock' and 'The Hollow Men' in *Collected Poems 1909–62* by T.S.Eliot, copyright 1936 by Harcourt, Inc., copyright © 1964, 1963 by T.S.Eliot, are reprinted by permission of the publisher. Excerpts from 'Burnt Norton' in *Four Quartets* by T.S.Eliot, copyright 1936 by Harcourt, Inc. and renewed 1964 by T.S.Eliot, are reprinted by permission of the publisher. Excerpts from 'East Coker' in *Four Quartets* by T.S.Eliot, copyright 1940 by T.S.Eliot and renewed 1968 by Esme Valerie Eliot, are reprinted by permission of Harcourt, Inc. Excerpts from 'On The Move' from *Collected Poems* by Thom Gunn, copyright © 1994 by Thom Gunn, are reprinted by permission of Faber and Faber Ltd. and of Farrar, Straus and Giroux LLC.

Excerpts from 'The Dwarfs' from *Plays:Two* by Harold Pinter, ©1977, 1990 are reprinted by permission of Faber and Faber Ltd. and of Grove/Atlantic, Inc.

Excerpts from 'Sorry, But Your Soul Just Died' by Tom Wolfe, copyright © 1979 by Tom Wolfe. Originally published in *Forbes ASAP*. Reprinted by permission.

Thanks too for permission to use extracts from lyrics of the following songs:

'Precious Angel' by Bob Dylan. Copyright © 1979 by Special Rider Music. 'Like a Rolling Stone' by Bob Dylan. Copyright © 1965 by Warner Bros. Inc., copyright renewed 1993 by Special Rider Music. All rights reserved. International copyright secured. Reprinted by permission.

'Prove It All Night' by Bruce Springsteen. Copyright © 1978 by Bruce Springsteen (ASCAP). Reprinted by permission.

'My Father's House' by Bruce Springsteen. Copyright © 1982 by Bruce Springsteen (ASCAP). Reprinted by permission.

'Living Proof' by Bruce Springsteen. Copyright © 1978 by Bruce Springsteen (ASCAP). Reprinted by permission.

Lyrics from 'The Fear' (Cocker/Mackey/Banks/Doyle/Webber) © 1998 by permission of Universal Music Publishing Ltd.

Lyrics from 'Feeling Called Love' (Banks/Cocker/Doyle/Mackey/Senior/Webber) © 1995 by permission of Universal Music Publishing Ltd.

Lyrics from 'Wannabe', words and music by Emma Bunton/Geri Halliwell/Melanie Chisholm/Victoria Adams/Richard Stannard/Matthew Rowbottom/Melanie Gulzar, © 1995, reproduced by permission of Universal Music Publishing Ltd and of EMI Music Publishing Ltd, London WC2H 0QY.

'Papa Was a Rollin' Stone', words and music by Norman Whitfield and Barrett Strong © 1972, Stone Diamond Music Corp, USA, reproduced by permission of Jobete Music Co Inc / EMI Music Publishing Ltd, London WC2H 0QY.

'Bohemian Rhapsody', words and music by Freddie Mercury ©1975, reproduced by permission of B. Feldman trading as Trident Music, London WC2H 0QY.

introduction

The madman thrust in between them and fixed them with his eyes. 'Where is God?' he shouted. 'I'll tell you! We have killed him – you and I! We are all his murderers! But how have we done it? How could we drink the sea dry? Who gave us the sponge to wipe away the horizon? What did we do when we uncoupled the earth from its sun? Where is the earth moving to now? Where are we moving to? Away from all suns? Are we not running incessantly? Backwards, sideways and forwards, in all directions? Is there still an above and a below? Are we not wandering through an infinite nothing? Is not the void yawning ahead of us? Has it not become colder?'

–Nietzsche

You know the question I mean, and its cumulative disquiet, its compound interest. You ask yourself the question ... as you walk the streets among sons of thunder. New formations, deformations. Yogi know the question. It reads: *Just what the hell is going on around here?*

–Martin Amis, *God's Dice*

This is a book for the dissatisfied.

It explores some of the factors shaping our world. There are times when we need to check what's happening to our lives, medium-term. We can speed down a motorway catching up on dictation, or floating far away with a personal stereo; but unless we check the road periodically, we end up wrapped around a juggernaut.

Our concern in this book will be for realism, and for hope. Realism, because, among all our era's advantages, we sense something going wrong, and it would be good to know what it is. The *Titanic*'s cooking was superb, but that didn't make up for their failure to notice the icebergs.

Yet also hope; because, as we look at the issues in our society, we begin to see them resolving into a pattern that might be understandable. Sometimes they appear incomprehensible: we sense something going wrong, but we fear that beneath the surface there is nothing we can put our finger on, nothing but uncontrollable chaos.

Yet perhaps it isn't so. Maybe we are not powerless; maybe there is a piece we can insert into the jigsaw that makes some sense of the whole.

This book will explore the idea that many of our difficulties are connected; and, that in various ways they relate to the profound 'turn' in our culture that we call the 'death of God'. If this 'death' lies at the heart of our contemporary dilemma – 'postmodernity', as fashion has it – we need to understand it for what it is.

Now, a cross-cultural point: this writer is English, and a cultural mark of the English is that we distrust wide-ranging explanations and universal open-sesames. We're not optimistic Californians; we mastered Murphy's law in our cradles; we believe deeply that the bigger the idea, the less likely it is to work. As an Englishman, therefore, let me suggest that there is a logic to this suggestion which makes it worthy of some attention.

For most of us, 'God' is a shorthand for things on a distant mental shelf; things that can safely be neglected, or that have no reality at all. Yet, curiously, throughout history the vast majority of our race has been convinced of God's existence. Even today, much of humanity retains a faith in the truth of God and the supernatural. In most of the two-thirds world – in Nigeria, say, or Brazil or the Middle East – it can be difficult to find really thoroughgoing materialists. We who live in the little European peninsula sometimes have an inflated view of the significance of our fashions of belief; assuming that what the North Atlantic countries affirm must always be the truth.

But what would it mean if the majority were right; if this fundamental, worldwide tendency to belief in God corresponded to some deep, accurate intuition of reality? 'Western civilization' – the culture being promoted in Rio, Manila, Lagos and Calcutta with all the impact our education and media systems can muster – obviously marginalizes God. It trains us to leave him out, forget him, carry on without him. God is simply not an issue: faith, where it exists, is a private oddity. (You believe, and that's OK for you; I don't, and that's OK for me.)

At a purely logical level, that attitude might not seem too clear-headed. After all, if there were a 'Maker', then he/she/it could not, by definition, be merely 'unimportant'. Ignoring 'it' might mean losing sight of whatever purposes our world was built around. It might be like tossing out the central pieces of a jigsaw puzzle, yet still expecting the picture to make sense. And a few pieces should, here and there; but our carelessness could mean that, as a whole, the puzzle failed to fit together. ('Things fall apart; the centre cannot hold', as Yeats put it early in modernity.) In so ultimate an issue, our choice could have far-reaching consequences.

These consequences are what we aim to explore. This book isn't an attempt to show the coherence of Christianity. It's more interested in the *significance* of the 'God-question' in the first place. It aims to try out some ways of thinking: to explore some contours of the crisis facing us (and our children), and to see if the 'loss of God' explains some of that data. If we know what the issue is, we can start to deal with it properly.

Inevitably, what follows is impressionistic. It would be impossible for any writer to be an expert in all the fields we'll touch (still less one who isn't a full-time academic). The book's endnotes provide some pointers for further exploration. But the big, wide-ranging questions are worth raising, even at the cost of academic delicacy. What I'm trying to ask is, Does it look this way to you? Do you think there's a trend here, a logical progression? Do you think this might get us closer to what's happening?

I'd like to dedicate what follows to the Russian, Baltic, Finnish, Belarussian, Dutch, German and Swedish students who provoked and endured its evolution. My hope is that readers among them, and elsewhere, will have their reflections on our culture – and its poets, philosophers, rock-prophets, social pressure-points – enhanced and stimulated. I hope, too, that some will catch a little of the excitement I've felt; glimpsing a possibility that the issues are starting to fit together; the possibility that, maybe, we can get it right ...

But now let's turn to what's going on around – and inside – us ...

identity after God

who am I? what am I worth?

> 'The point is, who are you? Not why or how, not even what. I can see what, perhaps, clearly enough. But who are you? It's no use saying you know who you are just because you tell me you can fit your particular key into a particular slot, which will only fit your particular key, because that's not foolproof and certainly not conclusive. Occasionally I believe I perceive a little of what you are but that's pure accident. Pure accident on both our parts, the perceived and the perceiver. It's nothing like an accident, it's deliberate, it's a joint pretence ... What you are, or appear to be to me, or appear to be to you, changes so quickly, so horrifyingly, I certainly can't keep up with it, and I'm damn sure you can't either ... You're the sum of so many reflections. How many reflections? Whose reflections? Is that what you consist of? What scum does the tide leave? What happens to the scum?'
> –Pinter, *The Dwarfs*[1]

What are the most important questions in your life?

Whatever they are, they probably wouldn't have been the

vital ones for most of our ancestors. During much of the history of the west, many of the crucial issues have had to do with appeasing – surviving the final encounter with – God, or the supernatural. From the pyramids to the English long barrows, the remnants of most ancient societies reveal an anxiety to get things prepared aright for the afterlife. The question from Philippi, 'What must I do to be saved?', stands central to the Christian tradition (and from one perspective was the source of decades of seventeenth-century warfare). 'How can a mortal be righteous before God?' is Job's version, from the heart of the Jewish tradition.

Not now, however. In our century, these questions are sidelined as meaningless, or too difficult. The 'big issues' for most of us are very immediate. The questions of *purpose and desire*: What shall I try to do? What do I want, where is my life going and why? The questions of *love and friendship*: How can I find intimacy, get into a relationship that works? What is real love anyway? The questions of *truth* and *ethics*: How do I know what is right? How can anyone know? And the issues Pinter raises that will be the theme of this chapter, issues of *identity and self-worth*: Who am I? What is my significance?

Unsettling questions that hang over many a bathroom mirror:

> The girl entered our hotel room. It was the day after my wife and I had given a lecture at one of the universities in northern Europe ... She was a beautiful Scandinavian girl. Long blonde hair fell over her shoulders. Gracefully she sat down and looked at us with deep and vivid blue eyes ... As we discussed her problems, we came back again and again to one basic issue which seemed to be the root of all the others. She could not love herself. In fact, she hated herself to such a degree that she was only one step away from putting an end to her life ... We asked her to stand up and take a look in the mirror. She turned her head away.[2]

Arguably, what has happened in the west over the last four hundred years is that the 'individual', the 'self', has become more and more important, more and more central, has been blown up like a balloon – and then, suddenly, has exploded. We need to understand why. Who am I now? What do I matter?

Blowing the man up

It was inevitable that identity should become a key pressure point for us. Nor is it merely an issue for sufferers of extreme trauma, where the individual loses track of who she really is, of what value he has. All too many 'ordinary people' know too well what it is to struggle with these questions.

Part of the reason is sociological. The sheer growth of our urban populations inevitably raises the issue, Am I more than a drop in all this ocean? Technology, reducing all that we are to a nine-figure number, makes the question more pressing still. But if we really want to understand what's happening, we have to look further back. What we're facing is a problem with a history. We inherit the struggles of four centuries as we peer uneasily at our reflections.

The issue has been building up at least since the sixteenth-century 'Reformation'. The Reformation was one of the political and artistic turning points of our history; but it was triggered at the level of spirituality. Under the influence of Luther, Calvin and others, Christians across Europe broke free from the papal hierarchy. Up until then, the church's authority had dominated medieval belief, defining what was true and what was acceptable to believe. But now the war cry '*sola Scriptura*' arose: the Bible alone, not religious tradition, as the source of God's truth. For the first time the Bible became available in national languages, and each individual had the astounding opportunity of hearing God speak directly to them through it. No longer did they merely have to accept definitions of truth from the establishment.

And Luther, the arch-revolutionary, took a further step that gave crucial importance to the individual. He pointed Europe back to the heart of the original Christians' teaching. Our being accepted by God – 'justification' – was not first of all a result of institutionalized church rituals, said Luther. Rather, it was above

all an issue of personal *faith*, of the individual's staking everything on the confidence that Christ had died to reconcile each of
us to God. This was radical enough; no other world religion had
ever dared to downgrade the importance of human religious
efforts in this way. It was radically democratic, too, for it meant
that heaven and hell hung on the poor man's decision as much as
on the king's; and in the years that followed this would have
major political implications. It was not surprising that the result
was fierce conflict all over Europe, and that those who translated
the Bible into the languages of ordinary people often did so on
the run from the authorities.

But above all, the spotlight was now placed firmly on the individual as the centre of the universal drama. It was no accident
that Shakespeare chose to make Hamlet a student of Luther's
university at Wittenberg, when he presented him standing alone
with the whole of his destiny in his hands: 'To be or not to be,
that is the question.' If Luther was right, and the early Christians
he looked back to were right, then each human individual, great
or small, stood at the crux of history, with their thoughts and
choices having enormous, eternal importance.

Another crucial development underlined the individual's significance. Modern philosophy is often seen as commencing with
Descartes (1596–1650), who sought to know truth by building a
logical system upon one of the most famous assertions of history:
Cogito ergo sum, 'I think therefore I am.' Once he had established the reality of the self, Descartes thought, he had a foundation for everything else he believed. Later philosophers would
note that instead of starting with 'I think' (which assumed the
existence of the 'I' that he was trying to prove), he should simply
have said, 'There are thoughts ...' But at the time, his choice of
method was historically crucial: the individual soul stood alone,
heroic, all-important, at the centre of the universe, gazing
outwards ...

Descartes himself moved immediately from his proof of the 'I'
to a proof of God. God was rather necessary for Descartes, to
ensure that what the individual self saw wasn't a delusion. After
all, unless our perceptions were guaranteed by God, they might be

deceptions from a malignant demon. (It's a possibility that has fascinated modern science fiction (e.g. *The Matrix*): what if the world is not at all as it seems to me?) But many of the thinkers who followed were less interested in God. Thus, after the Reformation came a period known as the 'Enlightenment', in which we see our modern 'loss of God' beginning. One aspect of this enormously fertile era was its commitment to 'reason' over divine 'revelation': we learn about the world firstly by following what is plain to our minds, not what is revealed to us from heaven. God, says Paul Hazard, 'was relegated to a vague and impenetrable heaven, somewhere up in the skies',[3] banished to the periphery. He was the clockwork-maker, the God who set the world in motion but then left it alone. Scientific arguments for disbelieving in God would not be available for another hundred years; but God was already being pushed out from practical experience.

In our day, that process is almost completed. But the implications for our identity and value are huge. Once, we could know ourselves as being, each of us, a uniquely valuable creation from the hand of a loving, almighty Creator, charged with a destiny of enormous meaning. Our Father was our Maker, the supreme Artist; we could rejoice in glad self-acceptance at having been made as we are, and with a deeply significant future ahead. As one children's song from the Protestant tradition puts it, 'I just thank you, Father, for making me me.'

But now those beliefs are gone. The sky is emptied; heaven has gone away. We no longer feel we can depend on the reality and purposes of God. From being a unique creature of God, for whom the all-wise, loving Father has designed a unique purpose in life, the individual finds herself merely the product of blind forces.[4] For millions of years, the evolutionary mud-pond has bubbled away; now we've clambered to the surface, to bask for a few brief moments in the sun. Tomorrow, the mindless process hurries on again. We're products of chance, without any special 'soul'; less durable than an oak tree, and maybe (since there are so many of us) of less value than an advanced computer. If we slip under a truck tomorrow, there should be flowers on a grave somewhere for a fortnight, but there are many others to take our place. By the law of supply and demand, we have very limited significance.

Here is a pattern that we'll see a number of times in this book. The consequences of the death of God in a particular area are announced first on the intellectual level – by the artists, the philosophers, or both. It takes time for the implications to work through to street level and to our everyday consciousness. What makes our present situation fascinating is that this is happening, explosively, in several key areas at once.

Thus, some years ago, the biochemist Francis Crick, famous for his work on the DNA molecule, assessed the human situation after the death of God with straightforward directness. 'In your stream of consciousness ... the person isn't there. Again man is made up of only these mechanical factors ... It isn't just that God is dead; man is dead as well, because he becomes simply the product of the original impersonal with only the addition of the equally impersonal time and chance.'[5] For Crick, and for many more recent biochemists who have followed him, the individual has no uniquely valuable 'soul', nothing beyond the 'mechanical factors'. Reith lecturer Edmund Leach stated a comparable position: 'There is no sharp break of continuity between what is human and what is mechanical', no radical difference between machines and ourselves. (In that case the technology I use may have more value than I do. We sometimes feel that that is the management's attitude, too.)

'All kinds of materialism lead one to treat every man including oneself as an object', suggested the French existentialist thinker Jean-Paul Sartre, 'that is, as a set of predetermined reactions, in no way different from the patterns of qualities or phenomena which constitute a table or a chair or a stone.'[6] It happens that we can walk and talk, but that does not alter what we are: chance objects of no inherent value in a chance universe. Hollywood screen-goddess Raquel Welch put it more bluntly still: 'I am just a piece of meat.'

All that may seem fairly abstract, until the unemployment market brings the issue into the everyday. What gives us value as individuals, since there is no God? The question is not just a philosophical conundrum; it comes down to street level in a culture with so many ways of denying our worth. The job market underlines how many people there are who are just as skilled, as *valuable*, as we are; the presence of so many competitors trumpets our own lack of distinctiveness. We are dispensable; we have no obvious intrinsic value. The marriage market can have the same effect.

And looking for the further logic of this: how do we, in Sartre's terms, 'treat objects'? What do you do with stones? What do you do with meat? Does Raquel Welch's remark give us one way to begin to understand what underlies the horrendous misery embodied in the sexual assault rate, for example? (A gang of Harlem teenagers – mostly 14- and 15-year-olds – picked on a woman jogger in the park, beat her senseless, dragged her into the bushes and then raped her repeatedly. '*She wasn't nothing*', said one afterwards.)

> We are the hollow men
> We are the stuffed men
> Leaning together
> Headpiece filled with straw. Alas!
> Our dried voices, when
> We whisper together
> Are quiet and meaningless
> As wind in dry grass
> Or rats' feet over broken glass
> In our dry cellar
>
> –T.S. Eliot, 'The Hollow Men'

Sorry, but your soul just died ...

This was the title of a 1997 piece by Tom Wolfe, renowned culture-critic and king of the 'New Journalism'. In it he described what he claims to be 'the great intellectual event of the late twentieth century'. What did he mean?

Other chapters in this book will focus on areas of rock, literature, and popular culture. But here it's essential that we realize what's being debated on the philosophical and scientific frontiers. That's the theme of this next section. Some of what's being argued may seem strange and abstruse, but sooner or later it will impact us directly. And, if we intend to preserve our self-image against the logic from those frontiers, we will need a good basis for doing so.

What's increasingly at stake is the suggestion that, as Crick put it, with God dead, 'the person isn't there'. The permanent 'soul' described in (for example) the Bible simply doesn't exist. For many thinkers on the cutting-edge, there is no real 'I'. A series of mental and bodily events take place within the same skin, but that may not amount to something stable enough to justify the notion of personhood.

The radical doubts about the self came into the arts first. George Steiner, in *Real Presences*, sees the trend starting a century ago. He points to the French poet Rimbaud and his famous statement '*Je est un autre*', 'I is somebody else'. This, comments Steiner, was a 'provocation' that 'is deliberately, necessarily, anti-theological. As invariably in Rimbaud, the target is God ... "*Je est un autre*" is an uncompromising negation of the supreme ... act of grammatical self-definition in God's "I am who I am" ' (God's self-revelation in the book of Exodus).[7] Rimbaud, says Steiner, was querying the self so as to deny God; that's where it starts.

The consequences of that denial of the divine 'I Am' for our human 'I Am' become clearer half a century later, in another anti-Christian French writer. In Sartre's novel *Nausea*, the central character Roquentin reaches this conclusion:

> Now when I say "I", it seems hollow to me. I can no longer manage to feel myself, I am so forgotten. The only real thing left in me is some existence which can feel itself existing. I give a long, voluptuous yawn. Nobody. Antoine Roquentin exists for Nobody. That amuses me. And exactly what is Antoine Roquentin? An abstraction. A pale little memory of myself wavers in my consciousness. Antoine Roquentin ... And suddenly the "I" pales, pales, and finally goes out ...[8]

But the experience of being nobody isn't always so amusing or voluptuous. Besides, Sartre is cheating: 'Roquentin' may be a piece of poor classification, but Sartre tells his story as if it had some continuous meaning and Roquentin himself had a real personality. Other, post-war artists would experiment with going further. There are the cardboard figures of Ionesco's plays, for example. In *Waiting for Godot*, Beckett reduces his human beings to a pair of tramps hanging around nowhere in particular, visited by people who cannot remember them from one day to another. Then, in Beckett's later works, the personalities, such as they are, disintegrate – for example into the mad voice gabbling away, disconnected from any mind, in *Not I*. ' "I," say I. Unbelieving,' Beckett writes at the beginning of *The Unnameable*; and later: 'I won't say "I" any more, I'll never utter the word again; it's just too damn stupid. Every time I hear it, I'll use the third person instead.'

That denial appears elsewhere. Sociologist Erving Goffmann, for example, in *The Presentation of the Self in Everyday Life*, viewed the self as a 'peg' on which the clothes of the various 'roles' we play get hung from time to time; little 'substantial self' exists beyond the role-playing. More recently, the respected British philosopher Derek Parfit argues powerfully, in his widely-acclaimed *Reasons and Persons*, that 'persons are not, as we mistakenly believe, *fundamental*.'[9] A conscious atheist[10], Parfit deliberately sets himself against his own intuitions of personal identity as traditionally understood, that depend on a notion of a non-physical soul.[11] He argues from the personality changes observed when the brain's hemispheres are split that persons such as we usually 'believe ourselves to be' exist only in the very loose, conventional sense that nations exist.[12] We have no lasting personal identity beyond the physical continuity of our brains, and the psychological continuity of our experiences and memories.[13] Both these sources of our connectedness are very much 'a matter of degree'[14] and tend to lessen over time; and if anything happens to disrupt either of them (such as the division of the brain hemispheres), the unitive 'person' supposedly underlying them is revealed as illusory. Thus whether my future self should be described as 'I' is an 'empty question', says Parfit; there is no absolute difference 'between some future person being me, and his being someone else'.[15]

'What you are, or appear to be to me, or appear to be to you, changes so quickly, so horrifyingly, I certainly can't keep up with it, and I'm damn sure you can't either' (Pinter). And the same denial of the 'person' marks the current of ideas evolving under such names as post-structuralism, deconstructionism, post-modernism: thinkers like Barthes, Foucault, Derrida, and more recently Lyotard or Baudrillard. Sturrock, writing a few years ago, observed in some of these writers 'a common ideology ... of dissolution, of disbelief in the ego'. Barthes, for example,

> ... professes a philosophy of disintegration, whereby the presumed unity of any individual is dissolved into a plurality and we each of us turn out to be many instead of one. Barthes will have no truck with oneness, and certainly not with God, the One of Ones: he supports whatever is plural or discontinuous. Thus biography is especially offensive to him ... because it represents a counterfeit integration of its subject.[16]

The 'individual' thus becomes little more than an illusion, an 'unstable, replaceable form within a soulless system', or, as Culler puts it, an 'unstable collection of fragments with no unity or centre.'[17] Sturrock links Barthes' thought to that of Foucault, to whom 'the self, in the traditional sense, would appear ... a "theological" notion, a false transcendence'.[18] For the neo-Freudian psychologist Lacan, the 'ego' is a false, if comforting, mental construct that we create because of such experiences as 'seeing ourselves reflected in mirrors and so assuming that we possess a permanent and unchanging kernel of identity'.[19] American postmodernist Rorty describes the self as 'a network of beliefs, desires and emotions with nothing behind it.'[20] Whereas in the 'modern' world the problem was the *alienation* of the self, argues Fredric Jameson, in postmodernity now the crucial issue is the self's *fragmentation*.[21]

Obviously such styles of thinking fundamentally challenge the assumption of the individual's coherent value. Not surprisingly, some of the most vocal objections have come from writers on the political left, who have seen that the 'end of the individual' might well mean the end of political ethics and morality. Sociologist Leo Lowenthal, one of the key figures in the Frankfurt School, has remarked,

> I am perhaps an old-fashioned man because I have the feeling that in the prevailing literary theory that is called post-structuralism, we are witnessing the further liquidation of the individual. And with that liquidation, we are losing all yardsticks of value, which connect aesthetic to ethical and political questions ... Nothing is very important, so anything goes. [22]

It is easy enough to understand his concern. Certainly the postmodernists have had a fascination for freedom, and an ideal of 'free play'. But the totalitarian possibilities of their denial of the individual are obvious. After all, if the 'individual' is an illusion, what price democracy, which is supposed to be based on the significance of the individual?

But the challenges to our 'sense of self' as a 'person' now come most overwhelmingly from psychology, where the idea of the individual 'mind', the 'ghost in the machine', has come to seem a clumsy and unscientific concept. As we grow more familiar with the workings of the human brain, we are increasingly able to identify what parts of the 'mechanism' trigger our experiences of pleasure, pain, fear, anger, sexual arousal, and so on. Indeed, as we become more aware of these triggers, the question arises as to how many can be duplicated, or even improved upon, by computers. Will computers soon be able to defeat any human chess–player (Gary Kasparov went down to Deep Blue in 1997)? Will computers – because they are 'better machines' – be able to synthesize a soundtrack giving greater stimulation to our pleasure-response than any human voice? Are human chess-players and human singers at the end of their respective reigns? Not only do we learn we are only machines, but it's doubtful whether we are even particularly competent ones.

But the behaviouristic school of psychology has asked more ruthless questions than these. John B. Watson, the founder of behaviourism, complained right back in 1930 that

> Human beings do not want to class themselves as animals. They are willing to admit that they are animals but "something else in addition". It is this "something else" that causes the trouble. In this "something else" is bound up everything that is classed as religion, the life hereafter, morals, love of children, parents, country, and the like. The raw fact that you, as a psychologist, if you are to remain scientific, must describe the behaviour of man in no other terms than you would use in describing the behaviour of the ox you slaughter, drove and still drives many timid souls away from behaviourism.[23]

What the 'timid souls' realize is, presumably, that this denial of any 'something else' – this insistence that 'morals, love of children, parents, country and the like' are no more than mechanical responses or animal drives – takes away much of their meaning. There is no reason why we 'ought' to act according to them, rather than by completely opposite stimuli and drives that might equally well be triggered within our mechanism.

Watson's most prominent successor was B.F. Skinner, famous for a book deliberately titled *Beyond Freedom and Dignity*. For Skinner, 'autonomous man', a person with a free will that is not determined by external causes, was 'a device used to explain what we cannot explain in any other way'. Now, however, we know that stimuli in our environment determine all our behaviour; ultimately, therefore, 'man is a machine', and the free individual is an illusion. So,

> to man *qua* man we readily say good riddance. Only by dispossessing him can we turn to the real causes of human behaviour. Only then can we turn from the inferred to the observed, from the miraculous to the natural, from the inaccessible to the manipulable.

But Skinner's attitude to that 'manipulation', in a world that denies the reality of individual freedom, had alarming, though logical, implications for democracy: 'A permissive government is a government that leaves control to other sources'.[24] A more logically-minded government might not make that mistake.

A final ingredient, however, comes with the development of sociobiology and genetic neuroscience over the last decade. These have switched the source of psychological control from the environments of the behaviourists to our evolutionary genetic inheritance – but in the process have made freedom, free will, even more improbable. 'Neuroscience, the science of the brain and the central nervous system, is on the threshold of a unified theory that will have an impact as powerful as that of Darwinism a hundred years ago,' argues Tom Wolfe.[25] The theory contends that our genetic history determines far more of our attributes than we will want to believe, determines them beyond our power to do very much about it:

> Many neuroscientists believe that genetics determine not only things such as temperament, role preferences, emotional responses, and levels of aggression, but also many of our most revered moral choices, which are not choices at all in any free-will sense but tendencies imprinted in the hypothalamus and limbic regions of the brain.

And younger scientists, says Wolfe, are now drawing the logical conclusion:

> Since consciousness and thought are entirely physical products of your brain and nervous system – and since your brain arrived fully imprinted at birth – what makes you think you have free will? What "ghost", what "mind", what "self", what "soul", what anything that will not be immediately grabbed by those scornful quotation marks, is going to bubble up your brainstem to give it you? ... You can look and look and you will not find any ghostly self inside, or any mind, or any soul

... just a genetic machine.

It is crucial to remember that all this follows from an assumption of the absence of God. Christians have always affirmed that a central aspect of the gospel is 'grace', the almighty power of

God's Spirit to break through any kind of determinism and create genuine free choice. Indeed, Christians would not be totally uncomfortable with the notion that, apart from the Spirit, psychological freedom is limited. St Paul described man's natural state as being in bondage to a process he termed the 'law of sin and death'; he used the word 'dead' to describe our natural condition, implying that only reunion with the 'Spirit of life' of God makes full personality possible. It is only 'if the Son sets you free' that 'you will be free indeed', in Jesus' words. There is also Paul's famous account of psychological determinism in practice: 'I am ... sold as a slave to sin. I do not understand what I do. For what I want to do I do not do, but what I hate I do.' He describes himself as 'a prisoner of the law of sin at work within my members. What a wretched man I am! Who will deliver me from this body of death?' – before adding, 'Thanks be to God, through Jesus!'[26] For Paul, the 'bondage' to physical drives is insuperable – until the supernatural (the 'miraculous', as Skinner terms it in the passage quoted above) is taken into account.

But now we know that there is no supernatural, what will all this mean in our culture? Wolfe's assessment is pessimistic.

The conclusion people out beyond the laboratory walls are drawing is: the fix is in! We're all hardwired! That, and: don't blame me! I'm wired wrong! ... The notion of a self – a self who exercises self-discipline, postpones gratification, curbs the sexual appetite, stops short of aggression and criminal behaviour – is already slipping away ... The male of the human species is genetically hardwired to be polygamous, i.e., unfaithful to his legal mate. Any magazine-reading male gets the picture soon enough. (Three million years of evolution made me do it!) ... Most murders are the result of genetically hardwired compulsions. (Convicts can read, too, and they report to the prison psychiatrist: "Something came over me ... and then the knife went in.") Where does that leave self-control? Where, indeed, if people believe this ghostly self does not even exist, and brain imaging proves it, once and for all?

(Other writers have observed that, if there is no such thing as free choice, it becomes much harder to distinguish murder from accidental stabbing;[27] it also becomes difficult to distinguish rape from normal sex.)

And where does all this leave individual significance? Wolfe continues,

> The peculiarly American faith in the power of the individual to transform himself from a helpless cipher into a giant among men ... is now as moribund as the god for whom Nietzsche wrote an obituary ... The most popular study currently ... is David Lykken and Auke Tellegen's study at the University of Minnesota of two thousand twins that shows, according to these two evolutionary psychologists, that an individual's happiness is largely genetic. Some people are hardwired to be happy and some are not. Success (or failure) in matters of love, money, reputation or power is transient stuff; you soon settle back down (or up) to the level of happiness you were born with genetically.

'Helpless ciphers'. Communist shop steward Jimmy Reid declared in his famous rectorial address at Glasgow University that the 'major social problem in Britain' was

> alienation ... the cry of men who feel themselves the victims of blind economic forces beyond their control ... the feeling of despair and hopelessness that pervades people who feel with justification that they have no real say in shaping or determining their own destinies.

Reid urged his students,

> Reject the values and false moralities that underlie these attitudes. A rat race is for rats. We're not rats. We're human beings. Reject the insidious pressures in society that would blunt your critical faculties ... This is how it starts, and before you know where you are, you're a fully paid-up member of the rat-pack. The price is too high. It entails the loss of your dignity and human spirit. Or as Christ put it, "For what is a man profited if he gain the whole world and lose his own soul?"

Fine words. But as we look back, Reid seems open to the accusation of talking mere emotive idealism. We *are* rats. Or have we any reason for believing – after the death of God – that we have a 'soul' to lose, that we can ever truly 'reject the pressures' in our environment or be anything but the victim of 'blind forces' beyond our control? What is this 'dignity' (the term Skinner hates) that Reid assumes as a given? 'We're not rats. We're human beings' – does that have defensible value, or does our increasing understanding reveal it as a sentimental slogan?

The issue we face, then, is that noted by Erich Fromm: 'In the nineteenth century the problem was that God is dead, in the twentieth century the problem is that man is dead.'[28] How long will all this remain a matter of esoteric doctrine, and how will it start to shape the ways we interact and care (or not) for each other? (Remember Sartre: 'All kinds of materialism lead one to treat every man including oneself as an object ... in no way different from the patterns or qualities and phenomena which constitute a table or a chair or a stone.') Do I have any true personality? Or am I simply lacking courage to face the conclusions reached by the 'cold realists' of the mind?

Humanistic psychologist Carl Rogers wrote:

> We are not fond of a mechanistically oriented, hard-headed empiricism. But what will we put in its place? An existential mysticism will not, in my judgment, be good enough. Private subjective opinion will not be good enough.[29]

So we arrive back from the scientific frontier to the bathroom mirror. Since we know there is no God, are my human 'dignity', my very individuality, merely comforting fables? Who, really, am 'I'?

Sorry, but your soul just died ...

What does it really mean when the concept of unified personality collapses?

One response: In a remarkable trial in Wisconsin, USA, Mark, a 29-year-old shop assistant, was accused of raping Sarah, 27. What made the trial unusual was that Sarah suffered from multiple personality disorder, and alleged that the sexual act they shared in his car was rape because it occurred without the agreement of her dominant, and indeed other, personalities. Mark, it was alleged, had summoned 'Jennifer', a 20-year-old personality who 'likes to dance and have fun'. But while they were having sex, a different personality called 'Emily' had appeared. (A psychiatrist told the court that Sarah's body was home to at least 48 different personalities.) 'Emily' informed the dominant 'Sarah' personality, and Sarah phoned the police to say that she had been assaulted.

As the trial proceeded, the judge and prosecutor questioned Sarah, and then 'summoned' and swore in both 'Jennifer' and 'Franny', a further personality inhabiting the same body (this time a '30-year-old').

Bizarre ... Yet if (as both psychologists and philosophers are telling us) none of our personalities are truly unified from month to month or even day to day, what is a judge – or anyone else – to do?

God and identity

'To treat every man, *including oneself*, as an object ... in no way different from a table or a chair or a stone.' In fact it is hard to live as if there were no coherent 'I' inside our skin. But the onus increasingly will be on us; we have to learn to handle the retention, or reconstruction, of identity after the death of God.

We have seen how the 'death of God' has led logically to the 'death of the "I" '. But it can also impact a related area that will decide our ability to feel comfortable about ourselves: our confidence of self-worth.

It's important to understand how much, experientially, the reality of God can mean for identity and self-worth. Sonship, and daughterhood, to the God who named himself 'I AM WHO I AM' can be a linchpin to the personality.

Several implications grow from the nature of God as Trinity.

First, Christians confess God as Father, as Creator. And if he is our Maker, then as we look at ourselves in the mirror, with all our follies and weaknesses, we know we are seeing a unique, eternal masterpiece ('fearfully and wonderfully made', Psalm 139), from the greatest craftsman in the universe.[30] Whether we like what we see or not, that gives us real worth – body and soul! If every least scrawl of a Picasso has tremendous value because Picasso made it, so we too as God's creations each have unimaginable, intrinsic worth. The nature of God as Creator also has enormous power to integrate and give value to our diverging roles. Because my Maker is my Father, then the many other parts of my life – my love, my work, my interests, my hurts – belong together and have significance, since they, too, are collectively foreseen and foreordained by a wise and caring God.

The word 'Father' presents another implication: that of profound and unconditional love.[31] It means that I am never truly alone, never truly lost: I can look up on a starlit night from a totally foreign city, and with me – yet also above the farthest galaxy – is one I can call Father, my Maker who loves me deeply as an individual, and on whom I can totally rely. 'I was built for infinite love from Someone who needs nothing in return, and for eternal impact through Someone whose purposes are supremely important. Only God can satisfy what my soul most deeply desires', writes Christian psychiatrist Lawrence Crabb.[32] To grasp that infinite, unchanging love is to begin to understand self-worth.[33]

Second, Christians confess God as revealed in Christ, God the Son; and a vital component of identity derives from the way Jesus treats people in the Gospels. Evidently his respect and his love do not have to be earned: we see this from the sensitive and affectionate way he relates to the poor, the aged, the failing and even the crooked. That, Christians believe, is the love and dignity with which we can trust him to relate to each of us.

But still more, self-worth derives from grasping the profundity of Christ's cross, and the forgiveness resulting from it. Christ's unimaginable agony on Calvary, dying (or, Christians believe, enduring 'hell') for each man or woman individually, shows the worth God sets upon every one of us. We learn that we are worth so much to God, loved so enormously, that the Father sent his own Son to die for us, exactly as we are. 'A friend is one who knows the worst about you, and loves you just the same'; that acceptance is both value and security.

As Keyes puts it,

> If your self-acceptance rests on maintaining an image of yourself as a nice, good person who never did anything wrong on purpose, then you cannot afford to allow much truth into your field of vision. True self-acceptance is in stark contrast to this self-delusion. Self-acceptance does not *survive* honesty; it rests on it ... The Christians are not people who are so brave or thick-skinned that they can face the truth about themselves unafraid; rather they are sinners who can face their sin because they have confidence that God has forgiven and accepted them in spite of it. The acceptance of God is the basis of self-worth.[34]

This sense of secure openness is the reverse of what sociologists such as Goffmann have described as the 'performing self', continually surrounded by scrutiny hence forever uneasily self-conscious. It is the haven that Bonhoeffer famously expressed from the Nazi jail: 'Whoever I am, Thou knowest, O God, I am Thine.'

Thirdly, identity and self-worth derive from God the Holy Spirit, whom Christians confess as God's presence in the soul of everyone who welcomes him. Each believer, says St Paul, now has a unique gifting from the Spirit 'for the common good', indispensable and irreplaceable.[35] Or, working with the different shade of meaning he employs in Ephesians: each believer *is* a gift of God to the total 'body' or community; and 'from him the whole body, joined and held together by every supporting ligament, grows and builds itself up in love' – but only 'as *each* part does its work'.[36] Each of us has value; each of us is unique; each of us is indispensable.

These elements don't constitute a simple, ten-minute route to a healthy self-image. They are concepts that take a great deal of reflection and meditation, amid ongoing life-experience, to internalize fully.[37] (That is why, for example, at the heart of Christian communal experience is the shared meal of bread and wine that Christ ordained as a symbol of himself and his cross, the broken body and the shed blood. As we partake of it, again and again and year after year, we reflect on its meaning for us from different angles, we come to grasp it ever more profoundly.)

DIY identity

But we now know none of that was true; we are merely products of an arbitrary process. We have bidden farewell to the loving Father-Creator who made us his masterpieces. The Christ who declared us worth hell on Calvary is also now dead for us. What this means is that our value has no *givenness*. Identity and self-worth become something we have to manufacture for ourselves, effectively or ineffectively, or else receive from others. What are the implications?

Many of us have friends who exhibit, say, aggressiveness, or depression, or unjustified insistence on their own failures – or we see traces of similar issues in ourselves. And we've found that these problems make sense when they're viewed in terms of self-worth and identity; just as physical symptoms make sense when fitted into, say, a framework of possible diabetes. Indeed, even truly healthy individuals can benefit from assessing where they're at with such questions – for example when we're taking time to reflect on the growth of our marriage, or on the kind of working situation in which we flourish.

And, culturally, these issues are becoming more urgent. It's widely recognized that the disintegration of stable parenthood, plus the dehumanizing pressures of contemporary life and the experiences of negation and rejection they bring, can pose a formidable challenge to our retaining adequate self-worth. And this experience of inadequacy may underlie a wide range of other problems: insecurity, self-disgust, over-anxiety, dependence, depression, self-pity, perfectionism, escapism, masochism, promiscuity, or a desperate quest to please others and find acceptance, if we blame ourselves; aggressiveness, resentment, hatred, the attempt to control or possess others, etc., if we blame our inadequacy on people outside us.[38] Keyes summarizes it like this:

> A person with a strong and true sense of identity will experience peace with self, others, and God. This person will have a certain self-forgetfulness, a lack of self-absorption and self-consciousness. By contrast, the person with a weak sense of identity is painfully concerned with him or herself. This person is keenly conscious of being one who is fragile, unreal, and unsubstantial and feels like a loosely held together collection of roles played to the audience of others' expectations and determined by forces outside of their control. They might describe themselves as masses of contradictory selves, or as several actors on a stage without a script or director. This lack of cohesion usually goes together with feelings of self-hate. Complaints of "I don't know who I am" often go along with "I can't stand myself".[39]

Reading these words after a discussion of postmodernism and neuroscience might well make us ask if the whole trend of western thought 'after God' isn't institutionalizing a broken sense of identity. Later in this book we'll see further grounds for such a concern. Keyes' useful study suggests that a sense of identity can be made up of four components: what he terms 'morals', or a clear sense of what things and values are 'more valuable than others ... worth living for, perhaps even worth dying for'; 'models', or examples ('heroes and heroines ... pictures, stories, images, things to aspire to'); 'dominion', or purposeful activity leading to 'mastery over some bit of the world to some degree'; and receiving and giving love. We shall see in the next four chapters that each of these has been rendered highly problematic by the 'death of God'. Purposeful activity is no longer easy to define;

values are notoriously unclear; the nature of the exemplary 'hero' is problematic; and we doubt whether love is anything more than a word. In all these regards, the contemporary west may have cut off the branches its identity was resting on.

If, then, self-worth is not for me a 'given', something intrinsic, it becomes something I have to earn, or construct. Thus our 'post-God' culture appears marked, all too often, by the pressures – and wrecks – of the battle to create our self-worth. How many ways are there in which different personalities respond to this dilemma? What (if not God, or besides God) are those things that make me feel good about myself, about being who I am?

Many of us find a real degree of identity in our job: *I have value because of my work*. 'I have that normal male thing of valuing myself according to the job I do', admitted Conservative politician Michael Portillo. John Thaw ('Inspector Morse') offered a particularly striking example in *TV Times*:

> I suppose I am a workaholic. It's all about needing to work to give yourself some importance, to prove that you exist. If I have a month or two off with nothing happening I get very fidgety, nervy, edgy. It isn't insecurity because I know there's work coming up. It must be, I suppose, that I need to work so as to be able to say to people: "Look, I'm here. I exist."

We would expect this to function as a significant area of identity for the craftsman, and for skilled – or powerful – professionals. (The apparently pointless nature of many contemporary jobs makes it less meaningful for others.) But it does leave us vulnerable: loss of work, through retirement or unemployment, comes to mean loss of identity. And since the one is inevitable and the other (now there are far fewer 'jobs for life') a strong possibility, to make our work the heart of our self-worth is to leave ourselves exposed. Hence, too, the fury of a Jimmy Reid against employers who 'see people as units of production' (that is, deny their value), and therefore disposable:

You have to see the hurt and despair in the eyes of a man suddenly told he is redundant without provision made for suitable alternative employment, with the prospect, in the West of Scotland ... of spending the rest of his life in the Labour Exchange. Someone, somewhere has decided he is unwanted, unneeded.

All of us rightly seek some self-worth in our achievements, what Keyes might term the 'mastery' element; that is, *I have value because I achieve.* The issue arising here is of a different kind: when success becomes not a component but a linchpin of our identity, we grow prone to the aggressive, stress-related 'Type A' behaviour that lies at the root of so much heart disease. The 'driven' personality, continually impelled to compete, to 'prove themselves', certainly hasn't 'achieved' one thing – self-worth itself. Schultze notes how this pattern is handed down in families where parents impose their own drivenness on their offspring, for whom it may have painful results – 'the common middle-class practice of imposing adult standards of competition and performance on young children, who then grow up to be fretful adults'.[40] Related, of course, is identity embodied in the accumulation of signs of past achievement – very precisely, of 'status symbols' (e.g. car size): *I must have value, because I possess.* That is a route to self-worth the marketing people want us all to follow. Schultze writes of American youth,

Having accomplished little with their own hands, their self-esteem is low and their dependence upon the products produced by others is very high ... Real joy is purchasing the latest product or catching the latest entertainment, especially if it bestows status. The pattern for finding identity and intimacy is increasingly clear: reach out and touch some*thing* – your wallet.[41]

('I shop therefore I am'; is the compulsive shopper using acquisition to try and fill a gap where the love of God could have been?)

For others, romance seems the most compelling route: *I have value if I am loved* – or alternatively, *I don't have value because*

I'm not loved. That is, 'If I could find the right partner, everything would be OK'; or even, 'A brief affair would put me right.' ('You're nobody till somebody loves you', to quote the title of a Dean Martin classic; or megastar Whitney Houston on her marriage: 'Women are supposed to have husbands; we validate ourselves that way.') Most of us will have experienced the sense of devaluation when a treasured love-relationship ends (or fails to come into being): maybe I have no value after all! ('Without you I'm nothing': the song title on Placebo adverts.) But to what extent does finding a partner solve the question in practice? Often a great deal; a positive, affirming relationship is an enormously healing contribution to a healthy self-image. The problems come when our sense of worth depends too strongly on our need to feel loved, leading us into unhealthy co-dependency (holding on desperately, by sex, to a poor relationship, because we dare not face losing it); or to draining our partner, putting demands on one relationship after another that destroy them. ('Prove to me you still care for me! Show me I am tolerable, loveable!') The situation is exacerbated now that sex no longer implies long-term commitment. The sexual embrace, where the ultimate openness could imply the ultimate loving security, becomes instead a proving-ground for technique, where once again value has to be earned. ('Did he think I'm good?')[42]

Are there pitfalls common to these DIY identities? Let's consider some others. *I have value because I look good*; in the mirror is a good body, accessorized with the latest styles – Comme des Garcons, Dolce e Gabbana, whatever. Great for clubbing, gym and disco culture; but trapped by the demands of this particular prison, we know, may be a 'poseur' – or an anorexic. (150,000 American women die of anorexia every year; up to 200,000 Britons suffer from anorexia or bulimia.) *I must have value because I am busy, because of my packed schedule*: the destructive self-worth of the workaholic. *I have value because people like (or respect or want) me*; leading perhaps to a different kind of vulnerability and servitude, where our self-worth depends on fulfilling others' expectations – but leading also, in some cases, to narcotics or unwanted pregnancy as we try to hold on to affection. (Marilyn Monroe became a supreme feminine icon; slept with a president, died in misery. 'Her sexual value to men was the only value she was sure of', writes Gloria Steinem. 'By exciting and arousing, she could turn herself from the invisible, unworthy Norma Jean into the visible, worthwhile Marilyn.') *I have value because I enjoy* – a sport, an art. This is maybe one of the healthiest approaches, because what gives identity is at a certain psychic distance from the self. Its disadvantage, albeit minor, is that my sense of identity becomes located largely in one segment of my time.

Then there is *I have value because I remember.*[43] For myself, photographs and souvenirs convey a real sense of the significance of the past, of meaning in the accumulation of experiences, in the binding together of memories. But there is vulnerability here too, once we cease believing in a loving, divine Providence who gives our lives significant direction. Does the past, indeed, have meaning? Or are all the memories and souvenirs merely a heap (as they may seem one day to my grandchildren) of pointless rubbish ... 'These fragments I have shored against my ruins' (T.S. Eliot)? (The question is answered clearly, and depressingly, in Beckett's glumly-titled play *Krapp's Last Tape.*) There is *I have value because of my pain*: where a hurt cannot be released, forgiven and outgrown, has to be remembered and cosseted, because it seems the only meaningful thing in a person's life. (An especially damaging variant is *I retain identity through my failure or my sickness*[44] – I am an alcoholic, I always fail, I am a depressive.) *I have identity because of what I belong to* – because of the party or the regiment or the religious sect, because I am gay, because of a Metallica jacket or a Millwall scarf ... Having a place where we truly belong is a basic human need, and a significant component of identity. But the need to turn it into a 'linchpin' for identity explains the bizarre degrees of loyalty we sometimes see; or the furious insistence on distinctness from other, similar groups. (Such tribalism seems an increasing feature of postmodernity.)

If 'creating our own identity' is a key issue in our culture, we might expect that the marketplace will attempt to satisfy our need (there is money in it) by offering a variety of off-the-peg identities. I am buying a new type of jacket; do I want to be that type of person? Reyner Banham wrote about the wide range of choice available in the purchase of a pair of sunglasses: 'That, probably, is what it's about anyway: instant role-playing. "Look, crowd, I'm John Lennon / Lolita / the dreaded Grimley Fiendish / les Tons-tons Macoutes / Beethoven / Brigitte Bardot / your Aunt Edna." '[45] ('You're the sum of so many reflections' (Pinter) . . .)

The snag with DIY

'*The point is*', asks Pinter in *The Dwarfs*, '*who are you?*'

What is happening in these examples? Nearly all the sources we have described have their place in a mature sense of identity. Even suffering, properly 'digested', is surely a component of mature identity. But one thing has disappeared with the 'death of God': the 'linchpin' to a coherent framework in which the different aspects of identity find their place.

In the Christian picture, our sense of identity is made up of numerous components, none absolutely crucial but each finding its place in relation to our inmost self's central, immutable relationship with God. (Bonhoeffer again: 'Whoever I am, Thou knowest, O God, I am Thine.') With that relationship gone, however, there is no centre to the framework. For some of us, then, a difficulty lies in retaining a sense of identity from various unrelated components, which come and go at different stages. The result can be that the framework lacks coherence; nothing quite brings the sense of identity, and we sense we're playing a fragmented, unstable hotchpotch of disconnected roles: 'several actors on a stage without script or director', to cite Keyes again. (Or we may feel like we're posing, or inauthentic; 29% of all

Americans say they feel like a fake, phony or hypocrite most of the time.[46]) Or, we may move different particulars into the central 'linchpin' role, the 'God-position' foundational to our identity. The result can be that good things become twisted and destroyed through carrying a weight they cannot ultimately bear.

What strain is created if we come to locate our self-worth and identity heavily in, say, our successes? To do so can involve the endless demand, Give me more: let me keep on achieving enough to reaffirm my value. Ordinarily, we may simply not get enough of the 'means' of identity to justify its central role in our self-worth. So we need more: more achievements, more assurances of love or likeability, more status symbols. A 'means' that could have been a simple source of pleasure becomes the source of a sense of failure, because it cannot offer enough to supply the self-worth we need.

From a Christian perspective, C.S. Lewis argued (for example in *The Great Divorce* and *The Screwtape Letters*) that putting anything other than God in the 'God-position' was an idolatry which ultimately both disappointed the idolator and distorted the idol. We can think of numerous examples. Children whose 'success' or 'happiness' is so central to the parent's self-esteem that the relationship becomes hopelessly controlling and unpleasant. Or, our identity so much needs the proof of love that our relationship becomes stifling; work means so much to our self-worth that it takes over our lives; the possessions or photos or souvenirs matter too much to be left where they can be enjoyed; the sporting ability matters so much that pleasure is destroyed because now 'winning is not the main thing, it's the only thing'. The same occurs in an identity-option we have not yet mentioned, *I have value because I help others*, when our need for self-worth manifests in a compulsion to know we have 'done good works'[47] – leading to a 'need to be needed' where our actions actually become counter-productive for others' self-reliance. Only God is big enough to fill the 'God-position'; but as God is dead we are forcing other things into his place, and that can destroy them.

Crabb comments interestingly about the need for us to take this weight off our relationships, if they are to be healthy. Inevitably, he suggests, there will be some sense of disappointment in any relationship, in any lover; the issue is what we do with that disappointment. It can lead us into bitterness, to a belief that no fulfilment exists anywhere. But if we cease making our relationship into an idol, and recognize its inadequacy to meet, totally, the thirst of our psyche, it frees us to receive the relationship, and the lover, for what they truly are. They can then be seen to have their own value, based on reality, but without having to satisfy all the demands of our psyche. 'When we learn to accept people who disappoint us by no longer requiring them to satisfy us, then we're free to love them, to reach toward them for their sake without having to protect ourself from feeling disappointed by their response to us.'[48] But Crabb writes as a Christian, assuming that we can find in God a deeper fulfilment for our identity.

There is a further snare to avoid. In locating our self-worth and identity within one area, we may create a prison for ourselves. If, deep down, our identity feeds on the thought, *I must have value since I have so much to do*, it creates a behaviour-pattern leading straight into servitude. But so too can I *have value because of my work* and *I have value if people like me*. Many of us have been down these roads.

And lastly, there is the issue of whether our source of affirmation will prove, if not a prison, then a house built on sand. 'I spent my years being a successful wife and mother. Is that it?' 'Did I want to spend my life getting to the top as a bureaucrat?' And we are vulnerable to their loss. Jesus told a famous story about the futile death of a rich man who had grounded his self-worth in his possessions. But the issue applies in numerous areas: we retire, or otherwise lose the work that is the base of our identity; our valued expertise grows obsolete; we grow bald, or pregnant, and no longer derive self-worth from our appearance; a lover or partner leaves us (one third of British marriages end in divorce), or dies. T.S. Eliot could write of being 'Fixed in the certainty of love unchanging', but Eliot believed in God.

In the absence of God, then, contemporary, postmodern (wo)man needs to be a skilled juggler: balancing value from various sources, over-committed to none. Here, perhaps, we see one of the roots of the 'cool', the detachment, that is a hallmark of postmodern identity. But here too is a root of that discontinuity in our sense of self that often seems to accompany it.[49] We are friend, lover, office performer, housewife, party girl, mother – depending on the occasion and the state of the hormones (and maybe someone different again on the internet). But we feel a lack of integrity, of a 'ground' on which all these hold together.

It should not be implied that the existence of God would provide instant solutions to these problems. Even the New Testament's concept of 'salvation' seems to be one where rebirth through the presence of God takes place at the core of our being, and then slowly spreads through different aspects of the personality. The 'ground' here is the conviction that there is a true and guaranteed identity that we grow into, and that, in time, integration will spread across the entire personality. We are loyal not to who we are (our genetics, environment, education, etc.) but to who we are becoming – the final integration towards which our identity develops, through all our diverse roles and experiences, under the lovingly creative hand of God. In his absence, however, no such final integration is guaranteed, and we are left with the discontinuities and inconsistencies on our own. To what extent can I then trust my intentions, make my promises? Who – or which – will I feel like tomorrow? Who will be inside this skin tomorrow?

The power alternative

There are also ways of resolving these tensions that are largely destructive – and for which our culture may pay a significant price.

Travellers in post-communist countries will have seen many cases of the self-worth of the bureaucrat, *I have value because I have power*; I can be reassured of my significance because I can keep people standing in line for hours. But in the west, too, the hunger for identity through power can lead to comical forms of status seeking. A Canadian friend, an office furniture salesman, expressed his amazement at the 'little opportunistic games' his business customers played. When a manager gets a new assistant, a new desk is needed, because his desk must be slightly bigger than his assistant's; his chair must not be quite the same.

But this can lead to something more serious. How do I know I have the power that gives me significance, unless I can see its effects experienced by someone else?[50] The obvious possibility is of a shift into *I have significance because I can cause inconvenience or pain*. ('Not to perish from internal distress or doubt when one inflicts great suffering and hears the cry of it', wrote Nietzsche, 'that is great, that belongs to greatness.'[51])

Many of the postmodernists, Foucault especially, would anyway insist that power-expression ('the endlessly repeated play of dominations') is the most basic reality of society. And all this is not restricted to the publicly powerful. Not long back I watched delivery men park a van in such a way that they successfully blocked a main street, including eight buses with all their passengers. The reaction, when they realized what had happened, was evident pleasure. Why is such a situation so satisfying? Or why is it enjoyable to block an underground train door, so preventing it from closing and the train from leaving? Surely the pleasure-element is the proof of my own significance through others' inconvenience.

And we can think of less petty examples. How far is this a key factor behind street violence ('Someone *is* going to notice me')?[52] Is it so unpredictable that a society which has lost its basis for identity as a 'God-given' should find its 'underclass' – those to whom it increasingly says 'You have no (spending) power, you have no value' – responding by proving their significance? If your name is visible in graffiti all over the Bakerloo line – or if you have broken someone's face – you have clearly shown that you matter, in their life at least; you are strong, semi-Stallone, quasi-Schwarzenegger. (Rape is often at root an expression of power.) The man who can halt a whole production process by putting glass in a tin of beans, or rat poison in a Mars bar, has likewise established his importance. A similar option is often celebrated in rap hits, where the musician's identity is affirmed in terms of competence for brutal violence.[53]

To the God-believer, there is a logic in why these things are so – and why they do not have to be that way. We don't have to be trapped in this wasteful battle to create worth and identity, if ultimately it's intrinsic, something given us forever by a God who loved us enough to die for us. Too many of us have become drawn into an exhausting struggle to validate ourselves, because we've lost that God.

But maybe he never existed. It does matter which is true.

> Here is a story told by Tony Blair, back when he was an ordinary Labour MP:
>
> 'Gary was walking home around midnight after an evening out in Spennymoor, Co Durham. He never saw his attackers clearly. They jumped on him from behind, stove in his face with billiard cues and left him bloody and unconscious. The object of the crime was not mercenary: no money was taken ... In another village only a few miles away, a different gang forced a car, driven by an elderly couple, to stop and smashed its windows and bonnet.'
>
> And what drove these gangs to violence? Their members, argued Blair, 'devoid of the discipline that comes from recognizing that the value of oneself is in some way related to the value given to others, prove their "worth", that they are "somebody", by inflicting fear upon someone else.'

Around the same time the trial took place of the 'Chelsea Mob', football supporters involved in brutal violence both in Britain and overseas. (During one ambush, of a Manchester City supporters' coach, they had kicked a policeman unconscious.) But the 'Chelsea Mob' weren't from the underclass; the leader was a solicitor's clerk with a respected City law firm. So what drove them on? At their trial, the police commented on the meticulous way the group recorded their deeds: 'A lot of these people are fairly insignificant individuals in their ordinary lives. Perhaps this was their way of achieving some glamour.' If significance can be found no other way, we may reach for it through 'inflicting fear upon someone else': self-worth through violence, identity through power ...

In summary...

Our loss of belief in God, and therefore in the 'soul', triggers major problems with questions like Who (or What) am 'I'? Dominant thinkers in contemporary psychology and philosophy are now sceptical whether there exists any 'I' to talk about. Even if there is, what value or 'worth' could 'I' possess? Self-worth, in our society 'after God', becomes something to be earned or constructed, with difficulty, rather than being gifted to us by a Creator.

The consequences, both personally and socially, can be painful and far-reaching. It matters very considerably whether there exists a God – and an 'I' – or not...

Additional note: Choice is all we need?

One other identity option, formerly quite significant, seems to be losing ground in our postmodern culture: the credo of existentialism, *I have identity because I create myself through my free choices*. In one sense this too derives from Nietzsche, the arch-exponent of the death of God. Nietzsche called for the emergence of the Superman who, knowing God is non-existent, knows too that all behavioural norms are buried in his tomb, and so steps out to create his own identity in his own way. Sartre was a key proponent more recently: 'If I have excluded God the Father, there must be somebody to invent values', he says.[54]

For this observer at least, there is doubt as to how far the act of choosing *entirely in itself* can now satisfy the need for assurance of identity at a gut-level. But there are three other points worth noting.

First, if the psychological determinists are right, the whole idea is absurd. If we have no free will, we cannot create our identity by our free choices. We do not 'decide'; at best we can 'predict' what we will do.[55]

Secondly, as the existentialists realized, if identity is created by free choice, then the originality of the choice is of prime importance. To fall in line with traditional ways of acting is an act of 'bad faith', is to forfeit identity. But then authentic, original action is defined not by itself, but by its opposition to or deviation from accepted norms. This creates a bondage – doesn't true freedom come when we do something neither out of subservience nor compelled by rebellion, but simply because it is the right thing? But the need to show deviation from accepted norms can drive us into dark places. The problems this creates are highlighted in Dostoevski's *Crime and Punishment*, where the key figure, Raskolnikov, murders a 'useless' old woman, to prove himself an individual of Napoleonic stature who can break free and create his own identity. Unfortunately, in the rest of the book he finds that good and evil are not dead, that crime is a reality.

If identity is something to be carved out in the face of the social totality, we would naturally expect the 'Rebel' to be a dominant mode. And so it was, in the period of mid-century modernity most influenced by existentialism. We find it in philosophy, in Camus (most obviously in *The Rebel*); in cinema, in James Dean (*Rebel Without a Cause*); in police thrillers, where the protagonist is so often a rebel-figure armed with a deft gun and equally deft one-liners (Clint Eastwood, Starsky and Hutch); in music, in Presley, Jagger, and successive subcultures – teddy boys, hell's angels, punk. The question is how far self-definition by 'rebellion' offers a lastingly satisfying base for identity on its own.

But thirdly, 'Create yourself by choosing' tends to be coupled with another contemporary commandment: 'Be yourself'. An episode of the American school soap 'Degrassi Junior High' presents a girl struggling to live up to an image that isn't really genuine, finally concluding 'I'm going to be myself'. When it's over, the announcer pauses before the next programme to tell his youthful audience, 'Being yourself is the most important thing, you know! ... I'm going to be me.' It appears so self-evidently right; yet it is a phrasing that would not exist in many cultural contexts. The Christian approach, as we noted above, would be significantly different. If there is a God who is steadily leading us into a glorious new identity, then the 'self' which deserves our loyalty is not one existing right now (which may well be scarred in all kinds of ways and trapped in self-destructive patterns; at best it is the product of our heredity and environment in a broken, 'fallen' world). Rather, we are called to be true to the self we will become. But all that presupposes the possibility of discovering the future identity and 'calling' that a God has purposed for us.

With God dead, therefore, 'Create yourself', or else 'Be yourself', became frequent guidelines for 'modern' identity. Yet don't these challenges sometimes sound like mockeries, when we are already doubting our self-worth and our ability to carve out our identity, as we take on the universe single-handed? And isn't that doubly the case when the brain scientists tell us we are merely being 'true' in our supposedly 'free choices' to the hidden stimuli of our genetics or environment; and the postmodernists explain that we have no stable core of 'self' to be 'true' to anyway?

Notes

1. Harold Pinter, in *Plays: Two*, pp.111–12.
2. Walter Trobisch, *Love Yourself: Self-Acceptance and Depression*, pp.7–8.
3. Paul Hazard, *The European Mind, 1680–1715*, p. xvii.
4. It is worth noting that this shift may also affect our perception of the whole natural 'creation' or environment. To call God 'Father' was to state that he alone was the one of whom the word could rightly be used; any earthly father merited the term only because, at his best, he might resemble the qualities of the divine Father. But the Bible presents God as the original, the archetype, of many other things: he is the 'true bread', the 'living water', the 'true vine', 'everlasting burnings', '*the* Rock', 'like a dove', and so on. It is as if God created a universe that is a colossal artwork full of revelations of himself! The loss of this vision turns the cosmos into something colder, less homely, more impersonal, more mechanical. Lynn Barber, in *The Heyday of Natural History*, points out that before the nineteenth-century loss of God, popular nature books sold almost as well in England as Dickens' novels. But once man no longer looked 'through Nature up to Nature's God', and 'the pious rationale had been removed, as it was so effectively after 1859 (when Darwin's *Origin of Species* was published), plants and animals lost their popular appeal.'

   The shift is obviously limited in its effect. But its end point would be the refusal of a postmodern novelist like Robbe-Grillet to countenance the use of the word 'sublime' for, say, Mont Blanc, which (he would argue) is imposing human categories of sublimity on something that existed without them for millions of years.
5. Quoted in Francis Schaeffer, *Back to Freedom and Dignity*, p. 19.
6. Jean-Paul Sartre, *Existentialism and Humanism*, p.45.
7. George Steiner, *Real Presences*, p. 99.
8. Jean-Paul Sartre, *Nausea*, p. 241.
9. Derek Parfit, *Reasons and Persons*, p. 445.
10. Cf. p. 454. Although Parfit presents his position as deliberately 'non-religious', he notes similar beliefs in the quasi-atheism of the original form of Buddhism, citing the following passages among others: 'Buddha has spoken thus: "O Brethren, actions do exist, and also their consequences, but the person that acts does not. There exists no Individual, it is only a conventional name given to a set of elements'

(p. 502). 'Here there is no human being to be found' (p. 503). ' "Nagasena" is only a name, for no person is found here' (p. 502). 'But when we use the expression "Caitra remembers", what does it mean? ... In the current of phenomena which is designated by the name Caitra, a recollection appears' (p. 503).

11. 'It is hard to be serenely confident in my Reductionist conclusions. It is hard to believe that personal identity is not what matters. If tomorrow someone will be in agony, it is hard to believe that it could be an empty question whether this agony will be felt by *me*. And it is hard to believe that if I am about to lose consciousness, there might be no answer to the question "Am I about to die?" ' (p. 280). But he adds, 'Instead of saying, "I shall be dead", I should say, "There will be no future experiences that will be related, in certain ways, to these present experiences". Because it reminds me what this fact involves, this redescription makes this fact less depressing. Suppose next that I must undergo some ordeal. Instead of saying, "The person suffering will be me", I should say, "There will be suffering that will be related, in certain ways, to these present experiences". Once again, the redescribed fact seems to me less bad ... The effect on others may be different' (pp. 281–82). This final sentence, at least, is probably correct.

12. Parfit, *Reasons and Persons*, p. 445. Cf. pp. 471–72: 'A nation is not a separately existing entity, something other than its citizens, and the land they inhabit. A nation's existence just consists in the existence of its citizens, acting together in various ways on its territory.' Parfit frequently selects the idea of the nation as a useful parallel for personhood.

13. Parfit, *Reasons and Persons*, p. 307.

14. Parfit, *Reasons and Persons*, p. 276.

15. Parfit, *Reasons and Persons*, p. 278. One of Parfit's qualities is his honesty about the weaknesses of his own position, and its potentially destructive implications. He cites his critics' claims that, if he was right, 'we would have no reason to be specially concerned about our own futures' (with indifference to continued life, or suicide, being a reasonable implication), 'and that most of morality would be undermined. These writers believe that it is only the deep further fact of personal identity which gives us reason for special concern, and supports most of morality. There seems to be no argument that refutes this view' (p. 445), although it can be 'defensibly denied' (p. 446). Even Parfit himself considers that the 'weakening

of psychological connections', and thus of our personal continuity, that occurs over time, may reduce the basis for both our 'responsibility for past crimes, and obligations to fulfil past commitments' (p. 446). (He is not the only one thinking in that direction: a recent postmodernist critic defended the wartime fascist outpourings of poet Ezra Pound by appealing to 'deconstruction's dematerialisation of an accountable self'.)

16. John Sturrock, ed., *Structuralism and Since*, pp. 15, 53. Terence Hawkes likewise links Barthes' undermining of human individuality with an assault on the Protestant notion of 'the individual's *personal* relationship to God' (*Structuralism and Semiotics*, p. 119).

17. Jonathan Culler, *Barthes*, p. 114. Culler cites Barthes' remark in *Le Grain de la Voix*: 'The subject that I am is not unified.'

18. 'Nothing in man – not even his body – is sufficiently stable to serve as the basis for self-recognition or for understanding other men', says Foucault in his essay 'Nietzsche, Genealogy, History'.

19. Sturrock, *Structuralism*, pp. 13–15.

20. Richard Rorty, 'Postmodernist Bourgeois Liberalism', *Journal of Philosophy* 80 (1983). This essay is reprinted in *Postmodernism: A Reader*, ed. Thomas Docherty, a fine selection which gives an excellent introduction to many aspects of postmodernism.

21. Fredric Jameson, *Postmodernism, or the Cultural Logic of Late Capitalism*, p. 63.

22. *California Monthly*, December 1984. Lowenthal described 'the work of all the members of the [Frankfurt] School' as focusing around the 'precarious fate of the individual in modern society', and added that, in his eighties, he wished to go on working on a counter-position to post-structuralism with regard to the 'concept of the individual', which 'has to be saved if everything is not to be allowed to go to pot'.

23. John B. Watson, *Behaviourism*, quoted in C. Stephen Evans' excellent study *Preserving the Person*, p. 46.

24. B.F. Skinner, *Beyond Freedom and Dignity*, pp. 191, 193. It is unsurprising that Skinner's rejection of the Protestant conception of the self should accompany a problematizing of democracy; there is a clear historical connection between the rise of Protestantism, with its emphasis on the value of the individual's choice, and the development of democracy.

25. I am deliberately using Wolfe's summary of the issues, because what is most important for our purposes here is not the precise

positions of scientific debate but the effect these have as they spread through the wider culture. Wolfe's article 'Sorry, But Your Soul Just Died' (which appeared first in *Forbes ASAP*) is alluding particularly to Edward O. Wilson, *The Insect Societies* and *Sociobiology: The New Synthesis*, and James Q. Wilson, *The Moral Sense*.

26. Romans 8:1; Ephesians 2:1; John 8:36; Romans 7:14–15,23–25. Of course the neuroscientific debate might well be viewed as irrelevant to the existence of God, since the maximum it could demonstrate was that the reasons why people believe or disbelieve in God were 'hardwired in' from the beginning. This would obviously not establish whether or not there was a God in the first place. It might even be congenial to the strictly predestinarian forms of Calvinistic Christianity.

27. Evans, *Preserving*, p. 72.

28. Erich Fromm, *The Sane Society*, p. 360.

29. Quoted in Mark P. Cosgrove, *Psychology Gone Awry*, p. 120.

30. The writer of Psalm 8 asks God, 'What is man?' And the answer comes back: '*You made him* a little lower than the heavenly beings and crowned him with glory and honour.'

31. In practical reality, any Christian pastoral worker will know how hard it is for many people to relate to the idea of God as being, in the richest sense, 'Father', because of their own experiences of negative or even abusive fatherhood. ('If he's like my father I sure would hate him', a New York kid told Carl Burke [*God is For Real, Man*, p. 133].) This can result in a series of dysfunctional relationships with authority figures – and with God. One book on this area that seems extremely valuable in practice is Floyd McClung, *The Father Heart of God*.

32. Lawrence Crabb, *Inside Out*, p. 82.

33. 'God's love is not only at the root of the divine decision to create the world (answering the question *why* God created) but also describes the most fundamental character of reality (*what* God created) ... It is, therefore, not trite to respond to Descartes' famous dictum *cogito ergo sum* (I think, therefore I am) with a more biblical *sum amatus ergo sum* (I am loved therefore I am).' (J. Richard Middleton and Brian Walsh, *Truth Is Stranger Than It Used to Be*, p. 149.)

34. Richard Keyes, *Beyond Identity*, p. 99.

35. 1 Corinthians 12:7,21–26.

36. Ephesians 4:7,11,16.
37. Keyes has an excellent chapter on this process in *Identity*, pp. 73–101.
38. This section draws heavily on material on inner healing developed by Jack and Mary-Anne Voelkel of the Unidad Cristiana Universitaria in Colombia, based on their extensive experiences with students in Latin America.
39. Keyes, *Identity*, pp. 4–5.
40. Quentin Schultze et al., *Dancing in the Dark: Youth, Popular Culture and the Electronic Media*, p. 257, citing *The Hurried Child* by child psychologist David Elkind.
41. Schultze, *Dancing*, pp. 11, 7.
42. African colleagues have mentioned another area in which relationships impact identity, *I have value because I have had a child* – or lack it because I haven't. In some countries, a woman could be a top lawyer, but without bearing a child she was a nobody. Indeed, a British Family Planning Association spokeswoman remarked recently, with regard to single mothers, that 'What is sad is that for some girls, a baby is the only possible way of giving their lives emotional meaning.' And remember the Burt Reynolds movie where its hero was desperately anxious to establish his identity by siring a child: 'He wants *you* to have his baby ...'?
43. 'Trained, shared remembrance ... safeguards the core of individuality. What is committed to memory and susceptible of recall constitutes the ballast of the self' (Steiner, *Real Presences*, p. 10).
44. A related variant is the therapy junkie: *I have value so long as a counsellor listens to me.*
45. Paul Barker (ed.), *Arts in Society*, p. 159.
46. James Patterson and Peter Kim, *The Day America Told the Truth*, p. 38.
47. A substantial part of St Paul's argument in Romans is directed against the misunderstanding that value can come from our own good works rather than from our acceptance by God through Christ.
48. Crabb, *Inside Out*, p. 108.
49. A number of ideas in this section derive from a valuable seminar led by Andrew Shudall of the Universities and Colleges Christian Fellowship.
50. Steiner notes that, from Hegel to Nietzsche to Freud, there is an influential theory of personality that is essentially a theory of oppression, of identity defined '*against* the identity of others ... The

consciousness of the full self will implicate the subjection, perhaps the destruction of another' (*In Bluebeard's Castle*, p. 46).

51. Nietzsche, *The Gay Science*, section 325.

52. In a perceptive chapter, Keyes comments on the way that anger, despite its destructiveness, can give a profound if temporary sense of identity: 'A particularly passionate expression of anger, especially if it involves physical violence, can have the psychological result of giving a person a sense of intense total involvement. They might experience an integration of their personality that they seldom find at other times. For this reason, some have compared violent anger to sexual and religious experiences of ecstasy. Rollo May points to a self-transcendence and total absorption that lies at the heart of many acts of violence and also explains the wider fascination with violence that most of us feel' (Keyes, *Identity*, p. 189; the reference to May is to *Power and Innocence*, p. 167).

53. For Surrealist leader Andre Breton, the ultimate expression of personal freedom, with God dead, would have been to take a gun and fire at random in the street. One British inner-city pastor remarked, after an outbreak of drive-by shootings, 'The problem is the young men have to have respect on the street. For the older community that means being Christian and having a good education. Now the young people earn this if they carry a gun.'

54. Jean-Paul Sartre, *Existentialism and Humanism*, p. 54. On p.28 he remarks that the individual's power to choose and so create himself is the reason why 'man is of greater dignity than a stone or a table … Man is, before all else, something which propels itself towards a future and is aware that it is doing so.'

55. 'It is not necessary to believe that a person's choices are always free to preserve the image of the personal, but it does seem necessary to believe that they are sometimes free. If [psychological] freedom is eliminated' (that is, if increasingly our 'choices' seem to be reactions to stimuli, internal and external, in a 'post-soul', totally material world), 'then the distinction between an action' (or an apparent choice) 'and a mere event disappears … Nor would the activity of deliberating or deciding what to do seem to have much point. It would seem more appropriate to attempt to *predict* one's future actions on the basis of past experience, just as one does not attempt to *decide* what a rock falling down a hill will do, but rather attempts to anticipate or predict its behaviour.' (Evans, *Preserving*, pp. 72–73.) But then no 'self' is being 'created by choosing'

(in Sartre's terms), in this world without God. (Remarkably, this 'predicting' emerges even at the close of Sartre's own *Existentialism and Humanism,* where he is questioned about a young man he had advised, 'seeking freedom', to 'choose, that is, invent' his future (p.38). Sartre's final words about this moment of 'choice' are 'Besides, I knew what he was going to do, and that is what he did.')

purpose and desire after God

'are we not wandering through an infinite nothing?'

What are we living 'for'? Where do we want to go, what is worth doing? 'Are we not wandering through an infinite nothing?'

It's Nietzsche's 'post-death-of-God' question; and it recurs in varying forms throughout our contemporary culture. A good example is the alien Wowbagger journeying through the 'infinite nothing' in Douglas Adams' outlandish and hilarious book *Life, The Universe and Everything*:

> Wowbagger the Infinitely Prolonged ... was a man with a purpose. Not a very good purpose, as he would have been the first to admit, but it was at least a purpose and it did at least keep him on the move. Wowbagger the Infinitely Prolonged was – indeed, is – one of the Universe's very small number of immortal beings. He had had his immortality thrust upon him by an unfortunate accident with an irrational particle accelerator, a liquid lunch and a pair of rubber bands ...
>
> To begin with it was fun. But things began to pall for him ... This was the point at which he conceived his purpose, the thing which would

drive him on, and which, as far as he could see, would drive him on for ever. It was this. He would insult the Universe. That is, he would insult everybody in it. Individually, personally, and (this was the thing he really decided to grit his teeth over) in alphabetical order.

Wandering through the emptiness, finding a purpose for the life I've got to spend. What is worth doing? Similar questions echo through Generation X novelists like Douglas Coupland and movies like *Slackers*. What is to be done? Can we do no better than divide our lives between McJobs that are meaningless, and relationships that reach the summit of desire one April and bitter disillusionment the next? What has gone wrong with us? Why is there so little left to dream for?

In any place, any century, anyone has to handle frustration. Yet now a deeper logic seems to underlie our sense of pointlessness, our feeling that so little is really worth doing.

French existentialist Camus, writing as an atheist, summed up the problem in *The Rebel*: 'Up till now, man derived his coherence from his Creator. But from the moment that he consecrates his rupture with him, he finds himself delivered over to the fleeting moment, to the passing days, and to wasted sensibility.' Camus' point is simple. Earlier in our culture's journey, we could feel deep confidence in a purpose that was in the truest sense a 'given': a God-created design for life that was knowable and worthwhile. Now, things are different, and pointless. 'A single sentence will suffice for modern man', Camus added in *The Fall*: 'He fornicated and read the papers. After that vigorous definition, the subject will be, if I may say so, exhausted.'

'From the moment that he consecrates his rupture with his Creator, he finds himself delivered over to wasted sensibility.' Again we're facing a theme crucial to the turbulent Reformation, with its rediscovery of the Bible. In the biblical world-view, we as human beings (no matter how infinitely prolonged) needn't struggle to construct our own purpose, wandering through a God-abandoned void. Rather, each of us can know what the Reformers termed a God-given 'calling'. The Latin for 'called' is *vocatus*; it's from the idea of God's specific 'call' that we get the term 'vocation', to describe any substantial sense of direction in our working lives. To Reformation thinkers, a job wasn't just a job: you were 'called' to it by God. Purposeful direction in life was the birthright of anyone within sound of the 'calling' of God. (A Californian expression of the same theme, popularized by the missionary organization Agape, runs: 'The first spiritual law is: God loves you and has a wonderful plan for your life.' The expression may sound crude, but the sentiments are historic enough.)

But things have changed. Now that design cannot be accessed; those 'callings' are vanished, inaudible. What results might we expect to follow?

This chapter explores that question. We will look first at some of the powerful ways it has been raised in literature and music; also some of the ways it's been answered. Then, we'll look at some of the alternatives that could replace God for us as 'sources of transcendence' and desire; and we'll consider what 'life-strategies' may become common if these solutions in turn prove unsatisfactory. Finally, we'll glance at the practical challenges all this is bringing to our lives.

The songs of the wanderer

Once again, it was the artists and musicians who saw the problem coming. The sense of loss is a mark of the arts of modernity.

'Droll thing life is', says the narrator of Conrad's novel *Heart of Darkness*, 'that mysterious arrangement of merciless logic for a futile purpose. The most you can hope from it is some knowledge of yourself – that comes too late.' 'Man's a useless passion', wrote Jean-Paul Sartre. Elsewhere he added, by way of diagnosis, 'A finite point has no meaning without an infinite reference point': if we have nothing eternal to measure our journeyings by, it becomes hard to perceive whether we are actually doing any meaningful travelling at all. In *The Sirens of Titan*, absurdist science fiction novelist Kurt Vonnegut offers the notion that the whole of human history has been masterminded to enable a stranded alien to get a spare part for his spacecraft; after that he can be on his way, and leave us (like Adams' Wowbagger) to our wanderings in the void.

Vonnegut and Adams are humorists and present Absurdity as comedy: the tragic Absurd can be found in (for example) Ionesco's brilliant play *The Chairs*. The old couple who are its central characters are cardboard cut-outs, scarcely human beings.[1] They are approaching the close of their lives, and the play's action concerns the arrival of an orator who will pronounce to the world their message, their whole lives' work. The orator arrives and the old couple jump into the sea. But the orator is incapable of anything but inarticulate grunts; and what he writes on the blackboard is jumbled rubbish.

If there is no meaningful shape to life, what stories have we left to tell? In France, this question has surfaced in a loss of faith in the whole notion of 'plot' – the idea that events can be depicted as a meaningful process that actually leads somewhere. In *Nausea*, Sartre makes his narrator Roquentin abandon his life's work on a historical biography for precisely this reason. However, later writers have accused Sartre of inconsistency: his own novels (*Nausea* for example) really do have plots and something meaningful does happen, even if it is only the gradual discovery of meaninglessness. More consistent might be a *nouveau roman* writer like Robbe-Grillet[2], whose fictions resolutely refuse to tell any discernible story. In the film *Last Year in Marienbad*, for example, for which Robbe-Grillet wrote the screenplay, it is impossible to know what is really going on. Or we might turn again to Beckett in *The Unnamable*: 'I invented it all', the narrator says of his story, 'in the hope it would console me, help me to go on, allow me to think of myself as somewhere on a road, moving, between a beginning and an end, gaining ground, losing ground, getting lost, but somehow in the long run making headway. All lies.' 'Nothing to be done', says Estragon in the opening words of *Waiting for Godot*; and, when the play ends, little or nothing has been.[3]

In the postmodern decades, that sense of 'plotlessness' has moved out into wider society. The ancient God-beliefs presented life as having a meaningful shape; with that gone, the value of almost anything we do becomes problematic. In an unexpectedly bleak finale to one of the Agatha Christie movies, the detective, having solved the murder, is leaving town. En route he encounters a Scottish policeman who has consistently hindered his investigations. 'You are right', he tells him. 'It wasn't worth it.' That doubt also creeps into the thriller, from John Le Carre onwards. *The Spy Who Came In From the Cold* closes with the killing of the girl who is the only lasting source of meaning in agent Leamas' life. In the chilling final sentence, Leamas' dying mind flashes back to an autobahn accident, a car full of laughing children crushed by blind and heedless forces: 'As he fell, Leamas saw a small car smashed between great lorries, and the children waving cheerfully through the window.' (The fatal loss of the lover in the story's closing moments is a powerful image in contemporary TV thrillers, conveying forcefully the ironic pointlessness of the whole activity.)

At the end of Bob Geldof's autobiography, Geldof tells the story of the magnificent Live Aid concerts that raised enormous sums for famine relief and were watched by more people than any other event in history. When it was all over, as everything was being cleared away, a kid shouted up, 'Hey! You! Is that it?' 'I wonder', wrote Geldof. *Is That It?* was the title of his autobiography.

In the absence of any end point, anywhere to journey towards, the journey itself becomes the only purpose remaining. 'To travel hopefully is better than to arrive', wrote Robert Louis Stevenson. Early last century, *The Journey, not the Arrival, Matters* was Leonard Woolf's version. Thom Gunn's famous bike-gang poem 'On the Move' strikes the same note:

One joins the movement in a valueless world,
Choosing it, till, both hurler and the hurled,
One moves as well, always toward, toward.
The self-defined, astride the created will
They burst away ...
At worst, one is in motion; and at best,

Reaching no absolute in which to rest,
One is always nearer by not keeping still.

The pilgrim-figure that embodied the ancient Christian image of life is replaced by the wanderer, the tourist, the sightseer. As far as any real point to the journey goes, you ain't goin' nowhere.

> To be on your own
> With no direction home
> Like a complete unknown
> Like a rolling stone
>
> – 'Like a Rolling Stone',
> Bob Dylan

Desire and modernity

Modern bureaucracy has its ways of turning the knife in the wound, of making our emptiness evident to us. Futility attaches to so much of our experience of employment. We have a job enabling us to work for money for food, to have energy to go back to work, to earn money for yet more food to go on working … For as long, downsizing and unemployment permitting, as we are a useful tool for someone else; then, after traversing that circle a few thousand times, what remains of us goes into a box, and the box goes into the ground. If we believed in a God, then we could believe in a purpose that made this activity 'vocational'. But if there is no such purpose, then the main function of work (for many of us) becomes securing a salary;[4] worthwhile activity we must seek elsewhere.

Other changes in society focus increased urgency on that search: the lowering of the retirement age to a point where many people finish their careers and still have energy requiring a meaningful outlet; the increase (for some) in leisure time; but also widespread unemployment. All these pose the question: If and when my life is not given direction by someone else's assignment of tasks, what is worth doing with it?

'You ain't goin' nowhere.' Unfortunately, of course, we are; to the six-foot wooden box, if nowhere else; and most of us dream of doing at least something worthwhile on the way. ('They give birth astride of a grave', says Pozzo in Beckett's *Waiting for Godot*; 'the light gleams an instant, then it's night once more.' 'Astride of a grave and a difficult birth', adds Vladimir. 'Down in the hole, lingeringly, the grave-digger puts on the forceps.') But 'worthwhile' implies some clear notion of 'worth', something that transcends its alternatives; something that is in its very nature worth doing. What can be transcendent in this way, what is there that deserves our desire? 'What to apply my strength to', says Dostoevski's Stavrogin, 'that's what I've never seen and don't see now.'

An inability to answer these questions of meaning can put heavy strains on our emotional integration. Therapist Victor Frankl insisted that the 'psychological health of individuals (and by extension, groups and even nations) depends on the degree to which they are able to discover the pattern of meaning ... of their experience'.[5] Jung was making much the same point when he reported that 'Among all my patients in the second half of life – that is to say, over thirty-five – there has not been one whose problem in the last resort was not that of finding a religious outlook on life.'[6] But where are such a pattern and direction to be found? What is it that is truly 'worth doing', worth living for? In which quarter should we seek the transcendent?

Surprisingly few authors have attempted a serious response to this question. One who did try to map the contemporary answers is Colin Wilson, whose fascinating best-seller *The Outsider* came out in 1956. (Reading Wilson, one becomes sharply aware of the difference between his anguished modernity, hunting for answers, and our ironically cool postmodernity, 'incredulous towards metanarratives', simply giving up on the big questions.) Surveying different areas of art and thought, Wilson attempted to summarize their approaches to the problem 'What should we do with our lives?',[7] and so define what gives life the sense of 'authenticity', of true 'freedom'. The result is a classic presentation of modernity's responses to the question.

Wilson points to music, dance and aesthetic experience – in Sartre, Hesse, Nijinsky, Van Gogh. Then, he examines sexual desire and experience (Barbusse); moments that make possible 'intensity of will', that offer 'a course of action that gives expression to that ... part of himself that is not content with the trivial and unheroic', for example in situations of danger, betrayal or death (Sartre again, writing about the wartime resistance movement: 'Freedom is terror'); courage, expressed in war, hunting or deep-sea fishing (Hemingway – to the point of 'Nobody ever lived their life all the way up except bullfighters'); and, indeed, sheer commitment for its own sake (Hemingway again: 'the feeling of unreality disappears as soon as he plunges into the fighting').

In his subsequent 1978 preface, Wilson comments on his earlier explorations. First, he draws a comparison between his own quest for authenticity and the notion of Desire in the Christian writer C.S. Lewis. 'Desire', or 'Joy', is a key theme in much of Lewis' work.[8] For him, it is a joyous yearning embodied in our responses to (for example) birdsong, far horizons, love, mythology, erotic or magical or aesthetic desire, and above all memory. But fundamental to Desire is the fact that it is never finally satisfied in any of these expressions; it points always to some further fulfilment, lying beyond. This dilemma leaves us with three alternatives, says Lewis:[9] to attempt to 'have again' the experience where we had it before, thereby discovering the anticlimax that 'joy' slowly vanishes with repetition; or, growing trapped in cynicism, to deny the possibility of fulfilment, and debunk the whole experience in psychological or biochemical terms; or finally, to follow the 'dialectic of Desire', through its partial embodiments, to its only ultimate and total fulfilment in God himself. For Lewis, the unattainability at any earlier stage is precisely the point.

Wilson's self-comparison to Lewis is not surprising, given his earlier definition of the issue as 'the fundamental religious idea of how to "live more abundantly"'[10] – alluding to Christ's 'I am come that they might have life, and have it more abundantly'. Wilson, like Lewis, has a sense of 'unattainability', that nothing human beings encounter in this world can ultimately prove capable of 'fully satisfying [their] desires'. But Wilson, unlike Lewis, cannot see desire as pointing towards a transcendent that has real embodiment. And so we find a deeply depressing remark in the 1978 preface where Wilson suggests that the whole quest for authenticity, freedom, 'abundant life', was fundamentally only an expression of sexual desire, which itself faces anticlimax in the moment of consummation.

A comparable sense of the unattainable dominates others among modernity's best writers: the sense of futile longing for something that will be an adequate embodiment of what we have dreamed. One of the great expressions is Scott Fitzgerald's simple but brilliant novel *The Great Gatsby*. Its central figure is a man with 'something gorgeous about him, some heightened sensitivity to the promises of life ... an extraordinary gift of hope, a romantic readiness', whose dreams do almost come true. He has 'made it', he has a marvellous house where he throws all kinds of glittering parties, and above all he meets again the girl of his fantasies whom he had lost years earlier, and seems about to win her back. But there is no reality anywhere that is adequate to the grandeur of his dreams. Ultimately they all turn out illusions, a 'rock ... founded securely on a fairy's wing'; Gatsby cannot escape from a 'foul dust' that 'floated in the wake of his dreams', eventually destroying them all.

At the close, with Gatsby shot dead and his girl, Daisy, disappeared back into an unsatisfying marriage, Fitzgerald broadens his panorama. The narrator compares the 'green light' that Gatsby saw on Daisy's dock to the 'fresh, green breast of the new world' that greeted the first sailors coming to America and encountering 'the last and greatest of all human dreams'. The missed fulfilment of the whole western vision is present, as well as Gatsby's personal tragedy, in the book's moving final sentences:

> I thought of Gatsby's wonder when he first picked out the green light at the end of Daisy's dock. He had come a long way to this blue lawn, and his dream must have seemed so close that he could hardly fail to grasp it. He did not know that it was already behind him ... Gatsby believed in the green light, the orgiastic future that year by year recedes before us. It eluded us then, but that's no matter – to-morrow

we will run faster, stretch out our arms further ... And one fine morning –

So we beat on, boats against the current, borne back ceaselessly into the past.[11]

The dreams don't come true. *Gatsby* is arguably the archetypal novel of the American 1920s, the first decade of modernity in the United States; and so it poses starkly the issue of purpose and desire in a world bereft of God.[12]

Restating the Christian option

Wilson's citation of C.S. Lewis leads us to an interesting question: Have we lost our way partly because of the contradictions of what was done by many Christians during the Reformation?

Lewis' vision of Desire is forever, by its very nature, 'on the move'. Desire always points away to a different order, longing for things to be 'on earth as it is in heaven'. By its nature, such a life-stance must be dynamic; it cannot be static. Indeed, because God's glory is infinite, heaven itself is a further exploration, not a static conclusion. The vision of the other world climaxing the last of Lewis' *Narnia Chronicles* embodies that dynamic in the clarion-call of Farsight, 'Farther up and farther in!'[13] (It is a note repeated in much recent Christian spirituality: in Graham Kendrick's songs, for example – 'We are marching, in the great procession / Ever further and deeper into the heart of God'.)

Now it's hard to avoid a sense of something much more static in the ethos that often came to dominate the Reformation.[14] What hymn, after all, better expressed the Reformation ethos than Luther's 'A Mighty Fortress'? We must be cautious here: first, because this highly influential image is primarily about God, not the church; second, because any complex vision has to be expressed by blending different images; third, because within the tradition that resulted there was scope for all kinds of highly purposive radicals.[15] But one cannot help sensing, in the retreat into a static 'mighty fortress',[16] a different concern from Lewis' ever-ongoing, purposive, adventurous Desire.

And perhaps a major problem with the Reformation was that, in the end, its reassessment of medieval religion was often seriously incomplete. Many of its dominant figures could as little resist the heady attraction of power on earth as had medieval Catholicism. The result, right across Europe, was the rise of the 'state church'. The notion of the 'pilgrim church', radical, dynamic, on the move because not really at home here, marked the Anabaptist 'left wing of the Reformation'; but across Europe their activities tended to be suppressed by force. (Wherein surfaces another fatal contradiction: in using the state's forces to suppress, by violence, those they disagreed with, some of the 'static' Reformation churches[17] were extraordinarily at variance with Christ's words about encountering evil and loving your enemies (Matthew 5:38–48). Disastrously so: the Europe-wide turn away from Christian faith that followed in the 'Enlightenment' was in good measure a nauseated reaction to decades of wars between religious armies.) Inevitably, the connection with political power led to the church embodying the dull, static conservatism and alliance with the status quo for which it has become stereotyped. What such a stereotype offered was a call to quiescence, rather than to prophetic, pilgrim radicalism shot through with a sense of specific purpose. Even the crucial concept of 'calling' became a tool for conservatism (and dullness), if understood only through a static vision of church and society: 'The rich man in his castle, the poor man at his gate / God made them high and lowly, and ordered their estate'.[18]

Strange, when one considers that much of the self-image shaping the New Testament church was thoroughly dynamic. We don't find much there about fortresses. Rather, the notion of a journeying 'pilgrim church' comes straight out of Hebrews 11:13 (and 1 Peter 2:11 in the classic King James translation). The one New Testament book that depicts the history of the church – Acts – is set in the shape of a journey, in which Jesus' gospel is carried from Jerusalem, across the eastern

Mediterranean, and finally to Rome. That in turn reflects the last words of Jesus, sending his followers out to be 'my witnesses ... in Jerusalem, and in all Judaea, and Samaria, and to the ends of the earth'; or Matthew's simple summary of Jesus' last six weeks of teaching: 'All authority in heaven and on earth has been given to me; therefore, go!' (28:19). (And when the journey had taken in all the 'ends of the earth', said Jesus, the end of history would come (Matthew 24:14); ultimately its goal is heaven, the 'city that is to come'.[19])

Two observations are in order. First, within the Christian tradition, the sense of purpose and direction seems clearest where that 'dynamic' summons to outgoing mission is felt most decisively and personally. Second, as a matter of historical fact, the Reformation synthesis was surprisingly weak in producing this sense of mission. Something was absent. There were numerous famous exceptions, of course, but in general the great 'journey' or 'outburst' of the Christian church that turned it into the largely two-thirds-world organism it is today began only in the nineteenth century, under the influence of rather different kinds of spirituality.

Considering that much of Lewis' theology was far from Anabaptist, it is striking that his art often embodies such a non-traditional, pilgrim spirituality. Most of his fictions are stories either of journeys, or of characters who subvert the status quo they find themselves in, or both.[20] (The paradox is even more evident in Lewis' friend and fellow-believer Tolkien; his theology was even less Anabaptist, but what gripped his imagination, in fiction such as *The Lord of the Rings*, was that salvation lies always in the quest into the open country;[21] not, for example, in the 'mighty fortress' of Minas Tirith.[22]) And this non-traditional spirituality was in fact the archetypal one: the authentic image of Christian life, one that gives the impulse of purpose to the imagination, is always journeying – going somewhere with God, with a destiny, always in motion.

It has to be so. In the nature of things – and this is why the whole notion of a comfortable alliance between state and church is problematic – Christ's community is not meant to fit in this world. ('Here we have no continuing city', says Hebrews 13:14, 'we are looking for the city that is to come.') To the biblical world-view, the world as a whole was condemned to purposelessness by the first humans' assertion of independence from God that we call the Fall. The results were meaninglessness, futility, entropy. Ecclesiastes 1 presents them in the passage made famous by Hemingway: 'The sun also rises, and the sun goes down, and hastens to his place where he arose; all the rivers run into the sea, yet the sea is not full; that which is done is that which shall be done; and there is no new thing under the sun.' If this sounds like the fatalistic vision of eastern religion, in bondage to cycles of meaninglessness where all action is futile,[23] that's because it is. 'Subjected to frustration ... in bondage to decay' is how Paul describes the natural, alienated order of things (Romans 8:20–21).

But now there are two competing systems in our universe: the natural, deterministic system of entropic purposelessness ('going nowhere') that is our natural habitat, and God's alternative system or 'kingdom' that is breaking into it since Jesus. The blind Cornish poet Jack Clemo defines the Christian proclamation in these terms: 'Your fate is unspeakably tragic, *but you need not fulfil it*. Surrender the self that would fulfil that fate and the fate itself collapses. You become a new creature with a new destiny.'[24] Where entropy multiplies decay and disorder, bringing nothing out of something, the new alternative of grace multiplies creativity, bringing something out of nothing ('God's jazz breaking into the mournful music of the spheres', Clemo calls it). Peter told his readers that they had been 'born again' through something within them that was beyond all corruption, the 'living and enduring word of God ... All men are like grass; the grass withers and the flowers fall' (entropy), 'but the word of the Lord stands forever' (1 Peter 1:23–25).[25]

It is in these terms that we see Jesus as the classic model of divine purposiveness. Unlike, say, the narratives of David or Solomon,[26] the whole shape of Jesus' life is a journey. Luke calls it an 'exodus', paralleling the archetypal journey of the Old Testament (9:31): with Jesus marching first through the opposition of the contemporary system to Jerusalem, then on via the cross and resurrection into the other world.[27] And where he went, the new 'kingdom' went too:

> *'The Spirit of the Lord is on me'* (Jesus announced)
> *'because he has anointed me to preach good news to the poor.*
> *He has sent me to proclaim freedom for the prisoners and recovery of sight to the blind,*
> *to release the oppressed,*
> *to proclaim the year of the Lord's favour'* (Luke 4:18–19).

And, his Old Testament original adds attractively, 'to bind up the broken-hearted, to comfort all who mourn, to bestow on them a crown of beauty instead of ashes ... a garment of praise instead of a spirit of despair'.[28] These are the works of the new 'kingdom'; and these are what he did. The Gospels narrate a triumphant, messianic advance – healing the sick, driving out forces of occult evil, helping his followers discover their life-direction, dealing with guilt, introducing truth, transforming legalism and dead religion, enabling forgiveness, raising the dead – 'proclaiming', says Mark, 'the good news of God', that his purposive 'kingdom' of goodness was right there to hand.

If in his life Jesus embodied – in the phrase Colin Wilson alludes to – 'life in all its fullness', then his death becomes even more crucial. It dealt with the sin-barrier between humanity and God, reopening the way for the transforming power of grace, enabling us to be 'born again' into the alternative order of the presence of God. That power, or presence, now re-enters our universe; and surrendering the autonomy that led to emptiness reconnects our destiny with both. Jesus pictured God's Spirit as life-giving 'rivers of living water' flowing out now from each person who genuinely believed (John 6:38).

That image – channelling life-giving water into a desert world – underlies the whole Christian life-stance of 'dynamic' purpose and desire. A spirituality based on passion first to 'love the Lord with all your heart, mind and strength', plus an equal passion to 'love your neighbour as yourself', will never lack for something worth doing. Clemo is relevant again for his exuberant assertion of the 'personal covenant'. Each individual, he insists, is being

> trained for a specific place in God's redemptive strategy. This is the next step beyond surrender. God takes the former rebel into his confidence and allots to him some stretch of existential territory where he can practise the divine presence.[29]

In other words, for everyone there is some unique sector of the 'kingdom's' frontier across which (s)he can desire, pray, and carry the presence of the 'kingdom' – creatively finding a way to add to the 'love', 'truth', 'respect', 'joy', present in that situation. (The fact that it is hard to write that sentence without inverted commas underlines the seriousness of our cynical situation. Yet can we imagine any place worldwide where no scope could exist for such creativity?) 'In everything', says Paul, 'God works together for good with those who love him'.[30] Because God is loving, there is at every point some creative purpose forward, if we choose to partner with it.

Paul insists that in the Jesus-community, each member is indispensable.[31] There can be no such thing as redundancy. The twin aspects of spirituality, the worshipper and the activist, extend to infinity together. There can be no end, ever, to our discovering and responding to the depths of God and his self-revelation ('ever further and deeper'); nor to our being reshaped, as gateways through which the powers of heaven break more fully into this world. So too there can be no end, ever, to people or situations where we can show respect, truth, or affection; and no completing the task of bearing Jesus-style love, gentleness and justice wherever it may be needed in a world like ours. By definition, genuine love is always reaching out, always open to expression, always purposive, always 'on the road'. To our last gasp there will be someone nearby worthy of affection, and truths and realities worth sharing.

It would be a huge (if common) mistake to see such a lifestyle primarily as 'sacrifice'. One finds that the everyday reality of this 'mission' lifestyle – whether for a businesswoman, a missionary or a housewife – is that its practitioners seldom wish any other destiny. Empirically, there is tremendous dynamism in the sense of shared purpose, and, purely and simply, a great deal of fun. Indeed, people living by this vision carry as many scars as anybody else: the impulses of 'needing to be needed' may be present still, the seductions of holy conceit, the possibilities of corruption by money, status or power. Yet it is striking to anyone in contact with communities inspired by such a lifestyle how unreal, or at least unusual, the Elmer Gantry caricatures seem. Rather, it has struck me how often agnostics who are close friends with people active in mission will remark wistfully, 'They're lucky to have a purpose like that'. Somehow, mistaken or not, it feels authentically human.

But if that is the credit-side of their life-stance, the tension in it is a very simple one. In postmodernity, we simply don't believe it's true; nobody believes all that any more. All the sacrifice, all the passion, is motivated by statements about Jesus that are, ultimately, lies. It is on that basis that the issue of purpose has to be faced.

> Bertrand Russell, one of Britain's key twentieth-century philosophers, phrased his loss of hope like this (in *Why I Am Not A Christian*): 'That man is the product of causes which had no prevision of the end they were achieving; that his origin, his growth, his hopes and fears, his loves and his beliefs, are but the outcome of accidental collocations of atoms; that no fire, no heroism, no intensity of thought and feeling, can preserve an individual life beyond the grave; that all the labour of the ages, all the devotion, all the inspiration, all the noonday brightness of human genius, are destined to extinction in the vast death of the solar system ... all these things, if not quite beyond dispute, are yet so nearly certain, that no philosophy which rejects them can hope to stand. Only within the scaffolding of these truths, only on the firm foundation of

unyielding despair, can the soul's habitation hence-forth be safely built.' (To our postmodern ears he sounds oddly like a liberal bishop having a rough time at a high-school assembly.)

Alternative transcendence

'Get a life', snarled *Star Trek*'s William Shatner (Captain Kirk) at an embarrassed group of Trekkie fans in a famous *Saturday Night Live* interview. But how and where? What kind of 'life' has value, in a way that mastering the nerdy details of *Star Trek* does not? What (switching to St Paul) is the 'life that is truly life'?[32]

What, post-God, are our options? (What kind of person am I?) One is to try to find something genuinely transcendent, some-thing inherently of value: for example, in the arts, romance, or a religious alternative that omits God. Or, we may finally assume that no genuine transcendent exists. In this case there are at least two possibilities: to overlook the issue, making the game of life as comfortable as possible while ignoring its ultimate meaning-lessness; or to take the deliberate, 'tough-minded' alternative, giving ourselves consciously to our material drives.

In Gatsby's world, the most promising embodiment of the transcendent is romantic – Daisy Buchanan. In our post-religious culture, the search for fulfilment, for something truly worth desiring and living for, tends often to embody itself in romantic terms (and the advertising and music industries recognize that well). Yet contemporary discussions of romance – *Cosmo*, *New Woman* – seem haunted by the sheer difficulty of maintaining fulfilling relationships. 'The cult of intimacy conceals a growing despair of finding it', argues Christopher Lasch,[33] adding, 'Personal relations crumble under the emotional weight with which they are burdened.' This whole issue of the viability of romance – and the extent to which God's disappearance affects it – deserves a chapter (Ch. 5, below) to itself.

What other routes to transcendence seem prominent? What else is there (or is the phrase outmoded now?) to 'live for'? Matthew Arnold suggested, as the loss of God grew evident last century, that poetry could take the place of religion. (American poet Wallace Stevens: 'After one has abandoned a belief in God, poetry is the essence which takes its place as life's redemption'.) For many of us, artistic experience offers a gateway into something of major, inherent value. The programme of the first Edinburgh Festival expressed the hope that visitors 'will find in all the performances a sense of peace and inspiration with which to refresh their souls and reaffirm their belief in things other than material'. Music, in particular, whether classical or rock, often performs this function. One of Anita Brookner's characters finds in music 'a world of feeling which she recognised as superior to anything she had ever known in life'. 'Some people pray, some people play music', said rock 'n' roller Chuck Berry; 'Rock 'n' roll was my religion for a long time', was Pete Townshend's version. 'I used to go to Sunday school. But the only thing I believe in now is music', was Jimi Hendrix's; 'I used to be a devout Catholic. Now I'm a devout musician' was Sting's.[34]

In one field after another, the last years of the twentieth century heard many voices (by no means mostly reactionary) debating whether entire art forms had died. Year after year the Turner Prize triggered discussion about the perceived irrelevance of modern painting. 'The line "the day the music died" echoes now through concert halls and opera houses', wrote Geoffrey Wheatcroft in Prospect; 'Has (classical) music anywhere to go, or is it the end of an old song?' Writers from Philip Larkin to Eric Hobsbawm bewailed the inability of contemporary jazz to match its past, while in rock New Musical Express triggered a major debate by declaring the 'great rock 'n' roll dwindle'. V.S. Naipaul, perhaps least plausibly, announced the death of the novel; in cinema, the respected critic David Thomson argued that the day of the great directors was past, indeed that we now face 'the death of film'.

For me, an especially striking example was Simon Callow's explicit comparison of the declining arts to declining faith, since Callow is a major figure in Britain's theatre and cinema scene. '"We must maintain the arts," cry all civilized commentators', he wrote.[35] 'But these cries have the forlorn quality of the Lambeth (Anglican bishops') Conference's resolution to return to traditional morality; the empty pews no doubt glow with self-righteousness, but the rest of the world goes merrily on its wicked way.' In his lifetime, he added, he had lived through 'the streamlining and glamorisation of the museums and galleries; the death or retirement of the generation of great musicians whose concerts were almost religious events and their replacement with non-threatening chaps with flawless techniques and wonderful cheekbones; the steady journey down-market of radio; the gradual abandonment of serious television arts coverage. It has, on the whole, been a gloomy journey ... Time is running out, faster than any of us know.'

'Forlorn quality'? The 'day the music died'? The 'end of an old song'? Yet few of these voices can be dismissed as 'diehard conservatives' ...

But there is a problem, and again it has to do with the loss of God. First, if there is no God it becomes increasingly difficult to know what we mean when we say great art is 'spiritual' or 'transcendent', in a way that (say) great cookery is not. Secondly, the whole area of aesthetic experience is currently in disarray. The question is whether the loss of God doesn't radically affect our whole sense of 'great art'. For the notion of 'great art' doesn't make sense automatically; and consciously post-Christian theory has become sceptical of the very idea. In particular, the radical postmodernists deny any 'canon' of supreme artistic masterpieces, insisting there is no timeless 'artistic' quality that is present in Shakespeare and not in, say, a TV soap. Andy Warhol's famous presentation of an exact copy of a Brillo carton as a work of art raised the same issues. Many of the more recent controversies over 'art' (Damien Hirst's dead cows, Carl Andre's bricks at the Tate Gallery, Helen Chadwick's cast of her urinations in the snow, Jeff Koons' giant rabbit; or, at the most extreme, junk artist Piero Monzoni who filled ninety cans with human excrement and sold them as art) have likewise had to do with the impossibility of defining what 'art' or 'beauty' are.[36]

> 'It was only in the nineteenth century that we became aware of the full dignity of art. We began to "take it seriously" ... But the result seems to have been a dislocation of the aesthetic life in which little is left for us but high-minded works which fewer and fewer people want to read or hear or see, and "popular" works of which those who make them and those who enjoy them are half ashamed ... By valuing too highly a real, but subordinate good, we have come near to losing that good itself.' This is C.S. Lewis;[37] was he right?

But the question goes deeper. Of course we have no definitive list that determines, for all time and all people, what are the 'greatest works of art'. To that extent the postmodernists are right. But the question is whether we are deluded, and talking nonsense, in affirming the objective reality of something outstanding in those few masterpieces whose glory we personally have been able to catch. If there were a God who created things and (as Genesis puts it) 'saw that they were good', then it would be meaningful to describe some things we humans create as likewise objectively 'good' or 'beautiful', in ways that other things are not. But God is dead. Then perhaps the statement that a Tolstoy novel or Bruckner symphony is 'good', in some profound way that a raunchy airport paperback or bubblegum single is not, conveys only a subjective preference. Perhaps it says more about the biases of our brain chemistry, and our personal background, than about the artwork itself. But somehow, in that process, the aesthetic experience is devalued. We no longer reach beyond ourselves, we no longer touch something of absolute value. So be it, the postmodernists would insist. But then, in this area too, experience of the transcendent slips beyond our reach.[38]

> I'm standing in a St Petersburg church. It's an October Sunday. I'm feeling massively uplifted as the gospel choir swings into worship with enormous gusto and commitment. And the thought comes: In the Christian system, anything beautiful or truthful is worth expressing yourself strongly about. But for a truly atheistic postmodernist, how many things are intrinsically worthy of praise or indeed of strong feeling? What is worth saying? As a result, postmodernist artistic expression usually tends to be flavoured by the artificial, the casual, the cool, the ironic. But what, ultimately, does that do for art?

Yet the thirst for the transcendent will not be denied. We see the growth of religion-substitutes and 'alternative spiritualities' – certainly in the United States, Germany or Scandinavia, and to a significant extent in Britain. 'New Age' attitudes tend often to be monistic, seeing all reality as one, and all reality as God. Consequently, they might seem to offer a route to the transcendent in the everyday. Whether they can deliver or not, they certainly offer a *terminology* of transcendence, enabling aficionados to think of themselves as 'getting into another reality' through, say, jogging, or even American football. ('You can get into another order of reality when you're playing, a reality that doesn't fit into grids and coordinates that most people lay across life', said ex-San Francisco 49ers quarterback John Brodie.[39]) Indeed, we might define 'New Age' as a collection of miscellaneous enthusiasms that have to do, one way or another, with finding transcendence: whether in Celtic or Native American mysticisms, holistic psychotherapy, Eastern meditation, *feng shui*, past-life therapy or outer space. In its sheer ecumenism, its ability to take on board all manner of resonant sources without worrying how they link together logically, 'New Age' might be well-placed to challenge for the position Christianity used to hold, underpinning the sense of transcendence in Western culture.

The issue between the two might appear to be one of truth. Was Christ really who he claimed to be, and did he rise from the dead, guaranteeing his presence as the personal source of transcendence now? Or have, say, the paraphernalia of 'New Age' crystals a more trustworthy claim? With the more coherent 'alternative spiritualities', this issue can be faced. All too often, however, the truth-question doesn't seem to matter; the bizarre fantasies of a Shirley MacLaine can take centre-stage despite their blatant improbabilities, and there are all too many other examples. That kind of inauthenticity seems a merely touristic spirituality,[40] and it can hardly be expected to be meaningful as a long-term source of transcendence. It now appears that the cultural high-water mark of 'New Age' may have passed, leaving behind (among other things) a monument to the way our hunger can turn into gullibility. (At the end of 1994, a major feature in Germany's *Der Spiegel* declared that the 'idea of a "New Age" has sunk out of sight', giving way to an 'Instant-Mystik' immediately attainable in a two-hour session or five weekend workshops. 'The new "Age of Light" is marked by "lightness" in the sense of Coca-Cola Light', it concluded caustically.) But the story is not over yet.

The urge towards the transcendent may also be expressed in the desire for direct encounter with the 'other', with what is 'beyond'. Is this a reason for the attractiveness of vast numbers of cults and fringe religions in our apparently secularized society? The Kevin Costner movie *Field of Dreams* presented a character receiving instructions through supernatural voices and visions, prophetic utterances from his infant daughter, and so on ('If you build it, he will come'). He remarks at one point, 'When the primal forces of nature tell you to do something, the thing is not to quibble about it.'[41] There is a sense of both relief and fulfilment if, at last, the 'beyond' speaks clearly. (The problem the film never faces is that the voice might be a deception.) The more comfortable arrangement is when the 'beyond' offers some direction to our lives at minimal expense in terms of disturbance or commitment. This seems to occur with many people loosely involved in 'New Age'; it may be the (optimistic?) hope of the dabbler in the occult; it is certainly true of the average horoscope-reader, from Nancy Reagan downwards. ('Of course' we don't believe it, but the illusion of significance is the vital anodyne.) In a different mode, the fascination with *The X-Files*, or Stephen King's novels, or the accounts of alien abduction, witness to a desire, yet fear, of encounter with the beyond. It is not much to live on, but it is what we can find to hand.

> Everyone's got a hunger
> A hunger they can't resist
> There's so much that you want
> You deserve much more than this
>
> –Bruce Springsteen, 'Prove It All Night'

Playing the game in postmodernity

The sense of dissatisfaction hangs over our era. 'I don't know what I want, but there's got to be more', to quote Bob Geldof.

There is in humankind a space in the shape of God, said Pascal three centuries ago. A Christian analysis of our culture might argue that, having lost God as the goal of our desire, we continually seek to fill that space with other things. We turn these things into idols, then find they aren't adequate, and that forcing them into such a role destroys what they might have been. ('We may give our human loves the unconditional allegiance which we owe only to God', writes Lewis in *The Four Loves*. 'Then they become gods: then they become demons. Then they will destroy us, and also destroy themselves.'[42]) But now this realization is being read the opposite way: in the end, there is nothing of ultimate, transcendent value to be found. The approaches we reviewed in the previous section might be described as classically 'modernist': the influential philosopher G.E. Moore suggested early last century that aesthetic pleasure and relationships were the two things genuinely worth living for. But now we have taken the 'postmodern turn'; the whole tendency in recent years has been towards the steady erosion of all structures of value or transcendence.

So be it, then. Think of it this way: You do not have to have a 'point to life' to go on living. Mid-century modernism tried to identify things that were ultimately worthwhile, even if there were no God. Now we know that things are worthwhile only insofar as we give them value ourselves. All is DIY. Nothing is, in itself, worth doing, but life goes on.

And you don't have to know what's worth doing to go on living – although it can help. We all know how it feels to have mundane, 'stupid' activities sucking away our disposable time (Parkinson's law: any task can expand to fill all the time available, unless there is something more significant that intervenes); leaving us with a vague feeling of rebellion, of never quite spending our time in ways we would have wanted. To solve that problem, however, we need to know what is 'significant', what it is we really value.

Guessing at our future is perilous, but nonetheless tempting. Now that we're 'beyond' both Christianity and its 'modern' alternatives, how will these issues be expressed? What might we logically predict to become the most widespread ways to respond?

A common solution, we might expect, would be to opt consciously out of the whole question; for our culture simply to stop thinking in terms of 'meaningful living'; to forget Wilson's question 'What shall we do with our lives?' We might likewise predict a change in attitudes towards drug legalization, since from a basically pointless universe it makes sense to escape to Prozac or Ecstasy or their successors.[43] There are other narcotics besides chemical ones. Media offer us a non-stop narcotic too ('Rent a little happiness from Granada TV Rentals'), filling our attention with alternative worlds where worthwhile things are happening, even if not to us; in which life is fundamentally happy and fulfilling (Australian soaps such as *Neighbours*)[44], or where there is the excitement of vicarious danger, of crimes to be solved and evils overcome by proxy – the illusion of meaningful activity. A further narcotic would be simple busyness: the more or less deliberate choice to work enough or party hard enough to forget the pointlessness awaiting us at the centre.

Meanwhile, out in the 'public' world, 'cool' would conclusively displace 'joy' as the keynote of our self-presentation. There's nothing left to get excited about, and to do so would be inexcusably gauche and naive. ('How I long for a little ordinary human enthusiasm', says Jimmy Porter in *Look Back in Anger*. 'Just enthusiasm – that's all. I want to hear a warm, thrilling voice cry out Hallelujah! Hallelujah! I'm alive! ... Oh brother, it's such a long time since I was with anyone who got enthusiastic about anything.'[45]) Indeed, one senses that it is becoming hard even to use the word 'joy' in the contemporary situation. Is the concept dying along with God? When do we see it used outside the contexts either of faith or eroticism (*The Joy of Sex*)? 'Happiness' and 'pleasure' we can contemplate; but maybe 'joy' is slipping out beyond our reach?

A second trend we could predict might be the spread of 'games' that have no intrinsic value, but that can give some shape to life: mastering the artificial complexities of bridge, chess, or fantasy role-play, or the cutting-edge intricacies of computer technology. They may represent a narrowing world, but they can be taken incredibly seriously if they are all we have. (The German novelist Hesse predicted this option last century in *The Glass Bead Game*.) Art, too, may function in this way – no longer as a glimpse of universal transcendence, but as a bigger, if ultimately pointless, game to keep meaninglessness at bay. British painter Francis Bacon put it clearly:

> Man now realizes that he is an accident, that he is a completely futile being, that he has to play out the game without reason. I think that even when Velasquez was painting, even when Rembrandt was painting, they were still, whatever their attitude to life, slightly conditioned by certain types of religious possibilities, which man now,

you could say, has had cancelled out for him. Man now can only attempt to beguile himself for a time ... You see, painting has become – all art has become – a game by which man distracts himself. And you may say that it always has been like that, but now it's entirely a game.[46]

The humanness in this 'game' approach lies in the skill, the mastery, no matter the narrowness of the arena. The tension lies ultimately in its sense of nerdiness (and if objective transcendence has disappeared from the arts, nerdiness is as much an issue for the denizen of the Tate Gallery as for the train-spotter on Waterloo Station); of living the sad life of the anorak. Yet the anorak might be right. Does 'maturity' really mean learning to be free from all such disproportionate attachments? Or is such a 'maturity', by definition, an equally sad loss of all enthusiasms and purpose, a loss of romance? But then again we face Lewis' question: is the whole meaning of 'game' slowly undermined by the pressures that ensue when what began as play has to carry a central role in life – when it is elevated to the place of an idol?[47]

A third possible trend: with the loss of purposiveness and the disappearance of transcendence, should we expect to see increasing numbers of people living simply and consciously by the basic biological drives? First among these might be the 'nest-making' drive towards security, the happy family in their DIY house. Ever since Dickens' *Little Dorrit*, the goal of an island of private relationship amid surrounding anarchy has been a commonplace of both art and popular culture. What challenges this objective may face after the death of God is a question we shall turn to in Chapter 5. Again, there may be a slow fuse of disappointment smouldering under so narrowed a world ('When you're no longer searching for beauty or love / Just some kind of life with the edges taken off'[Pulp]). A number of films in the last few years have asked how far this kind of 'getting by' amounts to dehumanization. *Educating Rita* is one; *Shirley Valentine* – with its fantasy of throwing everything aside, having an affair, making a fresh start – is another.

But should we also expect in the next few years to see a much more overt acceptance of basing life on the simple motivations of money, sex and power? (This is explicit in many of the high-selling, Grammy-winning hits of hip-hop; rap sex-symbol Lil' Kim summarized what she believed in as 'money, power and respect'.) Would that be crudity, the reduction to the 'animal option', or will it increasingly be presented as tough-minded realism? A feature of the last decade is the increasing tendency to define worthwhile experience purely in terms of brain chemistry – witness the emphasis on adrenaline rushes and 'endorphin buzzes' in the discourse of activities like aerobics and snowboarding. If 'joy' has vanished from our vocabulary, maybe the most we can hope for is stimulus for our physical drives;[48] if we no longer know what *is* good, let's at least ensure we *feel* good. Fabricate the feeling ... (In such a culture the therapist reigns.) But after all, we can view the last century of western intellectual development as resolving all our activity down to the basic drives. J.P. Stern, for example, presents the three key 'modern masters' as Marx, Freud and Nietzsche, and argues that each 'directed his thinking toward a single leading idea ... which was to unlock the secret of all that men do ... These leading ideas are: motivation through material interest' (Marx); 'sexual motivation' (Freud); 'the will to power' (Nietzsche).[49] A third 'unsentimental' trend, then, might be simply to 'face reality' in what we live for: 'Get rich, get famous and get laid' (Bob Geldof again in his punk-rock days), because that's all there is.

It may be – hard though we might find it to say so to our kids. Each of these needs some sublimation, some ornamentation. Few people can consciously live solely for the amassing of money, but it comes more easily if we express the materialistic drive in general terms: 'He who dies with the most toys wins' seemed quite acceptable as a slogan of the late '80s. The power-drive, again, is more acceptable if combined with an ostensible quest for rightful recognition and status. And the hunt for sexual fulfilment (rather than love) raises few eyebrows in its own right ('And you kiss the dames, but you don't ask their names; that's living alright' – *Auf Wiedersehen, Pet*). 'You only go around once in life', said a Schlitz beer ad. 'So you've got to grab for all the gusto you can get.'[50]

The issue might be how far disillusionment is inevitable when money, power or sex cease to be means towards some broader goal or relationship, and become an end. Do they then leave us feeling empty, needing ever more stimulus? (Why do we often feel dissatisfied at the end of a shopping spree? Why can cocktail sex feel so meaningless?) Diminishing returns, decreasing pleasure; Lewis would say that the 'idol' is being transformed to the point of destruction. One thinks of gay icon Robert Mapplethorpe, who proclaimed that sex was 'the only thing worth living for', but ended up having to seek his stimuli in bizarre extremes. ('So Mapplethorpe liked to photograph naked black men eating his faeces? OK', wrote the *Independent*'s art critic ironically.) If there is no higher goal, then at a purely logical level all there can be to aim at next is more money,[51] more shopping, more sex, more power. And yet that solution seems to betray its own emptiness;[52] with boredom, even anger, the results?

(It might have drastic implications in a society that continues to lose its ethical basis. As we'll see, a recurrent feature of postmodernity is pleasure through power.[53] Already Brazil's notorious 'corridor balls' take Europe's consciously-organized football violence one logical step forward, where Rio's underclass youth (girls as well as boys) go to fight in organized teams. The 'balls' attract thousands; the evenings start with high-energy funk and a dance style explicitly simulating sex (in the *Danca do Sexo* girls are paid to have sex with several men during a lengthy track, while other dancers mime their moves); then the DJ gives the signal for 'Mortal Kombat', where the aim is to drag members of the opposite side across the 'corridor' into your own

> 'There is only one thing to do in this world and that is to acquire money and more money, power and more power.'
>
> –Napoleon
>
> 'Man is for war, and woman for the recreation of the warrior; all else is folly.'
>
> –Nietzsche

territory and beat them, often to unconsciousness. Police believe such events may have seen dozens of deaths, besides other participants (female and male) paralyzed or blinded; but Rio's yuppie clubbers have been driving downtown in force to experience what they call a 'taste of reality'.[54] Alternatively, 'more sex' plus 'more power' lead easily to the sado-masochism that fascinates so many in Britain's media, arts and fashion; and in a culture where elements on the political right are already wanting to ensure that criminals are 'made to hurt', it's not impossible to foresee a scenario where elements disliked by the government actually become fodder for these drives. Let's not imagine that the equivalent of Roman gladiator circuses are inconceivable in our society – given, say, forty years' extrapolation of current trends. You only have to be in the home Shed of a London football club, hearing the savage chant of 'Let him die, Let him die' at an injured player on the visiting team, to know the old bloodlust is alive and well.)

One of the most famous songs of US west-coast rock is the Eagles' 'Hotel California'. This is Eagles founder-member Bernie Leadon:

> Ultimately [the Eagles' songs] offered no answer ... In the end we *do* want the things we can't get. Are we ever going to be satisfied? The ultimate answer must be no. In 'Hotel California' they ended up saying we're stuck, we can't get out. We're victims of our own appetites. We're on a treadmill where we just try to satisfy our physical desires or our emotional needs and so we need more sex, more money and more food. Then we need more exciting sex and better tasting food. I've heard people say, 'Give me more of everything and then I'll be satisfied.' But ultimately you're not.[55]

Pressure points

All this comes to a head in our culture in five key pressure areas, where the non-existence of a divinely-given purpose makes a major difference to our life-experience.

First, there is the issue of hope. With good reason, *Panorama* described the 1990s as the decade of fear: anxiety over possible joblessness; insecurities generated by the ubiquitous post-Thatcherite culture of audit and evaluation, by the struggle to retain your place through the 'bottom line' proving you a successful performer; anxiety and fear of AIDS, date rape, joblessness, street violence. ('Wherever you are, there's always a danger of a maniac in the shrubs', John Peel remarked.) And there are the broader fears: of ecological breakdown, anthrax-wielding terrorists, genetically-modified food, vaccine-resistant superbugs; the uncontrollable erupting on us in a world emptied of God's control. 'The only thing we can know with certainty is uncertainty', says management guru Charles Handy. In a paper on 1990s Europe, Nigel Lee recalled the widespread 1960s fear of the Bomb, and suggested there was a difference in our more recent concerns. At least the Bomb was under human control till the moment when it was fired, he said:

> Now, however, we are facing ... a "greenhouse effect" resulting from ozone destruction that will turn some of the planet's best food-producing areas back into dustbowls, the destruction of tropical rain-forests that will seriously deplete the world's oxygen supply, and the melting of polar ice caps producing a water level that threatens to overwhelm some countries like Bangladesh. And there is no one to blame or to whom we can complain. We are locked into a destructive process.[56]

Pressure for ecological responsibility is imperative, but we know that irreversible harm may already have been done: and there could be yet other areas where fatal damage will occur before we even notice. And our collective consciousness can no longer fall back on a caring, divinely-guaranteed purpose which will ensure it will ultimately turn out right. 'Fear', concluded Lee, 'is coming back.'[57]

A second pressure point might be silence. (We have 'knowledge of motion, but not of stillness', wrote Eliot in *Choruses from 'The Rock'*, 'Knowledge of speech, but not of silence'.)

Generation X, an American friend commented recently, longs for silence – but has no idea what to do with it. To Christian faith, silence, the 'still point of the turning world',[58] can be the presence of God, the possibility of meaning. I will not forget Koichi Ohtawa of Japan, co-ordinator of the IFES-linked Christian student movements in east Asia, challenging his hearers at a retreat in the Malaysian mountains to step out into silence and listen for the ongoing direction of their lives: 'What is the *meaning* of today? What has been the meaning of this month? What has been the meaning of this year?' But if no such purposes exist, silence can be painfully empty – whether at New Year's Eve or mid-afternoon without a Walkman:

> *Or as, when an underground train, in the tube, stops too long between stations*
> *And the conversation rises and slowly fades into silence*
> *And you see behind every face the mental emptiness deepen*
> *Leaving only the growing terror of nothing to think about ...*
> –T.S.Eliot, 'East Coker'

> ' Silence has become a very fearful thing', writes Henri Nouwen. 'For most people, silence creates itchiness and nervousness. Many experience silence not as full and rich, but as empty and hollow. For them silence is like a gaping abyss which can swallow them up.' For Nouwen as a Christian, however, 'Out of eternal silence God spoke the Word, and through this Word created and recreated the world ... The Word of God does not break the silence of God, but rather unfolds the immeasurable richness of that silence ... Silence is the home of the word. Silence gives strength and fruitfulness to the word ...'[59]

But thirdly: what does the non-existence of God mean for our experience of loss and suffering? If sunburn melanoma becomes an epidemic among our children, for example; or if we ourselves are diagnosed with cancer or multiple sclerosis? The Christian world-view held that 'in everything God works together for good with those who love him'.[60] That isn't to be mistaken for the blithe conservatism of deism, which held that God had designed the universe perfectly before retiring, so that now 'Whatever is, is right'. Rather, in the biblical picture, our repeated insistence on autonomy has turned our planet into a 'fallen', drastically broken world, full of futility and evil. But into this brokenness, as we have seen, erupts God's loving, creative purpose, always offering to bring something out of nothing, light out of darkness. It is up to us, says Paul, whether we opt into that new order: it is 'those who love him' who find God 'working together for good' with them in everything.[61]

This is not an easy creed. The biblical books of Job and Habakkuk deliberately show us faith being tested to the very edge of destruction. The words 'The just shall live by faith', so central to Christianity,[62] first crop up in Habakkuk as God's challenge to his prophet to stay faithful at a time of apparently unrelieved agony. Indeed, at the centre of Christian faith is a Man hanging on a cross shouting, 'My God, my God, *why?*'[63] But what such faith represents – if we have opted into the new 'kingdom' – is a trust that somehow, in whatever situation, God desires to 'work together' with us to bring something permanently meaningful out of black anguish. It is striking how often the New Testament writers – who knew brutal persecution very well – set 'suffering' and 'glory' immediately together, as if they were guaranteed to be two sides of the same coin.[64]

But all this is gibberish if there is no God.[65] What happens, then, to the experience of suffering? 'Pain is bad, so why should we suffer in heroic silence?', Sean French titled an article in the youth section of the *Guardian*:

When we describe people [who are suffering] in ennobling terms we believe that we are paying them a tribute, but in reality we are making things easier for ourselves. Bravery is the language of choice, and by describing victims in these terms we somehow convince our-selves that the suffering has a purpose.

And as it does not, he argues, we should choose to avoid the language of 'brave hostages or the brave families of hostages', 'heroic survivors ... noble victims'. The only 'appropriate reaction' to such suffering is 'rage'. Yet even rage is pointless unless we are crying out against the betrayal of an underlying order; if the universe is indeed impersonal, rage is a petulant demand for an order we know is lacking. There is a striking moment in the Australian movie *The Man from Snowy River*, where the central character's father is killed by a runaway stallion. He lifts his face to the sky and the camera pans upwards as he screams out, 'NO!' But if there is no God, the scream is wasted breath; there is no one to see your pain, no one there to notice your agony.

Without God, do we have any language for suffering? New York psychology professor Paul Vitz notes the inability of 'human-potential' therapies to speak to this area. In the absence of any notion of divine purpose, the keynote of humanistic therapy has been militant affirmation of the self's unlimited potential;[66] and, Vitz comments, the

> selfist position sounds optimistic and plausible particularly when advocated during materially prosperous times. But ... millions who enthusiastically endorsed optimistic selfism in the prime of life are now beginning to experience the ancient lessons of physical decline, of loss, sickness and death – lessons that puncture all superficial optimism about the continued happy growth of the wonderful self ... What does one tell a chronically overambitious man who learns at age forty that further advancement is over and that he has a serious, possibly fatal, illness? ... What does one say to the older worker who has lost his job, whose skills are not wanted? What does one tell the woman who is desperately alone inside an aging body and with a history of failed relationships? Does one advise such people to become more autonomous and independent? Does one say, "Go actualize yourself in creative activity"? For people in those circumstances, such advice is not just irrelevant, it is an insult.[67]

Meanwhile, postmodernism has been so shy of profundity that it has little vocabulary to handle the seriousness of suffering (gay responses to the AIDS epidemic being the most obvious exception). In an earlier period, suffering could be viewed as tragic, but tragedy demands a framework against which things might have been otherwise. Amid the meaninglessness of atheistic postmodernity, suffering is just 'stupid', to quote Douglas Adams' Random Dent; stupid, but little more.

A fourth pressure point, if there is no external, divinely-given purpose available to us, is the area of aging and maturity. In our society it is poor manners to publicly remind someone of their age; extra years are something to be concealed, pretended about. ('She has been thirty-five ever since she arrived at the age of forty', says Oscar Wilde's Lady Bracknell of an acquaintance, 'which was many years ago now.' Cary Grant received from a fact-checker the cabled query 'How old Cary Grant?', and returned the immortal reply 'Old Cary Grant fine how you?') We are so used to this habit of denial ('I'm in middle youth') that we forget how culturally-bound – and personally destructive – it is. How, in contrast, can the biblical writer of Proverbs see advanced years as a cause for deep thankfulness ('Grey hair is a crown of splendour'[68])? Has our society, with its loss of the spiritually transcendent, elevated sexual fulfilment and the 'body beautiful' to a point where aging can mean nothing but the slow loss of power to do everything that is truly worthwhile?

In a context shaped by belief in a divine purpose working itself out in our lives ('The Lord is my Shepherd'), extra years become something of which to be proud. They represent an extra degree of accumulated experience that is valuable because God-given; they represent further progress in the divine moulding and sculpturing. Age is not something to be denied ('I'm young at heart, really'). But once we lose the God who underwrites such a process, does 'old' merely come to mean 'obsolete'?[69] Does old age become the final defeat (President de Gaulle: 'Old age is a shipwreck'), rather than the final harvest?[70]

Sunday afternoons I visit my mother in the old folks' home. The strength has gone, and the mind has gone. Most of the time she 'talks' complete gibberish, repeating the same meaningless syllables: 'Radla radla radla radla radla', and so on and on all afternoon. The bad thing is when she apparently asks a question, but you've no idea what it is so cannot respond. That makes her furious. (But it's preferable to her haggard neighbour, who spends all her energy cursing.)

'Radla radla radla radla radla...' She used to be a poet, and a good one. Sometimes I think of a footballer laid up with a broken leg. Well, but he hopes to be back on the team in a year's time. But she? There's no God. She'll never be back.

'Maturity' likewise becomes a notion under pressure, now there is no meaningful direction in our lives to lend value to the 'experience' we accumulate. In limited areas of *savoir-faire*, technique, or behaviour, the value of 'experience' is still credible. Used more broadly, however, the notion becomes vulnerable, because of our lack of certainty as to what the personal growth presupposed by 'maturity' really means. ('Maturity', says Kurt Vonnegut's prophet-figure Bokonon, 'is a bitter disappointment for which no remedy exists.'[71]) And adulthood may simply mean the moment when one abandons the attempt to keep in touch with the cutting-edge. The contemporary teenager is more likely than any previous generation to have greater expertise than their parents in the areas they care about (computer literacy? video games? nuances of style?). Traditionally, this would be offset by the elders' accumulation of experience; but that has lost its value. Canadian youth worker Mary Dewar describes students she works with as having 'knowledge but not wisdom – they have facts but they don't have experience to know what to do with the facts.' But 'wisdom', like 'joy', is a word that seems to be disappearing from use; it implies some lost framework offering us a basis to organize the 'facts' and experiences we acquire, and so it gets used less and less except in Christian or 'New Age' contexts. Since there was no God leading us purposefully through life, what basis have we, as time goes on, to think we are any the 'wiser' or 'maturer'?

If we can't define maturity, then we find it harder to know what it means to 'grow' into an 'adult'.[72] 'To ask the question "What is an adult?" seems to put everyone at a disadvantage', says psychotherapist Adam Phillips. 'I know life has gotten so boring so quickly in so many ways – and that neither of us planned for this to happen', reflects the narrator of Coupland's novel *Life After God*. 'I never thought that we would end up in the suburbs with lawnmowers and swing sets. I never thought that I'd be a lifer at some useless company. But then wasn't this the way of the world? The way of adulthood, of maturity, of bringing up children?'[73] What else, with the disappearance of the loving and maturing purposes of God, is the 'way of adulthood, of maturity'? Not surprisingly, a number of feminist writers have complained that the contemporary male is a permanent adolescent. From the male side, Robert Bly (whose *Iron John* was a key text in the start of the debate on masculinity) agrees: 'Adults regress towards adolescence, and adolescents – seeing that – have no desire to become adults. Few are able to imagine any genuine life coming from the vertical plane – tradition, religion, devotion.' 'Perpetual adolescence – informally attired, developmentally-arrested and blithely irresponsible – seems to be the ideal state for young to middling adults', wrote Oliver Bennett in an *Independent on Sunday* survey of the '90s.

And whatever 'maturing' might come on the journey, at its end stands the final, unavoidable pressure-point: death. With God gone, death often seems to have become today's pornography, the ultimate unmentionable. (One of Noel Coward's characters demands honesty about death in the face of collective evasion: 'She didn't pass on or pass over or pass out – she died.') 'Civilisations before ours looked death in the face', wrote former French President Mitterand. 'For society and the individual they mapped a way through it. But now in this age of spiritual drought, never perhaps has our relationship with death been so deficient.' The ancient 'way through' is well summarized in the title of a Christian Medical Fellowship publication, *Dying: The Greatest Adventure of my Life*.[74] T.S. Eliot expresses the same sense of death as springboard as he climaxes 'East Coker':

> *Old men ought to be explorers*
>   *Here and there does not matter*
> *We must be still and still moving*
>   *Into another intensity*
> *For a further union, a deeper communion*
>   *Through the dark cold and the empty desolation,*
> *The wave cry, the wind cry, the vast waters*
>   *Of the petrel and the porpoise. In my end is my beginning.*

But this sense of adventure is grounded in faith in God and in an ongoing purpose that moves us on, 'farther up and farther in' ('Death is going home' – Mother Teresa). What happens now that is gone? 'Think at last', says Eliot's Gerontion, 'We have not reached conclusion, when I / Stiffen in a rented house.' What have we left but anger? 'Rage, rage against the dying of the light', wrote Dylan Thomas in one of the most famous poems of the mid-twentieth-century.[75]

It matters whether God is dead, and his purposes illusory. If they are, how should we describe what is left for us of aging and death? Anticlimax, struggle, termination, the cessation of hopes and dreams? At the end, perhaps, in our death as in our suffering, rage?

> It was not (to start again) what one had expected.
> What was to be the value of the long looked forward to,
> Long hoped for calm, the autumnal serenity
> And the wisdom of age? Had they deceived us
> Or deceived themselves, the quiet-voiced elders,
> Bequeathing us merely a receipt for deceit? ...
> The wisdom only a knowledge of dead secrets
> Useless in the darkness into which they peered
> Or from which they turned their eyes ...
>
> –T.S. Eliot, 'East Coker'

The loss of God inevitably made a major difference to our ability to feel a sense of meaningful 'purpose' and direction in life. So a feature of our culture is 'untargeted desire' – an unsatisfied hunger for something worthwhile or transcendent. Obvious alternative sources include the arts and romance; but these too have become problematic as a result of the 'disappearance of God'. Many 'alternative spiritualities' remain unconvincing in the longterm, while demonstrating the depth of our hunger. Some responses to this dilemma may become increasingly common in the next few years – deliberate escapism, the growing importance of 'game-playing', and the conscious self-surrender to the 'brute drives' of money, sex and power. Meanwhile, serious pressure points have resulted from our loss of the sense of God's loving purpose in areas like the meaning of adulthood, maturity, aging, suffering, death, and hope in a time of ecological crisis.

Once again, these pressures result logically from the disappearance of God from our world-view; it matters whether there is a God or not ...

Notes

1. George Steiner, in *The Death of Tragedy*, argues that tragic drama becomes impossible after the loss of all systems of belief such as Christianity, in terms of which human activity could have a tragic dignity. In general terms he has a point; as we saw in the previous chapter, human dignity becomes logically problematic after the death of God. But *The Chairs* offers us a different and powerfully tragic possibility. Watching Ionesco's characters, we become deeply aware, even by contrast, of the nobility that might have been.

2. Raymond Brazeau summarized Robbe-Grillet's stance in these terms: We now believe that 'Man and his factual world are the results of simple chance, arbitrary occurrences which happened to form a world. There is no substructure of order, no coherence ... All schematizations are falsifications, because they presuppose ...

the ability to interpret through language the existence of a universal reality.' Therefore, 'No longer is the novel a box in which various elements which appear merely to be heaped together reveal a neat order before the lid goes down.' There is no 'interrelation or unification'; ultimately the truth of what is going on 'neither matters nor exists'. The question is for how long art consistently building on the logic of postmodernity, and novels shunning any meaningful plot, can be worth reading, or whether (like tragic drama) the form dies. Brazeau comments that, as Robbe-Grillet's development continues, his novels become 'somewhat stiff and stereotyped', even 'ultimately sterile' (*An Outline of Contemporary French Literature*, pp. 40–42, 46).

3. *Act Without Words II* perhaps gives Beckett's presentation of life in its starkest terms: two figures clamber out of bags, perform a few trivial actions, clamber back into their bags.

4. It was, I believe, Emil Brunner who suggested that the unique thing about the view of work derived from God-centred Christian faith is that it gives a motivation for work as craftsmanship ('Do all things to the glory of God') that is more than purely economic. In contrast, both capitalism and Marxism tend in practice to view work largely as a means to economic and material gain.

5. The summary of Frankl's position is Mary Stewart Van Leeuwen's, in *The Sorceror's Apprentice*, p. 121.

6. Quoted in Os Guinness, *The Dust of Death*, p. 330.

7. Colin Wilson, *The Outsider*, p. 70.

8. Some of the clearest statements are in *Surprised by Joy*, the preface to *The Pilgrim's Regress*, and 'The Weight of Glory' in *Screwtape Proposes A Toast*. In *Surprised by Joy* Lewis describes the inmost essence of Joy as desire, 'an unsatisfied desire which is itself more desirable than any other satisfaction'. Henri Nouwen agrees: 'In every satisfaction, there is an awareness of its limitations ... In every embrace, there is loneliness. In every friendship, distance ... But this intimate experience in which every bit of life is touched by a bit of death can point us beyond the limits of our existence ... Expectation brings joy to the centre of our sadness.' (*Out of Solitude*, pp. 52, 60.)

9. Cf. C.S. Lewis, *Mere Christianity* (pp. 117–19). The 'trap' appears in the dwarves at the end of *The Last Battle* who 'refused to be taken in', and the prisoners who will not come out of the pit at the start of Book Four of *The Pilgrim's Regress*. 'But suppose infinite

happiness is there, really waiting for us? Suppose one really can reach the rainbow's end? In that case it would be a pity to find out too late (a moment after death)' (*Mere Christianity*, p. 118).

10. Wilson, *The Outsider*, p. 70 citing John 10:10.

11. F. Scott Fitzgerald, *The Great Gatsby* (pp. 8, 106).

12. The only eyes watching over the 'valley of ashes' (p. 29) are the unthinking, heedless eyes of a forgotten advertisement for an oculist; the man who appeals to them as divine authority (at some length, p. 166) goes off and kills Gatsby by mistake as a result. (The point is Henry Dan Piper's, in *The Great Gatsby: A Study*, p. 333.)

13. Or cf. Lewis' Teacher in *The Great Divorce*, p. 66: 'Every one of us lives only to journey further and further into the mountains.'

14. It should be added that at its best Reformed spirituality was, and is, something very deeply life-giving. For fine recent expressions, see for example Francis Schaeffer, *The God Who is There* and *True Spirituality*, Edith Schaeffer, *Hidden Art*, and Ranald Macaulay and Jerram Barr, *Being Human*.

15. Wilberforce's evangelical 'Clapham Saints', who campaigned tirelessly for the abolition of slavery, are an example, and many others to this day. In general these remarks do not apply so much to the state church's evangelical wing, with its much stronger commitment to mission. Anglicanism is highly diverse; Lewis was, of course, an Anglican.

16. Related, perhaps, is the image of the church (or even church-state) as 'city', which Alister McGrath sees as 'of central importance to Reformation spirituality' (*Roots that Refresh: A Celebration of Reformation Spirituality*, p. 114).

17. It should be said that, while we normally associate the Anabaptists with pacifism, parts of their movement fell into precisely the same trap of using physical violence for supposedly spiritual ends.

18. As Calvinism's spiritual passion dwindled, much of the dynamic inherent in the concept of divine 'calling' went into the emergence of capitalism: cf. R.H. Tawney, *Religion and the Rise of Capitalism*.

19. Hebrews 13:14. St Peter emphasizes this 'shape to existence' repeatedly in his first epistle, the classic 'pilgrim' letter.

20. At least the first two of Lewis' science fiction trilogy, four of the *Narnia Chronicles*, and *The Pilgrim's Regress*, are journey-narratives; at least five of the *Chronicles* and *That Hideous Strength* have to do with characters exploding the status quo in which they find themselves.

21. Time and again, powers for good in Tolkien are powers of the open road: the Rangers, the Nine Walkers, the Eldar or 'Wandering Companies', Gandalf the 'Grey Pilgrim', the Riders of Rohan.

22. This is the crucial choice at the close of book two of *The Lord of the Rings*. Cf. Peter Lowman, 'Supernaturalistic Causality and Christian Theism in the Modern English Novel', pp. 407–14. The quest into the open country is however motivated by a strong sense of calling, undergirded by prophecy.

23. Cf., for example, the classic Hindu teacher Shankara: 'By ceasing to do good to one's friends or evil to one's enemies, one attains to the eternal Brahman by the yoga of meditation' (quoted in Guinness, *Dust*, p. 224).

24. Jack Clemo, *The Invading Gospel* (1972 edn), p. 116. This exuberant, poetic, jubilant statement is one of the great out-of-print classics of contemporary spirituality, to which Clemo's own blindness and deafness give profound credibility. Clemo's powerful, earthy first novel *Wilding Graft*, with its defiant insistence that the dream ultimately finds fulfilment, needs to be read alongside *Gatsby*'s moving depiction of unattainability, referred to above.

25. Where Peter embodies the kingdom in the Word, his fellow-apostle Paul expresses it in terms of the Spirit of God, looking forward to a time when the 'creation will be liberated from its bondage to decay and brought into the glorious freedom' already possessed invisibly by 'the children of God ... who have the firstfruits of the Spirit' (Romans 8:21–23).

26. There is a difference here between the patterns expressed in the New Testament and the Old (at least once the 'exodus' is completed). In the Old Testament, God's 'reign' or 'kingdom' becomes embodied physically on earth – in Jerusalem, its king and its temple. So the Old Testament pattern of 'mission' is almost never to go out, Acts-style, but rather to invite the nations in to see the glory of God. The narratives of David and Solomon, climaxing in the building of the temple and the visit of the queen of Sheba, stand at the heart of this pattern. But see also, for example, Isaiah 2:1–4.

27. Cf. David Gooding, *According to Luke*.

28. Cf. Isaiah 61:1–4.

29. Clemo, *Invading Gospel*, pp. 43–44. Clemo himself relates this concept of the 'personal covenant' to Lewis' 'immortal longings' of Desire. Blackaby and King, in their stimulating book *Experiencing God*, speak in terms of sensing the divine invitation to become

involved with God in something he is *already* doing (p. 79). This is a helpful way of phrasing it, since the authentic Christian sense of calling stems not from an abstract doctrine that God has certain general concerns, but from relationship with a God who is active in specific and personal ways.

30. Romans 8:28.

31. Ephesians 4:16.

32. 'In order to make minimal sense of our lives ... we need an orientation to the good, which means some sense of qualitative discrimination, of the incomparably higher': that which we desire for our lives, and sense ourselves moving towards or away from (Charles Taylor, *Sources of the Self: The Making of the Modern Identity*, p. 47).

33. Christopher Lasch, *The Culture of Narcissism*, p. 320.

34. Steve Turner, *Hungry for Heaven* (1988 edn), pp. 26, 13, 17.

35. *Independent*, 15 August 1998.

36. In passing, the loss, post-God, of all notions of objective value also tends to undermine the idea of artistic self-expression as a life-goal, since in the absence of other values any expression tends to become meaningless. The act of 'self-expression' cannot *in itself* have value, unless joined with some other 'good'. (For example, the inherent value of the 'beauty' of what results.) If self-expression itself is ultimate in meaning, says Taylor, then the 'modes of life which this outlook encourages tend to a kind of shallowness ... Our normal understanding of self-realization presupposes that some things are important beyond the self, that there are some goods or purposes the furthering of which has significance for us and which hence can provide the significance a fulfilling life needs. A totally and fully consistent subjectivism would tend towards emptiness: nothing would count as a fulfilment in a world in which literally nothing was important but self-fulfilment' (*Sources of the Self*, p. 507). In practice, personal growth and self-realization probably come at times when they are not our prime goal (e.g. in parenthood). But if we deify self-realization and deny (or are unable to find) the reality of any other supreme value, we render meaningless our own self-realization.

37. C.S. Lewis, in *God in the Dock: Essays in Theology and Ethics*, p. 280. Lasch agrees, *Narcissism*, p. 218: 'The trivialization of art was already implicit in the modernist exaltation of art ... The modernist aesthetic guarantees the socially marginal status of art at the

same time that it opens art to the invasion of commercialized aesthetic fashion – a process that culminates, by a curious but inexorable logic, in the postmodern demand for the abolition of art and its assimilation to reality.'

38. The Christian would assume that, as men and women are made in God's image, they will continue to receive deep fulfilment from experiences of the creative gift their Creator has put within them, whatever orthodoxies dominate their thinking. But it will be interesting to watch how these intuitions are affected, long-term, by the current hostility to any expectation of the transcendent. In British arts television, for example, *Omnibus* editor Nigel Williams noted that 'There are now fewer and fewer arts programmes', adding, 'I and my fellow workers ... must bear a fair share of the responsibility', because of their postmodernist 'refusal to be reverent before the canon' and choosing instead to do 'programmes about things like the Ford Cortina'. During this process, he says, the 'arts programmes' began to vanish: '*Dejeuner sur l'herbe* gave way to the Ford Cortina. And after the Ford Cortina came a very large number of cookery programmes' (*Independent on Sunday*, 10 Aug. 1997).

39. Quoted in James Sire, *The Universe Next Door*, p. 164.

40. John Drane cites Carol Riddell of Findhorn expressing discomfort with the 'New Age' label (with which Findhorn has normally been identified), because of its association with 'sensation seekers ... whose interest lies less in seeking spiritual transformation than in dabbling in the occult, or in practising classical capitalist entrepreneurship on the naive' ('Methods and Perspectives in Understanding the New Age', *Themelios*, Feb. 1998, p. 23).

41. Where cinema is concerned with science fiction or the fantastic, it often has to offer some kind of statement as to where transcendence is to be found. Options in recent years have included ultimate technology ('Jim ... this is *transcendence!*', says Spock at the climax of *Star Trek: The Motion Picture*; the 'Genesis Project' has a similar function in *Star Trek III*); the mystical (the 'Force' of Lucas' *Star Wars* series); or even quasi-Christian content (*Tron* or *The Black Hole*).

42. C.S. Lewis, *The Four Loves* (1977 edn), p. 13.

43. Or a 'harder' escapism, into suicide. Almost certainly the crisis of purposelessness is one of the key factors in increased suicide rates; the rate among American 15- to 24-year-olds has apparently risen

by 300% over 20 years. A Samaritans survey of 16,000 British teenagers reported that 8% of boys and 17% of girls aged between 13 and 25 said they had made at least one suicide attempt, while just under half had felt there was no point in living.

44. The combination of media and drugs as twin narcotics was forecast years ago by Aldous Huxley in *Brave New World*.

45. Cf. *Generation X* author Douglas Coupland in *Life After God*: 'I was wondering what was the logical end product of this recent business of my feeling less and less. Is feeling nothing the inevitable end result of *believing* in nothing? ... I had been raised without religion by parents who had broken with their own pasts and moved to the West Coast – who had raised their children clean of any ideology in a cantilevered modern house overlooking the Pacific Ocean – at the end of history, or so they had wanted to believe' (pp. 177–78).

46. Quoted in H.R. Rookmaaker, *Modern Art and the Death of a Culture*, p. 174.

47. Lasch has an interesting analysis of how the 'attempt to invest sport with religious significance' ends up giving 'rise to its opposite ... ends with the demystification of sport, the assimilation of sport to show business' (*Narcissism*, pp. 218–19).

48. Lewis missed the point here. In *Surprised by Joy*, p. 136, he wrote that the essence of the experience he terms 'Joy' is that 'You desire not it but something other and outer. If by any perverse askesis or the use of any drug it could be produced from within, it would at once be seen to be of no value. For take away the object' (that is, the external source of 'joy'), 'and what, after all, would be left? – a whirl of images, a fluttering sensation, a momentary abstraction. And who could want that?' The answer is: anyone or any culture that has lost confidence in the value of anything external, and has nothing left for commitment but the internal 'rush'. (But if the 'rush' is indeed the name of the game, it can be obtained in more destructive ways, too: pornography and loveless eroticism, occultism, the excitements of danger or crime or football violence.)

49. J.P. Stern, *Nietzsche*, pp. 14–15. Cf. also Richard Foster, *Money, Sex and Power*.

50. Quoted in James W. Sire, *How to Read Slowly*, p. 15.

51. The 5 October 1997 *Independent on Sunday* quoted Paul Beresford, who had been researching the behaviour of Britain's wealthiest

families, as concluding, 'Money can never buy happiness for the future generations. You spend your life trying to get rich and when you get there you discover it's not worth it. You are even more insecure than when you were poor, you're fearful of losing it all, of being kidnapped and you worry about the effect it has on your kids.' Few children of post-war self-made millionaires managed to handle their riches successfully, he added. Geraldine Bedell wrote in the same newspaper a year earlier that the 'many studies of quality of life undertaken both in Europe and the United States all suggest that above the poverty line – say, for some 80% of the population – there is no correlation between increased income and increased happiness.'

52. 'I am absolutely convinced that meaninglessness does not come from being weary of pain', declares Indian Christian writer Ravi Zacharias, 'meaninglessness comes from being weary of pleasure' (*Can Man Live without God?*, pp. 178–79).

53. John Alexander offers another angle on how violence fits into what Ecstasy historian Matthew Collin (*Altered State*, p. 316) sees as the 'restless search for bliss' underpinning rave culture. 'Where do you get intense feelings?' asks Alexander. 'The obvious first answer is falling in love. The next answer is sex. And when sex fails, try drugs. And when drugs fail, try guns. And when guns fail, try death' (*The Secular Squeeze*, p. 101). The 'drive-by' violence of gangsta-rap culture shows how far along the process has already gone. Yet can you just step out of the 'search'?

54. This may sound implausible, but the corridor balls have been featured in various parts of the British media, including a thoroughly-documented piece by Nicole Veash in the 5 March 2000 *Independent on Sunday* and elsewhere.

55. Quoted in Turner, *Hungry for Heaven*, p. 112.

56. Nigel Lee, 'The Challenge: Europe in the '90s', in *Evangelicals Now*, Jan. 1990.

57. Of course this interplay of fear and the absence of faith may have health implications. In 1998, the *American Journal of Psychiatry* reported a Duke University (North Carolina) study of 4,000 over-65s showing that the stronger an elderly person's religious beliefs, the better they handled stress and depression, 'independent of medical intervention and quality of life issues'. Those with religious faith had 40% lower blood pressure than those who did not – significantly lowering their chances of a stroke or heart disease. Project leader Harold Koenig, himself not a Christian, saw this

as resulting from the way their faith enabled them to deal with problems and stress.

58. T.S. Eliot, 'Burnt Norton'.
59. Henri Nouwen, *Seeds of Hope*, pp. 55, 57–58.
60. Romans 8:28.
61. For a vibrant and moving expression of all this, see again *The Invading Gospel* by the blind and deaf Cornish poet, Jack Clemo, particularly ch. 7, 'The Rout of Tragedy'. Other deeply meaningful expressions are the quadriplegic Joni Eareckson Tada's books, *Joni* and *A Step Further*; also Edith Schaeffer, *Affliction*. Clemo in particular sets out to establish an approach to suffering based around the finality of the resurrection rather than the crucifixion, and around 'exuberance' rather than 'wistfulness'.
62. Hebrews 10:38; Romans 1:17; Galatians 3:11; Habakkuk 2:4.
63. Jesus' words in Matthew 27:46. Cf. also the 'sealed book' of war, famine, imperialism, economic injustice, disease and religious persecution described in Revelation 5 and 6: it is something 'sealed' to all – except Christ, 'because you were slain, and with your blood you purchased men for God' (5:9). Christ alone went to the utter heart of the darkness, Revelation implies, and he alone can understand all our suffering.
64. E.g. Romans 8:17–18, 2 Corinthians 4:8–12, 16–17, 1 Peter 1:6–7,11; 4:13–14; 5:1,10.
65. As Paul himself was well aware. If the resurrection never happened, he says in 1 Corinthians 15, 'We are to be pitied more than all men ... If I fought wild beasts in Ephesus for merely human reasons, what have I gained? If the dead are not raised, "Let us eat and drink, for tomorrow we die."'
66. Paul Vitz, *Psychology as Religion: The Cult of Self-Worship* (1994 edn). Vitz instances the work of Carl Rogers, Rollo May, Erich Fromm and Abraham Maslow.
67. Vitz, *Psychology*, pp. 139–40.
68. Proverbs 16:31; cf. 20:29.
69. Ronald Sider cites a Colorado state governor who suggested in a public speech that terminally-ill elderly persons 'have a duty to die and get out of the way' (*Completely Pro-Life*, p. 39).
70. Compare, again, Henri Nouwen's confident affirmation: 'Aging is the turning of the wheel, the gradual fulfilment of the life cycle' (*Seeds*, p. 185). Nouwen has an entire book titled *Aging: The Fulfilment of Life*.

71. Kurt Vonnegut, *Cat's Cradle*, p. 125.

72. Our culture's puzzlement at this question is a factor in the booming but confusing 'personal growth' industry (what is 'personal growth'? If I've taken courses in yoga and Moroccan cookery, does that constitute 'growth'?); and likewise in our inability to decide what education is 'for'.

73. Coupland, *Life After God*, p. 151.

74. A famous recent expression of the Christian confidence regarding death is the book David Watson wrote while dying of cancer, *Fear No Evil*.

75. Dylan Thomas, 'Do Not Go Gentle Into That Good Night'. Jack Clemo responds to Thomas directly in a poem in his 1988 Bloodaxe *Selected Poems* titled 'I Go Gentle', where he insists that this 'terminal rage gets us nowhere' – it leads only to the 'wrong grave, the dead end ...'

ethics after God

'is there still an above and a below?'

> *'There are altogether no moral facts ...* Morality is merely an interpretation of certain phenomena – more precisely, a misinterpretation ...'
>
> –Nietzsche, *Twilight of the Idols*[1]

'There are no moral facts.' The mother only left her toddler, fastened by the reins at the door of a Liverpool butcher's shop, for a couple of minutes. When she turned round, James Bulger was gone. Two kids had taken him. They dragged him weeping through the streets, and ended up stoning him brutally to death on a railway embankment.

It caused plenty of soul-searching. 'Evil is seeping into more and more people's lives', said one observer. Liverpool Football Club observed two minutes' silence. Tony Blair said that the atrocity challenged Britain to 'wake up and look unflinchingly at what we see', and he called for a reassertion of the clear difference between right and wrong.

The Bulger murder was only one of several such events sparking off anguished discussion of our 'ethical collapse' in recent years. A Gallup survey reported that most Britons 'believe concern for others and public-spiritedness has declined in the last decade'. As concrete evidence, it showed the great number of people unwilling even to report violent assault if it was committed by a friend or relative. The 'needs of your own folk' were now the main basis left for ethical life – and that was producing results rather different from our traditional ideas of 'public-spiritedness' and right and wrong. Strikingly, the same day's newspapers revealed the British government Department of Trade's 'dirty-tricks' handbook, written to teach Britain's entrepreneurs how to lie effectively when abroad. What's happening?

It isn't so easy to 'reassert the clear difference between right and wrong'. Once upon a time there was a God who showed us right and wrong, and why they mattered. But now we have jettisoned this God. So what, if anything, has taken his place? Moral values are merely interpretations, or, 'more precisely', misinterpretations, says Nietzsche; there are no 'moral facts'. Do 'right' and 'wrong' have any meaning now? Is there any compelling reason to be anything other than selfish?

Our schoolteachers, of course, taught us a soothing humanistic response. Right and wrong were what was good or bad for people in general, they said, or at least for the greatest number of them. You did what was good for society, and this was 'right'. But all that depended significantly on the conditioning left over from Christianity ('Love your neighbours as yourself ... Do as you would be done by'). As the conditioning receded, society became vulnerable to the rebel-challenge raised last century by Nietzsche, then more drastically by Hitler: Why should I play the game? Suppose I base what I choose to do, not on the needs of 'people in general', but on my own 'rules', my tribal – or even personal – urges and desires?

After all, why not? Anti-Christian writers like Richard Dawkins, proclaiming the ultimacy of the 'selfish gene' in our existence, have played into the hands of such attitudes. If the final reality is really the evolutionary struggle; and if that struggle is about the survival of the fittest, and the strong surviving at the expense of the weak; is classroom morality any more than one optional preference among others? Indeed, are we left with any real, objective moral case against fascism? Wasn't the argument of Nazism that the Jews were a degenerate people, and that therefore their destruction by a stronger race was entirely in tune with evolutionary nature? Why, in the end, should we care about 'everybody else', when nature doesn't?

It isn't merely a fascist question today. Many of the forces busy dismantling the welfare state, or fighting exclusively for their own 'special interest' group (whether religious, sexual, gender-based or ethnic), reveal the collapse of the old liberal consensus that based 'right and wrong' on the 'shared needs of society'. Just why, among all today's pressures, should we be expected to bother about 'shared needs'? Why should we 'put others first'?

Once again it was Nietzsche, German prophet of the death of God, who saw the ethical collapse coming:

> They are rid of the Christian God, and now believe all the more firmly that they must cling to Christian morality. That is an English consistency ... We others [in Germany] hold otherwise. When one gives up the Christian faith, one pulls the right to Christian morality out from under one's feet. This morality is by no means self-evident: this point has to be exhibited again and again, despite the English flatheads. Christianity is a system, a whole view of things thought out together. By breaking one main concept out of it, the faith in God, one breaks the whole; nothing necessary remains in one's hands.[2]

Nietzsche titled another of his books *Beyond Good and Evil*. This was to become a modish catch-phrase for rock groups and science fiction; and in the mid-twentieth century it sounded fine – provided we could safely reduce it to 'beyond traditional morality and conventional standards', but still keep our basic liberal norms (e.g. the outlawing of torture) intact. The postmodern world, however, is a chillier place. Increasingly we face the question posed by Raskolnikov murdering the old woman in Dostoevski's *Crime and Punishment*, and in a different way by the Marquis de Sade who genuinely seems to have enjoyed hurting people: What if, with God dead, we have no good and evil *at all*? What if there really is nothing bearing on our actions besides self-interest ... if there is indeed, as Nietzsche says, neither up nor down: what then?

Or to put the question in its most unpleasant form: if there is, objectively, neither right nor wrong; if this is just a planet working through an evolutionary process where the stronger race overcomes and devours or eliminates the weaker ... *Why was Hitler 'wrong'?*

And what happens in our culture – to our social support networks, to our police system, to our legal system – if there are no convincing answers to that question?

Why our rights aren't enough

If we want to 'look unflinchingly' at these questions, as Tony Blair suggested, we'll find that our current crisis began on the intellectual level.

Now, this book explores a very wide range of issues, so parts of it will be more relevant for some readers

> 'Why should people not steal if this is the only way they can consume? Why should they not drink in the streets and throw empty cans in the gutter if it suits their individual choice? Why should they have a mind for frightened old ladies if there is no economic advantage in doing so?'
>
> *–Independent on Sunday* editorial

than others; and it's deliberately written in sections that different readers can either use or omit for now. The first halves of these next two chapters will be the most intense sections of the book; some readers will want the complete picture, while others may find the goings-on of academic ethicists bizarre and uninteresting and prefer to skip down to the section titled 'Not my problem' (p. 115) or 'After morality' (p. 143), where we focus on the practicalities of all this. But if we understand what's happened on the academic level, we will have a better handle on the practical issues.

We'll tell the story in two parts: first, the inadequacy of 'human rights', and the 'contract' mindset that's dominated (and ruined?) Britain's 'post-God' conservatives; and second, what's gone wrong in the academic ghetto.

Alasdair MacIntyre's masterly *After Virtue*[3] records the long inability of post-Enlightenment thought to find a substitute for the moral framework previously supplied by Christian belief and the classical tradition. He describes the successive failures: Hume's attempt to show that morality coincided, in the long run, with our desires and passions (p. 49); Kant's attempt to show it was based on universal, self-evident, categorical rational principles (p. 46); and the 'utilitarian' tradition, arguing that personal happiness is attained by seeking general happiness. Unfortunately, that notion of general 'happiness' proved undefinable and inadequate (what if the public enjoys torturing Jews, or the killing of a minority promotes the general good?), and just why personal and general happiness were connected was also very unclear (p. 63). Thus the nineteenth-century tradition came to a close with Sidgwick accepting uneasily that, if there is no God, then moral beliefs do not form a coherent unity, and their acceptance is and has to be unargued (p. 65).

That wasn't a complete dead end; early in the twentieth century this very lack of a rational foundation for ethics was welcomed with enthusiasm, during the dominance of 'intuitionist' ideas such as those of G.E. Moore. Propositions declaring this or that action to be good are 'intuitions', said Moore; we recognize the 'goodness' of an act just as we recognize whether something is yellow (though Moore was unclear why, having recognized 'goodness', we should act upon it). But intuitionism proved thoroughly inadequate. As the century progressed, Moore's easy confidence in our ability to recognize and agree upon the meaning of 'goodness' vanished, and it became clear that these 'intuitions' varied from person to person. That pointed inevitably to relativism. Moral philosophy became dominated by 'emotivism', which saw moral statements ('This is good') as having no factual content at all. Rather, they become mere expressions of our emotional preferences and feelings: 'Hurrah for this!', or, 'I approve of this; do so as well!'

Obviously, says MacIntyre, such expressions of feeling can be neither true nor false. Nor can there be any rational way of settling disagreements between them; so agreement on an ethical issue is 'secured, if at all, by producing certain non-rational effects on the emotions or attitudes of those who disagree with one' (p. 12). Obviously this is a very serious point to have reached; moral persuasion stands revealed as either manipulation or a power play. Logically, 'if and insofar as emotivism is true, moral language is seriously misleading and ... ought to be abandoned' (p. 20). It is unreasonable, even foolish, for any of us to talk in terms of 'right' and 'wrong' any more.

All this may sound very strange. We speak so naturally of our 'rights'; indeed, 'rights' have been central to the 'modern' liberal's entire way of thinking. It comes as a shock when we first realize that 'right and wrong' in general, and our 'rights' in particular, have very little foundation.

'I have my rights': but where did I get them from? What (against Hitler, or the slave traders) gives me 'rights' that should not be violated? Are they just a comforting fiction, like one young child shouting 'You're not allowed!' to another? God is dead; who else can be a 'rights-giver'? Perhaps we awarded our 'rights' to ourselves. But then what gives human rights precedence over, say, the rights of fish not to be eaten? To say only human beings have rights seems almost as racist as arguing that only white humans have rights. Increasingly, many of us subscribe to some idea of animal rights. But which animals? How do we decide who or what has rights? By level of consciousness, perhaps? Chamberlain points out that we often base our own special 'human rights' on qualities that we possess but animals don't, like reason or creativity; but many animals possess equally impressive qualities that we lack. (He cites Taylor, who points to the speed of a cheetah, the abilities of birds to fly and of trees to photosynthesize light.[4]) No species has damaged the environment as we have; if lack of destructiveness were the criterion, humans should have the least rights. Presumably the smallpox microbe has no rights; in fact we will exterminate it if we can. But does a snake have rights? Does a lobster?

At any rate, all human beings, we may feel, have innate 'rights'. Yet this was just what Hitler denied – and what may well need defending soon, as the Christian heritage recedes into the past. Where do all these 'rights' come from, since they don't come from God? Bentham, the father of utilitarianism, spoke of the whole idea of rights as 'nonsense upon stilts'. Is all such talk purely arbitrary, a way of defending our own interests or, at best, expressing feelings that come with our more generous moods? The answers are scarcely self-evident.

One response that has been important in shaping Britain during recent decades has been the notion of 'social contract'. From this perspective, innate 'rights' and values don't exist; but we humans agree to award them to each other, since such a 'contract' will enable society to function smoothly. This way of thinking originated with Hobbes. The natural state of humankind, argued Hobbes, is an amoral war of all against all; such a condition was unliveable, so we invented rights and moral values. But there is nothing objectively 'real' about either; the 'contract' just makes life more liveable for the community that operates with it.

> 'I have often asked myself why human beings have any rights at all ... These values ... make sense only in the perspective of the infinite and the eternal.'
>
> –Vaclav Havel[5]

These ideas have an influence far outside the academic ghetto. But they are full of problems. First, as Mary Midgley points out, they are inadequate. A 'contract' can exist between articulate persons only; in such a system we cannot think of the 'weak and inarticulate' (for instance mentally defective people) having 'mutually-agreed' rights, nor indeed of the non-human world. Midgley tries to imagine Robinson Crusoe being tempted to devastate his island home, and notes that as a creature of his time he would have felt an 'invincible objection' to doing so, an objection arising from his 'duty to God'. However,

The language of our moral tradition has tended strongly, ever since the Enlightenment, to make that objection unstateable. All the terms which express that an obligation is serious or binding – duty, rights, law, morality, obligation, justice – have been deliberately narrowed in their use so as to apply only in the framework of contract, to describe only relations holding between free and rational agents ... Unless you take either religion or science fiction seriously, we can only have duties to humans, and sane, adult, responsible humans at that.

And she quotes Grice:

It is an inescapable consequence of the thesis presented in these pages that *certain classes cannot have natural rights:* animals, the human embryo, future generations, lunatics and children under the age of, say, ten. In the case of young children at least, my experience is that this consequence is found hard to accept. But it is a consequence of the theory; it is, I believe, true; and I think we should be willing to accept it.[6]

No rights for children, then? But that unpleasant result isn't the only inadequacy of this form of atheism. Ultimately, it's completely selfish; we accept the contract to make social life liveable for ourselves. Yet to work, it depends, like any other contract, on people keeping their word, keeping their side of the bargain. So then, as Hume asked two centuries ago: 'Why are we bound to keep our word?' The only answer (within this approach) is mutual – collectively selfish – advantage: 'Groups whose members adhere to such a practice' (that is, whose members abide by the contract and respect each other's 'rights') '...enjoy benefits in interaction that are denied to others.'[7] Now, it may be true that if we abide by the contract it will benefit our social group as a whole; it may also be true that individual members will benefit, so long as the groups are small and fairly egalitarian. But the larger a group becomes, the less clear it gets that sticking to the rules will lead to my benefit – or even to that of the majority of members. (So people begin to steal from the supermarket. They themselves won't lose by it, nor will anyone they know personally.) My 'doing what's right' according to the social 'contract' benefits society: so what? And the contract becomes doubly powerless when the obligations on my side of the contract were chosen for me by others, not by myself.[8] Why should I be bound by them? Why should I not abandon the contract just as soon as it suits me to do so? For self-interest was its ultimate basis anyway.

But thirdly, 'keeping our word' in the contract only makes sense when the participants are roughly equal in power; outside that situation it has little to say. Mutual advantage is the basis for a contract, but mutual advantage depends on mutual bargaining power. And the weak and infirm, Kymlicka notes,

> produce little of value, and what little they do produce may be simply expropriated by others without fear of retaliation. Since there is little to gain by co-operation with the infirm, and nothing to fear from retaliation, the strong have little reason to accept [or keep] conventions which help the infirm.

In the world of social contract, the weak have no innate 'rights'; 'rights' (and 'wrongs') are what we agree to make them. Our 'everyday' intuition is that our moral obligations are increased by someone else's vulnerability; but social contract gives no basis for this, and indeed offers no reason why we 'should' not simply kill or enslave them. (Hobbes himself was willing to say that irresistible power 'justifieth all actions really and properly'.) Thus 'There are no grounds within the theory to prefer justice to exploitation', concludes Kymlicka.[9] (For example, we can imagine a situation where a society decides to defuse its internal tensions by giving over the members of one weaker ethnic group for gang rape. Social contract morality has nothing to say to that at all.)

This may all sound theoretical; but aren't we seeing the consequences today, that community doesn't work if its only basis is the self-oriented negotiation of 'my rights'? Without a further, shared belief in something like the Christian ideal of 'love for your neighbour' or for the community, the rights-emphasis becomes inadequate, hyper-individualistic. We watch the law courts clogging up (and our own costs rising, as insurance premiums soar for public amenities as a result) through individuals' consistent pursuit of their rights. Aren't we finding that 'rights' need to be complemented (but this must be voluntary, empowered internally; it cannot be compelled) by an intelligent understanding of when not to insist on the letter of our rights?[10] Such a deliberate unselfishness is a strong feature of the ethics of radical love that Jesus teaches his community of discipleship (see the sermon on the mount, particularly Matthew 5:38–48). But with the 'loss of God', we seem to lack a basis for it. On its own, however, the contract-based rights system seems to turn into something greedily demanding, individualistic to the point of alienation.

'Contract theory has experienced a remarkable rebirth in recent years', says Kymlicka. Inevitably so: if there is no God, then the idea of ethics and 'rights' as things we choose to create (or negotiate) together becomes an obvious option. But the social contract idea gives us no real basis for fostering unselfishness; it needs some other moral basis to make it work. As we've seen, it is essentially optional, ultimately arbitrary, and fundamentally self-oriented; and its implications, followed through logically, could be poisonous. In the end, it isn't enough to live by, basic though it has been to much of the ethics of humanistic modernity. In postmodernity, however, 'rights' have begun to look like certain other features of the 'modern' period: concepts that liberalism inherited from its Christian heritage, but was quite unable, post-God, either to explain or to preserve. And what will happen, now in our 'postmodern' century, as the word gets around?

> Was their surrender to contractual thinking a major reason why Britain's conservatives lost their way in the last 20 years?
>
> Contract is an interesting model to choose as a basis for human life. Some would say its prominence

reflects an era dominated by capitalism – a drab time when, ultimately, commercial relations are all that counts.[11] But maybe the British education and health services still bear the huge bruises inflicted as these abstract ideas bore fruit.

The results of a situation where contract is all, where there is no other ethical basis, were highlighted in an intriguing *Times* article by Raymond Plant. Modern Conservatism often argues that public institutions such as education or the health service need to be governed by fixed contract rather than communal idealism (a 'sentimental public service ethic', as it gets called). To this way of thinking, those who work in such services are not ultimately motivated by a different set of goals from those in the market sector; both groups are essentially involved in a contractual relationship where they are motivated by their own gain. So in the public sector, neo-conservatives have argued, we need more market-type relationships, where all involved can be judged primarily by the efficiency with which they work towards the achievement of purely private – that is, self-oriented – ends.

Plant brilliantly analysed why this whole attitude was doomed. Ultimately, he noted, 'not everything in a contract is contractual ... The contractual relationship is actually based on trust, commitment, fair dealing, keeping promises, and so forth. These moral preconditions are indispensable if contractual relationships are to work.' Contract, in short, cannot be a sufficient basis for community on its own; it has to be supplemented by such things as trust, professional ethics, and the sense of vocation.

Plant then spelled out the consequences that many of us will recognise: 'I have recently heard many teacher and doctor friends say that, because of the way their professions are being taken over by the contractual model, they will stick to the letter of the contract and do what is required by it and nothing else. Ministers can hardly then appeal to professional ethics and duty, since it is they who have sought to replace them by contract.' (And, of course, the shift away from the 'public service' idealism that at least partly fuelled recruitment is an issue in Britain's critical shortage of teachers and nurses; a teacher's or nurse's life isn't so good a deal ('contract') if that's all it comes down to.)

Which is to say: one reason why Britain was left the worse (in significant respects) by Thatcherism was that, without the deep-seated ethical framework that we forfeited with the loss of God, the appeal to contract-based market forces alone doesn't work. Instead, society becomes increasingly individualistic, with everyone playing for himself by whatever rules may profit him. Long-term, the result could all too easily resemble the mafia-dominated jungle that followed the rise of the 'free market' in Russia, after so many of Russia's ethical foundations had been destroyed by communism.

The social contract works when there is something else underpinning it. But we don't seem to have found anything to do that since we gave up on God.

Voices from the ghetto

To oversimplify: broadly speaking, two or three basic options have dominated modern academic attempts to build a basis for ethics after the loss of God. And in our day, none have proved very compelling.

First, there have been the approaches based on *Kantianism*, with its famous 'categorical imperative'. 'Act only according to that maxim by which you can at the same time will that it should become a universal law', it reads in one version – that is, act in such a way that you can be comfortable with the thought of everyone acting the same way as yourself. In another version of the 'imperative', Kant insisted that we should always treat human beings as ends in themselves, not as means. It is ironic that Kant's system became a key God-substitute in western ethics, when Kant himself wrote that

> Belief in a God and in another world is so interwoven with my moral sentiment that, as there is little danger of my losing the latter, there is equally little cause for fear that the former can ever be taken from me.[12]

But with God now gone, various problems arise with Kant's idea. How far does he assume what he seeks to affirm? How far does his lofty insistence on the importance of treating humans as ends involve assuming that they possess a freedom about which postmodern psychology is deeply sceptical? And whence comes the authority of this abstract 'imperative'? That a moral framework (even, alas, a whole confusing range of contradictory frameworks) can be built on it seems clear; what is never clear is why anyone 'should' adopt and live by it in the first place. Kantianism resembles a religion that makes sense for its adherents. But it is not obvious why anyone else should join them, or live by their ethics when it hurts.

(The circular argument reappears in the best-known recent neo-Kantian, John Rawls. Rawls defines the moral act as the one we would choose in what he calls the 'original position', one where we are under a 'veil of ignorance' as to our actual strength, position or assets relative to others. In such a situation, he says, the acts I would choose will be those that benefit people in each situation in society, since I may end up as any of them; self-interest will dictate benevolence, impartiality and the promotion of liberty and substantial equality. But as Kymlicka observes, Rawls too assumes a prior commitment to the idea of justice he is seeking to support. If they share it, then someone in the 'original position' will indeed act impartially; but if someone held a different view of justice, what they would do in the 'original position' could be very different too.[13] For example, they might equally well (and equally 'rightly') act completely selfishly, gambling that they might benefit thereby. As Singer comments, 'Perhaps independent agents in this situation would choose whatever principles would maximise their prospects of getting what they want'.[14] In this case 'ethics' seems again to become no more than a contract, with its value judged by its ability to bring about the greatest (self-oriented) good for the contracting party themselves – with all the problems that we noted in the previous section. So Rawls' ethics isn't really helped very much by the 'original position'. As Kymlicka says, it fits the moral intuitions many of us (often) feel, but does little to support or defend them. Indeed, even if the 'original position' might point me towards benevolent impartiality, why should I live by that when my actual situation is very different? So, as with Kant himself, Rawls' neo-Kantianism seems to lack motivational power for the ethics he advocates.)

The second main group of options for a post-God ethics is those of *utilitarianism*. Here, right or wrong actions are recognized by their consequences. In the most classic variant, a right action is that which contributes to the greatest pleasure or happiness of the greatest number of people. (Or, in a more modern form, satisfies the preferences or interests of the greatest number of people.) Put like that, the principle may sound so obviously true (and has been taught in so many classrooms) that it can come as a shock when we first realize its weaknesses. But as Goodin observes, 'There is nothing in the theory that says that people should have these [particular] sorts of preferences'; the theory simply says that it is 'good – good for them – to have their preferences satisfied, whatever those preferences might be'. As Goodin adds, even John Stuart Mill, the author of *Utilitarianism*, 'could not help chafing at that conclusion. Surely there are some things – truth, beauty, love, friendship – that are good in themselves, whether or not people happen to desire them.'[15] And surely there are likewise things that are *bad* in themselves – the degradation of the environment, or the wiping out of the Jews in parts of medieval Europe – whether or not the majority of people prefer them. (Gang rape might in certain circumstances – on a desert island, for example – be argued to be conducive to the pleasure, happiness, and preferences of the majority; but can we then say it is 'good'?) Otherwise, 'good' becomes a word for that which is agreed upon as meeting society's needs and desires;[16] and then it is all about market forces, and can be fixed by whoever is best at mass manipulation. But utilitarianism gives little basis for asking these kinds of questions. Right and wrong have no other meaning than that which is desired, preferred or seen as needed – by the majority.

This can have serious implications for minorities and the marginalized. The forced sterilization over many years of gypsies and 'travellers' in famously liberal Sweden is a practical twentieth-century example. With God dead, our society needs some ethical basis to work on, but reducing ethics to the majority's concerns is a very wooden basis for handling human diversity and the claims of conflicting preferences or desires. Should we let a few hospital patients die to provide transplant organs and free up doctors' time for many others? Who decides, and on what basis? If utilitarianism is true, and you lose the vote, you are, in so far as the word has meaning, 'wrong', and there is not much more to be said. This could have unfortunate consequences, as we see from Sartre's statement of the communist variant of utilitarianism: 'A revolutionary regime must dispose of a certain number of individuals which threaten it, and I can see no other means of accomplishing this than death.' 'Twelve thousand scoundrels eliminated in time might have saved the lives of a million real Germans', wrote Hitler. In Russia, Zhirinovski said more recently that if he became president 'Those who have to be arrested will be arrested quietly at night. I may have to shoot a hundred thousand people, but the other three hundred million will live peacefully.'

Inevitably, in any system that defines 'right' as that which satisfies the preferences of the greatest number, the ends tend to justify the means. Might it be 'right' (as has been suggested) to outlaw famine relief if that was one way of reducing the global population and so contributing to the greater happiness of the majority? Is it 'right' (as has frequently happened) to torture the innocent so as to control terrorists who are related to them, if this will indeed increase the happiness of the vast majority? Or rather, on what basis could a utilitarian say it was wrong (and then agitate to prevent it recurring)? Would it be right (to quote a famous example) for a sheriff in a racist town to agree to – even carry out – the lynching of an innocent black man, if he knows that thereby a race riot will be prevented in which the entire black community might violently perish? The point here is not that allowing the lynching might in some horrific circumstances be viewed as the lesser evil, but rather that in utilitarianism's terms it is actually *right*.[17] There is a deeply unconvincing inadequacy about this whole version of 'right' and 'wrong'. And in the end there remains the other huge, unanswered question: Why, anyway, should I bother about the majority? If 'right' and 'wrong' are merely descriptions of what is best for others, and they do not happen to be what is best for me: why should I play the game? Why should I not put my own interests first?

> The second *Star Trek* movie got into this issue, when at the climax Spock sacrifices his life, giving voice to the creed of logical utilitarianism (as one might expect from a Vulcan): 'The interests of the many take precedence over the interests of the few – or the one.' Clearly its makers were uncomfortable with the implications of this, and *Star Trek III* saw Kirk and company turn thieves and deserters to bring Spock back to life. Kirk stated the motive for that unexpected villainy at the close: 'The needs of the one outweigh the needs of the many.'
>
> Interestingly, to make this reaffirmation of the individual work, the film's writers had to invoke the idea of a soul. It is initially to retrieve Spock's soul that Kirk steals the *Enterprise*; 'If there's even a chance that Spock has an eternal soul ...' is how he defends the journey to his unsympathetic Starfleet superior, and 'If I hadn't tried I would have lost my soul' is how he

describes his own situation. At least one Christian concept had to be reintroduced for the film's ethic to be able to reaffirm the individual's value against the primacy of the mass.

It seems to me that this applies even to the most convincing modern writer of this kind, R.M. Hare. Hare's work explores what is involved in a personal commitment to the use of moral language such as 'ought'. One is left wondering, however, whether in the end he is merely unpacking a verbal construct, the validity of which is presupposed. When he tackles the 'amoralist' in his book *Moral Thinking*, he concedes that he cannot 'see anything logically inconsistent in his position', and that 'amoralism is an option left open by our system of moral reasoning'. The argument he offers is that, in actual reality, the person thinking only of his own self-interest will still end up happier if he cultivates what are generally viewed as moral dispositions.[18] Which might be true; but it has little force when we must argue against the amoralist (particularly the amoralist inside our own head) who knows full well that a grossly selfish or cruel action will lead to the greatest personal happiness in the short- or even medium-term. Hare's work is impressive (to this reader anyway); but it again seems merely to be defining what ethics can mean for someone who already accepts the importance of moral concerns, and is willing to be morally motivated, rather than supplying any basis for that motivation. He seems to be exploring what is meant by 'I ought'; his response is not clear to '*Why* "ought" I?'

So neither Kantianism nor utilitarianism offer us notions of 'right' and 'wrong' that seem truly realistic and compelling. There are other possible approaches. Various liberal writers have tried to argue that rational thought itself provides a basis for morality; such thought necessitates a certain freedom and well-being, which a rational person must therefore view as a fundamental right. But, as MacIntyre points out, the fact that we need or want something does not mean we have some kind of 'right' to it,[19] nor need it imply that it should therefore be available, as of right, to others. Similarly, Habermas builds an ethic on what would emerge in conditions of unconstrained communication. The problem is that the value he puts (again as a liberal) on what emerges from human consensus is simply not self-evident. Indeed, it is precisely what many postmodernists deny.[20]

Ethics in disarray

To work one's way through contemporary books of academic ethics is to encounter a deep sense of powerlessness and confusion.[21] Until the 'death of God', we had a strong reason for unselfishness. But, since then, we haven't come up with much of a replacement.

Time and again, it seems that academic ethics can operate only by assuming beforehand that impartiality and unselfishness are good.[22] And that, as Nietzsche insisted, simply cannot be assumed, 'despite the English flatheads'. The attempt is what we should expect in the first century or so after the 'loss of God', when the liberal establishment have been trying to hold on to basically Christian ethics (love your neighbour) without their Christian underpinning. But now the weather is changing, and increasingly the 'realist' voices seem to be those of Foucault and his disciples, who see the world primarily as the arena of an unending power-conflict and 'play of dominations'. The academic ghetto has little to set convincingly against the selfishness that would seem normal in such a world. 'Clearly there is a gaping hole here', writes Charles Taylor. 'We might be tempted to put it this way: they [academic ethicists] leave us nothing to say to someone who asks why he should be moral.'[23] If Singer is right, that 'We have no need to postulate gods who hand down commandments to us, because we can understand ethics as a natural phenomenon that arises in the course of evolution ... Human ethics evolved from the social instincts that we inherited from our non-human ancestors', there is no automatic reason why we should continue to be bound by them – as Singer himself recognizes.[24]

At the close of one of his fine symposia, Singer faces the possibility that contemporary academic ethics is in a state of complete and irreconcilable disarray.[25] In fact he remains optimistic. (One suspects this is because Singer himself is driven by powerfully-felt intuitions about animal rights, and his sense of certainty about the 'truth' of these pulls him back from the relativistic brink.[26]) Singer sees increasing agreement among different thinkers that decisions taken in a position of pure, impartial decision-making could thereafter define for us what was moral.[27] But again, perhaps all that is resurfacing here is a shared intuition of the value of impartiality, a shared inability ethicists face 'after God' to work without an assumption that we 'should' value this over an egoistic perspective. And there are further problems. Singer seems especially attracted by Michael Smith's notion that a 'moral fact' exists when 'rational creatures would *converge* upon a desire' to act in a particular way. But Smith himself admits there is little sign of this happening in any widespread manner that might provide solid ground for speaking of specific, undeniable 'moral facts': 'It must be agreed on all sides that moral argument has not yet produced the sort of convergence in our desires that would make the idea of a moral fact ... look plausible.'[28] Indeed, Smith's confidence that such convergence would be both possible and valuable seems curiously 'modernist'. We are used, of course, to the 'modern' liberal humanist assuming that his values are not only politically correct but universally self-evident. But the more recent postmodern mood is deeply suspicious of any such 'totalizing' convergence, and of the manipulative forces that might bring it into being. And there would still remain the obligation issue: Even if 'convergence' did occur, why should I join in the game? Why listen to the majority? Why not tear up the rules?

There is of course an entire academic industry devoted to solving these issues. (Actually that is too idealistic a phrasing: 'furthering the discussion' is what most would say, as if time were not an issue.) And the industry will continue to produce. But at this point there seems some force in Anscombe's suggestion that moral philosophy should be laid aside now that we no

> 'The contemporary world has entirely lost its comprehension of morality. Though we continue to use ethical language, we have lost the philosophical context which gave it significance. Western culture committed a suicidal blunder when it abandoned its biblical heritage and sought to secularise the field of human knowledge.'
>
> –MacIntyre

longer believe in God, since the attempt to have moral law without a Lawgiver has proved meaningless. Sometimes it seems we have a whole slew of thinkers trying to make their sums add up so as to justify the inherited, Christian 'golden rule' they intuitively value. But intuitions are not enough to live by. Intuitions need a rational underpinning such as that which Christian faith used to provide, and this is lacking. Indeed, even the 'convergence of positions' that encourages Singer seems to point, bizarrely, to the need for a Christ. It focuses on defining 'right' as that action which would be chosen by an ideal observer, 'a person who was being as reasonable and impartial as it is humanly possible … whatever a perfectly rational, impartial, and benevolent judge would think best' (Rachels' version[29]), 'what an unbiased and otherwise perfect critical moral thinker would have them do' (Hare[30]). And, at the end of the day, it sounds bizarrely like a group of people stumbling towards the 'WWJD' motif espoused by many Christians: *'What would Jesus do?'*[31] The resemblance is clearest when we watch Hare in *Moral Thinking* grounding his ethics in what would be done by an imaginary figure he terms the 'archangel … a being with superhuman powers of thought, superhuman knowledge and no human weaknesses'.[32] That does sound rather like the Jesus Christians believe in. (It is not perhaps surprising that Hare's own son, also now becoming known as a moral philosopher, became a committed Christian.)

At this point Christians will affirm that such a Person genuinely exists, and that the reality of Jesus offers the ideal foundation for ethics. Such an approach is often called a 'Divine

Command' theory. That, however, betrays a complete misunderstanding of what's involved. A major purpose of the Old Testament is to show us that divine commands aren't enough to empower authentic 'goodness', and to drive us to realize that there must be radical change involving God's presence coming to be within us. We must be 'born of the Spirit', as Jesus termed it. [33] There is a huge difference between an ethic based on 'Thou shalt not', and one based on our participation in the life of God. 'Divine commands' are not what empowers ethics – not, as it were, the cure that enables health, but rather the essential thermometer that reveals our sickness. It may sound mystical, but for the Christian it is Jesus himself, personally, who is the foundation for ethics – and, ultimately, the only practical one.

To grasp this point is also to recognize the hyper-rationalism underlying the objection most often brought against an ethic grounded on faith. This argues that we can neither say we should obey God because his commands are good (since that still leaves goodness ungrounded and undefined), nor can we say that goodness is simply what God commands (since then he might arbitrarily command something terrible and it would still be 'good'). [34] But to the Christian, this question embodies complete incomprehension of what the God who actually exists is like. The notion of that God commanding evil is self-contradictory in the manner of 'What if a square turned out to be round?' Even to pose it – how to express this? – demonstrates we have not grasped the vision of the unimaginable, dazzling and unalloyed holiness of the Divine Majesty. 'God *is* Love': the two cannot be separated; 'God *is* Good'. For the person who has encountered Jesus, ethics is grounded not in philosophical abstraction but in adoration and relationship. Everything that is of value and beauty, all that is worthy of worship, love and emulation, converges in the glory of God at the heart of the universe; thus goodness is by definition relational, inextricably[35] bound up with the nature of God, with our participation in it, our reflection of it. [36] (And ultimately, the choice for or against that nature becomes, to Christian belief, the choice of life or death – the central and fundamental decision in every person's existence.)

What Christian faith claims to offer here is something deeply 'humanizing', a personal, holistic and practical grounding for life that stands in marked contrast to the sterile and powerless intellectualism of most academic ethics. In three further ways it earths the abstraction of ideas in a broader, richer context. First (and vital for postmodernity): what Jesus presented was not merely rules – impacting us, perhaps, at superficial levels only – but stories as to how to work out the principles; and, more important still, a lived-out example – we learn what goodness is by watching Jesus' life, and Jesus' death. The historian Lecky, a dedicated opponent of organized Christianity, observed that 'The simple record' (in the Gospels) 'of these three short years of [Christ's] active life has done more to regenerate and soften mankind than all the disquisitions of philosophers and all the exhortations of moralists.'[37] Secondly, Christian faith transcends the polarization between external, wooden principle and unanchored intuitive action. It offers both the Word and the Spirit, the eternal truths of God and also his guidance and companionship leading them to expression through the emotional, spiritual, and empathetic levels of our personality.[38] (Without the Spirit, Christians would immediately concede, 'Divine Command ethics' can and does deteriorate rapidly into legalism.) Thirdly, and crucially, the Spirit's presence means we not only have access to the wisdom to know what is right, but the motivating love and strength, case by specific case, to do it.[39] Word and Spirit, definition and motivation, mind and heart, wisdom and love and strength: here could be a holistic foundation that goes far beyond the aridly theoretical, an ethic empowered for real life. It matters whether it is truth or not; whether indeed that God is a reality to build our lives upon.

> The insistence that morality depends on God goes right back to the time of Plato. It can draw some emotional reactions, as if the implication were that only the religious were moral, and the non-religious always live immoral and selfish lives.
>
> But that would be absurd. A Christian might argue that she has a significantly better basis for reaffirming right

and wrong[40] than does a non-believer; but such thought by no means always translates into action. Nor could Christians think that, as a class, they (let alone the merely 'religious') always 'live better' than the non-religious.

Rather, the point is twofold. First, faith in God provides a basis for ethics that can point the way for any specific individual to live more morally than they themselves would otherwise. A believer struggling with major emotional wounds may still act nowhere near as unselfishly as a non-believer blessed with a healthy family background and deep psychological integration. But the difference, the believer will affirm, is that she has come to the place where healing and long-term growth can be found, rather than attempting to live morally by her own strength.

And second, just as statistical trends grow clearer in larger populations, so if we think of entire societies there begin to be certain discernible differences. One survey published by Social and Community Planning Research showed that only 11% of weekly churchgoers said they would pocket £100 found lying in the street, compared to twice that number in the general population. Similarly, far fewer weekly churchgoers would keep extra change given them by mistake in a shop. Those with no religion were, by every measure, the least honest. Again, a recent analysis showed that the majority of US charitable giving comes from active believers; weekly attendants at religious services gave an average 3.4% of their income to charity, occasional attendants 1.4%, and non-attendants 1.1%. 'One of the clearest findings of all research on giving and volunteering is that the volunteer or donor is likely to be an active Christian. More than income, age, race or education, faith predicts giving and volunteering.'[41] Again, the large-scale Patterson/Kim survey of 1991 showed that, among Americans, the 'very religious' were more 'moral' on 'questions generally accepted as defining citizenship', more truthful and less prone to petty crime. They were far less likely to 'have a price', that is, to express an openness to abandoning spouse or parents if the money offered them was high enough.[42]

The precise interpretation of all this may be debated, but it seems clear that, on a collective level, faith is linked to altruism and morality in some significantly supportive manner.[43] Indeed Lord Denning went a great deal further: 'Without religion there can be no morality; and without morality there can be no law.'

But the faith–question has been answered in our culture, at least for the time being: we are now turned firmly away from any such God. So where have we come to instead?

We cannot conclude that no workable, non-theistic ethical system exists; but the impression academic ethics gives us is one of deep powerlessness and disarray. Increasingly, our professional ethicists face the judgement of the 'anti-theorists' (with feminists prominent among them): the whole discussion is seen as abstract, rationalistic and taking place in a distant academic ghetto. Realistically, as we look at our post-God society, the charge seems justified. The impact of academic moral thought, even at its best, seems negligible. One meets many people whose lives have found ethical direction from Camus, or Jesus, or popularizations of Marx; but one meets very, very few for whom even Rawls or Hare have that kind of significance.[44] The entire debate seems utterly remote from ordinary people. It offers little practical guidance and almost no significant grounding for a counter to self-interest.[45]

Indeed, Singer may be right that, when academic ethics has had a cultural impact, its effect has most often been to deny any rational, objective foundation to right and wrong: Wittgenstein, Russell, logical positivists like Ayer, existentialists, and more recent postmodernists[46] and sociobiologists[47] have all agreed on that. Many of the last century's philosophers have argued that 'good' or 'bad' amount to no more than personal preferences, comparable to preferences regarding football teams. Or, as Mackie says, claims for the existence of objective moral value (his example is the wrongness of deliberate cruelty[48]) are, in the absence of God, simply false. 'It is important to note how often in widely different modern philosophical contexts something very like emotivism's attempted reduction of morality to personal preference recurs', says MacIntyre.[49] Meanwhile, attempts to re-establish ethics without God have turned out 'by and large to provide means for a more accurate and informed definition of disagreement rather than for progress towards its resolution'[50], serving up only a 'cafeteria of conflicting moralities'. Annette Baier argues that in practice the teaching of such approaches serves primarily to breed scepticism among its hearers.[51]

In short, then, whether it is deliberate or not, the practical effect of contemporary secular philosophy is to destroy any confidence that there are objective reasons for being altruistic or unselfish. As we will see later, cutting-edge evolutionary science is having the same effect. Ultimately, MacIntyre concludes, the only viable options are to recognize the death of all ethics, with Nietzsche, or else to find some way to restate the ancient frameworks.[52] But we no longer believe in God; and the academic ghetto has found nothing to put in his place.

Towards the end of his major study *Reasons and Persons*, Derek Parfit writes,

> When he was asked about his book, Sidgwick said that its first word was *Ethics*, and its last *failure*. This could have been the last word of my Part Four. As I argued, we need a new theory about beneficence … Though I failed to find such a theory, I believe that, if they tried, others could succeed.

Parfit recognizes that his own conclusions about ethics 'undermine our beliefs about our obligations to future generations'; he feels that there 'must be a moral objection' to policies such as carelessness about nuclear waste that jeopardize the world future generations will live in, but

Since I failed to find the principle to which we should appeal, I cannot explain the objection to our choice of such policies. I believe that, though I have so far failed, I or others could find the principle we need. But until this happens [mine] is a disturbing conclusion.[53]

Hare wrote in his introduction to *Moral Thinking* (p. v): 'I offer this book to the public now rather than later, not because I think it needs no improvement, but because of a sense of urgency ... These are issues over which people are prepared to fight and kill one another; and it may be that unless some way is found of talking about them rationally and with hope of agreement, violence will finally engulf the world. Philosophers ... have lacked any clear idea of what constitutes a good argument in practical questions. Often they are content with appeals to their own or others' intuitions and prejudices; and since it is these prejudices which fuelled the violence in the first place,[54] this is not going to help.'

* * *

'Almost every important tendency in modern thought has questioned the possibility of making moral judgments. Analytical philosophy asserts that moral statements are expressions of emotion lacking any rational or scientific basis. Marxism derides religion and morality as "phantoms formed in the human brain", "ideological reflexes" that are, at best, mere sublimates of material circumstances ... Existentialists argue that man must choose his values without having any sure compass by which to guide these choices. Cultural anthropology as practised by many of its most renowned scholars claims that amid the exotic diversity of human life there can be found no universal laws of right conduct ... All of science seems the enemy of moral confidence.'
–James Q. Wilson[55]

* * *

'An Asian couple were followed off a Harrow bus by five white thugs – two with knuckle dusters – who viciously kicked and punched the man in front of his petrified wife and finally booted him into the path of an oncoming car. Police ... have appealed for witnesses – especially a man and woman who were on the 340 bus at the time of the attack. When the terrified woman begged the male passenger to intervene, he retorted: "I don't want to get involved. It's not my problem." The victim was almost blinded in the attack.' (*Harrow and Wembley Recorder*)

Fear is understandable. And in what sense was it 'his problem'? What will be the results if we lack the 'moral confidence' to say?

'Not my problem'

So now back to the real world. But first let's recap, for readers who may be re-joining us. We jettisoned the God who embodied the heart of our ethics. The attempts of the academic ghetto to provide a replacement foundation for altruism, as against self-ishness, are in deep disarray. Major figures argue that moral values have no objective meaning and are entirely a matter of how we feel or what we prefer – preferences comparable to those of musical style or of colour.

But meanwhile, of course, life goes on. On what, then, should we base our morals?

Our first reaction may be that we can all go on living by our instincts, by following our 'hearts' (thus *Star Wars*: 'Trust your feelings, Luke'). Feminist writers sometimes come close to this position. Surprisingly, we find it even in Sartre: 'If values are uncertain, if they are still too abstract to determine the particular, concrete case under consideration, nothing remains but to trust in our instincts.'[56]

But that is a dire situation. At best, the appeal to instinct leads to unresolvable relativism. Some of us have the instincts of the wolf, the rapist or the paedophile. Many of us are good at feeling, instinctively, the need to put the family first, while having very little in the way of instincts that speak up for the unattractive stranger. The torchlight pageantry of 1930s Nazism depended quite heavily on racist instincts. When our instincts collide, what then? Without some additional way to distinguish between good and bad impulses, is there any recourse left but to fight it out?[57]

Many of us will stick with what we were taught in school: right or wrong is what is good or bad for society, for other people. Historian H.A.L. Fisher, for example, at the close of his *A History of Europe* (1936), speaks of the 'great democratic maxim' of 'securing the greatest happiness of the greatest number' (and shows his alarm at the rise of the very different attitudes of Nazi Germany). But now as we face the new millennium, Nietzsche's cold scorn for 'English flatheads' who have got 'rid of the Christian God, and now believe all the more firmly that they must cling to Christian morality' remains unrefuted at the intellectual level, and is increasingly finding echoes elsewhere. What price, then, the welfare of society as a whole? And how long should we expect it to take for the logic to work through from the academic stratosphere to street level?

Probably it has done so already. Gangsta rap lyrics by the likes of Tupac Shakur or Mobb Deep are as free from 'flathead morality' about society as a whole as Nietzsche could have wished. Was the unanswerable question asked during the riots twenty years ago? In the summer of 1981, Britain's cities exploded. Reports told of children looting shops and their parents arriving with prams to pick up the proceeds (as also, more recently, in Los Angeles). Let's imagine that a bystander had complained, 'But this is not good for other people! This is not good for society!' The response would probably have been 'Sod you, Jack', or something similar. But it could also have been: 'What has society ever done for me? Have you seen the house society has given me? Have you seen what "other people" have done for me in schooling and employment? Why should I care for them?' Rapper Ice Cube remarked in concert: 'Ask not what you can do for your country, ask what the f*** it's ever done for you.' God is dead: why, logically, should you expect altruism or communal responsibility from me?

Do we have a reply? Arguing with a vandal beyond the emotional level isn't easy; whether it's a graffiti sprayer or an executive carrying out the destructive mandates of an ecologically-mindless corporation. True, if we all operate like this the ozone layer and the rainforests will be destroyed, and that could be bad news for our entire race in a few decades; but that's someone else's problem, and I have the bottom line to look after. (As Groucho Marx observed, it's not obvious why I should bother about posterity when posterity's never done anything for me.) A Radio 4 interviewer discovered that *Look Back in Anger* playwright John Osborne didn't 'give a damn for the rainforest. It's nothing to do with him.' French gangster Georges Courtois told the judge at his trial for armed robbery: 'Society has never given me anything and I therefore have nothing to do with it.' After the more recent Hartcliffe riots, local councillor Paul Smith observed, 'Society's offering the kids nothing, so they have no stake in it. There's nothing tying them to the norms, so smashing their community causes them no problems.'

The shallowness of our concern for our society, or our human race, if it conflicts at all with our personal interests, is haunting our politics too. There are many fine things we would like to see happen, but not if they mean any increase in our taxes. *Times* columnist Barbara Amiel, writing as an unbeliever in 'metaphysical systems', had to concede the point:

> In fact, it remains ever true that if a leader wants to mobilize certain highly moral political programmes, it is insufficient to talk only of economic interest ... You may have to talk about intangibles such as Christian stewardship to get people to pick up litter or look after their children and ageing parents.

But since we don't now believe – not in the sense relevant here – in the 'intangible' God of Christianity, why should we put responsibility to society or parents above naked self-interest? And why should we forego our immediate satisfaction for the sake of the community or the environment? Some, undoubtedly, will – maybe enough for us to stagger on a bit longer; but many will not, and maybe logic is on their side. So why not 'vote self-ish' (altruism is fine providing the price isn't paid in *my* backyard)?

> Former British premier Harold Wilson chose to place, at the start of both volumes of his autobiography, the following quote from Aneurin Bevan's last parliamentary speech:
>
> 'There is one important problem facing representative Parliamentary Government in the whole of the world where it exists. It is being asked to solve a problem which so far it has failed to solve ... So far, nobody on either side of this House has succeeded ... I would describe the central problem falling upon representative government in the Western world as how to persuade the people to forego immediate satisfactions in order to build up the economic resources of the country ... How can we persuade the ordinary man and woman that it is worthwhile making sacrifices in their immediate standards or foregoing substantial rising standards to extend fixed capital equipment throughout the country?'
>
> (That was the '70s. The issue now is how to persuade people to 'forego immediate satisfactions' so that their descendants' environment is not permanently ruined.)

'Your-own-folk morality': Marxism

'The right thing to do is what's good for society.' We don't believe that any more. Indeed, it was British premier Margaret Thatcher who declared that 'There is no such thing as society. There are individual men and women, and there are families.' And plenty of other voices – left-wing voices this time – had long argued that 'what's best for society' usually meant 'what's best for those sitting on the top'. 'Society' has little chance of motivating our views of right and wrong action.

But then what alternatives do we have?

Three have been of particular significance during the last few decades. First, there are 'New Age' approaches that don't affirm God as such but still have an idealistic commitment to 'good' in terms of furtherance of the cosmic process – sometimes seen in evolutionary terms. Secondly, there is the 'tribalist' approach – no longer idealistic about humanity as a whole, but concerned to 'do what's right by your own folk'. And thirdly, there is that approach pared down to its simplest terms: what's right is what's good for my family. (Readers who want to skip all three will find we move on to the practical implications in 'After morality' on p. 143.)

We'll take the second, 'tribal', one first. It may seem easiest to forget about 'society' or 'the greatest possible number' and base our moral actions on the needs of people we know – people like us. This has recurred frequently since the 'loss of God', and it is stated quite explicitly in some variants of postmodernism. But it hasn't worked, and we need to understand why. We'll look at two examples of this approach that have looked well placed to take over the world in recent decades; first of all, communism.

For many Marxists, the only liveable basis for moral action is a class ethic: what's best for people like me, for my class, is what's right for me to do. What we need in parliament, Dennis Skinner, MP, told a British trade union audience some years back, is people 'who will fight for our class and to hell with the national interest'. (He got a standing ovation for that.)[58] And at the level of theory, Marxism is clear. 'We say, our morality is completely subjected to the interests of the proletarian class-struggle', said Lenin. 'We say, anything is moral which serves the destruction of the old exploiters' society and the alliance of all working people around the proletariat.' 'A Communist must be able to keep a pact or to break a pact', said Brecht; all our ethics are determined by the needs of the working class.[59]

Class morality is now utterly out of fashion. Yet less than forty years ago, around 1968, it all seemed so obvious; anyone who had a heart was a Marxist. But it may be back, one suspects. With the collapse of any real restraints on the greed of all-conquering global capitalism, Marxism, or something like it, could well start to sound cogent again – probably with a 'green', ecological tinge.[60] In the meantime, though, it's in eclipse. 'Doing what's right for your own folk' proved a grossly inadequate basis for ethical life. What is wrong with it?

Three answers stand out. First, it has a contradiction at its heart: its theory is about class morality, yet it fires up its adherents because it seems to embody a far more universal justice. Second, it never explains *why* you should do what's right by your own folk; it relies on you to know by intuition why it matters, why that should take precedence over self-interest. And thirdly, catastrophically, it provides no means of determining what the true interests of 'your own folk' really are – and, again, how to distinguish them from self-interest.

Let's take the first. The ethical motivation behind Marxism – the ethical 'god-replacement' – tends to combine two impulses. At the level of theory, as Lenin said, what mattered was what was good for the working class. But what seized the hearts of the '60s generation was *justice*: what mattered was what was *right* – or at the very least, what would advance the social evolution of the human race as a whole, because that was self-evidently 'right'. 'At least in many countries of the third world, before being a convincing intellectual challenge, Marxism is a challenge to action and commitment', wrote Samuel Escobar from Peru. 'The attraction of Marxism lies in the call to *do something* about social evils, to *fight for justice*, to *align with the poor and the oppressed*; especially in the third world where social evils can be so blatant.'[61]

But therein lay a fatal contradiction. I watched a Trotskyite selling the *Socialist Worker* a few years ago. Its front page was on racism: British immigration staff had abused and humiliated an Indian woman on the way through Heathrow airport. And I wondered what it meant for the newspaper seller. The Christian believes that persons of every race must be respected, because each person and race is made in the image of God. But this man believed in a totally evolutionary universe, where the survival of the fittest means, at bottom, the strongest race trampling the weak. So why, for him, was racism wrong? He answered me: Racism must be fought because it divides the working class. What really matters is the interests of the working class.

Well, it made me wonder. Suppose racism *unified* the working class (quite a possibility: it's not so many years since the dockers marched through London with placards declaring 'Back Britain not Black Britain'); would he be willing to use that to advance the 'class struggle'? And what about the woman herself? She, one imagines, would view her humiliation as a matter of fairness, as a universal moral issue. Could the Marxist explanation really be why her ill-treatment mattered – that such behaviour divided the working class? Surely the thing that fires us up to care – that motivated the newspaper seller to care, I hope and suspect – is not a morality of class interests, but a deep-seated intuition of human value and of universal morality for which Marxist theory had no place. In such cases, Marxist theory and the human intuition of justice are saying two very different things.

That brings us on to the second issue: Why bother? To some of us, it's overwhelmingly plain that something must ('ought to') be done about injustice. To others, the idea of 'siding with our class' is unworthy of a moment away from the MP3 or Nintendo. Worldwide, Marxism today is almost negligible as a force for justice. For successive 'me-generations', intuitions of global injustice have been blunted, or deafened: 'I want my MTV ...' An ever more powerful media system has trained us perpetually to consume, to look out only for our own interests. And so the question is: Why 'ought' I care about the needs of those around me unless they match my own? Why should I identify myself, expensively, with justice or progress?

It's not enough to say that someone who asks such a question doesn't deserve an answer. Hasn't Marxism always floated three feet above the ground? Wasn't there always a gap? Did it ever explain why the suffering of the individual – that tiny atom in the flood of the evolutionary process – should concern us? Interestingly, Marx's lack of faith in any God or 'transcendent norms' meant that he 'believed that in matters of conflict between social classes the appeal to moral judgments was not only pointless but positively misleading', notes MacIntyre. 'So he tried to excise from documents of the First International appeals for justice for the working class.'[62] But then why bother? If you could bring with you an awareness of the need for justice – a 'conscience', in fact – then Marxism would analyse what was going wrong for the poor, and tell you how to solve it. But you had to find that awareness elsewhere, because Marxism could never create it. South Wales, for example, became fertile soil for the growth of passionate communism, but it already had a strong chapel-going culture, and so Marxism could build on intuitions about justice that owed much to the Christian background. It's doubtful whether a socialist revolution has ever occurred where there hasn't been a strong religious culture first; idealistic socialism depends on people seeing the point of putting their neighbour's interests above their own, and that seems to need a religious background. (Maybe we shall only hear about socialism in future from countries where surviving religious consciousness undergirds the sense of community – Muslim socialism, African socialism? Maybe secularization destroys socialism because it enshrines individual selfishness?)

And so maybe it is too late now to define moral action by loyalty to class or loyalty to the poor; because their problem is not my problem unless it affects me as well. That, at least, was how the *Times* viewed one of the turning-points of British history: the fatal wounding in 1984 of the old political left, when Margaret Thatcher took on their elite, the hitherto-invincible miners' union. The miners were broken, the left was shattered, and a major reason was that they found no support from other unions.[63] Thatcher clashed with the dockworkers too, and broke them as well; the TGWU, to which the dockers belonged, proved unable to persuade their other members to support them. The *Times* commented that class solidarity and mutual support no longer functioned because of 'changes in society at large ... My problem is not your problem unless it impinges on you as well.' God was dead, yes – but now the old ethics of communal solidarity were dead too. Why bother with anything but self-interest? Am I my brother's keeper?

So here was the second reason why the class ethic died: ultimately, it couldn't compete with selfishness in a secularized society. Historically, British socialism had been rooted in the spiritually-based idealism of Wesleyan Methodism,[64] but its Marxist wing tended to talk (as indeed their theory demanded) as if economic issues were all that counted.[65] Ultimately, then, it seemed to offer little more than a way for those excluded by capitalism to compete afresh for the prizes. But in that case it's all about selfishness; so in a world where God is absent, why bother with communal solidarity any longer than it helps me grab the prizes? Surely the solution to my poverty isn't to fight for the poor but to escape from among them?

Here too, then, Marxism's ethical inadequacy, its inability to explain why others matter, became fatal. That was its 'external' problem: Why should I bother? But the final reason it vanished, an 'internal' reason, was still more serious: in practice, class-based morality was never enough to live by – indeed, it was catastrophically inadequate.

Ultimately, Marxism contained no ethics. Marx 'never discusses the question of what principles of action are to inform the working-class movement', says MacIntyre. Ultimately, there is no means of determining who 'your own folk', the true 'working-class movement', are, nor what their true interests are in practice – especially when they conflict with your own. And that became crucial when the class warriors had to decide what to do with real power. 'For us the duty of comradeship results from our duty to international Democratic Socialism and not the other way round', said Lenin. 'This means that loyalty to the aims of the revolution must, if necessary, break the loyalty to an individual comrade and even abandon to the enemy former comrades who have become liabilities', notes Bockmuehl. 'The end justifies even this means. This was stated early by Lenin in theory.' Bockmuehl adds that Brecht, in *Lehrstuck: die Massnahme*, 'tried to justify this ethic when he described a team of communist agents who decide to liquidate a young comrade (and even demand his approval of the act) by pushing him into a pit of unslaked lime because he has let himself be recognized by the police.'[66] The interests of the proletariat are the fundamental value; unless some other, alien values (like Christian ones) are introduced, they have tyrannical precedence over anything else – meaning anything smaller, more individual or more local.

But then it gets worse. For if we know no morality beyond our loyalty to 'progress' and to the class that stands in its vanguard – and thus to the leadership who 'know' what that class needs: how could we distinguish right from wrong methods, so long as the leadership's ideas of 'progress' are advanced? Doesn't the end result always justify the means? This is no idle question; perhaps its implications were what broke Marxism worldwide. For the story of communist totalitarianism has made the answers all too plain. 'From the slave revolts in the ancient world to the socialist revolution, the struggle of the oppressed has ended in a new, "better" system of domination', wrote leftist guru Marcuse. 'In this sense, every revolution has also been a betrayed revolution.'[67] Given the egoism in all of us, and given the fact that elite Marxist leaders tended to see themselves as embodying the revolution, and their factional interests as the revolution's own: wasn't their triumph almost doomed to result in elitism and authoritarianism?[68] Doesn't the repeated, colossal terror – the vast slaughters of Stalin's Gulag, Mao's cultural revolution, the Khmer Rouge killing fields – show Marxism's desperate lack of any counterbalance to human power-lust, selfishness and ruthlessness? Doesn't history show that 'class morality', morality based on the needs of 'people like us', can only be a disastrously unclear basis for our ethical action?

Ultimately, then, class morality was doomed to fall apart. Indeed, it only ever flourished among people whose ethics drew on something deeper, some intuitions or prejudices about universal justice. It was never able to explain why people of your class were really worth your self-sacrifice. It had no way of discerning violent, even horrific, selfishness when that masqueraded as the needs of the class. And it could never compete with the selfishness inculcated by the consumerism of secularized postmodernity.

'Your-own-folk morality': Fascism and the twenty-first century

'Doing what's right for your own folk' can still feel attractive when our self-interest needs the help of others. But then it can also turn out to be something very ugly.

We have Hitler to thank for demonstrating this most clearly. 'Whoever is prepared to make the national cause his own to such an extent that he knows no higher ideal than the welfare of his nation', he wrote, 'whoever has understood our great national anthem, *Deutschland Uber Alles*, to mean that nothing in the wide world surpasses in his eyes this Germany, people and land – that man is a Socialist.' Here, 'what's best for people like us' is indeed the 'highest ideal', the ultimate basis for ethics. Himmler stated the implications unflinchingly:

> Whether nations live in prosperity or starve to death like cattle inter-ests me only in so far as we need them as slaves to our Kultur ... Whether ten thousand Russian females fall down from exhaustion while digging an antitank ditch interests me only in so far as an anti-tank ditch for Germany is finished.[69]

Thus the theory. Death in the gas chambers for six million Jews, and millions of Slavs besides, was the completely logical result in practice.

What is astonishing as we read Hitler's *Mein Kampf* is to see how clear are its principles, and yet how the British liberal intelli-gentsia of the time refused to see the implications. (Just so, one suspects, we today see the collapse of ethics resulting from the loss of God, hear the many voices saying that right and wrong are illusory and that what is real is the 'play of dominations', and yet choose to think that somehow it 'won't matter', that life will go on as usual and the logical consequences will somehow never take place.) The fundamental idea running through *Mein Kampf* is one that pointed directly to Auschwitz: the community, the *volk*, is the absolute, and defines what is right and wrong.

'In giving one's own life for the existence of the community lies the crown of all sense of sacrifice', writes Hitler. '... The basic attitude from which such activity arises we call ... idealism. By this we understand only the individual's capacity to make sacrifices for the community.'[70] To such 'idealism' anything that is good for your own folk is justified. 'When the nations on this planet fight for existence ... then all considerations of humanitarianism or aesthetics crumble into nothingness ... The most cruel weapons were humane if they brought about a quicker victory.'[71] Within peace-time society the same consistent view prevails, where 'duty' to the 'nation' takes priority over abstractions of 'law and order'. Hitler writes of 1923,

> It was then the very first task of a truly national government to seek and find the forces which were resolved to declare a war of annihilation against Marxism, and then to give these forces a free road; it was their *duty* not to worship the idiocy of "law and order" ... No, at that time a really national government should have desired disorder and unrest, provided only that amid the confusion a basic reckoning with Marxism at last became possible and actually took place.[72]

When the interests of the community define what is ethical, then, almost anything can become justified. All this, Hitler knew, went totally against his country's Christian background. He complains that Protestantism 'combats with the greatest hostility any attempt to rescue the nation from the embrace of its most mortal enemy, since its attitude to the Jews just happens to be more or less dogmatically established.'[73] But Christian 'dogma' no longer shaped the national ethic. 'I cannot see', Hitler could argue as a result, 'why man should not be just as cruel as nature.'[74]

Let's not be naive about this. We would never, we may feel, go Hitler's way. An early draft of this chapter, written in 1989, read, 'Hopefully, in Europe at least, this mistake will not soon be made again.' But that was a foolish remark, as the mass murders and gang-rape camps in former Yugoslavia showed soon afterwards. 'All over the world', wrote Felipe Fernandez-Armesto in 1999, 'revived nationalisms are replacing dying ideologies. As superstates crumble, old ethnic hatreds crawl out of the woodwork.'[75] Russian Emergency Situations Minister Sergei Shoigu demonstrated Fernandez-Armesto's point in a speech that same year:

> Thank goodness we have come through that wonderful period when people's ideological and political convictions meant everything. Today we believe the main accent should be on professionalism, morals and, *above all* [my italics, but here it comes ...], patriotism.

But we're not just talking about the shift in mood in Russia or former Yugoslavia. All over the world, the collapse of beliefs that might have given us a broader vision has meant we tend to cling to some smaller group for survival, and our postmodern ethics can all too easily centre on 'our own folk'.[76] Here is leading American postmodernist Richard Rorty, advocating something rather too similar under the title of 'pragmatism':

> The pragmatist ... can only be criticized for taking his own community *too* seriously. He can only be criticized for ethnocentrism, not for relativism. To be ethnocentric is to divide the human race into the people to whom one must justify one's beliefs and the others. The first group – one's *ethnos* – comprises those who share enough of one's beliefs to make fruitful conversation possible.[77]

Rorty's 'ethnocentrism' embodies the nightmare the two-thirds world encounters over so many environmental and other issues. The postmodern west feels no need to justify our actions to anyone outside 'those who share enough of one's beliefs to make fruitful conversation possible' – meaning people like ourselves, people shaped by the same interests (and media) as ourselves. ('Such recommendations have a less than benign aspect when we consider how easily public opinion can be manipulated and con-sensus-based values engineered to serve some very illiberal forms of political behaviour', writes Sri Lankan Christian Vinoth Ramachandra. '... But how can such a critique emerge from intellectuals who can no longer distinguish between truth and what the majority have come to believe?'[78]) Rorty's denial of any ethical accountability beyond his 'own folk' may well sound like a kind of fascism. How can that be? Postmodernism is supposed to be violently anti-fascist, and Rorty presents himself as a liberal. Yet, if we are brutally honest, there are significant links between postmodernism and Nazism. The rhetoric of both owes a heavy debt to Nietzsche, while among the fathers of contempo-rary postmodernism both Heidegger[79] and de Man had clear Nazi ties. Remove Rorty's liberal intuitions, and his ethical method – divide the human race into the people to whom one must justify one's actions and the 'negligible' others – may suit something far more brutal. It did so in Europe, only 60 years ago.

We need to recognize what's happened. After World War II, both Christians and their liberal-humanist opponents agreed that right and wrong were things which anyone sufficiently enlightened, anyone sufficiently liberated from prejudice,[80] should be able to see and understand. Theoretically at least, then, both were committed to dialogue. But postmodernism is some-thing else. Here, it's argued that there is no longer an ethics for everybody; indeed Rorty implies that ethical issues may be beyond discussion unless you are 'one of us'. (Compare the slogans: 'It's a gay thing; you wouldn't understand.') You do what seems best to your own people; there is simply no point in trying to talk about it with anybody else.[81]

But if that's the whole story, it may not be long before the shooting starts.[82]

New Age ethics

So now we're 'without Marx or Jesus'; neither God nor loyalty to our 'own folk' is giving us much of an ethical base or counter to selfishness. But in the '80s, the swing of fashion brought a new option to prominence; in place of the hippie aligning his actions with the Marxist 'dialectic of history', there came the 'New Age' yuppie exploring alternative spiritualities and seeking to align with the 'cosmic process'.

'New Age' was a cover-all title for a wide range of attitudes, fads and philosophies. But certain ideas characterized many parts of it: the unity of everything, the divinity of everything, our divinity as human beings, the need for a change of consciousness to recognize this divinity, and the faith that this change in consciousness is beginning.[83] 'New Age' approaches offered a new optimism, a new sense of community, and a new foundation for ethics: the belief that a process is working itself out in the universe, and actions that advance or harmonize with that process are good.

How far did this give a genuine basis for a post-Christian ethics? Unfortunately two crucial 'internal contradictions' soon surfaced at the heart of much 'New Age' thinking. First, there is the idea that we are all God. ('Free will is simply the enactment of the realization you are God, a realization that you are divine', says Shirley MacLaine.[84])

On the surface, that's an attractive notion. And it might seem to have obvious ethical value, because then, as Blake said, 'Everything that lives is holy'. But deeper reflection soon reveals a problem. Can God sin? How can anything God does or wants be wrong? What values or 'checks' can possibly be set over against anything the God that I am may desire? But if there are no such checks, then whatever I desire is right: and an ounce of self-knowledge should dispose of that pretty falsehood.

Shirley MacLaine sets out the issues with enthusiasm in her series of best-sellers, and what emerges soon begins to sound like ego-worship. 'Each soul is its own god. You must never worship anyone or anything other than self. For *you* are God. To love self is to love God.'[85] 'I was beginning to see that we each did whatever we did purely for self, and that was as it should be.'[86] 'Purely for self': it is not surprising to find MacLaine reportedly saying on other occasions, 'I want to prove that spirituality is profitable', and, 'I've liked moderate success, but I've ... not wanted gigantic success. I'm changing now. I want gigantic success.'[87]

Many acolytes of alternative spiritualities would look down on MacLaine as a popularizer; but the lack of safeguards against selfishness surfaces elsewhere. 'A spiritual path is valid *for us* if it is appropriate to *our* needs as *we ourselves* define them', says Mark Satin in *New Age Politics*.[88] 'You know, God is everything – He is every thing', declares the 'channelled' spirit guide Ramtha. 'So any thing you do you have an inner action in divinity. Remember that, and do what you want to do' – adding elsewhere, 'Don't worry about your fellow man. If you become happy, however they look upon you doesn't make any difference. The fact that you are happy and in service to Self is quite enough.'[89] And this is Swami Muktananda, a key influence on Werner Erhard (founder of EST and Forum): 'Kneel to your own self. Honour and worship your own being. God dwells within you as You!'[90]

But what if, in reality, many of the problems in our culture are related to our egoisms – to our pride, greed, over-consumption, self-pity, self-centredness? How does 'kneeling to our own selves' help us in practice? There is huge credulity in 'New Age' at this point: that if we all pursue our own self-interest, everything will turn out all right. It sounds an improbable, even childish, utopia. (But there's a curious parallel with the optimism expressed by extreme *laissez-faire* capitalism, that the totally free play of economic self-interest will ultimately benefit everybody in society. 'New Age', unlike the '60s counterculture, fits and reflects capitalistic individualism in a number of ways – and hence offers all too little challenge to its excesses.)

A second strand of much 'New Age' thought makes matters worse, namely the attempt to 'transcend' or obliterate all categories, including those of 'good' and 'evil'. Marilyn Ferguson asserts in the key 'New Age' text *The Aquarian Conspiracy* that good and evil are to be transcended by an awareness that 'unites opposites';[91] Fritjof Capra, in the equally important *The Turning Point*, looks towards an ultimate consciousness 'in which all boundaries and dualisms have been transcended.'[92] 'Until mankind realizes there is, in truth, no good and there is, in truth, no evil – there will be no peace', Shirley MacLaine's 'Higher Self' tells her.[93] Eastern religious thinking lies behind this abolition of good and evil: 'By ceasing to do good to one's friends or evil to one's enemies [one] attains to the eternal Brahman by the yoga of meditation' (Hindu teacher Shankara). 'Conflict between right and wrong is the sickness of the mind' (Zen master Yun-Men). 'In this world nothing is wrong, nothing is even stupid. The sense of wrong is simply failure to see where something fits into a pattern' (Buddhist Alan Watts).[94]

But what if all boundaries really are gone, all opposites transcended? It might seem that our immersion in the divine order of creation points us automatically towards an ethic of right action. (Jonathan Porritt: 'Many Greens believe that salvation lies in opening our spirit to the presence of the divine in the world, acknowledging joyfully a sense of wonder and humility before the miracle of creation, and *then* going out and taking action to put things right, inspired by that vision.'[95]) But one wonders how far that 'sense of wonder' can function with any real relevance to the messy interactions of urban personal relationships. It helps our ecological commitment, but isn't it rather in a separate universe from the question of whether to be selfish in the home or the office, whether to attempt to steal someone else's wife? And again: does a voice whisper that, at bottom, this is all sentimentalism? That an ethic that truly arises from identifying with the developing processes of the natural world will simply be the survival of the fittest, in which the strong sustain themselves by devouring the weak?[96]

What, after all, is the ultimate logic of being 'beyond good and evil', of all opposites being transcended? Does 'New Age' talk of transcending the opposites in safety merely because it still smuggles in an ethic of love and goodness from discarded Christian beliefs? For it seems that the pantheistic, Hindu-oriented ideas that underlie most 'New Age' philosophies ultimately render moral issues irrelevant. If, in the end, all is one, what meaningful understanding can we have of 'good' and 'evil'? Brahma is revealed in Kali, the Hindu goddess of destruction, portrayed as smeared with human blood and chewing raw flesh,[97] as much as in more amiable expressions. As Davies observes, in Hinduism 'God is both good and bad ... Man does not have to try to be good, but is perfectly free to copy either side of God's nature.'[98] That possibility was raised bloodily in the 'Manson murders', when guru Charles Manson ordered his disciples to carry out the ritual murders of Sharon Tate and others. Manson, said an acquaintance, 'believed you could do no wrong, no bad. Everything was good':

> Charles Manson was absolutely sane: he had been *there*, where there is neither good nor evil ... If the ultimate truth ... is that "All is One" and "One is All," and that in this One all the opposites, including good and evil, are eternally reconciled, then have we any right to blame Charles Manson? ... Charlie, so far from being mad had a lucidly logical mind.[99]

'If God is One, what is bad?', Manson asked in an article in *Rolling Stone*.[100]

Nor is Manson the only straw blowing in this particular wind. The supposed spirit-guide Ramtha said through one 'channeller' that

> Every vile and wretched thing you do broadens your understanding ... If you want to do any one thing *regardless* of what it is, it would not be wise to go against that feeling; for there is an experience awaiting you and a grand adventure that will make your life sweeter.[101]

'There are no victims in this life or any other. No mistakes. No wrong paths', asserts Jack Underhill, publisher of *Life Times*.[102]

Ultimately, then, 'New Age' spiritualities seem to offer no real counter to self-interest. Not all religions are the same; what you 'worship' determines your moral vision. 'No mistakes. No wrong paths'; if, in the end, all is one, doesn't that make the rightness or wrongness of our actions unimportant? Does wrongdoing matter very much? Often (it seems to me) the kind of person drawn to alternative spiritualities may well be strongly motivated by intuitions that lead towards altruistic and admirable behaviour; but it is questionable if the 'New Age' beliefs help or hinder. Again, if the self is God, can the self's desires be, in any meaningful sense, 'wrong'? Indeed, doesn't a great deal of 'New Age' practice come down in the end to 'self-fulfilment' – either as a brief, undemanding 'tourist spirituality', or as a route to self-enhancement, 'self-actualization', increased efficiency or some other self-oriented aim?

'New Age' teachings are ecologically positive, certainly. But, in ethics as a whole, and as a counter to egoism, ultimately irrelevant?

Evolution and ethics

But the term 'New Age' feels outmoded now. In the last decade, yet another 'god-substitute' became fashionable: evolution. The respected Demos think tank suggested in 1997 that neo-Darwinism was becoming the dominant intellectual paradigm, taking over the central explanatory role that Freud or Marx or existentialism had held for previous generations. So what does it mean for ethics if evolution becomes the dominant way that we understand human life and society?

On the one hand, the evolutionary metaphor, combining physical, social, spiritual and cosmic evolution, is central to the vision of many 'New Agers'.[103] For them, 'evolution is God in process', to use Miller's phrase.[104] An ethic follows from that: 'Anything that moves a part towards its fullest development and fullest integration with the whole is good', says Lawrence LeShan – and anything that does the reverse is bad.[105]

But this ethical implication can come only because the 'New Ager' invests the evolutionary process with some wise, progressive purposiveness, seeing it as expressing, or undergirded by, the divine Self. Take that mystical confidence away (and it has its own ethical difficulties, as we saw in the previous section), and evolutionary theory begins to sound very destructive of ethics.

The driving force behind the recent prominence of evolution has been the new, high-profile field of the sociobiologists; and their assessment of morality isn't very conducive to our taking it seriously:

> Morality, or more strictly our belief in morality, is merely an adaptation put in place [by natural selection] to further our reproductive ends. Hence the basis of ethics does not lie in God's will ... In an important sense, ethics as we understand it is an illusion fobbed off on us by our genes to get us to co-operate.[106]

'Morality is just an aid to survival and reproduction, and has no being beyond or without this ... Considered as a rationally justifiable set of claims about an objective something, it is illusory.'[107] 'As any evolutionist will point out, often we perform better if we are deceived by our biology ... We think that we ought to help, that we have obligations to others, because it is in our biological interests [that is, our genes' interests] to have these thoughts'; if we ceased to believe in objective moral obligations, we would cease to act in the ways that our genes need us to act.[108] In short, our moral sense is merely, in Helena Cronin's phrase, 'just another of natural selection's tricks'.

So morality's claims to refer to objective right or wrong are illusory; and the fundamental reality is the struggle for survival of the genes. Richard Dawkins, author of *The Selfish Gene*, has done as much as anyone to popularize the idea that the blind, selfish processes of genetic evolution are the basic reality behind our existence. But he tries to deny the ethical implications. 'If we tried to learn personal lessons from evolutionary biology we would all the time be doing very unpleasant, very selfish things to each other', he wrote in the *Observer*; 'Fortunately, we do not live in a Darwinian world. Civilisation has changed it very radically.' And again, in an *Express* article,

It's very important that Darwinism, as a system of values, is deeply pernicious and evil and should be fought against. A Darwinian society would be a very unpleasant society in which to live ... We have been given our brains by selection. Now we can use them to rebel against the tyranny of our selfish genes.[109]

It's a remarkable idea, at a time when more and more areas of human behaviour are being seen as the fruit of our genetic inheritance. From where do we get the power, or desire, to transcend the dictates of our genes? (As Steven Rose observes, Dawkins can only make good his escape by invoking some mysterious 'non-material, non-genetic force moulding behaviour' – a dualism that sounds curiously similar to Christian faith.[110])

It is harder still, however, to see where Dawkins is finding his alternative ideals in the name of which we are to 'rebel against the tyranny of our selfish genes'. His own theory suggests that, first, any idea we adopt we may well be choosing not because it is true but for biological reasons; and secondly, the one thing we can apparently be sure of is the fundamental reality of universal struggle for the survival of the fittest. All of which leaves us almost naked against the impulse that, in the end, life is just an unending battle where 'you've got to stick up for your own'. This is doubly true when a different set of 'cutting-edge intelligentsia', the postmodernist followers of Foucault, are insisting that right and wrong are only artificial social constructions, and 'only a single drama is ever staged in the world of human relations', namely the power struggle, the 'endlessly repeated play of dominations'.

The fact is that evolution points easily to a set of ethical intuitions very different from the intuitive liberalism Dawkins seems to value. The vital chapter of Hitler's *Mein Kampf* titled 'Nation and Race' is grounded on evolution and the survival of the fittest. Hitler, as a racist, argues that mating of races at 'different levels' is

contrary to the will of Nature for a higher breeding of all life. The precondition for this does not lie in associating superior and inferior, but in the total victory of the former. The stronger must dominate and not blend in with the weaker, thus sacrificing his own greatness. Only the born weakling can view this as cruel, but he after all is only a weak and limited man ... Nature looks on calmly, with satisfaction, in fact. In the struggle for daily bread all those who are weak and sickly or less determined succumb ... When man attempts to rebel against the iron logic of Nature, he comes into struggle with the principles to which he himself owes his existence as a man. And this attack must lead to his own doom [or, as evolutionary theorists would say today, reduces his own fitness for survival]. Men ... owe their higher existence, not to the ideas of a few crazy ideologists, but to the knowledge and ruthless application of nature's stern and rigid laws ... This preservation is bound up with the rigid law of necessity and the right to victory of the best and strongest in this world. Those who want to live, let them fight, and those who do not want to fight in this world of eternal struggle do not deserve to live.[111]

He made the same point in a 1944 speech to officer cadets:

Nature is always teaching us ... that she is governed by the principle of selection: that victory is to the strong and that the weak must go to the wall. She teaches us that what may seem cruel to us ... is nevertheless often essential ... Nature knows nothing of the notion of humanitarianism which signifies that the weak must at all costs be surrounded and preserved ... On the contrary, weakness calls for condemnation. War is therefore an unalterable law of the whole life – the prerequisite for the natural selection of the strong and the precedent for the elimination of the weak.[112]

Quite apart from the slaughter of the Jews, these ideas found logical expression as between 80,000 and 100,000 physically and mentally impaired people were massacred.

We asked earlier whether post-God liberal humanism has any convincing basis for arguing that all this is not merely unpleasant, but abominably *wrong*. Here we face a related question: doesn't the dominance of the evolutionary paradigm serve to support Hitler's kind of thinking, and (in the absence of any powerful alternative) make it more difficult for us not to act in comparable ways? Later on in *Mein Kampf* Hitler returns to his theme of the 'obligation' to act in tune with the evolutionary process: our responsibility is to

> promote the victory of the better and stronger, and demand the subordination of the inferior and weaker in accordance with the eternal will that dominates this universe ... And so the folkish philosophy of life corresponds to the innermost will of Nature, since it restores that free play of forces which must lead to a continuous mutual higher breeding ... Such a reckoning of real world-historical import [follows] the eternal laws of life on this earth, which are the struggle for this life and which remain struggle.[113]

If we ask for the implications of evolution in ethics, there they are.

Finally, we should face the extent to which current cutting-edge evolutionary theory is placing a huge question mark over unselfishness, or 'altruism', in general. The major step here was the work of William Hamilton. Hamilton suggested that altruism might appear unselfish, but in fact it is just another expression of the survival mechanisms of the 'selfish gene'. Natural selection favours the genes 'for' altruism, in that a particular genetic population is more likely to survive if individuals within it are 'altruistic' in the sense of being likely to give up their lives for the community's benefit; by promoting such behaviour, the gene perpetuates itself. To this way of thinking, altruism becomes an expression of the fundamental 'selfishness' of our genes. And this applies even to parental affection: Hamilton has suggested that parental care is merely a special case of more general "altruism", in that the reason why parents are motivated to care for their own offspring is because those children are likely to perpetuate the existence of genes like their own. So not only can the evolutionary paradigm be read as legitimating selfishness or racism, its effect here is to actively undermine unselfishness (or at least to raise questions about it) as a sign of captivity to genetically-rooted drives – a genetically-inspired delusion. To the extent that we are persuaded that 'natural selection is both sufficient and true', says Ghiselin, 'it is impossible for a genuinely disinterested or "altruistic" behaviour pattern to evolve.' 'Evolutionary biology is quite clear that "What's in it for me?" is the ancient refrain for all life', writes Barash.[114]

But the argument then goes further. What is the root of counter-reproductive behaviour, of acts of radical self-sacrifice?[115] Not all such behaviour can be explained either in terms of the benefit to our kin or our group, or of the indirect benefits they bring to our own reproductive attractiveness. Thus many recent theorists have suggested that 'altruism' – that is, behaviour that decreases the agent's own reproductive success – must be the result of manipulation by the action's beneficiary. 'From this perspective nearly any interaction ... where one individual benefits at the expense of another, can be viewed as coercion or manipulation and take the form of parasitism, competition or predation ... In this way every act of apparent kindness becomes ultimately self-interested or involuntarily manipulated.'[116] Dennett cites George Williams: 'As a general rule today a biologist seeing one animal doing something to benefit another assumes either that it is manipulated by the other or that it is being subtly selfish.'[117]

Apply this to human behaviour (for how could it be different?) and you get Wright's position: 'What is in our genes' best interest is what seems "right" ... Moral guidance is a euphemism. Parents are designed to steer kids towards "moral" behaviours only insofar as those behaviours are self-serving.' Wright cites Christ as an instance of the manipulativeness involved: Christ's preaching, he says, took the 'form of exploitation ... amplifying the power of Jesus.'[118] Leading sociobiologist E.O. Wilson likewise argues that religious altruism such as that displayed by Mother Teresa is rooted ultimately in self-serving group loyalty.[119] But, argues Ruse, we must deceive ourselves into believing in the 'collective illusion' of morality, otherwise the system wouldn't work; self-deception is essential if we are to go on being manipulated by, and manipulating, others.[120]

What is the effect on us – or our culture – if we really come to accept (or even half-accept) these ideas? The belief that there are no disinterested behaviours, concludes Schloss, forces us to seek to explain or 'deconstruct those behaviours that appear disinterested'. The truly 'scientific' mind must look, under the appearance of unselfish actions, for the reality of 'manipulation, parasitism, competition, or predation'.

> 'Pity crosses the law of development, which is the law of *selection*. It preserves what is ripe for destruction; it defends those who have been disinherited and condemned by life ...
>
> 'The weak and the failure shall perish: first principle of *our* love of man. And they shall even be given every possible assistance.
>
> 'What is more harmful than any vice? Active pity for all the failures and all the weak: Christianity.'
> –Nietzsche, *The Antichrist*[121]
>
> 'The poison of the doctrine of "equal rights for all" – it was Christianity that spread it most fundamentally', said Arthur Gueth, director of public health in Nazi Germany. 'The ill-conceived "love of thy neighbour" has to disappear, especially in relation to inferior or asocial creatures.'[122]
>
> British society is now seen as a free-for-all where it is everyone for his or her self, according to 89% of the 1,130 people who responded to a Gallup poll carried out for Granada Television's *World in Action* programme.

The last sandcastle: the family

So then: There is no God who could show us today what is right or wrong, and why we should not be selfish. Nor will class loyalty, 'New Age', or our newly-dominant evolutionary theory. Indeed, 'New Age', and still more the cutting-edge of socio-biological theory, may logically encourage us to thoroughgoing selfishness. What then?

In practice, many of us look to the family as a final base for a post-God morality. When all else is gone, I may reasonably judge my conduct by what is best for my family.[123] After race ethics and class ethics, it is the final expression of 'doing what's right for my own folk' as the basis of right and wrong.

One suspects this is the functioning ethics of many Britishers. A top England cricketer, asked why he played in South Africa while the country was still under a UN boycott because of its immoral regime, is reported to have said, 'I don't know much about apartheid ... I did what was best for my family and therefore for me.' One of Scotland's leading footballers remarked likewise, 'A professional footballer has a duty to his wife and family to earn as much as he can from the sport as quickly as he can.' An extreme example was a man shown on television who made a living by kidnapping children in divorce cases. When the court gave the child to the mother, he would kidnap it for the father. When the interviewer suggested this was an unpleasant way to make a living, he replied, 'My family have to eat.'

What is good for my family is right; what is bad for my family is wrong. Here, at last, is something practical that we can and do set against self-interest. And it does seem a sufficient basis for many people's lives.

But it's very, very fragile – as is revealed by the divorce rates. Unfortunately, the family unit is in deep crisis too. In Britain, at least one marriage in three ends in divorce, and the trend continues to accelerate. 'What is good for my family' can no longer serve as a basis for our ethics when the family itself is gone.[124]

But where that last alternative to self-interest collapses, we may be losing our final sandcastle against the incoming tide. What will then be left?

With God dead and no other compelling basis for altruism, should it surprise us if we sense a trend towards evolutionary jungle law – the survival and indulgence of the strong, at the expense of the 'weakest links' in society? For one moment, we should face the worst-case scenario of what that means. Self-defence courses notwithstanding, the 'weak' in our society will include women, and children. Logically, then, with our ethics collapsing, we might expect there to be higher rates of rape and child abuse. And, as we know, there are.

Now ethical ideas aren't the only things that regulate our behaviour; most of us clearly have very deeply-felt, innate moral intuitions, and there are limits beyond which we just won't go. Yet taboo activities do fascinate and magnetize many of us. At this point sexual violence and paedophilia may lie outside the boundaries. But already we see 'daring' writers emerging who 'explore' for us the 'complexities' of these taboos also. *The People v Larry Flynt*, the Oscar-nominated bio-pic presenting a supportive image of the editor of porn magazine *Hustler*, was seen as right-on in many American circles, despite Flynt's reported use of pictures including women being forced into a meat-grinder, tortured or drinking from lavatory bowls.[125] (Flynt's opponent was a 'Christian fundamentalist', and it seems that the need for right-thinking folk to stand together against fundamentalism took obvious precedence over Flynt's treatment of women, revealingly.) As for paedophilia, there are numerous serious academics now questioning how – in the absence of a clear moral framework – we can 'know' the difference between a healthy and a 'sick and freakish' love for children. Such certainty, they argue, is in fact an arbitrary cultural agreement driven by fear, desire and denial; paedophiles are often gentle, loving, and non-threatening.[126]

Taboo actions fascinate; and taboos themselves shift, when there is no significant ethical force to maintain them. As we've seen, we do have very little left, post-God, to set against the evolutionary law. By that law the strongest do what they will, and the weaker suffer. Is this already happening? There were fifteen thousand indecent assaults on women in Britain in one recent year; a London survey found that one woman in six claims to have been raped.[127] Across the Atlantic, 13% of male under-graduates admitted forcing themselves on a woman physically; and more than 50% said they would if they could get away with it.[128] ('No Means No'? It doesn't, replied the jocks on one campus: 'No Means More Beer.') Child abuse is an increasing problem, with, according to some estimates, a million UK children being sexually abused before the age of 15.[129] 'In my work as an inner-city doctor', writes Theodore Dalrymple, 'every day I meet people who, earlier in their lives, were beaten unmercifully, locked in cupboards, tied to beds, scalded deliberately with hot water, and even permanently maimed by the vicious adults who brought them up.'[130]

Jungle law is already partly operative; the question is what we have left to set against it. The lasting wreckage in so many lives is already catastrophic. But we cannot regard it as illogical or incomprehensible; we've been choosing for this ethical jungle for a long time now.

It's seldom that Wales beats the All Blacks at rugby. But one famous occasion saw them coming very close indeed, then being 'robbed' at the last moment when All Black Andy Haden jumped out of a lineout, succeeded in persuading the referee that he had been pushed, and so secured the penalty that won the match. (Welsh friends of mine turned the TV off before the penalty: they knew Wales would lose now, and they knew why.) In a subsequent radio interview, Haden was unrepentant; anything that led to victory and was permitted by the referee was acceptable in modern sport. Commenting on this, star Olympic athlete Sebastian Coe observed that in fact modern organized sport first arose in a cultural context drawing heavily on the Christian moral code: 'A key word was "ethics" ... Fairness lies at the heart of sporting competition. Take this away and you have a very different activity.'

'Fairness', the commitment to the 'rights' of those opposed to you: is this a notion left over from a context prioritizing something other than the will to power, to victory? The postmodern alternative would be more about conflict: 'Winning isn't the main thing, it's the only thing.'

'You have a rival for promotion. When he loses the latest sales figures, do you produce them from the Atari Portfolio in your pocket?
'Well, you've got to look after No. 1 haven't you? It's war out there.'
–Part of the wording Atari Corp (UK) chose for their 'Business is War' advertising campaign. When ethics is dead, what's left is war. This, too, was foreseen by Nietzsche.

'After this war two torrents will be unleashed in the world: a torrent of loving-kindness and a torrent of hatred. And then I knew: I should take the field against hatred.'
–Etty Hillesum, in *An Interrupted Life*, writing shortly before she was sent to Auschwitz and murdered

'Future historians will record that we of the twentieth century had intelligence enough to create a great civilization but not the moral wisdom to preserve it.'
–Christian mystic A.W. Tozer, in *Man the Dwelling-Place of God*

After morality

We've watched so many sandcastles succumb to the incoming tide. God is dead and, 'post-God', we've found few compelling reasons for acting unselfishly. We aren't always logical, and from time to time we will be intuitively unselfish (African famines on TV, extinction of the whale), according to our moods. But from time to time we won't.

The logic works through slowly, of course. Older, Christian-based moralities will survive better in some areas (particularly rural ones?), though these differences are being eroded by our all-pervasive media. And all of us avoid meaninglessness; deep in our hearts we try to act as if our intuitive ethical frameworks were realities. Yet the lack of any real basis means we are going against the tide. The term 'moraliser', observes Melanie Phillips, is now a 'term of abuse which has become for the left what the insult "do-gooder" has long been for the right'.[131] Indeed, in some quarters we now find an almost knee-jerk reaction against thinking ethically. When some especially abhorrent crime gets committed, the humanist end of the media usually warns us frantically against 'moral panic'.[132] Not long back I was looking at posters for the charity 'Make Children Happy' and thought how absurd it would be to launch a charity called 'Make Children Good'. We aren't 'into' goodness today – not at all.

But what kind of consequences should we expect when 'thinking morally' and 'doing good' are both negative ideas? What results should we expect as the lack of any effective 'post-God' ethic becomes widely realized?

First, it adds to the loads on our consciousness that we examined in earlier chapters. 'Where men ... act in the conviction that "nothing is true, everything is permitted"', suggests Stern in his study of Nietzsche, 'that there is no authority to appeal to – their style of life is more troubled and more sordid than before.'[133] Stern is supported by Patterson and Kim's survey of American values, where they conclude that the loss of right and wrong

> raises fear and doubt, which often lead to depression: Did I do the right thing? Does it matter anymore? Does anything matter? ... In interview after interview, we saw men and women grappling with the consequences of their new freedom to define their own moral codes. If no one I can trust is available to counsel me, how can I be

sure that what I'm doing is right? Is the other person – my lover, my business partner – playing by some set of reasonable rules? What are the rules? Their rules? My rules? No rules at all?[134]

Second, there is likely to be a problem in the area of leadership. 'Today there is little shared sense of what it is to be heroic', writes Keyes,[135] citing Becker's observation that the contemporary crisis in youth culture is 'precisely a crisis of belief in the vitality of the hero-systems that are offered by contemporary materialist society'. 'Who are our heroes?' asked Polly Toynbee sadly in *Radio Times*:

> We no longer believe in altruism, which is the essential ingredient for heroism. Psychology has suggested to us that everybody does what they want to do, for their own personal satisfactions. Some want to be nurses, social workers and probation officers. Others want to make money in the City. There is less a sense of a value judgment in favour of those who devote their lives to helping others, because it is suggested to us that it is part of their inborn frame of mind to gain more satisfaction from that than from other apparently selfish occupations.

From India, Mangalwadi argues that 'Once the twentieth-century western world denied its transcendent faith, it lost its ability to produce heroes of its own'. The 'main heroes that the West celebrates', he adds, are Mandela, Gandhi and Martin Luther King – all of whom are from outside the post-Christian, de-ethicized mainstream.[136] If it exists for us at all now, 'heroism' has been divorced from goodness and has primarily to do with fame or novelty.[137]

'No More Heroes'; no more saints, either. In his eulogy at Princess Diana's funeral, Earl Spenser was anxious to distance his sister from any notion of 'sainthood', for example because of her 'mischievous sense of humour'. Somehow, 'saint' implied a lack of humanness. Ethicist Susan Wolf wrote a famous essay attacking the whole notion of 'moral saints' as being 'dull-witted, humourless or bland'. 'I don't know whether there are any moral saints. But if there are, I am glad that neither I nor those about whom I care most are among them', she begins, adding, 'By moral saint I mean a person whose every action is as morally good as possible, a person, that is, who is as morally worthy as can be.'[138] Wolf's idea of sainthood is a caricature (though medieval Catholicism did plenty to make sainthood and humanness seem incompatible), but it surely matches our cultural mood; we don't believe in saints, any more than in heroes.

All in all, then, as Blake Morrison says, we no longer know what a 'good' person is (in a genuinely Christian context Christ would provide that definition; but who now reads the Gospels?). But when we don't have much clue about 'good people', it becomes hard to believe in trustworthy leaders. Which in turn has implications for democracy – why should I bother to vote for Tweedledum rather than Tweedledee, if each is as crooked as the other? In a recent survey, 89% of Seattle teens said they knew of no leader of integrity. And there is an inevitable next stage: they didn't want to be leaders either.[139]

(But this leadership vacuum could be fatal in what may be our last chance to avoid massive environmental crisis. If we miss it, one suspects the next generation will view us as the ones who created huge problems for them by refusing the altruism of self-restraint; the ones who refused or denied the issues of moral justice that could have curbed our soaring population growth and pollution. As they grapple with the results of our loss of ethics, we must hope they do not hate us. For then we shall be the weak, dependent in our turn on their altruism; or, at any rate, on their paying us our pensions justly according to the promises we made to ourselves.)

But other consequences come much closer to home. One could be a loss of faith in the legal system, like that proving so costly in America. If there is no true ethics, it is hard to see how law can be justified; respect for law assumes an ethical basis to the system, and that assumes a 'real' morality. ('Without religion, no morality; without morality, no law', to quote Lord Denning again.[140]) With 'objective' morality gone, law becomes just a humanly-constructed game. Or, alternatively, it is merely an expression of the interests of the powerful; American Supreme Court Justice Oliver Wendell Holmes wrote as early as 1926 that 'When it comes to the development of a *corpus juris* [body of law], the ultimate question is what do the dominant forces of the community want and do they want it hard enough to disregard whatever inhibitions may stand in the way.'[141] Either way, law ceases to be an impartial public resource. In secularized areas of America we see already how far the legal practitioner has sunk in public esteem – from someone who applied the objective norms of justice to someone who gets rich by playing the system – hence *What To Do With a Dead Lawyer* and similar joke books. (Q: Why are scientists using lawyers instead of rats in experiments? A: There are more lawyers to begin with, they multiply faster, and laboratory personnel become far less attached to lawyers than to rats. Then, too, lawyers will do many things rats won't.)

> The crisis in law after the loss of God was particularly evident in the Nuremburg trials of those responsible for the Nazi Holocaust. Legal positivism – the dominant humanistic tradition that saw law purely as a human construct, with no basis in external, objective ethics – had no basis on which to judge the Nazis. Their actions may have been grossly immoral, but they had not been in any way illegal. Many of the charges brought against the Nazis 'could hardly be legitimated by positive law', notes Morrison.[142] Their actions had not breached any existing laws; their atrocities had been carried out according to a functioning legal system. On what basis, therefore, could they be found guilty? 'It was difficult to hide from the fact that from a legal positive perspective the decrees promulgated by the Nazis were valid law. Even the Holocaust was possibly legal, buttressed by the fact that it was carried out in the name of the (Nazi) good.'[143]
> In the ensuing debate, some argued for the Nazis' condemnation on the basis of 'natural law'. By

contrast Hart, the central figure of British legal positivism, took the view that human beings construct our own ethics; thus the legal system is a social contract without any metaphysical foundations.[144] But how then could the Nazis be condemned, if legal systems are merely something we construct according to our preference?

Clearly, the Nuremburg trials assumed that there was something deeper than our self-constructed legal structures; and indeed that each person was responsible to disobey a violently unjust legal system, in the name of a higher moral law. The Nazi mass murderers could only be judged (and were) as gross offenders against such a law. But where can we get such a law from, now that God is dead? If we have no answer, should not the mass murderers have walked out of Nuremburg free? And have we anything more to say to their recent successors?

But a society that has lost faith in its legal system, and has no universally-shared belief-framework to put informally in its place, is obviously headed for the jungle. Anyone who travelled much in post-communist Russia will know the situation where the law has become disrespected and been replaced by force and bribery, expressed in the omnipresent mafia and an often-corrupt police force. (' "Legal" is meaningless here', a Russian friend told me recently as we walked down the street in St Petersburg.) The Russian Interior Ministry stated in 1999 that 40% of the economy and 50% of the banking system was controlled by organized crime; 'Corrupt officialdom pervades the economy, organized crime pervades officialdom', concurred the *Economist*.

But all that is not limited to Russia. We sometimes wonder 'when Russia will catch up with the west'; yet the real issue may be how long it will take for the postmodern west, now almost equally short of ethical convictions, to catch up with Russia. Already in 1999 a British National Criminal Intelligence Service document suggested that police corruption had become 'pervasive', reaching 'two-thirds-world levels', and that lie detectors and drug testing were needed for police detectives. With the 'post-God' undermining of a 'love for your neighbour' public-service ethic, the number of people who go into police work motivated at least in part (as many have been) by idealism is likely to decrease. Police activity then can become a power game played by man-made rules with an ever-decreasing connection to objective ethics, or to any compelling sense of right and wrong. In the drug trade in particular, the sums involved are so huge that it can take an officer of real moral vision to resist being 'corrupted'; but from where is such a vision to be maintained?

At the least we should expect the 'kickback' and 'corruption' to become increasingly widespread. These things operate in any society; but if there is no convincing ethical reason for opposing them (and there is one for embracing them: the good of my family), they will logically become more common. If, as many postmodernists say, power is all there is, well, 'power corrupts'. So the ethical crisis, post-God, crosses the gap from the intellectual stratosphere to the universal street-level backhander. And at worst, a general collapse of ethics in the legal and police systems means, quite simply, a jungle for us to grow old in.[145]

The survey of American values by Patterson and Kim offers pointers as to what it can mean to be a western society that really disbelieves in goodness and badness. In America, 74% said yes to 'I will steal from those who don't really miss it'; 53% said yes to 'I will cheat on my spouse – after all, given the chance, he or she will do the same'. For $10 million, 7% of respondents said they would murder a stranger, 3% would put their children up for adoption, and 16% would leave their spouse. (For some reason, the figures stayed roughly the same for $5 million and $2 million but dropped sharply at $1 million.)[146]

That is what we admit to the pollsters; and it seems we have little now but social constraints to set against our selfishness. But, with their ethical basis disappearing 'after God', those social and legal constraints are crumbling too.

> 'No one has ever given an answer to the simple ques-
> tion, Why not? Why not do any evil I passionately and
> sincerely and "authentically" want to do, if there is no
> superhuman lawmaker and no superhuman law?
> Only because I might get caught, because crime
> doesn't pay? But crime often does pay: it is estimated
> that well over half of all crimes are never detected or
> punished. And if the only deterrent is cops, not con-
> science, what of the conscience of the cops? Who will
> guard the guards? And how many guards must we
> have to police a society of immoralists? A state full of
> moral subjectivists must become a police state.'
> –Peter Kreeft[147]

Beyond good and evil

Bonfire of the Vanities author Tom Wolfe, addressing Harvard
about contemporary America, observed: 'We have awarded ourselves the final freedom – freedom from religion and ordinary
ethical standards.'

Kirilov, in Dostoevski's *The Possessed*, moves logically from
the denial of God to the position that 'Everything's good ...
Everything.' 'And what about the man who dies of hunger, and
the man who insults and rapes a little girl. Is that good too?'
'Yes, it is. And the man who blows his brains out for the child,
that's good. Everything's good ...'[148] Nietzsche said the same:
with God dead, 'Nothing is true, everything is permitted.' Sartre
concurred: 'Everything is indeed permitted if God does not
exist.'

Few of us have read these passages outside a context still dominated, in practice, by 'ordinary ethical standards'. But if 'everything is indeed permitted', if God is dead and we are truly free to
(quoting Tina Turner) 'break every rule', what then? Presumably
the dominant factors become, again, the fundamental drives
such as money, sex, power. (Nietzsche once more: 'Thou goest to
woman? Take thou thy whip.') As we've said, it isn't good news

for the weak, but this is the reality of the 'animal kingdom'. De Sade: 'Whatever is, is right.'

However, Hitler's question may be the next on the agenda: 'I cannot see why man should not be just as cruel as nature.' As de Sade recognized, some people have a pleasure drive that genuinely receives satisfaction in cruelty. If 'everything is indeed permitted', what cruelties might logically lie ahead of us? The question may seem unnecessary. But can we be so complacent? Again we recall the 'games' of ancient Rome, the crowds entertained by seeing human beings ripped apart. And a look around youth culture might make us wonder: consider the success of mass-slaughter video games like 'Mortal Kombat', the best-selling comics (e.g. *Judge Dredd*) portraying amoral futuristic worlds dominated by bloodshed and 'might is right', the posed viciousness of much hip-hop and heavy metal. And what of the fascination de Sade exerts on writers from Foucault to Barthes to Angela Carter to Camille Paglia? Or Damien Hirst's art show *Some Went Mad, Some Ran Away ...*, which the *Independent on Sunday* described as combining 'fierce images of torture and violent sex, death, murder and decay'? Or the fashion for 'designer sado-masochism' (Amsterdam's beautiful Schiphol airport has a video store with a large section marked 'Bondage/ S/M'), when S/M so easily leads to pleasure at involuntary suffering, including rape? Or the evident attraction of 'slasher' movies, the endless gory remakes of *Friday the 13th*, *Nightmare on Elm Street* and so many others – or, at the 'classier' level, Quentin Tarantino and *Reservoir Dogs*, Harvey Keitel in *Bad Lieutenant* (to say nothing of the massive market for 'heavier' video nasties like *Driller Killer*)? In the Patterson/Kim survey, a remarkably high proportion of Americans reported regular fantasies of violence.[149] 'I wanna destroy', sang the Sex Pistols; the appetite seems to be there, biding its time.

'The strong men, the masters, regain the pure conscience of a beast of prey; monsters filled with joy, they can return from a fearful succession of murder, arson, rape and torture with the same joy in their

hearts, the same contentment in their souls as if they had indulged in some students' rag.'
–Nietzsche, *Genealogy of Morals*

'We want to exalt the movements of aggression, feverish sleeplessness, the forced march, the perilous leap, the slap and the blow with the fist. To glorify war – the only cure for the world – and militarism, patriotism, the destructive gesture of the anarchist, the beautiful ideas which kill, and contempt for women.'
–Marinetti, leader of the Italian Futurists

'Yes, I told him, I was a Nazi, I really believed it to be the ideal system ... I was completely committed to the whole philosophy. The blood and violence was an essential ingredient of its strength, the heroic tradition of cruelty every bit as powerful and a thousand times more ancient than the Judaeo-Christian ethic.'
–Alan Clark, minister in Margaret Thatcher's government, in *Diaries: Into Politics*

So it goes. The fact that the 'civilized' Nazis became a byword for darkness should not obliterate the memory of what they did: Polish rabbis forced to shovel out open latrines with their hands and mouths while Nazi officers observed and took photos for subsequent labelling; the torture and experimentation in the Gestapo cells, carefully recorded by stenographers (usually women); the drowning of so many in urine and ordure; Auschwitz, Dachau, Treblinka, Belsen.[150] 'We are British: we are different'? Perhaps.

But in Nottingham a few years back, a judge sentenced a family to prison after hearing how their children, some of them still in nappies, had been pulled from their beds late at night to be sexually assaulted as "playthings" at sex parties. He told two mothers, 'You must have sat there when these parties were going on and heard your children screaming and did nothing about it.'

America? A television programme recalled the incident when American GIs massacred 500 civilians in My Lai, Vietnam. 'I looked out of my house', said one survivor, 'and saw my sister Mui. She was 14 that year. An American was pressing on top of her ... At the time I didn't realise what that meant. My sister was trying to resist him. Afterwards, the American got up. He put his clothes on. And then he shot her.' American soldiers who had been present spoke of shooting women and children in ditches so that their corpses piled up tidily, and of slicing off victims' ears and hands. The officer who had trained them said he was 'very pleased with the way they turned out. They turned out to be very good soldiers.'

Back to Europe: 'Thousands of men executed and buried in mass graves, hundreds buried alive, men and women mutilated and slaughtered, children killed before their mothers' eyes, a grandfather forced to eat the liver of his own grandson.' This is from the UN's International War Crimes Tribunal report on atrocities in former Yugoslavia.

Back to Britain: according to evidence given to the Central Criminal Court, children of three families from New Addington, south London, suffered sexual abuse and torture sessions at the hands of their parents. The mothers encouraged the men to sexually attack the children in group sessions; the children were sometimes beaten, both for the adults' pleasure and to make them so frightened they would not tell anybody.

For most of us, gut intuition says: All this is abomination; these are evil. But to understand our real situation, we must face the issue of how (if God is dead) we can meaningfully call them evil; or whether, as so many of our post-God philosophers tell us, our intuitions here are just a matter of 'feeling', 'preference', taste. Richard Monk, head of Scotland Yard's anti-paedophilia unit, told a national police conference that paedophiles were 'evil like Hitler because they actually believe what they do is right. And because they are right and we are wrong they ignore conventional punishment, cover their tracks well and go on offending. The scale of offending is enormous.' Muswell Hill mass murderer Dennis Nilsen wrote to researcher Brian

Masters, 'No one wants to believe that I am just an ordinary man come to an extraordinary and overwhelming conclusion.' And here is postmodernist guru Baudrillard, in *The Transparency of Evil*: 'Everything we thought left behind forever by the ineluctable march of progress is not dead at all, but on the contrary, likely to return ... and to reach into the very heart of our ultra-sophisticated but ultra-vulnerable system.'

'Of course', writes Oxford determinist Wilfred Beckerman during an attack on the concept of 'moral responsibility', 'cruelty to children or anybody else is indescribably revolting.' ('If one likes to call the people who perpetrate such acts "bad", so be it', he adds. But 'passing moral judgements on people for acts we abhor' is basically an 'absurdity'.) But unfortunately not everyone agrees on what is 'revolting'. And while the fact that such cruelties 'sicken most of us', as Beckerman says,[151] may enable 'most of us' to feel good about imposing our tastes on their perpetrators, it certainly doesn't provide any reason why the deviant himself should not pursue his 'tastes'. Logically, we should not be surprised when we read of that happening. And if we intend judging such matters of 'taste' by popular consensus, we must think back to the Nazi era: there was a time when the savage degradation of an entire race became the fashion.

If there is no God, if 'good' and 'evil' cannot be known to exist, can we say more than this: I feel I have 'natural', 'wholesome' (altruistic) tastes; you have 'unusual', 'sophisticated', 'deviant' (e.g. sadistic) tastes:[152] and I will impose my tastes on you by force?

It matters if there is no God. My Lai, Belsen, Nottingham; these things are no longer 'evil'. There is no such thing as evil; just each to his own taste.

Hitler liked blue. Rapists like blue. I like green. God is dead. That's all there is?

God is dead: can we any longer say what is right and wrong? If not, what will be the results?

In the academic world, there is no consensus whatever about the meaning of 'right' and 'wrong' after the loss of God. Indeed, numerous voices declare that 'right' and 'wrong' have no objective meaning; they are merely matters of emotions or preferences. No self-evident motivation exists to restrain our selfishness.

So where do we find an alternative ethic? 'Right' is what is best for society, or for the maximum number of other people, we've been told. But there seems no self-evident reason why we should care about society. Or, perhaps right and wrong are what is good or bad for my class; but again, is there any clear reason why class solidarity should take precedence over my interests? Perhaps we could find a basis for ethics in the cosmic progression heralded by 'New Age'; but in actual practice, isn't much of New Age primarily about self-enhancement, self-actualization, offering no real counter to egoism? And evolution, if anything, undermines the basis for altruism.

Lastly there is the family: here, finally, is a value we can and do set against self-interest. But it is very fragile; we live in a culture of soaring divorce rates.

God is dead. So are 'right' and 'wrong' buried, obsolete and useless, in his tomb? Are they just words that are growing more and more meaningless, stupid, unworkable?

But if we are truly 'beyond good and evil' – once the generations pass that have Christian ethics embedded in their subconscious, once a generation arises that really accepts the logic that there is no 'right' and 'wrong', no 'justice', nothing but the compulsions of pleasure and power – what then? As we face the dawning of a violent world without ethics, it matters whether things really have to be this way. It matters whether there is a God.

Notes

1. In *The Portable Nietzsche*, ed. and tr. Walter Kaufmann, p. 501.

2. *Portable Nietzsche*, p. 517.

3. Alasdair MacIntyre, *After Virtue*. MacIntyre analyses the difficulties in a number of other post-Enlightenment alternatives in the second half of *A Short History of Ethics*.

4. Paul W. Taylor, *Respect for Nature: A Theory of Environmental Ethics*, quoted in Paul Chamberlain, *Can We be Good Without God?*, pp. 121, 200.

5. Address to the Canadian Senate, published in *New York Review of Books*, 10 June 1999. I owe this reference to Vinoth Ramachandra.

6. Midgley's essay 'Duties Concerning Islands' is reprinted in an excellent symposium edited by Peter Singer, *Ethics*, pp. 374–87. The emphasis in the Grice quotation is mine.

7. David Gauthier, in Singer, *Ethics*, p. 368.

8. In other words, if morality is a *social* contract, it is in fact chosen by and reflects the interests of the most powerful sections of society, not my own.

9. Cf. Will Kymlicka's essay in another symposium edited by Singer, *A Companion to Ethics*, particularly pp. 189–91. This fine volume contains helpful surveys by leading scholars of many areas we touch on briefly here, which readers wanting more in-depth coverage may well find helpful.

10. See St. Paul's attitude to his 'rights' in 1 Corinthians 9:3–23. Shakespeare's *The Merchant of Venice* can be read as a treatment of the insufficiency, for community, of insistence on one's rights; there must be something else, which Shakespeare presents as 'mercy'. Writing as a Christian, John F. Alexander expands the issue into the area of forgiveness with the comment that community inevitably depends sometimes on our 'allowing yourself to be wronged. In my experience, a church (or a marriage, for that matter) can never be at peace if the partners are concerned about their rights. You can only be reconciled if you accept the sins of others in your body, as Jesus did... Peace is not benign intentions but a cross with nails.' (*The Secular Squeeze*, pp.147–48.) Rights are not enough for community; but how, post-God (now we no longer believe in what 'Jesus did' on the 'cross with nails'), do we empower what is needed to complement it?

11. Allan Bloom, for example, writes of 'the attempt to found all human relations on contract, the discovery of complementary interests ... Abstract reason in the service of radically free men and women can discover only contract as the basis of connectedness – the social contract, marriage contract, somehow mostly the business contract as model, with its union of selfish individuals. Legalism takes the place of sentiment' (*Love and Friendship*, p. 28).

12. I owe this point to Ravi Zacharias, *Can Man Live Without God?*, p. 9, who cites here the close of *Critique of Pure Reason*. Kant incurred Nietzsche's wrathful scorn for postulating God to make his system work.

13. In Singer, *Companion*, p. 193. Indeed, evolutionary ethicist Michael Ruse suggests that it probably would be; the biological foundation of our behaviour makes it likely that the altruism we engage in would be limited to those most like ourselves (p. 505).

14. *Ethics*, p. 246.

15. In Singer, *Companion,* p. 243. The founder of utilitarianism was Jeremy Bentham, who took the bull by the horns quite unashamedly: 'Nature has placed mankind under the governance of two sovereign masters, *pain* and *pleasure*. It is for them alone to point out what we ought to do, as well as to determine what we shall do.'

16. This is more or less John Hartland-Swan's position in *An Analysis of Morals*.

17. Right, and, observes Bernard Williams critically (in Singer, *Ethics*, p. 340), *obviously* so.

18. R.M. Hare, *Moral Thinking*, p. 186, and ch. 11.

19. *After Virtue*, p. 67.

20. Cf. Lyotard's comment on Habermas in *The Postmodern Condition*: 'Consensus has become an outmoded and suspect value ... We must thus arrive at an idea and practice of justice that is not linked to that of consensus' (In *From Modernism to Postmodernism*, ed. Lawrence Cahoone, pp. 503–04.)

21. I invite the reader to check this perception by working through Singer's two excellent and comprehensive collections.

22. See, for example, the end point of James Rachels' exposition of ethical subjectivism: 'Thus, as our final attempt to formulate an adequate subjectivist understanding of ethical judgement, we might say: something is morally right if it is such that the process of thinking through its nature and consequences should cause or

sustain a feeling of approval to it in a person who was being as reasonable and impartial as it is humanly possible' (in Singer, *Companion*, p. 440). But why should they be impartial? The same is true with Sartre. 'One should always ask himself, "What would happen if everybody looked at things that way?"', he says in his famous essay 'Existentialism'; but the 'should' seems to come out of thin air. A third, more postmodern example is given by Linda Lange: 'Postmodern critique of universalism and "totalizing discourse" reads as a critique of power and domination ... Yet as such it is often highly inconclusive ... We are given a compelling analysis of how denial and silencing of "difference" has been done, but little rational reason why the practice should be given up!' (Quoted in Middleton and Walsh, *Truth Is Stranger*, p. 210.)

23. Taylor, *Sources of the Self*, p. 87. His targets at this point are Hare and Habermas in particular.

24. In Singer, *Ethics*, pp. 5–6.

25. In Singer, *Companion*, p. 543.

26. That would not be surprising. If human beings have no cause to consider themselves as qualitatively different from animals, then animal rights should indeed become a driving force behind ethics. 'Ideology is dead, long live animals', began a 1995 *Independent* editorial, summarizing the way that the 'struggle to save the whale, the elephant and the panda' had taken the place of religion and ideology in the contemporary mood. (But it will be interesting to watch how the refocusing of the animal rights issue that has arisen from an intuitive insistence on the value of consciousness will in turn refocus the foetal rights debate – or, if it doesn't, why not.)

27. Singer, *Companion*, p. 545, cites the moral realism of Michael Smith, Jonathan Dancy's assessment of what can be salvaged from intuitionism, Rachels' exposition of ethical subjectivism, and Hare's universal prescriptivism.

28. In Singer, *Companion*, p. 409.

29. Singer, *Companion*, p. 440. And cf. Michael Smith: the issue is 'what we would desire if we were in certain idealized conditions of reflection: if, say, we were well-informed, cool, calm and collected' (p. 406). (He does not add 'good-hearted'; does that weaken his position?)

30. Singer, *Companion*, p. 461.

31. Utilitarian J.S. Mill's words are striking: 'Nor even now would it be easy, even for an unbeliever, to find a better translation of the rule

of virtue from the abstract into the concrete than to endeavour to live so that Christ would approve of our life' (quoted in Josh McDowell, *Evidence that Demands a Verdict*, p. 109). In reality, the model of Christ is far more compelling, imaginatively and practically, than the various abstractions ethicists have advanced such as 'perfectly rational, impartial and benevolent judges', etc.

32. Hare, *Moral Thinking*, p. 44.

33. This is Paul's point in Romans 7; see also Galatians 3:24. The Bible is indeed structured to emphasize the consequences of wrong action in its early books – our 'first lesson', as it were. But it is the presence of the Spirit within us that actually brings power to enable changed behaviour, as Paul makes clear through Romans 6 to 8.

34. The form the conundrum takes in Plato's *Eutyphro* is 'Do the gods love holiness because it is holy, or is it holy because they love it?'

35. A vital aspect of the primal Genesis narrative is that it specifically rules out driving a conceptual wedge between 'goodness' and 'God'. The temptation to construct good and evil outside the context of loving trust in God constitutes precisely that fatal and unworkable snatching at independence that dooms the entire human race to misery (Genesis 3:5).

36. The two central ethical commands at the heart of the Old Testament, it may be recalled, were both 'You shall love' – the Lord himself, in the first, and my neighbour as myself, in the second. (See Jesus' words in Matthew 22:35–40.) God is love, and the ethic he calls for consists of absolute reflection of his nature. The New Testament then introduces the empowerment whereby that reflection can begin to come into being.

37. Quoted in McDowell, *Evidence*, p. 110.

38. At this point, it seems to me, Christian faith accepts and responds to the demand of feminist ethicists for a holistic approach that is not restricted to an arid rationalism in the manner of both Kantians and utilitarians.

39. Thus the God in whose nature Christians ground their ethical life is not merely a distant principle with the addition of a personal name. Instead, he is that multi-faceted, profound reality we term the Trinity: the Father in whom all value consists, the Word who in the fullest manner revealed the Father's nature, and the Spirit who works within us to bring the goodness of that nature into being now.

40. In other words, a non-believer may well have intuitions about right and wrong that are as accurate, or even more accurate, than those of a believer. But, they derive from the conscience that God has put within human beings, and may in many cases be difficult for an atheist to hold with consistency, as we have been suggesting in the preceding pages.

41. Cited in *Christianity Today*, 19 May 1997. This was not merely true of giving to religious causes; two-thirds of the money given to non-religious charitable enterprises came from church members.

42. Patterson and Kim, *The Day America Told the Truth*, pp. 201–02. This fascinating book reports on a survey of a large sample of Americans. It contains a vast amount of data and is highly recommended for anyone interested in the changing condition of American values. Patterson was chairman, and Kim a senior vice-president, of the J. Walter Thompson agency, and they appear to have gone to considerable lengths to ensure the survey's professionalism and accuracy.

43. We are using 'faith' in very general terms here: the impact of different forms of faith could usefully be analysed. For example, could it be documented that there is much less bribery in cultures with long-term exposure to forms of Christianity with a strong emphasis on biblical teaching, and on a 'new birth' leading to a radically new quality of life? I suspect that conclusion would emerge clearly from a comparison of the northern European countries with Catholic Spain and Italy, or with Orthodox Russia. The issue could also be explored at the level of comparative religion. Ancient Greek religion, for example, lacked the idea of altruistic *agape* love that is so central to Christian ethics. Does it make a significant difference to the effect of 'love' as a basis for ethics if one believes God 'is Love', existing from all eternity as a triune community united in mutual love, rather than being solely One, alone from eternity, as in Islam, which rules out 'love' as an ultimate divine attribute? Again, how true is it that the monism of mainstream Hinduism, denying the ultimacy of good and evil, cannot offer a strong basis for morality and law? (See in particular Vishal Mangalwadi's fascinating study *India: the Grand Experiment*.)

44. The exception here must be Singer, whose animal liberationism clearly does have major practical impact on the lives of many. But only, we must say, in one area – although it's a far-reaching one.

45. Charles Martin observed back in 1973 that a major weakness of overt humanism, and a reason why it was so uncompelling for most people, was that it was so desperately abstract and 'verbal'. (*How Human Can You Get?*, p. 135.) Fred Catherwood's assessment 27 years later is that 'It is easy to get a hearing for the removal of restraints, but to gain wide voluntary acceptance of a structure of individual duties to make those rights effective is beyond [the humanists'] reach' (*It Can Be Done*, p. 107).

46. 'The denial of the transcendance of norms is crucial to post-modernism. Norms such as truth, goodness, beauty, rationality, are no longer regarded as independent of the processes they seek to govern or judge, but are rather products of and immanent in these processes. For example, where most philosophers might use the idea of justice to judge a social order, postmodernism regards that idea as itself the product of the social relations it seeks to judge ... This greatly complicates any claims about the justice of social relations.' (Cahoone, in his introduction to *From Modernism*, p. 15.)

47. 'Human behaviour ... is the circuitous technique by which human genetic material has been and will be kept intact. Morality has no other demonstrable ultimate function.' (Edward O. Wilson, *On Human Nature*, p. 6.)

48. In Singer, *Ethics*, p. 163.

49. MacIntyre, *After Virtue*, p. 20.

50. Alasdair MacIntyre, *Whose Justice? Which Rationality?*, p. 3.

51. Cited by Dale Jamieson in Singer, *Companion*, p. 476.

52. MacIntyre, *After Virtue*, p. 117.

53. Parfit, *Reasons and Persons*, pp. 443, 451.

54. Hare's complaint resembles the comments we have made above concerning the assumptions (e.g. regarding impartiality) that take the place of solid substance in much current theory. Yet it is note-worthy that Hare assumes that the problem is linked with preju-dices, an intellectual failure, to which the answer is a clearer rationality, rather than the need for something to be done about the selfishness of the will.

55. James Q. Wilson, 'What is Moral, and How Do We Know It?', *First Things*, June 1993, p. 37. I owe this reference to James Sire.

56. Sartre, *Existentialism and Humanism*, p. 36.

57. And once again, modern psychology puts a huge question mark over the value of our instincts. If they are primarily triggered by our

genetic makeup and our environmental conditioning, it seems strange to put too much trust in them.

58. Cf. *The Times*, 24 June 1981.

59. Quoted in Klaus Bockmuehl, *The Challenge of Marxism*, p. 96. Lenin remarked on another occasion that 'Good is what advances the cause of the revolution' (quoted in David Lyon, *Karl Marx*, p. 168). Stalin's astonishing 1939 alliance with the arch-fascist Hitler exemplified that very well.

60. An example would be the anger stirred up by the apparent untouchability of the plans of multinationals like Monsanto for growing genetically modified food, backed by the legal force of transatlantic trade agreements. One suspects that if the European governments had not taken a stand on that issue, eco-terrorism would not have been far away.

61. Samuel Escobar, 'Marxist Ideology and Christian Mission', *In Touch* (IFES), Oct. 1981.

62. MacIntyre, *History of Ethics*, pp. 213–14.

63. No comment is intended about the rights or wrongs of the strike. The point here is simply the way that class morality has declined as a motivating force.

64. Keir Hardie, founder of the Labour movement, insisted that 'The Labour Movement is essentially religious. Christ's great work was to teach the oneness of the human race, to remove the abuses which divided man from man, to make it impossible for the strong to oppress the weak or for the rich to rob the poor.' Labour Prime Minister Harold Wilson said that his party owed more to Methodism than Marxism.

65. Just like their capitalist arch-enemies, of course.

66. Bockmuehl, p. 104.

67. Quoted in Guinness, *Dust*, p. 145.

68. Trotsky saw what would happen: 'The organization of the party takes the place of the party [that is, the working-class] itself; the Central Committee takes the place of the organization; and finally the dictator takes the place of the Central Committee' (quoted in Lyon, *Karl Marx*, pp. 168–69). They killed Trotsky with an ice-pick.

69. Quoted by Jonathan Bennett in Singer, *Ethics*, p. 299.

70. Adolf Hitler, *Mein Kampf*, p. 271. Zacharias (*Can Man Live without God?*, p. 23) cites some words of Hitler that now hang on the wall at Auschwitz: 'I freed Germany from the stupid and degrading fallacies of conscience and morality.'

71. Hitler, *Mein Kampf*, pp. 162–63.

72. Hitler, *Mein Kampf*, p. 621. Italics are mine.

73. Hitler, *Mein Kampf*, p. 103. One wishes that these complaints had been proved justified in the aftermath; in fact, the faith of many parts of the German church had been so weakened by 'liberal', doubt-oriented theologies that their resistance was minimal. But the so-called 'Confessing Church' offered a resistance, fuelled by their commitment to biblical ethics, that was as determined as Hitler had feared.

74. Quoted in Jacques Ellul, *Violence*, p. 130.

75. *Independent on Sunday*, 18 Apr. 1999.

76. Namely 'what is in the interests of our own folk'; or, what 'our own folk' or '*volk*' or 'tribe' hold to be 'correct'. Various postmodernist thinkers have argued that these two tend towards being much the same thing; and, unless there is some strong counterbalancing ethical force, this would seem to be the case. To quote the hip-hop slogan, 'There's no justice, there's just us.'

77. Richard Rorty, *Objectivity, Relativism and Truth*, p. 30. Actually, this community ethic is in the end no real counter to egoism. We all tend to belong to a range of different 'communities', and can usually find one to endorse what we really want to do.

78. Vinoth Ramachandra, *Gods that Fail*, pp. 5–7.

79. A good example of ethics as 'doing what's right for your own folk' is Heidegger's speech to the Freiburg students in 1933 when he told them, 'May you ceaselessly grow in courage to sacrifice yourself for the salvation of our nation's essential being ... The Führer himself and he alone is the German reality, present and future, and its law ... *Heil Hitler!*'

80. To the Christian, this would depend on the power and grace of God. To the humanist, 'enlightenment' was more a matter of progressive education.

81. I was troubled to read a recent piece in which an American feminist asked, 'How could you have a friend who belonged to the Christian Coalition and was an anti-abortionist?' It raised for me the issue of whether loving your enemy has become something so distinctively Christian. Empirically, a lot of us who are Christian genuinely love interacting with those with whom we profoundly disagree. It is the only way to carry on. (And how else could we learn?)

82. In other words: once what earlier periods saw as issues of truth become recognized (as postmodernists like Foucault say) as being

really issues of power, then the obvious conclusion is that they can only be settled in terms of power.

83. This summary is adapted from Douglas Groothuis' *Unmasking the New Age*, a book many readers may find a more useful introduction to the whole area than is implied by the aggressiveness of the title. It is worth reading alongside the helpful collection *The New Age: An Anthology of Essential Writings*, ed. William Bloom.

84. Quoted in Groothuis, *Unmasking*, p. 26. Our discussion here is directed at the mainstream of New Age thought, which tends to be monistic or pantheistic. There are exceptions, however.

85. Shirley MacLaine, *Dancing in the Light*, p. 358.

86. Shirley MacLaine, *It's All In the Playing*, p. 173.

87. Quoted in Russell Chandler, *Understanding the New Age*, p. 131.

88. Mark Satin, *New Age Politics*, p. 112 (emphasis his), quoted in Elliot Miller, *A Crash Course on the New Age Movement*, p. 30. Miller's book is an excellent survey.

89. Quoted in Miller, *Crash Course*, pp. 171, 239. Don Carson, in *The Gagging of God*, writes: 'Almost all of this multiplying thought is irremediably selfish. The aim of the exercise is self-fulfilment, self-actualization, serenity, productivity, power. God, if he/she/it exists, exists for me' (p. 331).

90. Quoted in Groothuis, *Unmasking*, p. 21.

91. Marilyn Ferguson, *The Aquarian Conspiracy*, p. 381.

92. Fritjof Capra, *The Turning Point*, p. 371.

93. MacLaine, *Dancing*, p. 357.

94. Quoted in an excellent survey in Guinness, *Dust*, ch. 6, and also p. 266.

95. Quoted in Michael Cole, *What is the New Age?*, p. 86.

96. The Christian, believing in a Creator God separate from his world, can hold together both insights – that creation is divinely created, suffused with the glory of God and therefore utterly valuable, yet also fallen and marked by a trend tending to destructiveness.

97. It is from Kali's devotees that we get the English word 'thug'. For centuries, the Thugs killed many of their fellow Indians in sacrifice to Kali.

98. Quoted in Groothuis, *Unmasking*, p. 154.

99. R.C. Zaehner, *Our Savage God*, pp. 69–72.

100. Quoted in Guinness, *Dust*, p. 192.

101. Quoted in Douglas Groothuis, *Confronting the New Age*, p. 24.

102. Quoted in Chandler, *Understanding*, p. 28.

103. See, for example, Barbara Marx Hubbard's essay 'The Evolutionary Journey' that William Bloom chose as the opening piece for his *New Age* anthology.

104. Miller, *Crash Course*, p. 65.

105. Quoted in Miller, *Crash Course*, p. 23. See also the writings of Ken Wilber.

106. Michael Ruse and Edward O. Wilson, 'The Evolution of Ethics', *New Scientist*, Oct. 1985, pp. 50–52. I owe this and the following reference to James Sire.

107. Michael Ruse, *The Darwinian Paradigm*, p. 268.

108. Michael Ruse, in Singer, *Companion*, p. 504.

109. But when Darwinian theory itself is under threat, writers of this kind can turn as Darwinian, and indeed as ethically totalitarian, as one could wish. Dawkins' American ally Daniel Dennett, in *Darwin's Dangerous Idea*, p. 515, draws a parallel between certain religious beliefs and dangerous animals, concluding, 'Safety demands that religions be put in cages, too – when absolutely necessary.' (His immediate examples are ideas from Catholicism, Mormonism and Islam.) But you can't put ideas in cages, of course; you can only put their adherents in gulags, like Stalin did. It's interesting to see where Dennett's avowed hatred of fundamentalism points him. The *Independent* cited another of Dawkins' supporters, this time in Britain, who has suggested it be made a criminal offence to teach children that the Bible is literally true (17 Oct. 1998).

110. Steven Rose, *Life Lines*, p. 214.

111. Hitler, *Mein Kampf*, pp. 259–60, 262.

112. Quoted in Wayne Morrison, *Jurisprudence: From the Greeks to Postmodernity*, p. 302. Morrison notes that the SS training manual stated that 'In so-called civilised nations, a false attitude of brotherly love, which the Church has been especially assiduous in fostering among the broad masses, operates in direct opposition to the selective process' (p. 304).

113. Hitler, *Mein Kampf*, pp. 348, 621.

114. Quoted by Jeffrey P. Schloss in an excellent survey of the altruism issue titled 'Evolutionary Accounts of Altruism and the Problem of Goodness by Design', in *Mere Creation*, ed. William Dembski, p. 238. One reason why this area is receiving considerable scientific attention at present is that, if it existed, genuinely altruistic

behaviours that decreased the agent's reproductive fitness would be highly problematic for evolutionary theory, at least in its atheistic forms. Darwin himself said that any characteristic which was 'formed for the exclusive good of another, would annihilate my theory, for such could not have been produced through natural selection' (quoted by Schloss, p. 238). Ruse likewise writes that, if there were any completely disinterested moral acts, they would be a 'clear refutation of the evolutionist's case'. Therefore, he logically concludes, although some people pay lip-service to such notions, nobody actually lives by them (quoted by Schloss, p. 251). (Considering what counter-argument might be set against this, one is reminded of John Stott's remark that the key challenge facing the contemporary church is to demonstrate a love so supernatural (and transcending the barriers of kinship to such a degree) that the world will be compelled to admit its divine origin.) Is Ruse right or wrong?

115. 'Much of the most recent work in evolutionary psychology and human moral behaviour attempts to address this issue' of how to explain acts of radical, unrewarded sacrifice for those who are not kin, says Schloss. 'Human behaviour regularly exhibits non compensatory sacrifice for nonkin'; for example, adoption, heroic efforts to help others across kinship barriers (for example protectors of Jews during the holocaust time), or blood or organ donation for strangers. 'Explaining such phenomena … is widely regarded as the last roadblock to the doctrinal completeness of evolutionary theory' (Schloss, 'Evolutionary Accounts', pp. 242–43).

116. Schloss, 'Evolutionary Accounts', p. 245.

117. Dennett, *Darwin*, p. 251.

118. Quoted in Schloss, 'Evolutionary Accounts', pp. 248–49.

119. Quoted in Schloss, 'Evolutionary Accounts', p. 250.

120. In Singer, *Companion*, pp. 507–08. Ruse is worth reading for the clearheaded logic with which he follows an argument through. He has an essay titled 'Is Rape Wrong on Andromeda?' (in *Extraterrestrials*, ed. E. Regis, Jr.), in which he builds on the position about morality expressed here by conceding that there is no reason why rape should automatically be 'wrong' for non-human organisms or extraterrestrials. (And after all, if the survival of the race is a supreme moral value, as seems to be the case with some sociobiologists, it does propagate the species. Cf. Chamberlain, pp. 154–60.)

121. *Portable Nietzsche*, pp. 570, 573.
122. Quoted in Sider, *Completely Pro-Life*, p. 42.
123. Some feminist ethicists such as Nell Noddings have adopted this as an intellectual position, explicitly denying the notion of universal caring: 'I am not obliged to care for starving children in Africa, because there is no way for this caring to be completed in the other unless I abandon the caring to which I am obligated.' (*Caring: A Feminine Approach to Ethics and Moral Education*, p. 86.) Noddings is addressing a real issue (that there are too many calls upon us for all of them to be addressed), but her either/or approach seems to leave the door wide open to collective selfishness – and it doesn't give much motivational basis for doing anything unselfish about the economic policies that cause these children to be starving.
124. We should note one final twist here. For many people, the family is being replaced in significant ways by variable combinations of 'friends' (hence the significance of *Friends* and other similar TV series). And we may well submit our ethics to this peer-group, in the way we might to a family: what my peer-group defines as good/bad, helpful/unhelpful, is what is right/wrong for me. But peer-groups are unstable and transient. We tend to choose them by how they meet our personal needs and desires; and if they no longer do this, they cease to matter for us. Which means that they tend only to offer very limited challenges to ethical selfishness?
125. As reported in *Independent on Sunday*, 6 Apr. 1997.
126. See, for example, the discussions in *Journal of Homosexuality* 20, nos 1/2 (1990).
127. Cited by Professor Anthony Clare in the 8 March 1986 *Radio Times*. Similar figures are reported across the Atlantic. The degradation and humiliation concealed in these statistics are hard to contemplate.
128. Cited by Robert Fryling in *Student Leadership*, Winter 1989, p. 8.
129. Estimates of the incidence of sexual child abuse in Britain indicate a rate as high as one in 50. About a third of victims are under ten years old. (Child Sexual Abuse Team at Great Ormond Street Hospital in London; *Times*, 25 Sept. 1985).
130. *Independent on Sunday*, 11 Mar. 1999. Dalrymple adds, 'There is no doubt that the extreme fluidity of personal relationships nowadays favours such treatment.'
131. Melanie Phillips, *All Must Have Prizes*, p. xxii.

132. It's worth looking carefully whenever we hear that phrase; it's usually the sign of a liberal-humanist not wanting to face the ugly results of something they've been advocating.

133. Stern, *Nietzsche*, p. 97.

134. Patterson and Kim, *The Day America*, p. 31. Another aspect of the problem is guilt: a sense of guilt can be a profound psychological burden, yet when our moral frameworks have disintegrated there is no way of facing the issue.

135. Keyes, *Identity*, p. 17.

136. Mandela's anthem was *Nkosi Sikelele Africa* ('Lord God, bless Africa'); Gandhi was a Hindu basing on Tolstoy's and the Quakers' Christian-pacifist ethic (Mangalwadi argues this point with some force, citing the critique by Hindu writers that Gandhi's pacifism was 'anti-Hindu' since 'the Vedas, Puranas, Ramayana and Mahabharata are written largely in the context of wars' [pp. 278–79]); and King, of course, was a Baptist pastor (Vishal Mangalwadi, *India: the Grand Experiment*, p. 36).

137. Keyes, *Identity*, pp. 17–20. The Patterson/Kim survey showed that 70% of Americans felt their country had 'no living heroes today'; about the same number felt that American children had no meaningful role-models (*The Day America*, p. 207).

138. In Singer, *Ethics*, pp. 345–61. Wolf's essay, it should be noted, is aimed as much at the legalistic inadequacies of utilitarian and Kantian ethics as at the Catholic notion of sainthood.

139. From Canada, Don Posterski warns that a relativist climate can create a generation of people trained not to believe anything strongly, incapable of anything but passivity: 'Relativism dooms rationality – it generates a reticent, tentative youth subculture. It takes away permission to hold convictions with passion; the antidote to passion is relativism.'

140. Wayne Morrison's massively thorough and fascinating *Jurisprudence* suggests that the history of legal theory can be viewed as a series of attempts to find alternatives to God as a foundation for a legal system that can command respect. (Morrison himself is clearly an atheist, p. 17.) In the medieval 'natural law' system, law had authority because it was directly linked to the will of God. But 'in the work of Thomas Hobbes ... who laid out a foundation upon which Austin was to build the modern approach of legal positivism' ('the dominant tradition in the jurisprudence of modernity', p. 4), 'the core of intellectual questioning turns its

back upon any other-worldly transcendental being – God – as the ultimate author of the pure or just ideal of law. Instead concern is transferred to the authority of the state' (p. 6). Since then, the history of legal theory can be seen (p. 9) as the 'search for some master-discipline ... for a replacement for the transcendental figure modernity dispatched when it turned religion from a relationship with "God" into a mere social and cultural practice. Modernity has thrown up many candidates', and indeed for many observers 'law has lost its identity, it has surrendered to new Gods: it is seen as a servant of economics, of policy, of utility, while we demand that it should be a moral phenomenon' (pp. 13–14). Yale law professor Arthur Leff concluded that 'The so-called death of God turns out not just to have been *His* funeral; it also seems to have effected the total elimination of any coherent, or even more-than-momentarily convincing, ethical or legal system dependent upon finally authoritative, extrasystematic premises' (quoted in Carson, *Gagging*, p. 383).

141. Quoted in Francis Schaeffer, *How Should We Then Live?*, p. 139.

142. Morrison, *Jurisprudence*, p. 314.

143. Morrison, *Jurisprudence*, p. 313. Morrison's whole treatment in pp. 312–19 is highly thought-provoking.

144. The positivist approach had in fact been particularly influential in Nazi Germany. After the war, leading German jurist Radbruch argued that it had left the German legal system defenceless against the Nazis. His own earlier writings had appeared to instruct judges that they could not resist commands of the legal order providing the commanding authority had the valid power to execute its orders. Postwar, he felt the legal system needed some kind of underpinning from a doctrine of natural or even divine right (Morrison, *Jurisprudence*, pp. 313, 327–8).

145. There can be major economic implications too, of course. Patterson and Kim even suggest that the 'number one cause of our business decline is low ethics by executives'(p.8), summarizing the findings of their surveys in these terms: 'Many American managers show little loyalty to their company, to their workers, or to the public that buys their products... "You want loyalty? Hire a cocker spaniel!"', to which the workforce responds ('They lie to us every single day') with 'absenteeism, petty theft, indifference and a generally poor performance on the job' (pp.8,147–48).

146. Patterson and Kim, *The Day America*, pp. 25, 26, 65.
147. In *Reclaiming the Great Tradition*, ed. James S. Cutsinger, pp. 18–19. Mangalwadi, writing from India, voices the same concern as Kreeft's final sentence: 'A denial of moral absolutes does not lead to tolerance of pluralism. Rather it produces social chaos, and is inevitably replaced by political absolutism' (p. 207).
148. Dostoevski, *The Possessed*, p. 243.
149. Patterson and Kim, *The Day America*, p. 123.
150. Cf. *George Steiner: A Reader*, e.g., pp. 211, 246.
151. *Times,* 17 Dec. 1986.
152. *Independent on Sunday* critic Quentin Curtis recently described Brian de Palma's films: 'A woman is murdered with a razor in a lift, her blood seeping into the corridor (*Dressed to Kill*); a man is killed with a chainsaw (*Scarface*); a woman is skewered with an electric drill (*Body Double*). De Palma apologists point to the style, indeed stylishness, of the execution (if that's the right word).'

truth after God

'there are no facts'

> 'What about these conventions of language? Are they really the products of knowledge, of the sense of truth? Do the designations and the things coincide? Is language the adequate expression of all realities? Only through forgetfulness can man ever achieve the illusion of possessing a "truth" in the sense just designated ... What then is truth? ... Truths are illusions about which one has forgotten that this is what they are.'
>
> –Nietzsche[1]

Does it matter whether there is a God or not? We turn now to the fourth of the areas we set ourselves to consider in response to this question. This is the most complex one, and again some readers may prefer to move ahead to Chapter 5, on love, relationships and intimacy. Yet this chapter's topic could be the most far-reaching of all for us. *If there is no God, can we really know the* truth *about anything at all?*

'There are no eternal facts, just as there are no absolute truths.' Thus spoke the nineteenth-century prophet of the death of God, Nietzsche. Kafka, one of 'modernity''s great novelists, told a parable expressing powerfully the 'modern' sense of truth's inaccessibility. In it, a peasant from the countryside comes and asks for entry to 'the law'. He is told to wait by the door.

> There he sits for days and years. He makes many attempts to be allowed in and wearies the door-keeper with his entreaties ... The man, who has equipped himself well for his journey, gives everything he has, no matter how valuable, to bribe the door-keeper. The latter indeed accepts everything, but, as he does so, he says: 'I accept this only so that you may not think you have neglected anything.'

Nothing can be done to further his quest. The long years pass by.

> Finally his sight grows weak ... He does not live much longer. Before his death everything he has experienced during this time converges in his mind into one question ... 'Everyone strives for the law ... How is it that in all these years nobody except myself has asked for admittance?' The doorkeeper realizes the man has reached the end of his life and, to penetrate his imperfect hearing, he roars at him: 'Nobody else could gain admittance here, this entrance was meant only for you. I shall now go and close it.'[2]

Thus Kafka: truth is tantalizingly close, but in the end inaccessible. And as modernity continued it became fairly fashionable to agree on the absence of absolute truths; for many liberals that absence itself is almost an absolute. But very few have taken themselves seriously in advocating such a position; scratch a mid-twentieth-century liberal and all kinds of self-evident absolutes would emerge just beneath the surface. (Indeed, when in *The Genealogy of Morals* Nietzsche sets himself against the 'absolute value of truth', it is the liberals who are his target, since they are working with a concept of truth that only makes sense if there is a God.)

But that was the generation now aging, the generation we now call the 'modernists'. They didn't quite believe in their own relativism. Things are changing. Now it is the postmodernists who have succeeded to the ideological supremacy; and they do. No God; no eternal truths and no way even of saying what is objectively true; few of us have yet grasped how deep run the implications of postmodernism. But in the next years, perhaps, we will learn what it really means never to know, or speak, absolute truth.

In this chapter, then, we'll seek to understand first how this situation arose, and look at its link with the 'loss of God'; then, we'll examine its massive and widespread implications for our contemporary lives.

Nothing more than words

If there is no God, can we know the truth about anything at all?

This basic question was raised years ago by Charles Darwin, the father of evolutionary theory. 'The horrid doubt always arises whether the convictions of man's mind, which has developed from the mind of the lower animals, are of any value or at all trustworthy. Would anyone trust the convictions of a monkey's mind?'[3] If all our thoughts are in the end just physical, chemical events inside our brains; if there is no revelation from outside; why should we consider that they bear any relation to objective truths about reality?

The issue is central for Nietzsche, as Ian Markham notes in *Truth and the Reality of God*.[4] Nietzsche too focused on the peculiar way that our 'reason' apparently arose from random evolution: 'If everything evolved, then human minds and logic must have evolved too.' But if 'rationality' emerged (or is emerging) from a purely random process, then why should its productions match up with 'truth'? Indeed our 'rational' statements about the world assume a whole range of things: that it is stable and coherent, that it is ultimately intelligible, that our brains can understand it correctly. But if, as Nietzsche says, there is no God, then the world's apparent coherence is fortuitous; likewise, if there is no ultimate cause for its intelligibility, then 'it would be just good fortune that we are able to explain anything at all'. But then the 'essential condition for truth is undermined'; for if the universe's intelligibility is just a lucky accident, how likely is it that it really is intelligible? And what then becomes of our attempts to explain it, or our hope that true explanations are possible? If God existed, it would not be a lucky accident that the world made sense: 'In a universe that God intends, then understanding and rationality are intended.' But in the God-less universe that Nietzsche believed in, 'understanding and rationality become accidents which might or might not be justified'; and in consequence 'argument, logic, truth itself have all become absurd'. (Markham cites Nietzsche's remark that this loss of truth extends to science: 'Physics too is only an interpretation and arrangement of the world (according to our own requirements, if I may say so!)'.)

We find the same question right back in Descartes, three centuries ago. As soon as Descartes had (he thought) proved his own existence from the existence of his thoughts, he hastened immediately to demonstrate the existence of a Creator God. This, thought Descartes, would mean that our created reason was a tool worth using. And so it might be – at least if it is operating in tandem with the divine reason. To the Christian, all knowledge is, in the long run, revelation; and it is almighty God, not us, who ensures we are able to know what we need to know.

But now that God is dead, what happens to our faith in reason?

It's a vital question. But a second problem follows it. In recent decades, the philosophical avant-garde have become deeply sceptical whether also the words we use can have any reliability as tools for expressing truth about reality.

To begin with, it was only religion that seemed under threat. Philosophers questioned whether language that arises within, and describes, the universe of our senses could be used to speak of anything beyond it, such as God. Some, such as Wittgenstein, implied that therefore the appropriate expression for God was the silence of ineffable mysticism. Others, such as A.J. Ayer, announced simply that any metaphysical or theological principles which could not be verified by the senses were meaningless nonsense (apart, of course, from this principle itself).

But more recently the high-profile emergence of the deconstructionists has taken matters a huge step further. Now it is questioned whether our language can speak of, or 'mirror', truth and reality at all; or whether it is not a self-contained system, forever ambiguous, forever undermining and contradicting its own meanings. Language, what we say to each other, is a 'self-referential' game. Words have no 'given' meanings rooted in external reality – they relate only to other words, their meanings 'slip' continually. Language does not 'converge' with reality; it is simply incapable of conveying unambiguous truths about the external world. Roland Barthes set out the consequences of this unflinchingly: it is the end, he insisted, of reason, of science and of law. And, we might add, of history, philosophy, sociology, politics and ethics, considered as expressions of objective truth about how the world was or is.

Our immediate reaction to such dramatic claims may be disbelief. Surely this is just the latest fashion?

Possibly. The fashions of the academic industry deserve a good deal more irreverent scepticism than they receive. In recent decades, we've seen styles of thought rise and fall like chart hits or skirt lengths: structuralism usurps the catwalk from existentialism, and is in turn displaced by post-structuralism, deconstructionism, postmodernism. To some degree the reasons are economic. Younger intellectuals need to make their names; publishers are pressed for new ranges of radical perspectives to publish. So, once a new thought-fashion attains a certain critical mass of media attention, its further development is guaranteed as herds of aspiring academics seize their chance to express, in their own area of speciality, the new outlook. But this reduction of knowledge to the exploitation of the latest fashion adds to our contemporary sense of the inaccessibility of truth: we know what is modish today, but we know too that some totally different way of thinking may have mastered the catwalk in fifteen years' time. The hemlines will have shifted, the thought-fashions will be new ones.[5]

Deconstructionism might appear one of the most bizarre thought-styles to snatch a place in the sun – the equivalent, perhaps, of hair dyed green. But in fact it represents a starkly logical development of the last century of western thought. Its current cultural dominance, particularly in the intellectual and media scene of North America and France, cannot be overstated. (Even as I write, there comes to hand a careful discussion of the Canadian academic scene that assumes the future ethos cannot be other than 'postmodern, deconstructionist'.) It is very hard to see the pendulum swinging back as if deconstructionism hadn't happened. So what is this movement whose assumptions of the inaccessibility of truth have become so dominant in the contemporary scene?[6]

Deconstructionism, or post-structuralism, grew out of the structuralist movement. Structuralism was described by David Lodge as the first intellectual movement to be born, flourish and die without anybody noticing; and indeed its esoteric French sages do seem a little like the mystical Eastern gurus who entranced the '60s hippies and then vanished. Nevertheless, it offered insights of considerable importance. One of its key hopes was to see how, underneath the various phenomena of human culture, there could be identified the 'deep structures' within the human mind. This approach became highly influential, for instance in the study of literature and popular culture. (Roland Barthes' brilliant *Mythologies* was a good example of what could be done with the latter.) Many practitioners of structuralism could be seen as attempting, in the footsteps of Levi-Strauss and Saussure, to put the 'humanities' onto a scientific basis.

But what Barthes and others ('post-structuralism') came to realize was that the thing could not be done.[7] The processes of interpretation they were employing could be made to yield not just one, objective, meaning, but any number of alternative or even contradictory understandings. They could see – and indeed desired – no place to stand outside the game of language, from which to 'fix' this 'play' of meanings and verbal signifiers. And what began as a change in the understanding of written literature soon generalized to a militant scepticism about the meaning of verbal communication as a whole.

Older approaches to literature had assumed that the meanings of what was written must largely be determined by the intention of the original writer. Yet there was always a problem: strictly speaking, we cannot know what that original writer intended except through the very words we are trying to understand. By the 1950s this insight had become part of orthodoxy, and over-emphasis on the author's intended meaning was being rejected as the 'intentional fallacy'.[8] But then another issue arose: if the meaning of a set of words is not determined by the author's inten-tion, then perhaps any reader can make what she chooses of it. Deconstructionists like Barthes took this idea to its logical con-clusion. Interpretation becomes less a search to understand some original idea or 'truth' underlying the words; it is more a per-sonal, even hedonistic, game,[9] in which the reader, as much as the original writer, reinvents or re-creates their own meaning. Words carry no absolute, 'given', external meaning,[10] no unalterable 'message' about the world from writer to reader, they simply 'are' in themselves.

Or let's put it another way. One of the valuable insights deriv-ing from these thinkers is a more sophisticated understanding of the role of the reader (or hearer) of a communication. It is obvious that different readers can interpret a message in many different ways. In other words, the meaning of the text in itself is inaccessible; we have only what results from the text's interac-tion with the expectations and 'pre-understandings' of one or another reader. No text ever has a 'single valid interpretation'. Thus the word, the message, is inevitably cut adrift from any-thing it might have signified; it is subjected to a free play of inter-pretation, in which we cannot speak of right (that is, truthful) or wrong understandings – only of more or less interesting ones.

One may respond that this is not how communication works in everyday life. We all know, more or less, how to interpret someone who cries out, 'Help, my daughter is drowning in the lake.' But, the deconstructionist might reply, the greater the quantity of 'text', the greater the degree of 'slippage', of indeter-minable meaning. So, when we come to the 'big questions' of history, philosophy, ethics, the degree of 'slippage' is such that the 'texts' of our world cannot be read as saying anything specific, definable and coherent about anything. About the big questions of the world, we can never learn, nor speak, what is 'true'. None of us can 'catch truth by the tail'; there are only words, gyrating in their own self-contained universe.

Words, then, are not mirrors through which we perceive eternal, coherent 'truths' about a 'present' reality that preceded the words and is reliably expressed through them. They have no fixed meanings; they 'slip' around, they can indeed be 'pushed' around if we have the power. Power, not some eternally existent truth, determines what we come to understand as meaning. And on a broader scale, our interpretations and belief-systems are likewise not mirrors of what is 'really there' beyond our language; they too are verbal constructions, which means that they are shaped for us by whatever are the most powerful forces in society.[11] And, since all of them are 'man-made' rather than 'realistic', they will all equally be revealed as incoherent as the words begin to 'slip'. In fact, 'deconstruction' takes its name from the aim of these writers to 'deconstruct' and reveal the self-contradictory falsity of the supposed truths and belief-systems which each of us constructs within the 'prison-house' of our own language. We distort and contradict ourselves all the time, because our words will not stay still, and their tendency to 'slippage' negates any possibility of their expressing any coherent picture of truth-about-reality. 'Truth' of any objective kind remains inaccessible; 'to write' is (says Barthes) an intransitive verb, because there is nothing external to language that can truly be written about. Foucault insists on the folly of the 'will to know', as if what is 'out there' could somehow be known and expressed. What he is writing, he says in *The Archaeology of Knowledge*, 'does not set out to be a recollection of the original or a memory of the truth'.

The Christian will respond that it is indeed only because there is a God that we can pass beyond our 'prison-house' to know (or communicate) anything; that all knowledge, of whatever topic, is ultimately revelational, given to our individual minds through God; and that it is because God the Holy Spirit is almighty that he can overcome (or orchestrate) the inadequacies of our minds and our words to reveal truth when he so chooses.[12] Because God is 'the Word', and because language is something he created for a purpose, communication is possible. Genesis begins, 'And God said, Let there be light, and there was light'; language matches reality.[13]

Thought and speech are God's gifts to creatures made in his image, wrote the evangelical mystic A.W. Tozer:

> These are intimately associated with him and impossible apart from him. It is highly significant that the first word was the Word: "And the Word was with God, and the Word was God". We may speak because God spoke. In him word and idea are indivisible.[14]

Because there is a God, certain things are either true or false; and we can (at least sometimes) know which are which.[15] But all this is nonsense if God is dead.

> To the Christian, deconstructionism is intriguing from another angle. As we have noted elsewhere, thinkers like C.S. Lewis (and, from a different perspective, the Dutch philosopher Dooyeweerd) have argued that the history of human culture can be seen as an attempt to 'fill in' the space left by the loss of God, by 'deifying' or making idols of particular aspects of the world. But the problem with turning something into an idol is that nothing but God is big enough to take God's place; by turning something into an idol, you risk distorting and destroying it.
>
> With structuralism, we may say that the thing idolized was language: much of human culture – fashion, car design, wrestling – was understood through the model of language, of *langue* and *parole*. Isn't it interesting, then, that structuralism's exaltation of language led directly into a movement that denied the ability of language to function at all for communicating real information?

And that is exactly the starting-point for deconstructionists such as Barthes and Derrida. Quite overtly, they take their cue for the death of language as communication of reality from the death of God. So Derrida, in *Of Grammatology*, draws heavily and overtly on Nietzsche. When Derrida denies that a word can be a 'sign' pointing unambiguously to an external reality, what he is really refusing is the notion of 'a sign signifying a signifier itself signifying an eternal verity, eternally thought and spoken in the proximity of a present logos' ('logos' being the Greek for 'the Word' from John's Gospel). In the 'epoch of Christian creationism', he says, reading and writing were 'preceded by a truth, or a meaning already constituted by or within the element of the logos'. And it was because, or if, God's truths, God's 'eternal verities', were there first that our words could function as trustworthy signs: 'The sign and divinity have the same place and time of birth. The age of the sign is essentially theological.'[16] But now we no longer believe in a God who is that 'Logos', that 'eternal Word'. Language and reality are not, as we had believed, two created systems that match each other. So the death of God is fundamental to the divorce of language from truth. Barthes was equally plain:

> We now know that a text is not a line of words releasing a single "theological" meaning (the "message" of an Author-God), but a multi-dimensional space in which a variety of writings ... blend and clash ... Once the Author is removed, the claim to decipher a text becomes quite futile.

His choice of expression is clear about both cause and effect: the cause is the lack of an Author-God, paralleling the real God; the result is the reduction of the text to a variety of meanings in insoluble conflict. And this is truly far-reaching:

> Literature (it would be better from now on to say writing), by refusing to assign a "secret", an ultimate meaning, to the text (and to the world as text), liberates what may be called an anti-theological activity, an activity that is truly revolutionary, since to refuse to fix meaning is, in the end, to refuse God and his hypostases – reason, science, law.[17]

From the other side of the Atlantic, Richard Rorty makes a similar point. 'The suggestion that truth, as well as the world, is out there is a legacy of an age in which the world was seen as the creation of a being who had a language of his own.'[18] But 'The pragmatist ... wants us to give up the notion that God, or evolution, or some other underwriter of our present world-picture, has programmed us as machines for accurate verbal picturing.'[19]

Renowned culture-critic George Steiner summarizes the deconstructionists' position: 'God the Father of meaning, in His authorial guise, is gone from the game; there is no longer any privileged judge, interpreter or explicator who can determine or communicate the truth, the true intent of the matter.' We have broken with the 'Logos-order as Western thought and feeling had known it since, at the least, the tautology spoken from the Burning Bush', where God declared himself 'I am who I am'. 'The issue is, quite simply, that of the meaning of meaning as it is re-insured by the postulate of the existence of God. "In the beginning was the Word." There was no such beginning, says deconstruction; only the play of signs and markers amid the mutations of time.'[20] Jean Baudrillard, radical postmodernism's most flamboyant guru, has argued the same way:

All of Western faith and good faith was engaged in this wager on representation: that a sign could refer to the depth of meaning, that a sign could *exchange* for meaning, and that something could guarantee that exchange – God, of course. But what if God himself can be ... reduced to the signs which attest his existence? Then the whole system becomes weightless ... There is no longer any God to recognise his own, nor any last judgment to separate true from false.

Elsewhere he adds,

This is where we are today, undecideability, the era of floating theories ... All contemporary theories are floating and have no meaning other than to serve as signs for one another. It is pointless to insist on their coherence with some "reality", whatever that might be.[21]

God is dead; interpretation is up for grabs. Make of the world what you can; you will never know if you were right or wrong.[22]

And all this can go a long way further. 'I'm very far beyond issues like whether I'm writing about factual reality any more', Whitley Streiber told an interviewer regarding his book on his supposed childhood experiences with alien beings. At the more serious end of the spectrum, Sokal and Bricmont's book *Intellectual Impostures* documented the tendency of key postmodernist writers (Lacan, Irigaray, Baudrillard and others) to illustrate their culture-criticism with scientific or mathematical material that, carefully examined, bore little relation to reality: Baudrillard's phrase about the 'multiple refractions of hyperspace' being a good example, since hyperspace is a concept established in science fiction but not in science fact. (It was Baudrillard who made a name for himself by his argument that the Gulf War never happened.) A.N. Wilson, in a polemical attack on postmodernism, cited an English archaeologist who 'considers it perfectly "valid" to accept the American Indian myth that their people rose to that continent from a subterranean spirit-world, rather than having crossed the Bering Straits 10,000 years ago. In the "post-modernist" view, one idea is just as acceptable as another'; indeed, adds Wilson, from a 'politically correct' perspective the narrative of the Zuni tribesmen has an attractiveness that the 'western scientific outlook' lacks.

If, then, the deconstructionists are right; if there is no God and nothing to distinguish 'true' from 'false' and 'realistic' from 'unrealistic'; if language no longer brings with it a 'single valid interpretation', so that we have no possibility of any truly accurate 'theories' or understandings of objective fact or reality; if, in short, we must with Barthes 'refuse' God, reason, science, law – what then?

> The best-selling mystery novel *The Name of the Rose* was written by Umberto Eco, an Italian scholar linked with the structuralist movement and its successors. It's an interesting example of how these ideas translate into the terms of mainstream fiction.

Eco's preface begins by quoting the opening of John's Gospel: 'In the beginning was the Word, and the Word was with God, and the Word was God. This was beginning with God, and the duty of every faithful monk would be to repeat every day with chanting humility the one never-changing event whose incontrovertible truth can be asserted.' But, he continues, 'We see now through a glass darkly, and the truth, before it is revealed to all, face to face, we see in fragments (alas, how illegible) in the error of the world.'

And that is the keynote of the action. When the narrator's master, William, exposes the villainous Jorge's plot, he concludes, 'I arrived at Jorge through an apocalyptic pattern that seemed to underlie all the crime, and yet it was accidental ... I behaved stubbornly, pursuing a semblance of order, when I should have known well that there is no order in the universe.' The narrator asks if William is not more or less concluding that God does not exist: 'William looked at me without betraying any feeling in his features, and he said, "How could a learned man go on communicating his learning if he answered yes to your question?" '

Truth is illegible, pattern illusory, order non-existent, and all learning under question in the absence of God. And, in the end, fire consumes the abbey, along with the 'greatest library in Christendom' – in other words, the repository and summation of western learning. Years later, however, the narrator returns to the abbey. He finds scraps of parchment in the rubble, and begins painstakingly to collect 'every relic I could find ... the glimpse of an image's shadow, or the ghost of one or more words ... sometimes a half page had been saved.' He studies them with love, seeking to reconstruct the text from which they came.

At the narrative's poignant conclusion, he realizes that this search for the lost truth is fruitless. 'The more I reread this list the more I am convinced that it is the

> result of chance and contains no message. It is a hard thing for this old monk, on the threshold of death, not to know whether the letter he has written contains some hidden meaning, or more than one, or many, or none at all ...
>
> 'It is cold in the scriptorium, my thumb aches. I leave this manuscript, I do not know for whom; I no longer know what it is about; *stat rosa pristina nomine, nomina nuda tenemus.*'[23]

Truth is impossible

Deconstructionism has come to dominate the intellectual scene only in the last couple of decades. Yet it is not alone. As the 'loss of God' gathered pace, other twentieth-century trends moved us in the same direction. Together they have led us towards a profound 'death of hope' as to whether the truth really is 'out there'; as to whether we can ever really know truth about anything that matters.

At least nine major factors have conspired to dissolve our hope.

(i) We are heirs to a century-long process: the nineteenth-century 'loss of faith' in traditional Christianity, and the subsequent exploration of alternatives. Last century there flourished the great mythic alternatives to Christian faith: utopian Humanism, utopian Freudianism, utopian Fascism, utopian Marxism. It is important to grasp how different is our atmosphere now from that time when so many huge, confident dreams were in the air. We cannot imagine anyone today writing with the blithe assurance of, say, communist J.B.S. Haldane: 'Mammon has been expelled from one sixth of the planet's surface. It was men, not angels, that cast him out.' All that is over. It seems, to quote the sad finale of Hardy's *Collected Poems*, that 'We are getting to the end of dreams'. 'Those who speak do not know; those who know do not speak.' The competition of utopias left us profoundly doubtful that anybody knew the truth.

(ii) At the same time, the two great atheistic faiths of Marxism and Freudianism had a deep and lasting effect in making us aware of the non-intellectual factors that affect our beliefs. Marxism introduced the concept of 'ideology': we are strongly motivated to hold beliefs that will safeguard our economic position. Freudian psychoanalysis reminded us of the many factors from our familial or sexual experience that drive us to 'believe' what we do; what we think are beliefs are often only rationalizations, and concealed beneath them are the real motives for our conduct. Both approaches put a question mark over the value of any deeply-held belief. (Translated into its most knock-down mode, this produces: 'You think you believe in God, but it's only because of your neurotic need for a father-figure'; 'You think you're an atheist, but it's only because of your neurotic need to protect your independence'; 'Freud only "believed" his own theory because he disliked his father and hated his Catholic nanny.') Both Marx and Freud are outmoded now, but they have played a major role in undermining our belief in serious intellectual exploration as a way to truth.

(iii) To this we must add the aftermath of the Second World War. Fascism and Nazism were self-evidently 'big ideas' that thought they were right. The result, among many '50s intellectuals at least, was a deep distaste towards any such confidence. For a while, indeed, certain kinds of academics had an almost neurotic(!) tendency to use the term 'totalitarian' (or 'fascist') for ideas claiming any degree of certainty. Except, of course, for their own; they did not intend the uncertainty to spread to their basic humanistic assumptions. But no one is secure from challenge; they were setting the tone for our own much deeper collapse of certainty.[24]

(iv) The overwhelming influence of our era, therefore, a generation later, is the profound scepticism of 'postmodernism'. Jean-Francois Lyotard, author of *The Postmodern Condition*, singled out this hopelessness as the key feature of our time, when he spoke (in the postmodernists' best-known phrase) of our 'incredulity towards meta-narratives'. We have, he was saying, become deeply sceptical towards any 'big stories' that might 'explain it all'.

He is not talking about religion here. In context, Lyotard is observing the failure of the 'big ideas' of modernity – Marx, Freud, Darwin. In 'Note on the Meaning of "Post-"' he emphasizes particularly the 'disappearance of the Idea that rationality and freedom are progressing ... We can observe and establish a kind of decline in the confidence that, for two centuries at least, the West invested in the principle of a general progress in humanity.'[25] It is the humanist dream that we no longer believe: we have little trust in science, little hope in progress, little faith in the welfare state. We don't believe in any big solutions. The bureaucrats and the detail managers have now inherited the earth; and we don't trust them either, but anyone with big ideas is absolutely beyond the pale, and only the naive listen to them.

(v) Other social forces have combined to make it almost ill-mannered to believe anything too definitely. Modern western society is increasingly pluralistic. Ethnic diversification has made the tolerance of multiple belief-systems more and more important for social stability. (In the coming years we may see the social fabric strained most where two belief-systems collide – for example in Islamic and liberal approaches to animal rights, or the enforcement of homosexual equality, which was a key flashpoint when President Clinton clashed with the east Asian governments.)

Now, it is true that one does not have to lack strong convictions in order to be tolerant (and supportive) of individuals holding very different ones. Nonetheless, pluralism has created a context where it is 'socially useful', and may well be seen as 'progressive' or 'helpful', to be unable to pronounce a verdict on the claims of any of the great belief-systems. Liberalism has been defined as a system in which you can believe whatever you like so long as you don't believe it's true. The social pressures are on us to deny the possibility of truth; the ideal liberal 'pillar of the establishment' (in education, for example) is someone incapable of making up their mind too definitely on fundamental issues.

(vi) There are still other factors in our loss of confidence about knowing and expressing truth. Western culture has always had an anti-rational side, which surfaced in Romanticism, and later in Futurism, Surrealism, Dadaism; thence into pop culture – M.S. Escher posters, the Goons, *Monty Python*; or Douglas Adams' brilliant *Life, the Universe, and Everything*:

> 'And when the trial continued,' he said in a weeping whisper, 'they asked Prak a most unfortunate thing. They asked him,' he paused and shivered, 'to tell the Truth, the Whole Truth and Nothing but the Truth' ...
>
> ... Arthur shone his torch full on Prak's face.
>
> 'We thought,' he said, 'that you were meant to be telling the Truth, the Whole Truth and Nothing but the Truth.'
>
> 'Oh, that,' said Prak. 'Yeah. I was. I finished. There's not nearly as much of it as people imagine ... I can't remember any of it now. I thought of writing some of it down, but first I couldn't find a pencil, and then I thought, why bother?'

Why do we enjoy the surrealist overturning of reason? Partly for its imaginative adventurousness: the creative joy of newness, of seeing things other than as they are. But it has also to do with freedom from what Weber called the 'iron cage'. With the loving providence of God long vanished, what modern rationality has created is an enormous, soulless technological system, turning us into pawns, ciphers, computer numbers. And science: science has given us the Bomb, BSE, genetically-modified food – all kinds of horrors. All this has made us hostile to reason in general. We feel a sense of relaxation in the Zen offer of truth that is no truth: 'What is the sound of one hand clapping?' ('Something like this', Tallulah Bankhead answered the sage, slapping him round the face.)

(vii) Yet even science moves now in regions where the concepts of human reason begin to seem woefully inadequate tools. Quantum physics in particular has encountered situations in which there are things it is impossible to know, observations it is impossible to make. (If you think you understand quantum mechanics, it has been said, it simply shows that you don't.) Again, theoretical developments such as Heisenberg's uncertainty principle (which is primarily concerned with what it is possible for an objective observer to measure) need not necessarily be viewed as pointing to a wider nihilism. New Age pantheists like Capra have claimed these developments as support for their approaches; so have some Christians. Nonetheless, quantum mechanics has filtered into the wider culture primarily as a metaphor for denying the accessibility of truth, or even the existence of objective reality at all.

Tom Stoppard took the idea up in his entertaining play *Hapgood*. Stoppard brilliantly presents a spy comedy involving attempts to tell whether Kerner, a defected Russian scientist, is a double agent. To this, he links the idea of the inaccessibility of truth in the physics that is Kerner's work. Does light come in waves or particles? Experiments can prove either, says Kerner – the observer can choose. And similarly, 'A double agent is like a trick of the light ... You get what you interrogate for.' Blair, the old spy catcher, won't have it, and to the end of the play he's insisting explicitly on the importance of an 'either/or'. 'One likes to know what's what', he says firmly on another occasion. Kerner laughs at him: 'Oh yes! Objective reality. Objective reality is for zoologists. "Ah, yes, definitely a giraffe." ' And later, offering a clear definition of what science is perceived to say about truth: 'Your certainty is also amusing – you think you have seen to the bottom of things, but there is no bottom.'

(viii) But if, in high science, language is proving no longer adequate for truth, we have also created other contexts fairly central to society that break the link between language and truth in deeply personal ways.

Two obvious examples might be the institutions of marriage and the church. For many of us in the west, marriage vows are now accepted as having a strange linguistic status. It is important to commit ourselves verbally 'Till death us do part', for example; yet at many weddings everyone knows that those five words are hedged around, modified almost out of existence, with a host of ifs and buts. It might be different if we believed in real divine providence in the decisions leading to marriage, but we don't. At the heart of our sexuality, therefore, stands a communal moment marked by the fact that our words do not and cannot match what is true. And the deep significance of the event to us – and, too often, its associated pain – surely means that our inability in this case to trust words, to 'mean what we say', will spill over into the way we grow to view language, truth and promising in general.

Alongside this we should set other activities in many parts of the official 'church'; most obviously the repetition of the creed. A profound divorce between language and truth is created by bishops and priests who state, each week, 'I believe in God the Father Almighty, and in Jesus Christ his only Son ... On the third day he rose again from the dead; he ascended into heaven; from thence he will come to judge the quick and the dead' – when they simply don't. The issue is not merely one of intellectual dishonesty. The crucial point is that, since these often-recited creeds are treated in the rest of life as having only a very limited truth, the words are being used to express something markedly different from their face value. Thus many parts of the church establishment institutionalize a use of language which clearly does not (for them) convey truth, but is its own self-referential game; deconstructionism encore.

(ix) A final factor dominating our attitude to the possibility of truth is the triumph of visual media over the written word.

Television and related media are notoriously poor at handling complex idea-structures. As a result, the whole social position of such structures is threatened in a culture that these media dominate. Image tends to displace verbal content, observes Neil Postman in his important study *Amusing Ourselves to Death*; and if the link between language and truth has grown tenuous, that between image and truth is weaker still. Words do not guarantee their truth content, says Postman, but they do at least tend to 'assemble a context in which the question, Is this true or false? is relevant'.[26] The visual image, in contrast, raises no such question: 'There is no beginning, middle, or end in a world of photographs ... The world is atomized. Here is only a present and it need not be part of any story that can be told', whether true or false.[27] Overtly at least, the image makes no truth-statements; it is disconnected; it has the status of a dream, a vision, a fantasy. To an increasing degree, therefore, the most compelling impressions around us are precisely not to do with reality, or with truth.

Postman observes how in recent elections the short 'soundbite', the telling visual image wrapped up by a brief punch-line, has become far more important than carefully-planned statements of policy.[28] Such trends were evident in British politics from at least the 1980s. Did Thatcher triumph, or was it Saatchi and Saatchi? In Labour's renaissance, the 'new image' (Brahms in the background, red rose replacing red flag) preceded the policy review, both in time and importance. Even if we had anything to say that was true, it is hard to say it audibly in such a situation; even when there is genuine substance, and the language seeks to convey something that is true-to-reality, the media context makes it very hard to recognize. What is sincere or truthful comes across instead merely as a good image of truthfulness. (Was this a problem faced by Tony Blair in the last British election? That a man who, it seems, genuinely was sincere found it impossible not to come across merely as someone good at pretending to be sincere?)

In the media context, then, even verbal language ceases to be 'about truth'. In a consumerist society where language is the only 'reality' we can grasp and image is all-important, the advertisers will tend to dominate;[29] but when we watch advertisements, we don't really expect them to be 'about truth', or even about their products' qualities. Propaganda tends to replace persuasion, because persuasion is about asserting that certain things are objectively true.

Likewise we permit the *Sunday Sport* to be sold in the same newspaper racks as 'quality papers', not so much out of pleasure at such mind-bogglingly wonderful headlines as 'Space Aliens Turned My Son Into An Olive', but rather because we doubt if any of the newspapers really 'tell the truth'. That's not what the media are for.

Jesus, it will be recalled, was the Word;[30] not, firstly, the Image. Martin Buber told of a rabbi so dumbfounded by the implications of the huge words, 'And God said', that he never got beyond the opening verses of Genesis where they occur.[31] At the heart of Christian faith was the belief that God speaks, to each individual, and that therefore reality can be expressed, and known. But there is no revelation now. Now, so many pressures conspire to make truth seem impossible: the bedlam of competing ideologies, the doubts about the reliability of our reason, the misuse of science, the misuse of language, the pressures from multiculturalism, and the flood of images that simply marginalize any question of truth. We have abandoned the notion of a loving God as Revealer,[32] but it grows harder to believe we will find truth otherwise; if it must be done DIY, carrying it through against the social pressures may be a task for the master-spirits only. The rest of us will live as victims of an indistinguishable swirl of part-truths, lies and videotape. Somehow we thought that anyway.

And so we return to Barthes: the farewell to God was a farewell in general to expression of truth in language, and thus to reason, to science, to law.

We still have to confront the issue of what it will mean to live in a world where we will never know what is true.

'Westerners are usually so shallow', complained one of a group of teachers to whom I lectured at Moscow Linguistic University. And what else, given the thought-world we live in, should one expect? What, and whence, is depth?

Style triumphant

So much for the philosophical background story. Now for the life-implications.

We don't normally think of *The X-Files* as optimistic. Yet the slogan, 'The truth is out there', is a sign of refusal of despair. It offers the hope that, against all the odds, two people might come to know reality. But that, we may feel, is where the fantasy-element comes in. We find it all too easy to believe in the other side of the coin – Mulder's enemies, all the systems and people out to obfuscate things. According to postmodernism, the death of God means we cannot know the truth; the very 'will to know' is folly. And among all the social pressures to the contrary, there is little to give us back a faith that we really can know.

What shall we do then? If we cannot learn the truth, then neither can we speak what is true. But we will still go on speaking, and writing and selling print – for economic reasons if for no other. So, among the hallmarks of a culture marked by post-God despair about truth, we will tend to find: a dominance of style in the absence of content or substance; a focus on the media of communication, rather than on any messages they might have contained; a dominance of image and surface over depth – whatever that might be.

Medium plus message equals Marshall McLuhan, another of the gurus who had 15 minutes on the catwalk in recent decades. McLuhan's famous epigram 'The medium *is* the message' was a perceptive observation that what the newer media primarily communicate is themselves, rather than some external, detachable message about the world. But it extends further: it could have been a motto for a whole culture distrustful of 'message'. Is it not a recurrent feature of the post-war decades that 'medium' has displaced 'message' in one field after another?

Philosophy, for example, has largely given up on discussion of the historic 'big issues' (particularly in the Anglo-Saxon world). Most of the past decades' major movements have poured scorn on the idea of inquiry into the nature of reality or the meaning of existence, becoming dominated by analysis of language. In literature, a dominant force has been various types of formalism. Modern painting has often been concerned to give attention to the medium of the painting itself, rather than any thing represented.[33] '*I have nothing to say and I am saying it and that is poetry*': avant-garde musician John Cage.

Now the postmodernists have taken the trend further, with their overt denial that there is anything coherent to be said.[34] Indeed, some have cultivated a near-impenetrable style (Derrida, Lacan, Foucault and Baudrillard all spring to mind) that seems almost a rejection of comprehensibility. Some of this is the element of showbiz that seems part and parcel of Gallic intellectualism, but it is also a logical development of their atheism.[35] In discussing purpose in Chapter 2, we noted how Robbe-Grillet ruthlessly pursued the implications for plot of Sartre's atheistic disbelief in a patterning of events – and nearly strangled the life out of his own novels. So too here: if truth is inaccessible and reason (as Foucault insists) untrustworthy, then the near-incomprehensibility of the radical postmodernists comes close to expressing these realities,[36] even at the price of their own ability to communicate. (But not, the cynic might add, at the price of their ability to market books.)

But something still remains, and that something is style. It is a mark of this group of thinkers (and Barthes and Foucault in particular) that they have deliberately avoided a consistent, definable position. Yet, observes White, as they have moved through a variety of stances, what has given unity to their work has not been a set of beliefs but rather a certain intellectual style.[37] 'One thing is needful', wrote Nietzsche in *The Gay Science*, ' "giving style" to one's character'.[38] When reason cannot be trusted and knowledge is ambivalent, when there is nothing truthful to say, still there is style.

And as elsewhere, what begins in the intellectual stratosphere finds its parallels in popular culture. Is it coincidence that, after the death of the big ideas of the '60s, we moved (via the backlash of '70s pessimism) into an era where designer style became far more central to culture than at any previous stage in the century?[39] It's been a theme of youth culture for the last two decades, from the New Romantics (whose icon was Boy George, the self-proclaimed 'man without convictions') onwards. Disco replacing message; nothing to say, nothing to believe; but when all else is lost, still there is style? MTV has been incredibly influential in setting the tone of recent youth culture. And here too, said one of its co-founders, 'We're talking about dealing a mood to you. It's the style, not the substance.' 'When you get down to it', said MTV's president, 'the only thing we have is image.'[40]

The Word is dead. But if you have nothing to say now, say it with style. And if indeed we have seats booked on the ecological Titanic, let's at least dress up for dinner.

Living in a world without truth

But the loss of truth impoverishes.

Indeed, taken to its logical end (and in the absence of God it is unclear how we find our way back), the collapse of truth-knowing means the loss of the distinction between reality and illusion. That, in turn, means nothing less than the collapse of sanity. But this would be the end-point; no one suggests we are going that far.[41] Instead, we need to look at specific losses – because we do pay the price for the death of truth in a wide range of important areas.

First, and self-evidently, the loss of confidence in meaningful communication shuts us up in the prison-house of the self. Friendship depends on genuine communication.[42]

Second, loss of faith in truth-speaking soon comes to mean loss of truth-speaking itself. In North American intellectual life, postmodernism increasingly controls the agenda. It may not be entirely coincidental that the Patterson/Kim survey of American attitudes showed that 20% of the citizens of this culture that is increasingly dominated by disbelief in absolute truth reported themselves lying every day, consciously and premeditatedly. (75% have regularly lied to their friend, 73% to their lover, 69% to their spouse, 58% to their best friend.) 'We lie, and we don't even think about it. The people we lie to most are those closest to us', concluded Patterson and Kim. 'Lying has become a cultural trait in America. Lying is embedded in our national character. That has not been understood around the world.'[43] (Anyway, 'One should ask oneself carefully: "Why don't you want to deceive?" ', says Nietzsche during his sustained attack on the 'will to truth'; 'especially if it should appear – and it certainly does appear – that life depends on appearance ... and when life has, as a matter of fact, always shown itself to be on the side of the most unscrupulous ...'[44])

Third, loss of truth leads to captivity in other ways – to subjectivism, and thence to egoism. Truth is whatever you like; thus one reading of quantum mechanics has given the Shirley MacLaines fuel for a faith that they can turn the universe into whatever they want it to be – New Age egoism.[45] The same captivity to egoism grows visible elsewhere in postmodernity, when we note just what it is that the deconstructionists finally make of the arts. As John Carey has observed, very few deconstructionist critics actually serve to lead the reader into a new affection for a book; in general they write largely for their own sake.[46] (There seems an egoism even in the apparent goal of dazzling opacity.) The loss of truth about the world beyond words risks the steady loss of the universe outside the self; experience of the real grows rare and becomes 'epiphany' (James Joyce). Or as the Christian would say: the prison of hell is one in which the self is left with itself alone.[47]

'You will know the truth and the truth will set you free', said Jesus. Again, truth delivers from the captivity of deceivers. Or as St Paul put it, truth ensures that we 'will no longer be infants, tossed back and forth by the waves, and blown here and there by every wind of teaching and by the cunning and craftiness of men'.[48] We cannot simply live without truth. As Chesterton said, when people stop believing in God, it doesn't mean they believe in nothing – it means they believe in anything. Paradoxically tied to postmodern scepticism is the gullibility of a new gnosticism: we feel there must be some spiritual secret, and we'll seek it almost anywhere – in the extraordinary rigmaroles of UFOs in New Age cults, for instance – because we no longer really hope to distinguish what is true. (This is particularly true of the overload of information on the internet.) An alternative twist, in North America at least, is when a significant proportion of the culture starts to welcome our ignorance. We need no 'big ideas', no 'master narratives'; 'dumbing down' is fine, and a simpleton like Forrest Gump is as worthy to shape the nation's destiny as, ummm, a Reagan. Why watch the news?[49] You won't understand, and anyway they're lying; All I Really Need To Know I Learned In Kindergarten. But then the doors seem wide-open for deception.

But there is more. 'We're looking for the truth of ourselves, not other people's truth', artists Gilbert and George told interviewer Wolf Jahn; so even scientific truth 'is only for the moment, isn't it? It wasn't always true that the earth goes round the sun ... Maybe we've got it wrong even now, maybe there's some completely new way of seeing it.'[50] Too bizarre? But Nietzsche argued a century ago that our modern `faith in science' inevitably rests upon a 'metaphysical faith ... that Christian faith, which was also Plato's faith, that God is truth, that truth is divine.'[51] And as we saw, Barthes is very direct about the implications of postmodern atheism in this regard: 'By refusing to assign a "secret", an ultimate meaning, to the text (and to the world as text)', we liberate 'what may be called an anti-theological activity, an activity that is truly revolutionary since to refuse to fix meaning is, in the end, to refuse God and his hypostases – reason, science, law.' Indeed, postmodern writers such as the followers of Feyerabend have expressed scepticism as to whether our scientific beliefs are anything more than that: our own subjective, institutionalized constructions, products of our will to power.[52] Even the respected Thomas Kuhn argues that we 'have to relinquish the notion, explicit or implicit, that changes of paradigm carry scientists and those who learn from them closer and closer to truth'. For Feyerabend, meanwhile, scientists are 'salesmen of ideas and gadgets ... not judges of truth and falsehood.'[53] (Postmodern analyst Adam Phillips likewise says he views psychoanalysis as 'poetry, so I don't have to worry whether it is true or even useful, but only whether it is haunting or moving or intriguing or amusing.'[54] The modernist Freud, father of what he thought of as the science of psychotherapy, would have been amazed at this disinterest in truth; one wonders how Phillips' patients feel.) If it is not moving ever closer to 'truth', what then drives the scientific enterprise? Lyotard's assessment in *The Postmodern Condition* is brutally frank. 'Scientists, technicians and instruments are purchased not to find truth, but to augment power ... The games of scientific language become the games of the rich ... An equation between wealth, efficiency, and truth is thus established.'[55]

The loss of truth from the scientific world might not seem too pressing an issue for many of us. But what happens to us when the same loss of truth-knowing comes to dominate the legal system too? We saw in Chapter 3 how our 'post-God' collapse of ethics poses major problems for law's credibility; but what if we now lose our commitment to truth as well? After the O.J. Simpson murder trial, Simpson's lawyer, Robert Shapiro, was asked by television interviewer Larry King whether the defence was in pursuit of the truth. 'Absolutely not,' Shapiro replied. King then asked Shapiro what he personally thought of Simpson's guilt or innocence. 'It doesn't matter what I think,' Shapiro replied. 'What I believe is something that really is of no importance.'[56] Such words could only be said in a certain climate, where truth is ceasing to be the issue at law. But what if, besides this, the dominant postmodern attitude to texts grows accepted, that there is anyway no 'single valid interpretation' of the text of the law? We recall Lewis' prediction of a time coming when 'rival readings would ... cease to be "right" or "wrong" and simply become more and less brilliant "performances" '.[57] That could be entertaining as literary theory but terrifying as legal practice. Foucault would be right: not truth but power (the power to pay for the star 'performer' as your lawyer) would determine what interpretation of the law the judge and jury find most 'interesting'.[58] Several high-profile trials in America have come close to this already; and the important point is that, if the deconstructionists are right, such a situation merely reflects the reality of what it means to interpret texts, after the death of God.[59] In full postmodernity, the legal system could prove a death trap for those who do not have power.

(But that returns us to another unsettling question raised, for different reasons, in Chapter 3. If, in so many areas of post-God postmodernity, we are finally believing that truth is largely inaccessible, and the only reality in our disagreements is power, then how long is it likely to be before the shooting starts? To quote a British railway-line graffiti: 'Don't Argue; Destroy'.)

Nothing to pass on

But for now, the loss of truth-knowing impinges most seriously on those groups of people whose task it is to pass on an understanding of the world to the next generation. This is part of the reason for the crisis in contemporary teaching, and contemporary parenting.

It's important, and it should be obvious. To question whether we can ever know a coherent body of objective truth, whether we can express to one another a coherent understanding of our world, is also to put a massive question mark over the value of our 'experience' or 'knowledge' or 'wisdom'.[60] What, then, are teaching and parenting *for*? By what right can one carry out these roles, if our authority[61] flows not from the possession (even if partial) of a true understanding of reality, but merely from our possession of power?[62]

Some commentators affirm that the results of this loss of objective truth have become plain in both higher and primary education as postmodernism has grown in influence. First, if truth cannot be known, then obviously there is a limited value in knowledge for its own sake. Increasingly, therefore, the purpose of education is merely to enable the student to get a job (again, not truth but power).[63] A *Guardian* article cited Orlando Figes complaining that Cambridge students 'only want to know that what they are reading will give them answers for their exams'. Richard Hoggart likewise complained about 'vocationalist policies in education that have convinced people that they should only learn what is immediately useful to them'. But that impoverishment becomes reasonable if truth is inaccessible, and knowledge is to be judged primarily by what it means for our empowerment.[64]

The real impact of the loss of objective truth comes in much younger age groups, however. Melanie Phillips' angry and well-researched critique of the marked decline of the British school system, *All Must Have Prizes*, focuses on the 'fundamental uncertainty over adult authority' at the heart of a rapidly-increasing breakdown in primary school discipline.[65] She notes in particular the influence of the pragmatist philosopher Dewey, who rejected the idea that the teacher had objective knowledge to impart because that would be to act as an 'external boss or dictator'.[66] She also identifies as a major factor the flight away from study of any 'objectively real' rules, for example the rules of mathematics: 'Maths teaching in Britain has effectively been deconstructed.'[67]

Phillips continues,

> The collapse of the teaching of literacy and of numeracy is a matter of profound significance for our society. It tells us not merely about educational fashion but about some of our deepest human values ... At the most immediate level, it deprives children of their elementary entitlement to gain some control over their own environment and handicaps them in their initiation into the adult world ... Instead of authority being located "out there" in a body of knowledge handed down through centuries, we have repositioned it "in here" within each child. In doing so, we have deprived those children of the structures through which human beings have traditionally made sense of the world. Instead, children are having to make it up for themselves as they go along. They are being abandoned to disorder, incoherence and flux.[68]

Phillips links these philosophies directly to the deconstructionist disbelief in any truths as objective and external, and sets out the drastic consequences this has had for a whole generation's mastery of the subjects concerned.[69] Enormous responsibility rests on those who train future generations of teachers in approaches based on such a disbelief in truth, she suggests. This is scarcely 'just a game', and it could have huge social consequences.

In parenting, even more than in education, much is involved besides merely passing on a wise and realistic understanding of the world. But surely it is a central component. And the belief that no such understanding can exist – that we cannot say much to our children with certainty – can only lead to a collapse of parenting confidence. This point is highlighted in Lasch's *The Culture of Narcissism*. Lasch criticizes American parenting fashions that emphasize only the subjective need to '"get in touch with your feelings" and to base everyday intercourse on the communication of these feelings to others', leaving no place for objective truths of which the parent may be aware and the child may be ignorant. ('Objective statements should be excluded from this discourse with the child ... because no one can argue rationally about beliefs.') This flight from objectivity, says Lasch, 'confirms ... the parent's helplessness to instruct the child in the ways of the world or to transmit ethical precepts',[70] with at least two major consequences. First in the area of discipline: where there is no clear, objectively-justified framework of boundaries or standards, 'the parent's failure to administer just punishment to the child' actually 'undermines the child's self-esteem rather than strengthening it', because the child comes to realize that nothing he or she does 'really' matters.[71] But equally, if truth cannot be known, there can be no 'true' framework to justify the restraints needed to develop the art of self-discipline in a culture increasingly bad at it.[72]

Lasch observes perceptively that the exception to all this is in sport, where there is a built-in 'resistance to the erosion of standards ... Excellence is relatively uncontroversial as a judgment of performance',[73] because in this area objective 'truth' can obviously be known. Significantly, athletic achievement constitutes a key source of self-worth and self-discipline for many dispossessed youth; and it does so because it offers achievement based on objectively true, accessible standards. Thus the accessibility (or otherwise) of truth impacts directly on the effectiveness of parenting and teaching in cultivating robust self-image.

A final aspect here is our difficulty in knowing what a word like fatherhood 'truly' means anyway. Throughout the last decade this question has been the subtext to a whole series of films; Geraldine Bedell wrote in the *Independent on Sunday* of taking her children to *The Lion King*, for example, and realising it was 'a parable about fatherhood, made for a market terrified that men no longer know how to be dad' – especially 'dads who can heal fractured families by combining toughness and tenderness.' (She went on to instance *Look Who's Talking, Shadowlands, Sleepless in Seattle*, and *Mrs Doubtfire*.) Toughness and tenderness: how to combine them? How to learn tenderness? And – the key issue for us here – when, and to communicate what, does anyone have an objectively-grounded right to be `tough', and how are they to go about it? Here the 'external truths' of the nature of God as Father could offer a redefinition of fatherhood. From one angle, the issue I struggle with as a father can be seen as learning to imitate the one all-loving Father; learning slowly to interweave unstinting love, mercy and justice, and freedom and intervention. (For myself at least, that helps me understand the task I face as a parent.[74]) But the 'loss of God' has left the 'truth' of such models under heavy question. Yet we lack any clear alternatives; and we may wonder who ends up paying the price.

The definition of fatherhood by reference to God is typical of the person-based Christian concept of truth. To Christian faith, truth-principles alone are vital but insufficient; truth divorced from spiritual life becomes destructive, bones devoid of flesh. (A classic example would be how the 'true' principle of human need for a weekly Sabbath-rest turns, outside the context of genuine spiritual life, from being life-restoring to being life-denying.)

As St Paul put it, 'The truth is in Jesus'. Truth is first of all a quality of a Person, rather than an abstraction; because, if Christ is God, is infinite, then what is ultimate in the cosmos is personal rather than abstract. (Truth is a characteristic of the ultimate Christ, rather than Christ being an instance of the absolute of truth.) Jesus' words 'I am the Truth' affirm a personal quality to truth that is far removed from the impersonal rationality of Weber's 'iron cage'.

Therefore, the truth about what kind of authority a teacher, or a father, has, or what the interplay of justice and mercy mean, lies also, firstly, 'in Jesus'. Teaching, at its profoundest, is what Jesus did – so how did Jesus teach? Love is what Jesus did – how did Jesus love? Or lead? Or discipline? How did Jesus handle the Sabbath? The same principle extends to many other areas of 'truth'. How did Jesus treat women?[75] What was Jesus' attitude to the Bible?[75] What were Jesus' priorities in religion?[76]

Or, to put it another way: reality is the world as God sees it. And because God is personal and has spoken to us, we now possess genuine and trustworthy (if imperfectly-grasped) fragments of a total and true 'meta-narrative'. It isn't entirely accessible yet. For the time being, as St Paul says, we 'know in part and we prophesy in part'.[78] But what we've been given, we can depend upon; and if we don't see everything clearly, still we *'see Jesus'*.[79] And we see him pre-eminently and definitively in the Bible; the written Word, opened to us by God's Spirit, is indispensable if we are to know what the living Word was like, how he lived, what he taught. This therefore defines the heart of authentic Christian faith and truth ...

A world gone flat

Our loss of the divine Father as archetype of human fatherhood is an instance of another aspect of our impoverishment. Our crisis of knowing has deprived us of many of our structures of symbolism.

The world no longer *means* for us and our children in the way it did for pre-'death-of-God' humankind. To the biblical-Christian mind, God had created for us a world full of pictures of himself, as we have noted. He is the *'true* bread', the *'living* water'. He is the *'true* vine'. He is *'the* door'.[80] Things 'resonate' in such a world-picture – a lamb is a lamb, yet also a reminder of Christ the Lamb of God; a lion is a lion, yet also a reminder of Christ the Lion of the Tribe of Judah. To the God-centred imagination, mountains have a beauty in themselves, yet in addition 'I lift up my eyes to the hills; where does my help come from? My help comes from the Lord, maker of heaven and earth.'[81] The sea becomes a symbol of God the Father, glorious in majesty, unfathomable in his wisdom ('Your justice is like the great deep'[82]) – boundless in itself, yet also a provocation to worship the even more boundless God. But all of these are lost with the disappearance of the truth-structures that give them meaning.[83]

But that is a minor example of our more general loss of depth. Fredric Jameson speaks of the 'flatness or depthlessness, a new kind of superficiality in the most literal sense – perhaps the supreme formal feature of all the postmodernisms ... Depth is replaced by surface, or by multiple surfaces.'[84] As Seamus Heaney has suggested, our postmodern era is marked by a loss, even a fear, of profundity. With the loss of truth we forfeit profundity; we are deprived of depth.[85]

A more crucial example would be the loss of history. Of course, knowing the truth of history is always difficult – there are variant understandings, and all too easily history is written by the victors. But still we could have believed that, if all that is true in each reading were combined, we could move towards a truly accurate model of what occurred – the truth as seen in God's eye, we may say. Postmodernism denies this hope because, once again, history comes down to us primarily through words – and words continually slip and slide, words have unending interpretations and variations. No event within history contains any more significance than another. 'The true historical sense confirms our existence among countless lost events, without a landmark or a point of reference.'[86]

But here again we are deprived of depth. We will develop, perhaps, our own myth of history, with no real prospect that it matches the reality of the past. Instead, it serves primarily as a consoling story we tell ourselves to satisfy our needs. What results is the loss of the past. History becomes forgotten, we universalize the local and contemporary, and we lose touch with all alternative ways of thinking and feeling.[87] Nothing is passed on: again the word for this is impoverishment.[88]

And that doesn't refer only to a loss of enjoyment in visits to medieval castles. Rather, it means that arguments about whether the holocaust happened, whether the resurrection happened, whether or not communism was a disaster in practice, can never be settled. Those who ignore history, it has been said, are condemned to repeat it. But without God and without truth, what we believe about any such matters we will believe for no real reasons.

Locked into the dreamworlds

In one practical area after another, then, it makes a huge difference whether there is a God who speaks and who makes it possible for us to know truth from falsehood.

Perhaps the truly 'god-less' world is recreated in a product like Resnais' famous film *Last Year in Marienbad*.

What is it about? The film's action is difficult to describe. Certainly we see a man urging a woman that a year before in Marienbad she promised to go away with him. But who is he? A deceiver? Her husband? Her psychiatrist? A rapist? Is what he says true?

We do not know, we cannot know. We watch different versions of the same events; we cannot tell fantasy from reality. And at the end of the film, when the woman leaves with the man, we do not know whether what we see has really occurred or whether it too is a fantasy in the mind of one of the characters.[89] Certainty and reason are obliterated; the world cannot be interpreted. Is that the point of the film? Or is it to take away all understanding of content so that our attention can be held solely by the surface, the medium, the style? Probably both? We are locked into contemplation of the dream-like silver screen, because the world itself has passed beyond our understanding.

And meanwhile, maybe the man was a rapist. How different is our situation on this side of the screen? Truth matters. The current global crisis in areas like the environment might surely demand hard thinking as to what is going wrong; what is true, how we can understand it, how to respond, how to live. But maybe there is no truth to say or hear or propound. God is dead, reason is unreliable and truth inexpressible. We have got a problem.

In summary...

Postmodernist thinkers have been absolutely clear that the loss of God leads inevitably to the loss – or the 'unspeakability' – of truth. Which sounds like a piece of mere academic weirdness until we see how its logic completes many of the past century's trends, and also how major and wide-ranging are its implications. As Barthes says, the 'refusal' of God leads directly to the refusal of 'reason, science, and law'. And there are more: substance displaced inevitably by style, message by medium, depth by surface; and huge question marks over whether we can ever speak of knowing the truth – in science or the legal system, in teaching or parenting ... Or whether, in all these areas, truth is inaccessible since there is no God; and as a result the only reality is power.

And there is more besides. It seems a heavy price to pay for the loss of God. Have we made sure that the price is unavoidable?

Notes

1. *On Truth and Lie in an Extra-Moral Sense*, in *Portable Nietzsche*, pp. 45–47.
2. Franz Kafka, *The Trial*, pp. 166–67.
3. Quoted in Colin Chapman, *Christianity on Trial*, p. 197. For a presentation of the major philosophical difficulties involved in believing in rationality (at least in its more theoretical activities) in a purely materialistic universe, see J.P. Moreland, *Scaling the Secular City*, pp. 92–96. No one would trust the printout of a computer, he notes, if they 'knew it was programmed by random forces or by non-rational laws without a mind being behind it' (p. 97).
4. Ian Markham, *Truth and the Reality of God*, cf. pp. 90–91, 101, 105, 114–15.
5. Popular science sometimes seems the big exception. The intellectual dinosaur who argues that the supernatural 'conflicts with modern science' usually assumes science to be a static body of knowledge that has now mastered 98% of what there is to know, and is threatened by the idea that 22nd-century science may be preoccupied with ideas as

radically different from our own as ours are from Newton's.

6. This section unavoidably falls into the trap of attempting a coherent account of a school of thought that deliberately shuns coherence in its theory. But it is not unreasonable to sketch in the ways in which the deconstructionists have been most commonly understood, since what we are trying to do here is understand their impact on the wider culture. We can try to 'make sense' of them, even if they themselves deny that that 'making sense' is possible.

7. Culler, *Barthes*, p. 76, cites Barthes' dismissive remark in 1971 that in his earlier work he had 'passed through a euphoric dream of scientificity'.

8. The classic expression is W.K. Wimsatt Jr. and Monroe Beardsley's essay 'The Intentional Fallacy', published in 1946 and subsequently reprinted in *The Verbal Icon*. Other components of the mid-century liberal literary-critical mentality can be seen as paving the way for the deconstructionists' denial of words as expressions of univocal truths – Cleanth Brooks' emphasis on the importance of paradox, for example, or William Empson's on ambiguity. Or, in philosophy, liberal guru Isaiah Berlin's insistence that truth is not a unity but is made up of irreconcilable insights and values.

9. The notion of what constitutes pleasure here is a significant one. The alternative might be that aesthetic pleasure comes from contemplation of an observed external reality (a landscape, a harmonic progression, an artwork) – the joy, as Lewis puts it, of experiencing things that are 'so and not otherwise'. In Barthes, pleasure comes instead from manipulative power. It is a recurrent postmodern motif; pleasure from power through technology, pleasure from power in sado-masochism.

10. 'In the multiplicity of writing, everything is to be *disentangled*, nothing *deciphered*; the structure can be followed ... but there is nothing beneath ... Writing ceaselessly posits meaning ceaselessly to evaporate it, carrying out a systematic exemption of meaning' (Roland Barthes, *Image – Music – Text*, p. 147).

11. It was at this point that the post-structuralist critique made common cause with neo-Marxism.

12. This is also a starting-point for a Christian response to the similar denials of the possibility of knowing truth that come from some varieties of determinism. The Christian accepts that, normally, our minds may be limited in all kinds of deterministic ways (educational, genetic, ideological) from perceiving what is true. But, this

does not rule out the possibility of 'grace': the moment when the supernatural power of God's Spirit creates, through his Word, the freedom to see, to know and to choose. 'Where the Spirit of the Lord is, there is freedom', said the apostle Paul when discussing how God enlightens minds that are normally blinded to a right understanding of their 'texts' (2 Corinthians 3:14–17). D.A. Carson summarizes the issues very simply: Christians believe that God is personal, and he speaks.

13. But see also Michael Edwards, *Towards a Christian Poetics*, who concedes much of the radical case about the non-transparence of language and then proceeds to construct a Christian equivalent of these theories on the basis of the disintegration of language since the Fall and Babel, and its incipient reintegration at Pentecost.

14. A.W. Tozer, *The Knowledge of the Holy*, p. 12, quoting John 1:1. Tozer died in 1963; evangelicals have tended to foresee the deconstructionist issues before they arose. In 1954, in his essay 'De descriptionis temporum', C.S. Lewis asked why there should not come a period when the art of writing would stand lower than the art of reading, and 'rival readings would then cease to be "right" or "wrong" and simply become more and less brilliant "performances"'; exactly the postmodern position on interpretation.

15. D.A. Carson sketches the contours of a Christian response to deconstructionism in chs. 2 and 3 of his massive and brilliant assessment of contemporary pluralism, *The Gagging of God*. A fuller, ground-breaking study is Kevin Vanhoozer, *Is There a Meaning in This Text?*.

16. Jacques Derrida, *Of Grammatology*, pp. 14–15. This divine underpinning of meaning remains fundamental, says Derrida, 'even where the thing, the "referent", is not immediately related to the logos of a Creator God'.

17. Barthes, *Image*, pp. 146–47.

18. Richard Rorty, *Contingency, Irony and Solidarity*, p. 5.

19. Richard Rorty, *Consequences of Pragmatism*, p. 165.

20. Steiner, *Real Presences*, pp. 127, 96, 120.

21. These quotations are taken from essays excerpted in two excellent and thorough anthologies that give a fine introduction to postmodernism and its antecedents. The first is from Baudrillard's *Simulations*, reprinted in Docherty, *Postmodernism*, pp. 196–97; the second is from *Symbolic Exchange and Death*, in Cahoone, *From Modernism*, p. 459.

22. Barthes suggests that the written word, with its endless interpretations, might well 'take as its motto the words of the man possessed by devils: "My name is legion, for we are many"' (quoted by D.S. Cartwright in *Gospel Perspectives*, III, ed. D. Wenham and R.T. France). The example is suggestive: the demon-possessed man is a truly 'decentred self' living out an absolute loss of God.

23. Umberto Eco, *The Name of the Rose*, pp. 3, 599, 600, 609–11. (The last words mean, approximately, that the name (the verbal label) for the rose is all that we can have.) In Eco's subsequent novel, *Foucault's Pendulum*, he turns to the occult (kabbalah, tarot, numerology, diabolism, Aleister Crowley, voodoo), with its offer of a secret knowledge that would make sense of the apparently unconnected world. But at the close, beneath all the complexities of secret lore, there is again a void, an inaccessibility of truth: 'I have understood. And the certainty that there is nothing to understand should be my peace, my triumph.' This, it is worth adding, is what we also find at the end of Nobel prize-winner Gabriel Garcia Marquez's *One Hundred Years of Solitude*; Aureliano attains truth on the book's last page when he finally reads the prophecies of Melkiades' parchments, and it is a final mockery: he learns only of his own death. The reading act is achieved with a final reward of futility. Beneath all the explorations and seductive fascinations of occult knowledge is a final reality or fate that is foretold but meaningless; at the centre, nothing but death.

24. There was, of course, an interlude (it seems we cannot live long without idealism): the blossoming of a whole bouquet of 'big ideas' in the 1960s, each confident of transforming the world. Most obviously there were eastern religion (e.g. the Maharishi's transcendental meditation), LSD-based hallucinogenic mysticism, and the New Left ('Marx, Mao and Marcuse') of student revolt. All three had less than five years between upsurge and burial. Was this the overall 20th-century process repeated in miniature? The 1970s that followed were a profoundly cynical decade.

25. In Docherty, *Postmodernism*, pp. 47–48. Lyotard continues, 'This idea of a possible, probable, or necessary progress is rooted in the belief that developments made in the arts, technology, knowledge, and freedom would benefit humanity as a whole ... After two centuries we have become more alert to signs that would indicate an opposing movement ... It is no longer possible to call development progress.' C.S. Lewis made similar observations two decades

earlier in 'The Funeral of a Great Myth' (reprinted in *Christian Reflections*).

26. Neil Postman, *Amusing Ourselves to Death*, p. 61.

27. Postman, *Amusing Ourselves*, p. 75. Schultze et al note how in MTV 'Although some songs and artists attempt to make statements about life, politics, and the environment, the channel's carefully crafted ambience isolates these statements from any kind of meaningful community discussion or debate' (*Dancing*, p. 205).

28. Postman, *Amusing Ourselves*, pp. 99–100.

29. Cf. the editors' introduction to *Christian Apologetics in the Postmodern World*, ed. Timothy R. Phillips and Dennis L. Okholm, p. 14.

30. Cf. the first chapter of John's Gospel.

31. Quoted by Os Guinness, in *The Anglican Evangelical Crisis*, ed. Melvin Tinker, p. 162.

32. Jesus presented himself as the 'light that gives light to every man'. The point of the central Christian discipline of daily, prayerful Bible reading is precisely this continual, personal exposure to revelation.

33. 'It does seem to me that most of the art of this century has been about "making"', painter Bridget Riley told an *Independent on Sunday* interviewer. The same point could easily be argued about other arts.

34. This happens to varying degrees. Baudrillard says that 'The absolute rule of thought is to give the world back as it was given to us – unintelligible. And, if possible, to render it a little more unintelligible.' In contrast, Lyotard begins his 'Notes on the Meaning of "Post-" ' by saying he is writing 'in order to avoid confusion and ambiguity'.

35. There is, it should also be said, something about the French intellectual tradition that can prefer to dazzle by extreme subtlety than to convince by clarity. To such a mindset, deconstructionism is obviously germane. But might we also speculate that most French intellectuals are Jesuit atheists rather than Protestant atheists? They owe their roots to a culture prizing brilliance of casuistry, whereas an Anglo-Saxon, post-Protestant culture sets a higher value on clarity of exposition? (Of course we should be alert to the possibility raised by Galen Strawson in an *Independent on Sunday* review, that the obscurity arises because Derrida is a 'nice man but simply not very bright'.)

36. Cf. Sturrock, *Structuralism*, pp. 16–17.
37. Culler makes this point about Barthes in *Barthes*, p. 13; Hayden White says the same about Foucault in Sturrock's *Structuralism*, p. 86.
38. In *Portable Nietzsche*, p. 98.
39. In other periods too, a move away from faith in truth has been succeeded by an emphasis on style. The 1890s of Wilde and Beardsley would be an obvious example. One of Oscar Wilde's characters is challenged about a remark he has made in *The Importance of Being Earnest*. 'It is perfectly phrased,' he defends himself, 'and quite as true as any observation in civilized life should be.'
40. Schultze, *Dancing*, pp. 205, 178. Kevin Ford applies this to politics: 'We don't know who's lying and who's telling the truth. So we vote for the one with the most attractive image. Issues are complex. Image is simple' (*Jesus for a New Generation*, p. 60).
41. However, it is worth noting here a comment by Doug Schaull of InterVarsity-USA, that relativism in truth has a major effect on the 'emotional complexities' afflicting students he works among in the Los Angeles area, because 'their world is continually in motion'; nothing in it is stable, and that has major psychological repercussions.
42. Allan Bloom makes this point precisely in response to the deconstructionists and to Nietzsche: 'For Nietzsche, language can be no more than the oracular expression of absolutely individual selves and hence can never reach beyond mere perspectives to true universality, which would be understanding ... Socrates talks of his good friends, Nietzsche of his best enemies. Friendship is that relation constituted by *logos* and is logocentric' (*Love and Friendship*, p. 543).
43. Patterson and Kim, *The Day America*, pp. 44, 48, 236, 49. The 'national character' comment should be qualified by a 1997 survey from an Italian psychological review showing that 70% of Italians confessed to telling between five and ten lies a day.
44. From *The Gay Science*, in *Portable Nietzsche*, p. 449.
45. This way of thinking has become surprisingly influential in some areas of management theory. The idea (present in many areas of New Age thought) that imagination can reshape reality is of course a further cultural force contributing to the loss of the notion of truth, where reality has an objective givenness that can be known but is independent of ourselves and our wishes.

46. Again we might see here the pattern of the self-destruction of idolatry that we have noted at several other points. In the absence of truth, postmodernism almost deifies the category of story and narrative. But postmodernist criticism too often comes close to stifling the stories we have.

47. Francis Schaeffer's way of describing this would be to say that, first, the 'upper storey' of values becomes divorced from the 'lower storey' of empirical reality, and then the lower storey reality itself becomes lost. C.S. Lewis, in *The Screwtape Letters*, saw the renewed experience of real pleasures and pains as one of the surest anchors against such deception.

48. Ephesians 4:14. Tana Clark, regional director of InterVarsity in Alberta, Canada, has commented on the potency in the postmodern context of the notion of truth as anchor; truth as that which holds us fast amid so many forces that would manipulate or exploit. (Truth, we might add, set again as an alternative against the Foucauldian crosscurrents of power.)

49. *Time* reported in 1990 that the generation then under 30 'knows less, cares less and reads newspapers less' than any in the past 50 years, and warned that they were therefore an 'easy target of opportunity for those seeking to manipulate public opinion' (quoted in Schultze, *Dancing*, p. 201). All the main British news programmes lost viewers in the later 1990s.

50. *Independent on Sunday*, 3 October 1999.

51. From *The Gay Science*, in *Portable Nietzsche*, p. 450.

52. See, for example, David Bloor, *Knowledge and Social Imagery*.

53. Both these quotations are taken from chs. 6 and 7 of Ramachandra, *Gods that Fail*, which offers a perceptive Christian response to the radicals' scepticism concerning the scientific enterprise.

54. Quoted in *Independent on Sunday*, 26 Nov. 2000.

55. One could agree with Lyotard's words, as a critique of the workings of public science, without denying objective truth as something that nonetheless exists. But the postmodernist marginalization of truth removes that possible counterbalance, so that what is left in the world of science is merely the play of power. And the displacement of truth by power changes the whole nature of scientific debate. 'As Max Planck said of disputes in theoretical physics, "One can never manage to convince one's opponents, only to outlive them"', writes Charles Jencks in *What is Post-Modernism?*

56. Quoted by Ravi Zacharias in 'The Court of Last Resort', in *Just Thinking*, Spring/Summer 1996, on the stimulating website www.rzim.com.

57. This is recognized explicitly in Morrison's legal textbook *Jurisprudence*, p. 294. In postmodern perspectivism, says Morrison, 'each and every view is one among many possible interpretations ... There are obvious applications to the understanding of legal texts and legal material ... Perspectivism holds there are no independent facts (in the sense of facts that do not need themselves to be interpreted) against which the various interpretations can be compared so that we can agree on which interpretation is "correct". In this case, the task of making sense of processes or sets of institutions, such as the legal system, or reading texts, such as legal texts, may be a question of obeying certain methodological rules and/or imposing order among many possible interpretations.' 'Imposing order': law is determined not by truth but by power.

58. We should note, however, the validity of the postmodernist critique that this was equally true of modernist legal theory. Morrison notes the 'intimate connection between legal positivism' (the 'dominant tradition' in jurisprudence in the last 150 years, p. 4) 'and power' (p. 346). Once legal positivism cut itself loose from the 'natural law' tradition of law reflecting the will of God, it became a purely human construction – or, one might say, a construction of some humans for others – with no intrinsic connection to morality (p. 218). Even Hart, the doyen of legal positivism, admitted that 'Here all that succeeds is success' (p. 375). But at that point its entire moral legitimacy becomes questionable; and this has become a central concern for much of modern jurisprudence. Derrida himself observed (in a symposium titled *Deconstruction and the Possibility of Justice*) that 'Since the origin of authority, the foundation or ground, the position of the law can't by definition rest on anything but themselves, they are themselves a violence without ground. Which is to say that they are themselves unjust, in the sense of "illegal"'; they are always dependent on issues of enforceability, hence of power. (Quoted in Morrison, *Jurisprudence*, p. 522.)

59. The goal of deconstructionist legal theorists, says Morrison, is to show that 'any settled law of the text is open to destabilisation. Every interpretation which tries to replace the openendedness of the basic text with a final – authoritarian – interpretation usurps

the life of the text' (p. 521). We recall the postmodern president Clinton's famous statement to the Senate hearings on the Lewinsky affair: 'It depends on what the meaning of "is" is.'

60. We noted a related problem earlier, in our section on purpose. But there the cause was the lack of reason to believe, after the loss of God, in the value of the process of maturity; whereas here the issue is whether truths that matter can ever really be known or spoken anyway.

61. It is difficult even to state the issues here. In our culture it is hard not to feel a built-in, knee-jerk reaction at any defence of 'authority'. In fact, as Lasch points out, the loss of 'truth' does not remove the realities of control from our society; they merely reappear in a therapeutic guise. ('The popularization of therapeutic modes of thought discredits authority, especially in the home or the classroom, while leaving' their own forms of social control and their own 'domination uncriticized' [Narcissism, p. 315].) Somewhere beneath the mid-century liberal allergy to all 'authority' lay a fantasy of everyone eating their sandwiches in the sun together, rather than the law of the jungle which the true negation of all authority creates. (The triumph of the mafia in post-communist Russia has shown that all too clearly.) Here again, mid-century liberalism indulged in easy rejection of the notion of authority without really thinking through what follows; again, it is postmodernists like Foucault who are drawing out the full results of this kind of atheism.

62. A good example of the resulting confusion is the following quotation from an Open University senior education lecturer: 'Instruction is a term that is very rarely used in the British context ... Any conception of accuracy in the teaching of reading will be based on unequal power relations between the reader and the arbiter of accuracy' (quoted in Phillips, Prizes, p. 87). The consequences are predictable.

63. One must also bear in mind here the enormous influence of the 1980s new-right philosophy that measured everything in economic terms, by the 'bottom line'. But if there are no other standards (such as the value, and possibility, of learning 'truth for its own sake'), then the only feasible criterion for assessing an education is financial. 'Let the market decide' is centrally postmodern.

64. Lyotard argues that this also inevitably characterizes the entire research system: with 'truth' no longer a prime value, 'In the

discourse of today's financial backers of research, the only credible goal is power' (Cahoone, *From Modernism*, p. 497).

65. Phillips, *Prizes*, p. xviii.

66. Phillips, *Prizes*, p. 212.

67. Phillips, *Prizes*, p. 13. In noting Phillips' identification of the problem, we aren't implying a particular view regarding the present government's solutions. But in case Phillips sounds unduly concerned, it is worth noting the development of 'ethnomathematics' – feminist and ethnic-specific approaches to mathematics – under the auspices of the USA's National Council of Teachers of Mathematics. One leading figure in ethnomathematics argued recently that students' 'thinking or approach must not be structured for them, so that they are not being led to "the right" ' (that is, objectively true) '"way" of solving a problem'. Meanwhile, an American Federation of Teachers report found that in every respect US maths students lagged far behind their counterparts in France, Germany and Japan.

68. Phillips, *Prizes*, pp. 27–28.

69. One response to this would be that education has to do with internal growth as well as with mastery of external facts and principles. This is certainly true; but it is hard to imagine personal growth that does not include a maturing understanding of how the world really is – again, what our loss of truth denies.

70. Lasch, *Narcissism*, pp. 286–88. Phillips adds, 'The child has become an autonomous and solitary individual, left alone to construct his or her own meaning from the world ... Children have been saddled with a burden of adult responsibilities well beyond their years. What child-centred theories have done is to destroy the very concept of childhood itself' (*Prizes,* pp. 235, 271).

71. Lasch, *Narcissism*, p. 316; cf. p. 308. Cf. also the impeccably liberal Miriam Stoppard on the need for discipline based on clear standards: 'Research has shown that children do not actually like a lack of discipline nor do they thrive when they are undisciplined. In fact they do best when the limits of behaviour are clearly defined for them. It is your role to set standards for behaviour and conduct appropriate for the age of your child ... When aggressive behaviour in a child becomes a regular feature, however, it is usually a response to two things: a lack of effective restraint and discipline from the time he was born, and a feeling of insecurity in the child' (*The New Baby Care Book* (1990 edn), pp. 17, 283).

72. Cf. Lasch, *Narcissism*, p. 304. This chapter was drafted soon after

the 1998 football World Cup, from which England were eliminated partly (and dramatically) because one of their most gifted players, Beckham, lacked self-discipline in the area of retaliation.

73. Lasch, *Narcissism*, p. 190.

74. Cf. McClung, *Father Heart*. Obviously the model of God as Father must be balanced in its application to human fatherhood by recognition of our human tendencies to misunderstand, mistreat and dominate. But its loss is serious. Mark Simpson asked, in the *Independent on Sunday* (4 Feb. 2001), 'What is it that boys are supposed to grow into these days? Masculine certainties have vanished, in many cases, along with dad', going on to suggest that homosexual identity often 'represents a solution of a kind to the problem of being fatherless in a fatherless world, and the bastard boy's hollow ache for male intimacy.' That 'ache' isn't helped at all if the world is Father-less as well as fatherless.

75. Cf. Ann Brown, *Apology to Women*, ch. 7.

76. Cf. John Wenham, *Christ and the Bible*.

77. Cf. John Stott, *Christ the Controversialist*.

78. 1 Corinthians 13:9,12.

79. Cf. Hebrews 2: 6–9.

80. John 6:32–35, 7:38–39, 15:1, 10:7.

81. Psalm 121:1.

82. Psalm 36:6.

83. Cf. Derrida's remarks about the 'book of Nature' as the 'book of God' in the first chapter of *Of Grammatology*.

84. In Docherty, *Postmodernism*, pp. 68, 70.

85. Obviously this issue relates to our discussion in Chapter 2 regarding our culture's loss of transcendence, of anything of supreme value that is worth living for.

86. The classic postmodernist statement here is Foucault's essay 'Nietzsche, Genealogy, History', from which this sentence is taken. Once again, the issue is rooted in Foucault's explicit denial, following Nietzsche, of any 'theogony', of the Christian story of 'the origin ... the site of truth ... the point where the truth of things corresponded to a truthful discourse'; thence, of the Fall where this truth was lost, and of history as 'a field of knowledge whose function is to recover' this place of origin. (Which, incidentally, could also describe Marxist or Freudian history.) 'The traditional devices for constructing a comprehensive view of history and for retracing the past as a patient and continuous development must be

systematically dismantled. Necessarily, we must dismiss those tendencies that encourage the consoling play of recognitions.' (Foucault's essay is reprinted in Cahoone, *From Modernism*, pp. 360–79.)

87. This seems a hallmark of the rise of 'cultural studies' and 'media studies' in the western university system, at the expense of disciplines such as literature and history. (One can say that without denying the value of the newer disciplines, from which, obviously, this study itself has benefited very significantly.)

88. Hence C.S. Lewis' insistence (in *The Screwtape Letters*) on the need to read writers of different eras, so that we see beyond the false certainties of our own culture.

89. The screenplay was written by the renowned French novelist Alain Robbe-Grillet, whose hatred of meaningful plot we touched on briefly in Chapter 2. In Robbe-Grillet's novels, likewise, it can be impossible to reconstruct what has occurred.

5

love after God

'has it not become colder?'

Maybe there's a God, maybe there isn't. It doesn't matter much.

But as we've seen, it does matter. And the long-term loss – or gain! – to us looms largest in the area of life that has become central to our culture: personal relationships.

The final shelter

Intimacy embodies so much that matters deeply to us.

We've looked at the issue of *identity*, and seen how the experience of love forms a vital component of a healthy self-worth. (The advertisers are aware of it too: 'Don't let love and life pass you by', runs a Dateline ad.) It's scarcely the whole story, of course – yet most of us have known what it is to feel our loneliness consuming our self-worth from within.

And doesn't *purpose* in life also focus, to a significant extent and for plenty of us, into the discovery and development of 'real' relationship? But so, increasingly, does *ethics*; as we have seen – 'What's right is what's right for my family...'

So it is that relationships have often become our final citadel in the twilight of the west, after the death of God. This is Matthew Arnold:

...The sea of faith
was once, too, at the full, and round earth's shore
lay like the folds of a bright girdle furl'd;
but now I only hear
its melancholy, long, withdrawing roar
retreating to the breath
of the night-wind down the vast edges drear
and naked shingles of the world.

Ah, love, let us be true
to one another! for the world, which seems
to lie before us like a land of dreams,
so various, so beautiful, so new,
hath really neither joy, nor love, nor light,
nor certitude, nor peace, nor help for pain;
and we are here as on a darkling plain
swept with confused alarms of struggle and flight,
where ignorant armies clash by night.
–Matthew Arnold, 'Dover Beach'

Love, let us be true to one another: that will be left when everything else is gone. This is D.H. Lawrence:

"I know," he said. "It just doesn't centre. The old ideals are dead –
nothing there. It seems to me there remains only this perfect union
with a woman – sort of ultimate marriage – and there isn't anything
else."
"And you mean if there isn't the woman, there's nothing?" said
Gerald.
"Pretty well that – seeing there's no God."
"Then we're hard to put to it," said Gerald.
–D.H. Lawrence, *Women in Love*[1]

When there is nothing else left to believe in 'seeing there's no God', love remains. The pattern recurs in a singer central to more recent decades, John Lennon, whose haunting melody 'Imagine' was arguably the most beautiful denial of Christian beliefs ever written. 'Imagine' didn't stand alone; other songs by Lennon demonstrate profound unbelief, not only in Jesus and the Bible but in many other kinds of ideals besides. One thing, however, he still expressed particular faith in: his relationship with Yoko Ono. 'Love, let us be true to one another' (Arnold); that is where we look for shelter when everything else is gone.

Candle in the dark

But will our shelter hold as the 'night-wind' turns chillier?

We do seem to face a problem. As Lewis would say, often we find love when we're looking for something else; once love itself becomes our goal, it gets harder to find – or even to understand.

A historical example: the artistic movement known as Romanticism often sought fulfilment in human impulses such as love, after the sterility of eighteenth-century rationalism. Somehow, however, it didn't work; it all ended up in tortured excess and twisted relationships, over which stands the shadow of the cruelty of the Marquis de Sade. The love-god turned out to be broken or unattainable. (The whole development is charted in Mario Praz's thorough if unpleasant book *The Romantic Agony*.)

To D.H. Lawrence, too, the man-woman relationship offered so much creative potential. But his novels' relationships usually seem unsatisfying, his lovers devouring-and-devoured. And in 1921 we find him writing of love more broadly,

Why is everybody always caring so hard about somebody else? Why not leave off? In short, why not have done with Jesus and with love and have a shot at conscious proud power. Why not soldiers instead of lovers? Why not laugh, and spit in the eye of love. Really, why not laugh? ... Kick the posterior of creeping love, and laugh when it whimpers. Pah, it is a disease love ... give me henceforth Mars, and a free flight.[2]

Later still, the 1960s placed 'free love' at the centre of a culture whose anthem was 'All You Need Is Love'. But somehow it turned into abuse and whips, children with vanished fathers, planeloads of pornography leaving Europe each day for the two-thirds world, where their effect is colossal. (Of course the rate of women being gang-raped has shot up in places like Port Moresby, New Guinea; but that's how the free market works. The west feels sometimes like an open sewer to the rest of the world.)

Somehow we wanted love, but we've failed to get it right. Singers like Alanis Morrisette have a strong sense of the failure of relationships, and the damage they can do. 'This isn't what the movies tell you', sang Pulp in 'Feeling Called Love'. 'The cult of intimacy conceals a growing despair of finding it', writes the respected American commentator Christopher Lasch; 'Isolation seems to be the disease of our time', confirms Allan Bloom.[3] One of the things that made the 1990s collapse of the British royal marriages so significant – Diana and Charles, Fergie and Andrew – was the sense of representativeness: the royals couldn't make it work either. According to Andrew Motion, the night Charles proposed to Diana, she told him in response how much she loved him. 'Whatever love means', was his reply.

So what does it mean? – after the death of the Christian God from whom the term was historically defined? The Christian world-view didn't merely describe love ('Love is patient, love is kind. It does not envy, it does not boast, it is not proud. It is not rude, it is not self-seeking, it is not easily angered, it keeps no record of wrongs. It always protects, always trusts, always hopes, always perseveres'[4]). More crucially, it affirmed – uniquely among world religions – that God actually '*is* Love'; and it pointed to Christ's ultimate act of love on Calvary as the pattern for all relationships – and for sexual and marital lovers in particular.[5] But God doesn't exist. So, in a world of disposable marriages and cocktail sex, what should we use the word 'love' to mean?

Is love anything more than a word? Does 'love' mean any more than the mere hunger for sex and company ... more than a temporary tactical alliance with sex included, accompanied by pleasurable but passing feelings? Actress Joan Collins once admitted, 'I've never been able to figure out what love means.'[6] Novelist Julian Barnes has an answer for her: love is just a way of getting someone to call you darling after sex. Camille Paglia is equally tough-minded: sex is combat. Feminist writer Andrea Dworkin: 'Romance is rape embellished with meaningful looks.'

And if you don't believe that, still what does love mean? We've learnt sex: now where do we learn tenderness? How can you tell whether or not your relationship is a destructive 'co-dependency'? How far should love extend – what does it entail in terms of commitment or forgiveness? ('I would have thought *not* forgiving was a sign of love', said a character in a recent TV drama about marital unfaithfulness.) And how do we find the strength – or will – to (truly) forgive anyway? Again, is love something that can last? Can it coexist, long-term, with marriage? Medieval 'courtly love' poets denied it; and the clear message of films like *Falling In Love* (Meryl Streep, Robert de Niro) is that 'love cannot endure in the humdrum atmosphere of married life, it needs the secret hothouse excitement of an affair'.[7] 'Modern marriage is in chaos. We no longer have a clear concept of what marriage means', says Penny Mansfield of One to One. 'That's what marriage is – concentrated lust', says a character in 'Mary Hartman, Mary Hartman'. How do find our definition – or should we each make our own? Is the story of many broken relationships that of the fatal combat of different ideas as to what 'love' and 'marriage' mean?

Or is there simply something scientifically inevitable about the decline of love into exploitation and domination? We could recall Sartre's comment: 'All kinds of materialism lead one to treat everyone, including oneself, as an object.' What, then, is this 'love'? One problem posed by the new psychology and brain genetics is whether 'love' is any more than a sentimental gloss to dignify the evolutionary mating drive, and the reactions certain sights or scents trigger in our chemistry so that our genes get passed on. '*Why* is love?', wonders biologist Colin Tudge provocatively:

> ... The point of sex is to mix genes. The constant supply of novelty provides the raw material for evolutionary change... But no creature in its right mind would risk sex, no matter how worthwhile the biologists might show it to be. So natural selection has ensured that we are not in our right minds: passion for motivation, ecstasy for reward – testosterone, adrenalin, endorphins. That's about all there is to it, really.[8]

But where does that leave us? William Barrett writes,

> Suppose, out of a moment of theoretical austerity ... we strive to consider those close to us "as if" they had no minds and were not conscious, but were only behaving bodies. We would very shortly be schizoid, deranged. Or, to make the illustration as plain and grotesque as possible, you are approaching a moment of tenderness and passion with the woman you love, but for a moment you stop to reflect that theoretically you can treat her words and caresses as if there were no consciousness or mind behind them. That way madness lies![9]

But it doesn't, of course; that way, quite probably, the future of psychology lies, with its assumption that (now God is dead) 'love' means only a loaded term for triggered but mechanical responses. How the woman might feel about it is another matter, of course; the 'moment of passion' might well not be repeated.

But facts remain facts. Unless, of course, our intuitions are perhaps in touch with realities deeper than our atheism?

I remain self-possessed
Except when a street piano, mechanical and tired
Reiterates some worn-out common song
With the smell of hyacinths across the garden

Recalling things that other people have desired.
Are these ideas right or wrong?
–T.S. Eliot, 'Portrait of a Lady'

Where did our love go?

Kurt Vonnegut's nihilistic classic *Cat's Cradle* offers us a way of looking at our confusion about love.

'Is – is there anyone else in your life?'

She was puzzled. 'Many,' she said at last.

'That you *love*?'

'I love everyone.'

'As – as much as me?'

'Yes.' She seemed to have no idea that this might bother me ...

'I suppose you – perform – you do what we just did with – other people?'

'*Boko-maru*?'

'*Boko-maru*.'

'Of course.'

'I don't want you to do it with anybody but me from now on ... As your husband, I'll want all your love for myself.'

The speaker isn't expecting the disagreement that follows:

She stared at me with widening eyes. 'A *sin-wat*!'

'What was that?'

'A *sin-wat*!' she cried. 'A man who wants all of somebody's love. That's very bad.'

'In the case of marriage, I think it's a very good thing ... Is that clear?'

'No.'

'No?'

'I will not marry a *sin-wat*.' She stood. 'Good-bye.'

'Good-bye?' I was crushed.

Then comes the cause of the problem:

> 'Bokonon tells us it is very wrong not to love everybody the same. What does *your* religion say?'
> 'I – I don't have one.'[10]

Step by step, the lovers' relationship heads for impasse. And the reason emerges in the final question: 'What does *your* religion say?' 'I – I don't have one', replies the helpless male. The implication seems clear: inconsistencies in our deepest worldviews can lead to radically divergent perceptions of what 'love' involves; and if we've never thought around that level we may not understand why our love has gone wrong. But what are these 'divergent perceptions'?

Let's get historical again. Allan Bloom, notorious for his provocative *The Closing of the American Mind*, has an equally thought-provoking analysis of these uncertainties in his book *Love and Friendship*.

Bloom's story sees two forces at work. First, he links the 'death of eros' with the triumph of the outlook generated by 'materialistic science'; particularly in the powerful form of Freudian psychology, and the mechanization of sex symbolized by surveys like the incompetent but influential Kinsey report. Their result, he contends, has been an 'impoverishment of feeling'. 'Everything is so routine and without mystery'; the 'risk and the hope of human connectedness' have been replaced by an 'appalling matter-of-factness ... A description of sex is no different from a description of eating habits, and the object of desire is essentially indifferent.'[11] Consumption has replaced affection, he suggests; and at the intellectual cutting-edge, what we used to call love has turned into either a contract-relationship or a power-struggle.

Bloom is very good at linking this 'fall of eros' with the megatrends of the broader cultural scene. He notes the influence here of 'the hot new principle that all human relations, especially sexual ones, follow from the one motivating principle in man, the will to power. Everything is power-relationships, crude power, the will to dominate.'[12] The key prophet of this 'hot new principle' was of course the atheistic postmodernist Foucault again; and Foucault's own erotic life was deeply involved with sado-masochism. (As Sturrock has commented, Foucault lived out in S/M what he set forth in theory in his philosophical work, the 'rigmaroles of domination and submission he had earlier uncovered in symbolic form'. He died of an AIDS-related illness in 1984.)

Power, the will to dominate, to keep control – that is one contemporary 'aspect of love'. And in this 'war of all against all', says Bloom, the 'only possible peace is to be found in artificial constructs ... Abstract reason in the service of radically free men and women can discover only contract as the basis of connectedness – the social contract, marriage contract, somehow mostly the business contract as model, with its union of selfish individuals. Legalism takes the place of sentiment.'[13] Bloom probably has in mind the bizarre contracts suggested as frameworks for relationship in America's more postmodernist colleges. But we might also recall the well-meaning British liberals who suggest that newly-married couples should sit down and work out the contractual rules for when they break up (surely an approach tending towards disastrously self-fulfilling prophecy).[14] Nor is it only liberal postmodernists who turn so quickly to contracts as a basis for relationship. We saw two chapters back how the post-Christian New Right has gone in the same direction, with unfortunate effects on the vital intangibles of idealism and generosity.

Now if these two factors summarize the reality of 'love' – contract with no ultimate commitment, and power as the hidden driving force – it obviously raises the issue of security: how can I avoid ending up as the loser here? Thus the 'sexual talk of our times', says Bloom, 'is about how to get greater bodily satisfaction (although decreasingly so), or increasingly how to protect ourselves from one another ... Ours is a language that reduces the longing for the other to the need for individual, private satisfaction and safety.'[15] This sense of fear, of the need for self-protectiveness, features in many contemporary discussions of relationship. 'Of *course* men betray you', writes Edmund White in *The Farewell Symphony*, 'of *course* love is an illusion dispelled by lust, of *course* you end up alone.' 'For both sexes in this society, caring deeply for anyone is becoming synonymous with losing', wrote Hendin in his survey of American students, *The Age of Sensation*.[16] And Christopher Lasch's famous study *The Culture of Narcissism* suggests that

> Both men and women have come to approach personal relations with a heightened appreciation of their emotional risks. Determined to manipulate the emotion of others while protecting themselves against emotional injury, both sexes cultivate a protective shallowness, a cynical detachment they do not altogether feel but which soon becomes habitual.[17]

Thus we find the Spice Girls singing, 'If you wanna be my lover, you gotta get with my friends', because it is friendship that is safe, friendship that 'never ends'. Friends are people you can trust; lovers may well not be. Friendship is safe; love is not.[18]

Still, this is not the whole story. Perhaps the tradition of 'materialistic science' has indeed led us to treat each other as objects; perhaps mechanistic psychology has replaced 'love' with an atmosphere of power-struggle in a jungle of selfish-gene Darwinism, restrained only by our self-protective contracts. But, says Bloom, there has also been a second, humanizing alternative in our culture. This is the Romantic tradition, deriving from Rousseau in the eighteenth century.

Rousseau comes after the 'loss of God'; he was seeking to 'reintroduce eroticism in the context of Enlightenment materialism', says Bloom.[19] Both Rousseau and his era had turned away from Christianity, so what he did was replace that earlier faith in God with 'sincerity in the profession of faith' itself; 'sincerity puts the onus on the subjective certainty of the self'.[20] And that subjective sincerity became the heart of the whole Romantic tradition of love and relationship.

Here too, however, there was a problem. Rousseau assigned a central place in love to 'imagination unsupported by reality.

He, of course, did so because he was persuaded that in fact imagination has no such foundation in reality for its creations.'[21] Thus the imagination central to Romantic love is one unrelated to reality. Bloom quotes Rousseau as observing, 'This beauty is not in the object one loves; it is the work of our errors. So, what of it? Does the lover any the less sacrifice all of his low sentiments to this imaginary model? ... In love everything is only illusion. I admit it. But what is real are the sentiments.'[22] They are ultimately unrealistic, but they are what really matter in love.

Give it a slightly more positive spin, and we recognize Rousseau's Romanticism, and his sadness, as contemporary 'aspects of love'. 'Love is blind', we smile tolerantly – as if the alternative is a realism of disillusion, but the illusion is worth having so long as we can believe in it. The Christian idea of love was different; it was founded, not on the improbable perfection of the partner, but on the active lovingkindness of God who brings imperfect partners wisely together. Love then becomes the emotional counterpart of something objectively real, a shared lifelong calling from God. But in our Romantic tradition, love tends ultimately to be 'a rock built on a fairy's wing'; at its heart is unreality. It is the greatest of dreams, but in the end we will know it for an illusion, and expect marriage to be something different. The Romantic hero and heroine will ride away into the sunset when the movie ends. Their 'love' belongs on another planet – it will not have to face the nappies and the conflicts over decoration. But we will. And at such times, if 'love' is only illusion then it may collapse under us. If that be 'love', we need some other word for the realities of relationship. And so 'love' loses its meaning.

That illusion is all too clear in the drastic gap between Rousseau's romantic rhetoric and his repeated habit of abandoning the children he fathered. Bloom goes on to show how the Romantic ideal fascinated, and failed, the following generations (for example in *Pride and Prejudice* and *Anna Karenina*). Above all, says Bloom, Flaubert's Madame Bovary marked the inadequacy of the romantic hope:

Love had, it appears, no foundation in nature ... Emma [Bovary] and Flaubert are full of longings for ideals that cannot be and are really, from the standpoint of reason, foolish. The aspiration of author and heroine is impossible to fulfil, and the world they look at in terms of it is dreary past endurance. They share defeat.[23]

The writers that followed, he adds, were bitter.[24]

So neither the materialistic nor the Romantic tradition give our hearts what they call for. Seen in this light, our 'love problem' becomes a classic instance of the 'split' Francis Schaeffer sees as haunting Europe's culture, ever since its loss of the Reformation's biblical world-view.[25] Up to and during the Reformation, says Schaeffer, God's reality underpinned and unified both the world of God's science and the world of God's values; they fitted together. In contrast, our post-Reformation, 'god-less' world-views contain a disastrous chasm. On one side are the ideals and values we long for, that turn out, fatally, to have no true foundation in any reality. On the other side stand the brute facts of materialistic science, which offer no values at all. Bloom's presentation of 'love' seems to exemplify this.[26] Between the romantic ideal we imagine, and the brute facts of life as seen through our dominant, mechanistic world-view, stands an enormous gulf; and neither side is enough for us to live by.

It is particularly interesting that Bloom (who does not appear to be a Christian) sees the most coherent presentations of love coming in the work of Shakespeare – written, of course, when that unified, Reformation synthesis was dominant. Shakespeare, says Bloom, is neither a materialist nor an advocate of a ground-less romantic imagination. He does not have to start from human 'isolation and selfishness'; but nor does he 'begin, as does Rousseau, from a Cartesian radical doubt and then try to put the machine back together again'. Instead, says Bloom, Shakespeare's 'premodern view' leads to a 'naturalness' about human connectedness.[27] We should not overstate the case here; yet if Shakespeare's ability to make this fusion work has any-thing to do with the Reformation, then it becomes of particular interest when set alongside the idea of Linda Grant (author of *Sexing the Millennium*) and others that 'companionate marriage', based on intimacy and devotion, was also an invention of the seventeenth century. Somehow the God-oriented Reformation world-view offered a coherent base for the meaning of love-as-marriage, and for thinking and writing about love.

If that is so, then the post-Reformation 'death of God' is highly important for understanding our problems in 'love' today. In what ways might the death of God have contributed to the death of love? How might the rediscovery of God help me to be a good lover?

Intimacy and the death of the Father

There are at least three key areas where the presence of God significantly empowers our approach to relationship. First, the sense of calling that comes from faith in God the Father as sovereign Creator; second, the understanding of love that comes from faith in Jesus as God the Son; and third, the confidence that comes from faith in God the Spirit.

Most simply, our attitude to 'love' is profoundly affected by the notion that God himself 'is Love'. If that is true, love is not merely a piece of unscientific illusion; nor is it just a construct of the adolescent imagination, ungrounded in reality. Instead, our love would partake of reality in some very profound manner. That would be very significant. We are used to living with a huge chasm between two worlds that seem diametrically opposed to each other, even in denial of each other: the world of scientific objectivity that matters so much to us, and the world of authentic feeling that matters equally. The reality of a God who himself 'is Love' bridges that chasm. If true, it validates our emotional and sexual life, and challenges us to believe that love is more than just a word.[28]

But secondly, the belief in God the Father as Creator offers us profound confidence in God's loving sovereignty within our own lives and relationships. He is *good*, he is almighty, and he is always 'working together for good with those who love him', in our marriage as in everything else.[29] Psychologist Lawrence Crabb points to such faith as one of the strongest motivators for rekindling a disintegrating relationship.[30] Faith in a loving God's goodness brings us to believe he will not lead us, in so vital a matter, into something totally destructive. In some sense at least, we are in our right place; our marriage is one he has lovingly foreseen, and indeed (unless we entered it without seriously seeking his will) created. ('Like meeting on board a ship; knowing you're bound for a long journey together', it's been said.) God surely desires, then, to provide ways to develop this marriage he has given us into the kind of marriage he would want us to have. So many times this writer has talked to partners who are working through significant relational issues, and in the end they have concluded on an upbeat note with, 'But I'm sure God has brought us together.' 'Three things are essential for a good marriage', said a writer in *His*, 'commitment, commitment, and commitment': a sense of the calling of God is a powerful encouragement that this kind of creative commitment is worthwhile. (It is also a complete response to the pessimists who regard long-term marriage as unrealistic because it assumes that two different people will grow and mature in tandem. Belief in God implies faith that our growth process has been designed precisely to unfold in tandem.)

Related to this is the psychological effect of faith in the biblical teaching on marriage. Jesus taught clearly that divorce was unacceptable – that is, in view of God's supernatural power, no marriage was irretrievable – except in situations of adultery.[31] In a difficult marriage, then, the only way out is forwards. This might seem a stimulus to despair if divorced from its all-important companion, faith in God's absolute goodness. But paired with that, it becomes enormously motivational. Include the possibility of divorce, and the option exists of playing the spectator: 'Well, let's see if she changes over the next months. If not, I can think about getting out.' But if that option doesn't exist, there is no alternative but to make the marriage work. It becomes more 'profitable' to contemplate the difficult actions –

swallowing our pride, forgiving, apologizing – that may in fact change the situation. Again, whether the Bible's marital teaching comes from a real God, and whether it is backed by real supernatural power, can make a huge difference in how we are motivated to act. (It is interesting that Zelda West-Meads of Relate – formerly the National Marriage Guidance Council – reports, 'When people with strong religious convictions encounter problems in their marriage they try harder to resolve them ... Register office marriages are more likely to end in divorce than those conducted in church.'[32])

At this point God's loving calling goes to the heart of the problem expressed by *Generation X* author Douglas Coupland in one of his later novels: 'She says: I'm sorry, but I just stopped being in love. It happened. I woke up and it was gone and it scared me and I felt like I was lying and hollow pretending to be "the wife." And I just can't do it anymore. I love you but I'm not in love.'[33] What is love? 'I love you but I'm not in love.' Which 'love' matters most as foundation for truly fruitful long-term relationship? Taking Jesus' teaching seriously transforms this particular issue. The two 'great commandments' of the Old Testament are both 'You shall love' (God in the first instance, your neighbour as yourself in the second).[34] Thus 'love' in its primary meaning is something we choose to exercise (or not), rather than something we either have or haven't got spurting up inside us. 'Love is a decision', says Gary Smalley; or in Trobisch's words, love is a 'feeling to be learned' and fostered, rather than simply observed. When St Paul writes about marriage, the main thing he wants to tell husbands – no less than three times – is, '*Love* your wives'.[35] Evidently he thinks they can decide to! Christian belief has always been that emotions follow the will; God gives the feelings as we set out to love him and do his will, rather than in advance of our obedience. Counsellors confirm this as a common pattern in marital love too;[36] the issue is finding the power to get the process started. So here again our loss of God will logically have significant results in our relationships.

> Ironically, commitment to marriage as a lifelong 'safe place' can make it a lot easier to handle conflict. 'We never dared to fight', Kathy told me after her live-in relationship broke up. 'Because any conflict might be the one that broke us apart. So I had to cut off any area where we might fight. In the end there was less and less for us to talk about. We never had the security to face conflict openly.'

Faith in marriage as God's lifelong calling transforms it in a fifth way. Very few people get married without intending a serious commitment. But knowing it is truly 'till death us do part', and death alone, takes it onto a different level. It means we are saying: Whatever happens to either of us, with God's grace I will be there for you. If you have an accident or disease that leaves you physically scarred and sexually unattractive, still I will be there. If you have a deep depressive or mental illness, I will be there for you. If for a while we can't seem to work things out, I won't take it as an excuse to find someone else, I will stick with it and you and do everything I can to make things work. If you have a car crash and end up paralysed, I will still be there for you. If someone more attractive comes into my range of vision, still you can trust that I will be there for you only. Because that is how God loves us. In our consumer society, marriage all too easily becomes another 'disposable' – except that, this time, we are what gets thrown away. But that is a result of the banishment of God from our mental horizon. Lifelong marriage in the sight of God is an unlimited commitment to the other.

And this in turn transforms the meaning of sex. If marriage is a growing into total and lifelong oneness, sex is the physical expression and symbol of that oneness; an act of unlimited openness and self-giving, in a context of total mutual commitment, security, and trust. But with the 'death of God', the focus in our culture has moved away from sex as emblem of lifetime commitment – emphasizing self-fulfilment instead,[37] making sure I get my orgasm. (In the process, sex itself seems changed; in novelists like Jay McInerney, its natural context has shifted from the bedroom to the bathroom.) But this too may be self-defeating. Instead of finding a place where there is space and time to learn sexually (and many of us need that), we're back into performance: Was I good? Was his/her last partner better? Will the next one be better? The performance element was clear in a *Mail on Sunday* feature that suggested that 'Few today would marry without knowing how a potential partner shapes up in bed.' They failed, of course, to add 'shapes up in bed outside the security of marriage'. Yet the premarital context has its own peculiarities; it is scarcely a safe guide to what long-term sex together will be like. (The 1993 Janus Survey showed 61% of American women and 59% of men experienced sex as better after marriage.) The 'loss of God' contributes to a shift from sex as expression of totally secure relationship to sex as the unpredictable fee for relationship.

We have raised these issues here primarily in terms of how the loss of the sense of God's calling affects the development and survival of relationships. However, we should also note the fascinating conclusions of two American surveys, including a large study by *Redbook* magazine, that for women

> sexual satisfaction is related significantly to religious belief. With notable consistency, the greater the intensity of a woman's religious convictions, the likelier she is to be satisfied with the sexual pleasures of marriage ... Strongly religious women (over 25) seem to be more responsive ... She is more likely than the non-religious woman to be orgasmic.[38]

This is not something one is likely to read in *Cosmopolitan*, but it raises intriguing questions. More than one factor could be involved; but it seems the loss of God might have implications not only for women's relationships, but also concretely for their sexual experience.

Intimacy and the death of the Son

In a number of ways, then, the reality or absence of God the Father-Creator has major implications for our commitment and motivation in relationships, and hence for whether these last or not. But there is a deeper level for us to explore. Commitment to, or disbelief in, Christ as God the Son can affect enormously our approach to the whole issue of 'What is love in my life?'

Jesus' followers look to the Gospel stories as models of what love means in practice. We look to his life – particularly the way he treats a whole range of diverse and not very loveable individuals – and, most of all, to his death. For Christians, the cross is the ultimately profound moment that defines and brings together all that is at the heart of relationship.

The classic biblical statement comes in St Paul's celebration of sex and spirituality in Ephesians 5. Here, Paul challenges us to understand the deepening oneness of marriage and sex through the ever-deepening oneness of Christ and the Church. Christ's death, where he poured out everything he was for us, is the pattern for our love too, says Paul. ('Husbands, love your wives, *just as* Christ loved the Church and gave himself up for her ... In this same way, husbands ought to love their wives as their own bodies.'[39]) So when a man asks, 'What does it mean for me to really love a woman?', he should look to Christ's creative, total self-giving. And the early church to which Paul wrote knew just what that crucifixion involved: the church's central meal of broken bread and poured-out wine recalled joy that was won only through a body broken and blood shed in hours of agony.[40] This, says Paul, is how far Christ loved a people who had wronged and rejected him: and this is the unconditional, unchanging love that we should seek to embody for our partner. Paul doesn't spell it out further, but the principles of that '*just as*' are, for any husband or lover, frustratingly clear! (Particularly if coupled with Christ's teachings that radical discipleship involves going the second mile for someone who asks you to go one.) There are many other aspects to fruitful relationship; but someone who sets out, creatively and genuinely, to love his woman (or her man) in so total a way, is surely less likely to end with a broken marriage.

But there are several more issues here for the understanding of love. First, there is the assertion that openness, risk-taking, is central to love. To be open to love is to be open to hurt. And that isn't easy. We noted Lasch's words in *The Culture of Narcissism*: 'Both men and women have come to approach personal relations with a heightened appreciation of their emotional risks. Determined to manipulate the emotion of others while protecting themselves against emotional injury, both sexes cultivate a protective shallowness, a cynical detachment.'[41] Jesus' cross is a statement that the risk of pain is inseparable from the experience of love: insofar as I maintain my armour against pain, in some measure I exclude the other person. So faith in the presence and goodness of an active God is vital for love; what empowers our risk-taking, our openness, is faith that all experiences God allows us must ultimately, somehow, be positive. In the gospel's terms, if we are living with God then any experience we face of 'death' must ultimately lead to experience of 'resurrection', because that is the universe's basic principle – even if there is no guarantee when it will be.[42] On that basis, love can risk openness; as St John puts it, 'Perfect love' – in this case, faith in the perfect love of God – 'drives out fear'.[43] It is the opposite of self-protection.

Second, the cross, if we 'believe' (the word is weak) in it, redefines love as pre-eminently self-giving. Love is that condition in which our own interests are not the priority (or, more exactly, are a forgotten issue). Without the cross, that understanding becomes debatable. It is not by accident that the 'loss of God' is associated with the dominance (in America especially) of self-fulfilment therapies arguing precisely the opposite.[44] Lasch's *Culture of Narcissism* again:

> Even when therapists speak of the need for "meaning" and "love", they redefine love and meaning simply as the fulfilment of the patient's emotional requirements. It hardly occurs to them ... to encourage the subject to subordinate his needs and interests to those of others ... "Love" as self-sacrifice or self-abasement, "meaning" as submission to a higher loyalty – these sublimations strike the therapeutic sensibility as intolerably oppressive, offensive to common sense and injurious to personal health and well-being. To liberate humanity from such outmoded ideas of love and duty has become

the mission of the post-Freudian therapies and particularly of their converts and popularizers.[45]

Vitz draws the conclusion for practical relationships:

> The values of selfism are not conducive to the formation and maintenance of permanent personal relationships or to values like duty, patience, and self-sacrifice, which maintain commitment ... With monotonous regularity the selfist literature sides with those values that encourage divorce, breaking up ... in the name of growth, autonomy, and "continuing the flux"

– for example the kind of assertiveness training that emphasizes 'escaping the compassion trap', presenting compassion and assertiveness as inherently contradictory.[46] You pays your money and you takes your choice. Compassion, patience and self-sacrifice are values at the very heart of the universe, if the crucified Jesus is indeed God's Son. But, if he isn't, maybe these things could stunt your growth – though they might maintain your marriage.

A third issue that the cross would make fundamental is that of forgiveness. In any relationship, we are occasionally going to lose control. Anger, carelessness and jealousy are realities; and families break up because of inability to deal with these things. Inability to forgive generates inability to apologize or, indeed, to resolve anything. Besides, many of us bring into marriage a subconscious naïvete; somehow we dream that, right from the start, our partner will be an untiringly creative companion, a patient and sensitive soulmate, an expert and unselfish lover, a flawless manager, a support to our career, and several other wonderful things too. And either the marriage will break, or we must learn to accept, and forgive, our partner as (s)he is.[47] ('A lot of women have to realise they're not marrying their sisters', Philadelphia youth worker Marcia Hopler once remarked to me, 'but people whose socks smell.') The skills of compromise, apology and forgiveness are essential to long-term relationship. But they don't come easily, and they do demand practice; many of us need all the help we can get, and the 'loss of God' removes a vital model and motivation.

For there are other ways of thinking about forgiveness. Novelist Helen Zahavi speaks of 'not just the right to avenge oneself but the duty – a physical, psychological necessity.' The proud Corsican 'vendetta' system, handing grudges down the generations, is an extreme case of this – but its diluted version, 'I don't get mad, I get even', seems widely acceptable. 'In a secular age', writes Blake Morrison, 'Christian notions of atonement, redemption and "turning the other cheek" seem archaic, even craven ... To forgive is to be "soft". It's to let yourself be walked over. You only do it if you're lacking in self-assertion and self-respect.'[48] In Canada, Posterski and Bibbey's[49] authoritative youth surveys reveal a wide diversity of attitudes as to whether forgiveness is a good thing, and show a clear correlation between commitment to the value of forgiveness and commitment to Christian faith. This is not surprising; Christ's cross[50] embodies the overwhelming importance of our forgiveness by God; and the regular celebration of communion is an ongoing reminder of that and of the importance of our learning to forgive. Here again, faith in the cross leads to an understanding of love conducive to lasting relationships.

But what will become the norm as the cross recedes into unreality for us? For Nietzsche, the dynamic of self-sacrifice, apology and forgiveness was precisely one of the things that made Christianity redundant, since the individual's will to power was the only reality. Christian ethics, he declared, was the morality of the weak, revealing no more than an 'inability to take revenge'. 'Never apologize; never explain', was Edith Piaf's watchword. Again, we pays our money and we takes our choice – and the choice will have far-reaching effects.

To all of this we must add the question of empowering. Jesus' teaching is clear that right principles alone are insufficient; indeed, the prime thing they do is clarify our inadequacy to get things right without supernatural help.[51] 'Total self-giving love' is pitifully easy to chatter (or scribble) about; and much more so in the first ardours of romance than in the horse-trading of needs and wants that comes later, especially with the advent of children. Actually noticing, in the heat of the moment, the need to love in the sense Paul describes, and then finding the strength from somewhere to do it – we can imagine a particularly impressive partner succeeding here, but for ourselves it requires a bit of a miracle. The same can be true of finding the strength for self-control, forgiveness, or humility:[52] to be the first to apologize; to back off a demand, knowing your partner knows you are doing so; to be the one who buys the flowers or makes the conciliatory gesture in a clash-situation.

The point cannot be proven, but Christians will insist that here too the 'loss of God' is significantly damaging to relationships. 'Young people have seen thirty years of marital breakdown ... they are afraid to start on a journey which may end in tears', says Jack Dominian. Where then can we find confidence? Jesus offers a response: to be 'born of the Spirit',[53] as his follower, means that the supernatural power of God the Spirit comes within us, empowering us, situation by situation and issue by issue, to live the 'Christ lifestyle' – and increasingly so, as (or if) he fills and transforms our minds. Love, self-control, gentleness and humility are 'fruits of the Spirit', adds St Paul.[54] To have the Spirit, Christians would testify, is not to become an effortless relational maestro, but rather to be offered a growing empowering for getting it right – in creativity, mutual forgiveness, perseverance, communication, devotion.

None of this is to say that faith in God is essential to a good marriage. It obviously isn't (though Christians will insist that they themselves would – or do – make a much worse mess of their own relationships if God were out of the picture). Nor is it to claim that earlier cultures generally had better relationships than we do; anyway our predecessors lived with the confusion of attitudes to love that Bloom describes. Our point is rather that – as any reader of *Cosmo* or *Marie Claire* will know – we clearly have problems in making our relationships work; and the loss of faith in God's calling, and the 'disappearance of the cross', remove a number of very powerful forces for healthy relationship that we can ill afford to spare.

Love in a cold season

But as the Americans say: 'Deal with it.' We now know there was no 'divine hand' overruling our path through the mating game; and that, whatever happened on Calvary, it wasn't the act of total, atoning, self-giving love that the Bible said, and it has no 'authoritative' status for us. So how shall we determine what it really means to love?

'His love of France is matched only by his love of women', said the adverts for a TV drama on a wartime resistance fighter. Can we speak that way? Is a 'great lover' someone who can envisage romancing a whole sequence of women, one tasted and cast aside after another? Clearly yes, for whatever adman designed the slogan. The *Love Story* version, 'Love means never having to say you're sorry', is self-evidently stupid. But is 'love' a bargain where both partners get what they want in care and fulfilment? Possibly; but then what happens when the fulfilment doesn't materialize? The husband is under work-pressure, the wife is pregnant, one partner has severe depression, 'fulfilment' is unavailable: is love, by definition, dead (and therefore replaceable)? Why – and how – should we work at rekindling it? Does the 'needs'/'rights' approach inevitably emphasize not what we give but what we get – or use, consume – and collapse when the getting stops? In that case, has love been swallowed up in narcissism – or were we always merely bargaining across a counter? Setting aside Jesus, how should we find our definition of love? Or do we each make our own? Maybe one of the biggest difficulties in many decaying relationships comes because the two partners mean different things by 'love', and have different expectations.

> Freddie Mercury: 'I've had more lovers than Elizabeth Taylor. I try to hold back when I'm attracted to someone but I just can't control love. It runs riot.' He died of AIDS.

More and more, the term begins to disappear. As we noted in Chapter 2, certain words like 'joy' and 'wisdom' seem to be falling out of use with the deepening loss of God. Perhaps 'love' is going the same way

– except in songs that we know are 'sentimental', that is, unreal. In a recent TV programme discussing the experience of adultery, almost none of the participants used the 'love' word. Perhaps, to them, it was too much to hope for. And perhaps we wonder, deep down, if 'love' isn't a word belonging with the dramatic but immature passions of teen infatuation. Realism, maturity, means thinking more in terms of 'steady relationships' that – for the time being – offer good contexts for fulfilling both parties' needs ...

When we had a God we had a reason to celebrate the reality of love. But that is past. Critics such as J.B. Broadbent have noted that love poetry, as a literary form, can die out, and maybe it is doing so now. In the novel, writes Bloom, 'There have been hardly any great novelists of love for almost a century.' R.B. Kitaj remarked in 1994, 'It occurs to me that men and women are rarely seen together in paintings any more. At least, they are not depicted together in heterosexual relationship in the work of the dozen or so very well-known painters I most admire.'[55] Does our culture have a basis for talking about, believing in, 'love' any more? Or is love dying with the death of God? And if our love-relationships were the prime shelter (and maybe goal) left us in the darkness, and they too disintegrate – what then?

A farewell to love

In the classic love song 'The Lady in Red', Chris de Burgh describes the moment when he suddenly realized how blind he had become to his wife's beauty: her hair, her dress, her eyes. It's an emotional cry of joyful affection, and probably de Burgh's most famous track.

It got a rough ride, however, at the hands of *Guardian* journalist Desmond Christy. Christy coupled his attack on de Burgh's song with a crack at the Catholic church's attitudes to love and sex (which haven't been too biblically-based, and made a fairly easy target). He then added cynically:

What amuses me – a little – about the Church's attitude to pop music is that the Christian churches and rock stars are often in the same business – that is, the idealisation of love … It isn't just a feeling to them. It's Real … So when you marry you have to promise that it's until one of the partners dies. And from the little country and western I hear, it is expected that a woman put up with her man no matter how late he comes home. She must stand by her man … One of the worst culprits was, in some of his moods, Shakespeare. "Love is not love/Which alters when it alteration finds" … There is, then, a huge pressure of culture to regard love as some supreme force, probably God-given even though experience shows the opposite …[56]

Yet perhaps – just perhaps – the intuitions of Shakespeare, country music, Chris de Burgh and Christianity were right? That love is 'real', it isn't 'just a feeling'? That real marriage is precisely about the security, the sheer relaxation, of emotional and sexual commitment that lasts till death us do part? That the whole point may be that there is a place somewhere where we will still be loved, still stood by, no matter what? Where we are `fixed in the certainty of love unchanging', in Eliot's evocative phrase?

Unfortunately, Christy has the facts on his side. Shakespeare is dead, and so is God, so logically `just a feeling' is all we are left with – that, and perhaps a piece of paper. We may not want to believe it; Camus, one of the central voices of 'post-God' modernity, presents Marie in *The Outsider* reacting as most of us will …

Marie came that evening and asked me if I'd marry her. I said I didn't mind; if she was keen on it, we'd get married.

Then she asked me again if I loved her. I replied, much as before, that her question meant nothing or next to nothing – but I supposed I didn't.

"If that's how you feel," she said, "why marry me?"

I explained that it had no importance really, but, if it would give her pleasure, we could get married right away. I pointed out that, anyway, the suggestion came from her, not me; as for me, I'd merely said, "Yes" …

She kept silent after that, staring at me in a curious way.[57]

'This isn't what the movies tell you' indeed, but these might well seem the facts of the case. The death of God logically leaves us with the experience, says Christy, that love is not 'some supreme force, probably God-given'. We can more realistically redefine it in terms of mutual satisfaction of needs; in which case, as Christy concluded, 'There is no need to go on loving when the love isn't returned'.

And, statistically, that's quite likely to happen. 'Loving isn't easy' ('Hell is other people' – Sartre, and a currently chic T-shirt). Stress, role conflict, financial problems, overwork, young children, immaturity, carelessness in communication, over-familiarity and neglect: many relationships go through – or come to – a moment when 'love' seems no longer there, on one side or both. The divorce rate is already one in three in a country like Britain. With the 'death of God' removing most of the supports discussed above, that rate should rise further.

But then comes the next acceleration to the cycle: 'As any counsellor can tell you, the most important factor in your marital happiness is what models you have had in your parents, and how you are reacting to them.'[58] Parental and grand-parental marriages that terminate in divorce will very probably be replicated in the next generation; the hurt creates a deep assumption that marriages can't be expected to last, which in turn affects the children's commitment to making their own marriages work – or even to taking such a step at all.

'If as a child your parents divorced', writes Zelda West-Meads of Relate,

> this can affect your adult relationships. Cohabitation can seem a solution. You long for intimacy and commitment to repair the damage done to your own emotional world, but you fear giving it as you may end up being hurt again. People with that experience will often opt for live-in relationships.[59]

But cohabitation accelerates the process yet further. West-Meads was commenting on a British government survey showing that couples who live together before marriage are up to 60% more likely to divorce than those who do not; more recent figures show that married couples are more than five times as likely to stay together after ten years, compared with cohabitees. The massive 1994 survey funded by the Wellcome Trust revealed that people cohabiting were far more likely than married people to have multiple sexual partners (one in seven cohabiting men as against one in twenty married; one in twelve cohabiting women as against one in fifty married). Further, 'Cohabitation does not seem to exert any strong influence on monogamy – indeed [astonishingly], cohabiting men were *more* likely to report concurrent relationships than single men.'[60] Domestic violence affects 6.4% of female cohabitees, compared with 2.7% of married women. A Swedish survey showed cohabiting couples to be six times more likely to break up than married couples. It isn't just marriage, but partnership in general, that seems to be breaking down; and increased cohabitation merely deepens a cycle of breakdown of intimacy that will now take a miracle to halt.

The social consequences of this cycle are all around us.[61] Journalist Polly Toynbee (who seems happier about it than most) has termed it 'an astonishing social revolution ... more far-reaching than any political revolution ever could be'. In education, any teacher will confirm that the pupils who most overburden the system are those coping with the hurts from broken family backgrounds. The plight of a health service increasingly short of resources is worsened by unavoidable commitment of resources to sexually-transmitted diseases that would be greatly reduced if relationships were more monogamous.[62]

But it is individuals who handle the deepest results of loneliness after relational break-up in our answerphone-and-intercom society. Divorced or separated people are four times as likely as married people to need psychiatric help (single people are only twice as likely); married people also adjust better to illness or disability.[63] In particular, behind the statistics lie enormous pressure and dehumanization for single mothers, particularly when illness hits their family, and particularly in a country like Britain still poor at ensuring equal pay for women. And matters get worse as the cycle accelerates. 'Women have always got pregnant', said one man interviewed by the *Independent on Sunday*, 'the problem now is that the men leave them. With the easing of moral restrictions, they just don't hang around very long.' Yet surveys show, too, that six years after divorce the majority of ex-husbands wish they had never let it happen; while further still down the road we see the ever-increasing host of aging divorcees battling through life on their own. (Many people remarry after divorce, but the breakdown rate for second marriages is even higher than for first marriages – about 50%).[64]

> After God, what is love? 'Bonk', 'shag' and 'screw' fit what we think about sex more accurately, in their gruff, mechanical character, than the strange, older phrase 'making love', or the biblical 'know'.
>
> Italian film director Federico Fellini: 'Women are presented on television ... as if they are something to eat ... They are treated the same way as hamburgers or, for that matter, nappies or stain-removers ... A young boy makes love standing on a street-corner, munching a pizza, a tin of beer in his hand, stereophones over his ears and his other hand on the girl's backside. And what used to take us a week takes him a quarter of an hour to finish everything – he has had a drink, something to eat, he has made love and is ready to jump back on his motorbike.'
>
> Andy Warhol: 'Brigitte Bardot was one of the first women to be really modern and treat men like love objects, buying them and discarding them. I like that.'

But the ones who really pick up the bill are the children. 'All the available evidence suggests that divorce makes children extremely unhappy even where the father has been very distant, has sexually abused the children or has been violent to their mother', says Penelope Leach in *Baby and Child*.[65] In Germany, Professor Joest Martinus of Munich's Max Planck Institute observes that 'Children of divorced parents suffer particularly serious damage in their social development', finding it 'extremely difficult to integrate into a community or to develop lasting relationships with a partner'. And they come 'into contact with the law a lot more often than children from intact families ... 5% of all children in the Federal Republic of Germany suffer from some kind of mental disturbance; in contrast, 35% of the children from broken homes suffer from such disturbances.'[66] In Canada, a study of 4,500 students by Montreal University's Jean-Francois Saucier showed teenagers from divorced families to be less confident about their lives and more likely to have psychological problems causing them to seek professional help.[67]

> 'I asked the kids of Highgate Wood School what was the thing that scared them most and they said, something happening to my mum and dad. My parents splitting up. What was the most important thing in their lives? "My parents, family. Being wanted. Family."'
>
> –Linda Grant[68]

In Britain, a 1994 study funded by the Rowntree Trust, comparing families that divorced with similar troubled households that stayed together, found children even in conflict-ridden but intact families to be far better off in terms of health, schoolwork, self-esteem and friendships than those whose parents divorced. Dr John Tripp of Exeter told a BBC *Panorama* interviewer,

> What the study has shown us, which is surprising, is it's the loss of a parent which is much more significant than other factors, such as conflict ... Our data suggests that's a very minor effect compared with when a parent leaves a home. In almost all cases the children would have preferred the parents to stay together.[69]

Five years after divorce, only one child in ten enjoys a warm relationship with the absent parent (and one in four never accept their parent's replacement partner).[70] A 1997 National Family Mediation group survey of 11,400 British children showed that children of divorced parents did less well both economically and socially.[71] Eighty-six per cent of teenage suicides happen in fatherless families. As regards the boys, respected psychiatrist Anthony Clare argues that the presence of a father is central for a healthy male growth process, and the lack of fathers is strongly linked to 'spiralling' young male violence: 'Poor parenting and detachment, a destructive or absent father, and you end up with a damaged, aggressive male with a massive sense of shame, a desperate fear of weakness and an entrenched sense of injustice.'[72] Baby battering and sexual abuse are far more widespread in families without two natural parents; such homes accounted for almost two thirds of the 6,000 cases catalogued by the National Society for the Prevention of Cruelty to Children between 1983 and 1987, although they make up only a minority of families with children under sixteen, while a Canadian study by Martin Daly and Margo Wilson showed that children under two were 70 times more likely to be killed by step-parents than by natural parents.[73] The accelerating cycle of divorce also swells the ranks of the next generation of violent child abusers. Sixty per cent of sexually abusing fathers had divorced parents; a stepfather from such a background can be one of the biggest dangers a young woman can encounter.

And so the cycle continues. Dr Sebastian Kraemer of the Tavistock Clinic told an interviewer on the same *Panorama* programme, 'There's a collective wish not to look at children's pain – because we would really need to have a social revolution in our attitudes if we took it seriously.' He's right, of course: too many people in the media feel too much guilt and pain themselves to be able to face the issues.[74]

The *Independent on Sunday* is, to my mind, Britain's most intelligent liberal newspaper. So we can get some idea of the consensus on this issue from the following sentences of an *IoS* editorial:

This is a complex subject, which is not easily debated in the age of the sound-bite. Suggest that children are better off with two parents and you will be accused of insulting single parents. But it is not an insult to single parents to argue that, because bringing up children is labour-intensive and emotionally draining, two pairs of hands will find it easier than one ... The effects of divorce and single parenting are, according to research on both sides of the Atlantic, devastating and long-lasting; on average, the children perform worse at school, get into more trouble with the police, suffer more mental illness and earn less when they grow up. Class and poverty are part of the explanation, but not the whole.

The statistics are inescapable; and behind them lies a colossal quantity of individual hurt. Our broken relationships matter enormously. But when they are causing so much pain, we must surely look again at anything that could help them work. Our contemporary 'death of love' seems linked in several ways to the 'death of God'. We are paying a high price; so whether we were wise to do so – whether God, and the support he could provide for love, really is 'dead' – cannot be a trivial question. It may underlie much of our pain; for ex-partners, and especially their children, who might not have lost their relationships if they could have rediscovered faith in God's good calling; if they could have found fresh, life-giving meanings for love in Jesus; or if, indeed, they could even have found supernatural strength to recreate love, empower forgiveness and apology, discern what is possible, energize creativity and affection.

> 'I used to be intrigued by things that ended relationships. Now I am most fascinated by what allows them to continue.'
>
> –Erica Jong

Evidently it matters greatly whether these things are realities or not. The 'loss of God' is far from being the only explanation for our hurts. But the truth of God offers enough healing to our intimacy for a casual ignorance of whether he is real or not to seem small-minded and costly.

Does it really have to be that way?

In summary…

'All we need is love.' In our post-God culture, relationships and intimacy are enormously important to us. But because of the 'loss of God', the meaning, attainability, and even existence of love have grown highly problematic. As we re-examine God's Fatherhood and Jesus' cross, we see numerous aspects that could help empower our relationships to survive and flourish … except we don't believe in them any more.

But that becomes serious when intimacy is (for many of us) the 'final shelter', often the most meaningful area in our lives … and yet it 'doesn't work'. Looking more widely, our relational breakdown is causing widespread social damage – and profound, far-reaching personal pain.

And here we must pause to look back at the enormous significance of our relational crisis for the issues we considered in earlier chapters. For many of us in western culture after the death of God, our identity and self-worth have found their prime underpinning in loving relationships. So too, after the loss of God, may purpose and desire. Loving relationships may also be the final shelter for our ethics.

But love isn't working. The trend of failed relationships in the west cuts, therefore, at the very heart of our futures. It exacerbates the identity crisis, and the purpose crisis; and it points us beyond an attempted ethics based on the family, out into the void …

In short, the loss of God has pointed to alienation on an epidemic scale. Nietzsche's question: Has it not grown colder?

Notes

1. D.H. Lawrence, *Women in Love*, p. 64.
2. This is the final letter of vol. III of *The Letters of D.H. Lawrence*, ed. James T. Boulton and Andrew Robertson.
3. Lasch, *Narcissism*, p. 320; Bloom, *Love and Friendship*, p. 14.

4. 1 Corinthians 13:4,5,7.

5. John 13:34–35; Ephesians 5:2,25–33.

6. *SAS Scanorama*, Feb. 1987, p. 70.

7. Alan MacDonald, *Films in Close-Up*, p. 51.

8. *Independent on Sunday*, 9 February 1997.

9. William Barrett, *Death of the Soul*, p. xiii.

10. Kurt Vonnegut, *Cat's Cradle*, pp. 130–32.

11. Bloom, *Love and Friendship*, pp. 13–14, 19–20.

12. Bloom, *Love and Friendship*, p. 27. Christianity does not deny the huge presence of this aspect of sexuality. Indeed, Genesis 3 presents the replacement of ideal sexuality by a dialectic of desire and domination as one of the key consequences of the break in relationship between God and humanity at the Fall (Genesis 3:16).

13. Bloom, *Love and Friendship*, p. 28.

14. Cf., for example, the astonishingly negative mindset recommended for those in relationships by Polly Toynbee in the *Independent on Sunday*, 2 Apr. 1995: 'Face up to the prevalence – and thus the probability – of divorce and separation; and learn to separate elegantly, without fighting.' Rather than, say, learning to work doubly hard at marriage-building.

15. Bloom, *Love and Friendship*, pp. 13–14. The safety issue is underlined by the increasing prevalence of date rape: Patterson and Kim found that 20% of American women reported that they had experienced being raped by their dates (the figure rose to 37% within the gay/bisexual community) (Patterson and Kim, *The Day America*, pp. 7, 130). One might add that, in a culture shaped by postmodernism's scepticism about love and its belief that domination is the final reality of all human social interaction, the rise of date rape is scarcely surprising.

16. Herbert Hendin, *The Age of Sensation*, quoted in Vitz, *Psychology*, pp. 116–17. Hendin's book was a survey of several hundred college-age young people. A telling (if welcome) side-effect of this emotional disengagement from romance, he adds, is the decline in student suicides over heterosexual love affairs – coming at a time when overall college-age suicide has increased. Vitz comments that 'Today's students resist letting the opposite sex mean too much to them, and only homosexual men and women seem to interpret failed love relationships as significant enough to touch off a suicide attempt.' In general, concludes Hendin, 'Men seem to want to give women less and less, while women increasingly see demands men make as inherently

demeaning ... The scale of value against which both sexes now tend to measure everything is solitary gratification.'

17. Lasch, *Narcissism*, p. 330. Elsewhere he notes, 'The progressive ideology of "nonbinding commitments" and "cool sex" makes a virtue of emotional disengagement, while purporting to criticize the depersonalization of sex' (p. 339).

18. Space doesn't allow us to explore the questions of loneliness and inability to make lasting friendships, which also seem major contemporary issues. Several of the 'skills', or principles, that we shall look at in the following section are relevant to friendship as well as to romantic and sexual/marital love – for example, self-giving, openness, forgiveness, and commitment. (In this connection it was striking to see Alex Comfort, author of the 'swinger's Bible', *The Joy of Sex*, musing in a recent interview, 'I haven't got any friends. Not many.')

19. Bloom, *Love and Friendship*, p. 433.

20. Bloom, *Love and Friendship*, p. 75, drawing on Arthur Melzer, *The Natural Goodness of Man: On the System of Rousseau's Thought*. A key aspect of Romanticism is the way it often enthrones subjective sincerity in the place of objective faith. Keats, for example: 'I am certain of nothing but of the holiness of the heart's affections and the truth of imagination.'

21. Bloom, *Love and Friendship*, p. 151.

22. Bloom, *Love and Friendship*, pp. 112–13.

23. Bloom, *Love and Friendship*, p. 209.

24. Bloom, *Love and Friendship*, pp. 259–60. 'The prevailing mood was disappointment ... The search for the beautiful ended in the triumph of the ugly ... Novels, the privileged form of Romantic communication, in the twentieth century ceased to celebrate love ... An angry "I told you so" announced the dashing of Romantic foolishness. The reality is that all the beautiful talk exists only for the sake of seducing others and oneself.'

25. Cf. F. Schaeffer, *The God Who is There*; also his *Escape from Reason*.

26. Cf. Bloom, *Love and Friendship*, p. 260.

27. Bloom, *Love and Friendship*, p. 270. 'Shakespeare seems to have thought that Christianity effected a deepening of women and a new sensitivity of men to them' (p. 391).

28. An important aspect of Christian faith is that it holds God to be a Trinity, three Persons in one eternal Godhead united in mutual

love. If he were not so, then the only kind of love that could have existed before the world would have been self-love. But as a result, says Schaeffer, we can say that human love 'is not a product of chance ... Though I am very far from plumbing all its depths when applied to God Himself, yet the word love and the reality of love when Christ spoke of the Father loving Him before the foundation of the world, has true meaning for me.' (*The God Who is There*, pp. 97–99.) In contrast, in many forms of eastern religion 'God' is not truly personal; nor, consequently, is the human person, the potential object of affection, ultimately 'real' either. And this has implications for the meaning of love. For Gautama Buddha, for example, true wisdom ultimately involved renouncing his wife and family to meditate in solitude.

29. Romans 8:28.

30. Lawrence Crabb, *The Marriage Builder*, ch. 7. Personally, I have found this idea – that strength for relationship-building, and particularly for forgiveness, come from our assurance of the long-term goodness of God – to be very helpful in other relational situations too.

31. Matthew 5:32. Obviously space does not permit us to go into the complexities here, such as the role of separation in a situation of abuse.

32. A related point was made by a Moscow psychotherapist in *Moskovskii Komsomolyets* in a 1986 discussion of Moscow's 50% divorce rate: 'There is no fear before God or before people ... The external mechanism for keeping families together has weakened.'

33. Coupland, *Life After God*, p. 152. Miriam Stoppard wrote similarly in *TV Times* about *Coronation Street*'s Deirdre Barlow: 'If you don't love [someone] any more, it won't work. You can't recreate love.'

34. Jesus' comment in Matthew 22:35–40.

35. Ephesians 5:25,28,33.

36. See, for example, Crabb's *Marriage Builder*, and Gary Smalley, *Love is a Decision*. A number of other points in this section derive from a seminar given by Nigel Lee of the Universities and Colleges Christian Fellowship.

37. Cf. Henri Nouwen, in his book *Intimacy*: 'When the physical encounter of men and women in the intimate act of intercourse is not an expression of their total availability to each other, [it] ... is still part of the taking structure. It means "I want you now but not

tomorrow. I want something from you, but I don't want *you*'"
(excerpted in *Seeds*, p. 74).

38. Robert J. Levin and Amy Levin, 'Sexual Pleasure: The Surprising Preferences in 100,000 Women', *Redbook*, Sept. 1970, pp. 52–53; quoted in Tim LaHaye, *The Act of Marriage*, p. 9. (Robert Levin co-authored *The Pleasure Bond* with leading sexologists Masters and Johnson.) LaHaye gives details of his own survey in ch. 12 (particularly pp. 211–12, 227–28), claiming that strongly Christian women in their twenties reported a higher figure of orgasmic satisfaction than any survey of the overall population that he had access to.

39. This is part of a much longer passage. Besides illustrating Christian sexuality from spirituality, Paul is also doing the reverse – illustrating Christ's relationship to the collective organism ('his Body') of his people by comparing it to bridegroom and bride.

40. 1 Corinthians 11:23–26.

41. Lasch, *Narcissism*, p. 330.

42. Once again blind Cornish poet Jack Clemo provides an enormously moving affirmation as he describes his own love affair in these terms in *The Invading Gospel*.

43. 1 John 4:18.

44. Vitz's useful study *Psychology as Religion* documents the extent to which key figures in the 'selfist' or 'human potential' movement, such as Carl Rogers and Erich Fromm, were reacting strongly against Christian faith.

45. Lasch, *Narcissism*, pp. 42–43.

46. Vitz, *Psychology*, pp. 81, 27.

47. Here the presence or absence of God is again important. The Christian relationship is designed to be a triad: because my wife relates not only to me but also to a God who does not share my inadequacies, our emotional 'eggs are not all in one basket'! – and accepting the partner's insufficiencies is easier.

48. *Independent on Sunday*, 3 May 1998.

49. Cf. Don Posterski, *Friendship*, pp. 33–34.

50. Other belief-systems can have a different effect. Nation of Islam leader Leo Muhammad rebuked his fellow-Muslims, 'You talk about loving everybody, but the holy Quran don't talk that language.' Christianity had taught forgiveness and turning the other cheek, he added, but Islam says 'You smack my cheek, I kick all

four of yours.' A Muslim leader made an almost identical comment after ethnic conflict in the Crimea.

51. This is St Paul's point in Galatians 3:24, and in the flow of thought from his description of failure to live aright in Romans 7 to the presentation of the power of the Spirit in Romans 8.

52. Humility itself is not a universal, but a virtue recognized within a Christian context – particularly as a reflection of Jesus (cf. Philippians 2:5–8). Classical Greeks, in contrast, despised it (cf. John Stott, *God's New Society: The Message of Ephesians*, p. 148), as did Nietzsche.

53. One of Jesus' ways of describing what is involved in 'believing in' him, John 3:8,16.

54. Galatians 5:22–23.

55. On the homosexual side, Francis Bacon remarked of his own art that 'Most couplings are violent, more or less.'

56. *Guardian*, 20 June 1989.

57. Albert Camus, *The Outsider*, pp. 48–49.

58. Doug Stewart, writing in the IFES magazine *In Touch*, Oct. 1988, p. 3.

59. Kevin Ford cites clinical psychologist Paul Osterhaus on America's 'Generation X': 'An entire generation grew up lacking the skills of intimacy, feeling wary in relationships, approaching each other hesitantly, defensively and with little intention of making any lasting commitments' (in *Jesus for a New Generation*, p. 159). Alongside that may be set the following summary of distinguishing marks of the present Canadian student generation, from a seminar convened by InterVarsity Christian Fellowship: a lack of security caused by lack of solid relationships, both parents working in stressed environments, and the increasing incidence of child abuse; leading to a longing for intimacy matched by a fear of intimacy and entrapment, resulting in turn in a pattern of brief, unsatisfactory relationships; and, growing within that, a hardening distrust and a deep-rooted anger.

60. Kaye Wellings et al., *Sexual Behaviour in Britain*, summarized in *Independent on Sunday*, 16 and 23 Jan. 1994.

61. Relate chairman Ed Straw has suggested that public expenditure payments in Britain arising from broken homes amount to £4 billion a year.

62. AIDS, herpes, and other sexually transmitted diseases will obviously be drastically limited to the extent that there is genuine and

widespread belief that sex belongs within a lifelong, exclusive relationship.

63. Patrick Dixon, *The Rising Price of Love*, pp. 34–35.

64. There is much more to be said about the social impact of the 'sexual revolution'; for example about the increase in childlessness directly related to the spread of sexually-transmitted pelvic inflammatory disease, the commonest cause of infertility. Cf. ch. 4 of Dixon, *Price of Love*. Dixon's study is an outstanding and highly thought-provoking treatment of the social and (massive) medical consequences of the shift away from Christian sex ethics. He also documents in great detail the research findings on the effects of marriage breakdown on children (ch. 6); and the causative link with poverty, and increased rates of criminality, in the children involved (ch. 7).

65. Penelope Leach, *Baby and Child*, p. 279.

66. *Idea*, 18 Aug. 1980.

67. *USA Today*, 12 Oct. 1984. Asked how successful they thought they would be in life, students rated their prospects from a low of 1 to a high of 7. Girls from divorced families rated their prospects lowest (4.14), followed by boys from divorced families (4.31), then boys from widowed families (4.46), girls from intact families (4.49), girls from widowed families (4.56), and boys from intact families (4.66).

68. Quoted in Phillips, *Prizes*, p. 249.

69. Cf. Monica Cockett and John Tripp, *The Exeter Family Study: Family Breakdown and its Impact on Children*.

70. Dixon, *Price of Love*, p. 131. Indeed, child survivors of divorce become more likely to lose contact with *both* parents (p. 132). Also, 44% of those with a step-parent at 16 had left home three years later, compared to just 27% having both parents at home; and 25% of those under 18 who left through domestic tension then became homeless (p. 144).

71. Fred Catherwood, in *It Can Be Done*, describes the Stepping Stone Project for job-seekers in East Belfast and how they added a children's homework club to their activities designed to help unemployment, sensing that many single parents had all too little time to help their children. But when the homework issue was tackled, there was a marked effect on children's attention-span in school, and their general educational progress (p. 28). There are inevitable limits to what the normal single parent can do.

72. 'Is there any way we can pull back from spiralling violence in the home, in the cities, in school ...? Evidence, both scientific and anecdotal, suggests that fathers – male role models – may hold the key', he concludes (*Independent on Sunday*, 23 July 2000). By their presence or their absence, we might add – that is, male violence may be an increasing part of the bill our culture has to pay for our inability to help our marriages last.

73. Studies from Britain and America confirm the pattern. A step-relationship is, Daly and Wilson conclude, 'the single most important risk factor for severe child maltreatment yet discovered'. However, a 1994 study also showed that children were 20 times more likely to face abuse if their natural parents were cohabiting rather than married (Phillips, *Prizes*, p. 240).

74. Former *Guardian* journalist Melanie Phillips describes the hostility evoked among critics she knew personally by the remarks about family life in her book *All Must Have Prizes*: 'It was almost impossible to discuss this issue in the way other topics were debated ... More and more apparently "neutral" commentators were personally compromised. Ostensibly arguing about policy, my critics almost invariably were disguising expressions of their own personal pain, defiance or guilt' (p. xxii). She gives an interesting example on p. 248.

6

'one by one our gods have failed us'

Can we do without God in the twenty-first century?

At the end of the millennium, our western culture feels, as Thomas Hardy suggested, like a cemetery of dreams. And the dreams have died at a moment of global environmental crisis, when we need vision to motivate us for change more than ever before.

It wasn't always so. For centuries Europe saw a 'dialogue of visions' as to the nature of life, truth and meaning. We inherit that debate; but what marks our own time is that the dialogue has ground to a halt – not because it has been resolved, but because we have seemingly run out of ideas.

As we said earlier, this book is a resource with topical modules that different readers may find fruitful or prefer to skip; what follows here is a thought-experiment, a speculative chapter. Some readers less interested in history may prefer to move on to p. 267 ('From dream to dream'), where we focus on more recent politics and rock'n'roll. But, at the start of a millennium, it's good to grasp how we got to where we are. To understand our postmodern west, we need to understand what we've inherited.

The story that follows isn't offered as infallible. But isn't it roughly what happened?

The long road out

It's not easy to make sense of history. But the Dutch philosopher Dooyeweerd[1] offers a helpful way of bringing together our understandings of the past.

We can re-express it like this: In each era since we turned away from the Bible's God, our culture has been shaped by one or more 'god-substitutes'. These aren't gods that we actually 'worship', but they're the next thing to it. They're the things that 'matter most' to us, the principles that dominate our lives, determining our sense of what's important and the sources we look to for truth and meaning, for the understanding of right and wrong. Our culture's story is, among other things, the history of successive 'god-substitutes', and of how well they 'reign' as our gods. One after another they hold this role, until their inadequacies become obvious; then we lose faith in them, they are replaced by a different 'god', and the story begins again.[2]

It's a fruitful way of thinking, focusing our attention on what matters most for the hearts, minds and imaginations of an era. It's one an atheist or Christian can be equally comfortable with.[3] Let's give it a try.

Our long 'succession of gods' can be illustrated from Britain's arts and literature. When an artist writes a poem or a novel, she has to decide what to write about. That is, to choose what is worth celebrating: what is most significant in the world, what is most worthy of record.[4] So may we see the story of our art as a series of judgements as to what really matters? That could chart for us the 'gods' we've used to replace the Father we no longer believe in.

The seventeenth century is a good place to begin: that crucial period when the Bible first became widely available to ordinary people, resulting in a joyous, Europe-wide rediscovery of individual faith. Of course, the Reformation was a muddled amalgam of political, economic and religious factors, with religious banners masking loyalties of many kinds. Yet still it was a crucial historical moment, when the 'nearness of God' – God relating directly to us as individuals, rather than via a cumbersome and dubious religious structure – suddenly became vital to Europe's consciousness. With the liberation of the biblical text, each individual's response to God was seen to stand at the heart of existence. The individual received a significance that was dramatically new.

Such a change of consciousness had massive repercussions. For example, in the growth of democracy: if God reveals his ways to individuals, not just to the authorities, and if the most important thing in the world is our individual response, then that has political implications; our own views have significance just as much as those of the authorities. Of course the Reformation left British politics a long way from universal suffrage; but the link between the rise of Protestantism and the rise of parliamentary democracy is not coincidental. There were implications for art as well. As Dooyeweerd's fellow-Dutchman Hans Rookmaaker points out, in the painting of this period we see a marked shift in what is thought to be worth depicting. Where earlier painters had chosen to paint the saints or the heroes of Greek legend, now the ordinary individual seemed worth celebrating. Artists in the Protestant culture of Holland like Jan Steen, or indeed Rembrandt[5], become concerned to paint realistic scenes of ordinary people going about their ordinary lives. They were working within a culture that grasped that God was deeply interested in ordinary people, not just in heroes and saints.[6]

And when we look at the literature of this period, don't we see that same re-valuing of the ordinary person? We find Christian poets like Donne, Herbert or Marvell, writing about love or worship as they feel to ordinary people. It is in the Reformation context, too, that the novel arises – perhaps the branch of literature pre-eminently interested in the development of the ordinary individual. The English novel may be said to emerge with the radical Baptist preacher John Bunyan, then more clearly with Daniel Defoe (also beginning clearly from a Protestant background, e.g. in *Robinson Crusoe*).[7] The clarity of the sense of the biblical God at the heart of the Reformation world-view affected their politics, their painting, their literature – it mattered what God they worshipped.

Today, postmodernity has subverted much of this. We saw in Chapter 1 how our loss of the Reformation confidence in individuality has implications for democracy; we saw in Chapter 2 how our loss of confidence in any direction or 'shape' to individual life has (among other things) eroded the feasibility of the novel. To be westerners is to be great-grandchildren of the God-centred Reformers; but it is also to be heirs to the dialogue that has happened since.

For in the late seventeenth century, the Reformation world-view was replaced by other ways of thinking. Why? Was it because of fatal contradictions in the thinking of too many 'Christians'? – for example in their failure to take seriously Christ's apparent outlawing of force?[8] They taught, indeed, that personal faith was all-important, and this emphasis on individual choice implied diversity; yet many sought to impose a state church into which all were coerced by law, and were even willing to use the sword to further their religion. Too often, the Reformation was simply incomplete. It was a paradox as brutal as an Ulster 'Protestant' carrying a Bible saying 'Love your enemy' yet hating his 'Fenian' neighbour; and it could lead only to conflict worsened by passionate conviction. It is true that the bloody Civil War in England and the Thirty Years' War on the Continent were at least as much about new political forces and nation-states consolidating their power as about doctrinal disagreements.[9] But did the long years of conflict under religious banners leave a climate of weariness with anything approaching a clear religious stance? At any rate, by around 1680 there came a reaction against much that the Reformation had stood for, with the period we call the Enlightenment.

This, we might say, was the west's first major attempt at a 'god-substitute', centring its culture on faith in 'natural' human reason, rather than faith in divine revelation.[10] Christians insisted that unaided human reason, being part of a broken world, has a fundamental problem in perceiving ultimate truth.[11] Enlightenment thinkers tended to deny the problem; natural human rationality, for them, took the place of a 'nearby' God, and was thoroughly trustworthy as the pointer towards a new dawn of civilization.[12] ('We hold these truths to be self-evident', the starting-point of the American Declaration of Independence, is a quintessentially Enlightenment statement.[13]) We see this optimism in much of the work of Pope, perhaps the most important English poet of the early eighteenth century; a similar easy confidence marks a novelist like Fielding.[14]

But soon there began to be bad dreams as to whether this was enough to live by. At the end even of Pope's *Dunciad*, a nightmare of chaos overwhelms human society, and the closing words are 'universal darkness buries all': instead of the clarity of human rationality, the night of Dulness falls on humanity. The terrible final book of Swift's *Gulliver's Travels* offers a parallel nightmare: human beings, devoid of true reason, are merely animals wallowing in the mud. In both these masterpieces we sense a shared fear: what if reason is not enough? What if humanity will not be governed by it? The anarchic brutality of the world depicted by Hogarth, or by Smollett, undermined Pope's easy confidence that 'Whatever is, is right'.[15] And as the century continues we find writers sensing that rationality isn't enough (see *Tristram Shandy*), and looking elsewhere for different principles or values around which to orient what they depict: the 'sentimental movement', rediscovering the value of feeling (Mackenzie or Sterne; or, from a different angle, Hume); primitivism (Macpherson's *Ossian,* looking back to the world of Celtic myth, and even, in a sense, Walter Scott); or the dark side of the psyche, in Gothicism. The rationalistic 'god-substitute' had proved insufficient; Enlightenment simply didn't satisfy the intuitions which insisted that, somewhere, there must be more. But this breakdown – first, of the old consensus that God's revelation held the key to truth; then, of the replacement faith that human reason is an infallible guide – triggered the search for alternatives that has characterized our history.

So at the end of the eighteenth century[16] comes the emergence of themes we associate with Romanticism, in poets such as Blake, Wordsworth, Coleridge, Shelley, Keats; writers marked by a rejection of what Blake calls the 'mind-forged manacles' of the Enlightenment, and the rules of neo-classical poetics (as subverted by Wordsworth and Coleridge) and conventional behaviour (see Byron and Shelley) that went with them. The result might have been a whole 'rediscovery of God', and indeed that did take place to a certain extent.[17] But, in general, the 'marginalizing of God' that began in the Enlightenment continues in the mainstream of Romanticism.[18] As American postmodernist Rorty rightly argues, Romanticism attempts to salvage the spirituality of Christianity by placing it in a de-supernaturalized context – by giving it, in effect, other 'gods'.

What, then, replaces God, for the Romantics, as source of the ultimately significant? Perhaps childhood, considered as something pure ('trailing clouds of glory') before it is ruined by society (Blake's *Songs of Innocence*, Wordsworth's *Prelude*); the natural world, considered now as something untamed, supra-rational, beyond humanity, but also unfallen (Wordsworth again);[19] visionary experience attained through drugs (Coleridge's *Kubla Khan*, supposedly); the individual consciousness,[20] embodied particularly in the Imagination (Keats, Coleridge).[21] In various ways, Romanticism offers to find what is truly significant and worthy of celebration beyond the world of everyday reason, but with God continuing to be marginal. (Can we see a parallel with what happens in Kant's philosophy, where the things that really matter – freedom and ethics, for example – likewise belong to a realm 'independent of the whole world of sense'?)

But it didn't last. As a thought-experiment it would be worth reflecting how the elevation of these qualities to 'god-substitutes' ultimately distorted or destroyed each of them. We could consider how idolization of childhood led to the sentimentalizing of children in Dickens, perhaps a prime factor making him unreadable today; or, how treating nature (divorced from God) as the source of life turned into its becoming the unfeeling source of death in later authors like Zola; or again, how the emphasis on feeling over thought led to the utter degradation of feeling in de Sade. But a deeper and tragic question lurked beneath the Romantic vision: do we really find a higher truth as we look beyond the rational to the Imagination; or are we just 'imagin-ing' it, wandering in our own daydreams?

The question is put powerfully by Keats, at the close of *Ode to a Nightingale*.[22] Keats listens to and celebrates the beauty of a bird's song. But at the end of the poem the bird is gone, and Keats asks, 'Was it a vision, or a waking dream?' Was it a truly signifi-cant glimpse of ultimate beauty, or just the kind of fantasy that comes between sleep and waking?[23] As the nineteenth century continues, the issue becomes more urgent. In Tennyson, guru-bard to the Victorians, we often sense the despair of a man who hardly dares hope that the things he most cares about have ulti-mate reality. In Browning, too, isn't there a deep sense of loss, of seeking to forget the big questions in the rush into action – every-thing is lost, but anyway keep riding?

For at the heart of the apparent confidence of nineteenth-century Britain was a violent collapse of certainty. Up till now the Christian framework had underpinned the dominant values, even though in many ways the culture had moved far from com-mitment to the biblical God. But now came the first really major intellectual assault on Christianity – from German biblical criti-cism and from Darwin's theory of evolution.[24] It was the age of the 'loss of faith': just when the Romantic dream was seeming a fantasy[25] and dwindling into sentimentalism, so too the Chris-tian framework appeared to be collapsing. Don't we see in many Victorian writers – in Tennyson's *In Memoriam*, in Arnold's 'Dover Beach' (quoted in Ch. 5) – a profound sense of loss and doubt as to whether any foundation is left for significance? And is there not doubt, too, as to whether goodness is something with any real basis or source or power? (That is, is there really any 'god'?) Dickens' villains, for example, have tremendous vitality, but his good characters seem pale by comparison (e.g., in *Oliver Twist*); it is very hard to understand why in the end they triumph.[26] The reason, one suspects, is that Dickens himself didn't know. (Dostoevski's *The Idiot* poses a similar problem.)

So doesn't much of the major literature of the last 150 years reflect a quest for new 'god-substitutes', for alternative bases for values and significance? We see the Pre-Raphaelites – William

Morris, Christina Rossetti, Dante Gabriel Rossetti – looking back to the Middle Ages. George Eliot is almost an early liberal-humanist: for her God is 'inconceivable', immortality 'unbelievable', yet still there remains duty, 'peremptory and absolute'. Others look to science as the key: but the French Naturalists such as Zola reveal the scientific universe as a machine pursuing its impersonal, deterministic purposes, with no care for the human beings trapped in the process. (At the end of *L'Assommoir*, for example, the heroine is found dead and 'turning green already'.) And none of this quite suffices; towards the end of the century a different alternative appears, with the swing away from visible reality among the first precursors of the modernist movement.

'God is silent and that I cannot possibly deny – everything in me calls for God and that I cannot forget ... As a matter of fact, this experience can be found in one form or another in most contemporary authors; it is the torment in Jaspers, death in Malraux, destitution in Heidegger, the reprieved-being in Kafka, the insane and futile labour of Sisyphus in Camus.'

–Jean-Paul Sartre[27]

Even if there is nothing to live by in the mundane world, they seem to say, at least we can look for something meaningful and significant in the separate universe of art and in the personal aesthetic consciousness; in France with the Symbolist poets, in Britain somewhat differently with the Aesthetic movement – 'art for art's sake', that being all there is to truly celebrate.

Twentieth-century literature offers a vast proliferation of 'god-substitutes', responding to the issue of what is worth living for.[28] But don't we find many of modernism's greatest literary achievements building on this 'aesthetic god'? In different ways Joyce, Yeats, Woolf and Pound seek an autonomous aesthetic construct that will somehow make sense of this meaningless world, or contain an order and meaningfulness that this one lacks. The influential philosopher G.E. Moore pointed to two spheres as containing that which was truly worthwhile: art and relationship. E.M. Forster gave expression to the latter in his famous remark that, faced with the choice of betraying his country or his friend, he hoped he would betray his country. (Perhaps these two remain the central 'god-substitutes' for modernity: Posterski and Bibbey's recent surveys of Canadian youth values likewise highlight music and friendship as the things that really matter.)

> Communism and Fascism are two great myths of 'modernity'. Ultimately, didn't they both destroy the 'gods' they had deified? Communism deified the State, the collective – and by the time Russian Communism finally fell, it was obvious to any visitor how anything public, that belonged to the State, was completely neglected by the average citizen. Nazism deified Germany, the 'master-race' – and left Germany divided in two for the next 40 years. What we deify, we destroy?

But these two 'god-substitutes', like their predecessors, had their problems. So many of the best novels of this period struggle with the inadequacy of human relationships (the devouring relationships in Lawrence, Conrad's themes of betrayal and isolation, or the sense of failure in the close of Forster's *Passage to India*). And art:[29] what is art? In the autonomous universe of art, how do we know what is significant and worthy of record? When we believed in God, we could go back to the beginning of the Bible and see a Creator who makes things and declares that they are very good; beauty had real meaning because it came from God. But now that God is dead, what is beauty? Is it purely subjective? Is there any difference between the sound of a Beethoven concerto and of a concrete mixer? What (if anything) is of value? What is genuinely worth the artist's celebrating?

The last thirty years crystallized this problem with the shift to postmodernism. Postmodernism is a complex phenomenon, but isn't one of its characteristics precisely this doubt? Andy Warhol produces a sculpture that is an exact replica of a box of Brillo pads. And why not? In the past we made sculptures of human beings. But what is so special about them? In a chance universe they are no more significant, no more worthy of celebration, than anything else. Jeff Koons made a name for himself with (among other things) a giant stainless steel rabbit. Earlier in the century, Marcel Duchamp presented a toilet as a work of art; in the 1960s, Piero Manzoni tinned and sold his own excrement. ('Of course it's art', says Damien Hirst, famous for his dead shark in formaldehyde and his cow's head being eaten by maggots, 'it's in an art gallery'.)

The music of John Cage poses a similar question. Beethoven might write symphonies for violins, clarinets, flutes; but why are these sounds more 'privileged', more significant, than anything else? In Cage's famous piano piece *4'33"*, he does not even play the piano. Why, after all, should we give the term 'music' to pieces of wood striking pieces of wire? The sounds of people laughing or jeering, arguing or demanding their money back, would be as much an expression of music as the wood and wire. The reasoning is logical enough. Cage once wrote, 'I have nothing to say and I am saying it and that is poetry.' All that is left at that point is the act of speaking, of words without meaning. It is the last extremity of formalism: the medium is the message because there is nothing else. Many of Beckett's writings present only a voice speaking in the dark (surprisingly often in hell), with nothing worth saying, wanting indeed to stop but unable to do so, therefore going on, meaninglessly, hopelessly, for page after page after page. That end-point is all there is left to be said. And we have to ask: if there is no God, what else is there to celebrate and believe in as a source of significance? Have we any logical alternative to postmodernism?

At the end of a millennium, then, we are heirs to an extended but failed dialogue: from the excitement of the Reformation, with the rediscovery of the individual's enormous significance before God; through the Enlightenment's turning away from

God's revelation in the name of autonomous human reason, then the swing in turn from the inadequacies of that 'reason', to non-rational sources of significance; then on through the searchings of the nineteenth century, through the modernist era often seeking meaningfulness or order in separate universes of art; and now postmodernity, when those myths too have lost their meaning. Today, all the syntheses and 'god-substitutes' have broken down; we are 'incredulous towards meta-narratives'; we have little left to build upon, celebrate or rejoice over, little to say except to go on saying very little. In such a world, art may become increasingly difficult; so, too, may life. We live in the 'twilight of the gods', as heirs to three centuries of failed 'god-substitutes'.

But perhaps youth culture has taken up the search where its elders failed. Let's explore the story again, starting this time in the '50s.

Once again, we can guess at the 'god-replacements' that briefly flavoured our world before giving way in inadequacy to their successors. Once again, what follows is hypothetical. But we're asking the question: isn't this roughly what happened? Might this story explain where we are?

In the previous section we focused on 'high culture', but many aspects of 'high culture' have lost their significance now. (Dickens is far better known in Russia than in England, though Russia is changing too.) So this time we'll focus more on popular culture – on rock and fashion and politics. In particular, postmodern art seems, to many people, totally irrelevant; if the collapse of values means there is nothing left to celebrate, nothing to say, then the whole enterprise of 'high art' is meaning-less. Dripping paint on the canvas? Sitting by a silent piano? Nice work if you can get it; nothing in it for me. But in this same period there burst onto the scene a new set of impulses, and par-ticularly a new music, that clearly could find something to shout about. This was a new beginning; this was the time for rock 'n' roll.

From dream to dream

In many ways, 1950s culture reflected a blithe new confidence. The west had been through a bad time. The late '40s mood contained a sense of something gone wrong beyond the power of idealism to set right: in the bestiality demonstrated at Auschwitz, Belsen and Buchenwald, and the fearful power for destruction revealed even in the Allies' triumph. We can see something of an attempt to confront these issues in the arts – for example, in the poetic movement known as New Apocalypse; and, more generally, in a brief return among the intelligentsia to Godward faith. This was the heyday of C.S. Lewis' championing of 'mere', original Christianity, for example, and of T.S. Eliot's *Four Quartets*.

But as the '50s proceeded, it seemed that humankind, empowered by science, was really putting its world in order on its own. Germany saw the *Wirtschaftswunder* or economic miracle, Britain the rise of the welfare state. At the end of the decade, John Kennedy could tell America that the world's problems had been created by man, and could be solved by man.[30] British premier Harold Macmillan told his electorate, 'You've never had it so good'. And, compared to the mass unemployment of the '30s, the privations of the '40s and the austerity years of the early '50s, the point carried weight. Fascism had been defeated; communism was contained; standards of living were rising continuously.

In Britain at least, this confidence in humanity's resources was reflected in the rise of a new god-replacement, an overt humanism. In the arts there arose a deep distrust of 'big truths' of any non-humanistic kind; hence a dominance of formalism, or (in English poetry) of the Movement – poets who denied any role as 'seer' and disdained the grand concerns of an Eliot or an Auden. ('Nobody wants any more poems on the grander themes for a few years', wrote Kingsley Amis in 1955.) No outside revelation was needed. Even the religious establishment was in heavily liberal, non-supernatural mode; when Billy Graham was invited to address the student Christian Union at Cambridge, his message of the need for 'new birth' was denounced by Michael Ramsey, soon to be Archbishop of Canterbury, as 'heretical'.[31]

Yet soon there were widening cracks in the temple of this humanistic confidence. If the '50s saw the emergence of humanism as 'god-substitute', they soon saw also its implosion. In literature, Leavis became the guru of taste, but his uncompromising humanism was coupled curiously with an insistence that British culture was in its death-throes. Clearly the facade of '50s humanism could conceal unresolved contradictions. (Few things would be more characteristic of the '60s than a loathing of the 'Great Society' that '50s humanism could be so proud of.) Elsewhere the '50s saw a sense of unfocused rebellion, distrustful of an establishment incapable of living up to the ideals it proclaimed; and a sense of fresh energies seeking an alternative. John Osborne's *Look Back in Anger* is the classic expression of the frustration, even if he and his fellow 'Angry Young Men' had little positive to say. The same note sounded through James Dean (*Rebel Without a Cause*); through the beatniks ('I saw the best minds of my generation destroyed by madness, starving hysterical naked' – Ginsberg in *Howl*); through the teddy boys. And, most of all, through Elvis and the rest. Beat and rock 'n' roll were controversial from the outset; revolting impatiently against the old gods, against the '50s establishment that was modernity's final fling, against liberalism's old order that thought it knew all the answers. Rock 'n' roll is rebel-music – 'Move over, daddy-o!' As in Osborne, as with Dean, there was no new big vision to follow – not yet. But there was radical dissatisfaction with the complacencies of the reigning 'gods'; and a hunger for something new.

Early in the '60s, new idealisms – new 'gods' – began to emerge. In America, the inaugural speech of Kennedy's 'New Frontier' administration was marked by words like 'new', 'anew', 'renewal'; the dominant image was of dynamic youthful energy taking over at the top. Of course we now know of the mafia links that lay behind the image, and the sleazy relationships – both Kennedy brothers sleeping with Marilyn Monroe, JFK's chronic gonorrhoea. But that wasn't how it seemed at the time; Samuel Eliot Morrison's 1965 *Oxford History of the*

American People climaxes with the *Camelot* song that came to stand for JFK, about 'one brief shining moment'. ('The hardest thing now is to explain how we once felt about the Kennedys', reflected one recent writer. Rauschenberg's *Retrospective II* (1964), featuring a spaceman and a shot of JFK, was 'the last affectionate tribute to a political figure produced by an American artist', suggested *Time*; after JFK, no more heroes.) In Britain, too, the tired and scandal-prone Conservative administration was swept aside by a young Labour government mouthing idealistic rhetoric about the 'white heat of the technological revolution'. 'It seemed the time had come for young men to take over the world', Roy Hattersley wrote later. (The same optimism was mirrored exuberantly in pop art.)

And in pop music, four young men from Liverpool seemed to be doing just this, with the worldwide triumph ('bigger than Jesus') of the early Beatles. That soon merged into the broader '60s counter-culture.

What were the '60s about? They weren't just a period of sexual libertinism, nor of mere overthrow of traditional standards. The culture of these years – hippies, 'flower power' – has taken a great deal of sarcasm, but they were in many ways an era of hope compared to the decades that followed. They were years of conflict, certainly, but also confidence – now almost unimaginable – that new possibilities were available, pointing the route to a better world. New principles arose as foundations for identity, action and ethics; new 'god-substitutes' overthrew those of '50s liberal humanism. There was the political New Left inspired by Mao and Marcuse, unifying black power and student power, powerful enough almost to bring down the French government and certainly to terrify the American one. There was the hippie culture, proclaiming not only sexual liberation but a whole new order of 'love and peace'; the drug culture, offering complete transformation right down to the cellular level ('Grass will grow in Times Square within ten years', promised Timothy Leary); and the assured proponents of Eastern religion. Indeed, rock music itself was 'going to become the answer to the day's problems', affirmed Pete Townshend.[32] Gods a-plenty; and when

Eric Clapton's Blind Faith, or the Rolling Stones, played totally free before a host of flower children in Hyde Park, and still more at the quasi-religious atmosphere of the Woodstock festival attended by half a million, it did seem that there was a 'whole generation with a new explanation'.

But what was that 'new explanation' to be? Bob Dylan had been the voice of the simpler political protests of the earlier '60s, but soon he was concluding that 'Politics is bullshit. It's all unreal. The only thing that's real is inside you.'[33] The Beatles moved in the same direction, from the simple pop of 'I Wanna Hold Your Hand' through the existential questioning of 'Eleanor Rigby' and 'Nowhere Man', thence to confidence in the power of hallucinogenic drugs to unlock reality ('A Day in the Life', 'Strawberry Fields Forever'), culminating in the full manifesto of the *Sergeant Pepper* album. 'All You Need is Love' became the anthem of the hippie movement, sung on international telecast to an estimated audience of 400 million. Many other voices proclaimed drug experience as the source of meaning – Jimi Hendrix, Pink Floyd, Jefferson Airplane, the Grateful Dead.

For an artist like Hendrix, drugs were not merely a mind-trip; rather, blended with music and new sexual freedom, they offered a source for mystical liberation on a cosmic scale. Back in 1963 Paul McCartney had written God off ('I don't think about religion. It doesn't fit into my life'); now, he declared, he had found God after swallowing LSD. The 'god-substitute' was everything we could need: LSD 'could heal the world ... I now believe the answer to everything is love.'[34] Bryan Wilson of the Beach Boys agreed: 'My experience of God came from acid. It's the most important thing that ever happened to me.'[35]

But still one 'god-substitute' gave way to another. If drugs pointed to God, maybe God pointed beyond drugs, to India. The Beach Boys got into transcendental meditation, with the Maharishi opening the concerts in their May 1968 tour; Pete Townshend of the Who was into Meher Baba, and Baba's ideas would turn up in *Tommy* and *Quadrophenia*. 'We're all searching for something called God', said George Harrison; 'We are all trying to get where Jesus Christ got'[36] – although his fellow-

Beatles hit the end of that particular road after their frustrating visit ('just like Butlins') to the Maharishi's Indian headquarters.

Cooling off

But there was a darker aspect to the decade: the nihilism of the Velvet Underground, singing of heroin and sado-masochism, setting out to reflect the 'wild side' of New York which was hookers, junkies and cross-dressers. Heavily influenced by pop artist Andy Warhol, they became a gateway through which the nihilistic conclusions of 'high art' would move across into the mainstream. Unfortunately, they had truth on their side.

As we look back now to the '60s, there is a delightful childlikeness about the optimism; but none of the ideals quite worked.[37] Politically, the vicious 1968 brutality of Mayor Daley's Chicago police, followed by the re-election of Richard Nixon, showed that the old order was quite capable of resisting the new left; the left itself turned now in an increasingly autocratic direction, confirming Marcuse's comment that every revolution is a betrayed revolution. (The Beatles set their faces against the new, destructive mood in Lennon's song 'Revolution'.) LSD likewise didn't deliver; the girl who wrote down the secret of the universe while tripping, then found that what she had written was 'If I stand on the tips of my toes I can touch the ceiling,' was not the only one to find how this god had failed. George Harrison visited the psychedelic heartland of Haight-Ashbury and reported, 'That was the first thing that turned me off drugs. I expected them to be all nice and clean and friendly and happy and the first thing you see is lots of dirty people lying around on the floor.' One of LSD prophet Leary's original disciples, Allen Cohen, remarked, 'One of the fantasies we had is demonstrably false. This is the belief that if you take enough psychedelic drugs you will become holy ... love will flow from you. It doesn't work ... You can't carry over even the profound experiences you have. You can feel very loving under LSD but can you exert that love to someone who previously you didn't like? The long range answer is no.'[38]

If Harrison was unimpressed by Haight-Ashbury, his fellow-Beatles became equally underwhelmed by Eastern religion – expressing their deep disillusionment in 'Sexy Sadie', originally titled 'Maharishi'. All they had needed, seemingly, was love; and, unable to figure that one out, they broke up. Most painfully, the mass idealism of the free Woodstock festival proved to be built on sand; reality broke in four months later at a similar event in Altamont, California, as Mick Jagger sang 'Sympathy for the Devil'. A man was beaten to death by the Hell's Angels the Stones had brought in to police the festival, and Jagger was left pathetically pleading, 'I mean, like people, who's fighting and what for? Hey, people! I mean, who's fighting and what for? Why are we fighting? We don't want to fight ... I mean, like every other scene has been cool ...'[39] 'It was like a nice afternoon in hell', said Jerry Garcia afterwards, 'It was so weird.'

Altamont, the Grateful Dead's manager remarked later, was the end of the '60s; the day the music died. Bob Dylan had retreated into country pastoralism on *Nashville Skyline* (1969), the Byrds likewise with 'Sweetheart of the Rodeo'. Back in the cities, a craze for witchcraft began to sweep the counterculture. (This was also the heyday of the 'Jesus movement': things were tending to go one way or the other.) As the '70s began it became clear, as John Lennon said, that the dream was over. The deaths within ten months of Jimi Hendrix, Janis Joplin and the Doors' Jim Morrison symbolized the end of an era; Paul McCartney began proceedings to dissolve the Beatles in the same period.

The gods had failed.[40] 'Won't Get Fooled Again', sang the Who. To Frank Zappa the 'whole hippie scene' was 'wishful thinking. They wish they could love, but they're full of ****'.[41] Lennon's summary of the counterculture was deeply depressed:

> Nothing happened except that we all dressed up. The same bastards are in control, the same people are running everything ... I no longer believe in myth and Beatles is another myth. I don't believe in it, the dream is over. And I'm not just talking about the Beatles. I'm talking about the generation thing. The dream is over. It's over and we've got to get down to so-called reality.[42]

(Somehow a straight line leads from that to the greed-is-good 'realism' of more recent times.)

'Talkin' 'bout my degeneration.' Jesus dead, '50s humanism dead, and now the '60s dreams vanished too. These were the days of the scandal of Watergate, and idealism gave way, if not to the outright courting of corruption, then to cynicism and an overt loss of hope for any real meaning. (And, in fashion, an almost deliberate tastelessness.) The cover of the 1963 edition of Colin Wilson's best-seller *The Outsider* had announced, without irony, 'an inquiry into the sickness of mankind in the mid-twentieth century'; an emblematic '70s moment came when *Monty Python* denied any such inquiry, recycling the phrase at the close of one episode as patently ludicrous. Something had grown old and died in the meantime – or between the days of '60s songs like 'Blowing in the Wind' and 'Where Have All the Flowers Gone?', where the ideals and values seemed so real, and the '70s dominance of 'cool', pessimistic, uncommitted, maintaining a safe distance. Logically enough, on the religious scene the huge promises of the Eastern-based cults of the '60s (TM, Divine Light Mission, Zen Buddhism) gave way to psychotherapeutic self-help groups (EST, Synanon, Insight). With so many other dreams dead, what remained to foster was the self – self-expression, self-discovery. The '70s became known as the 'Me Generation' (Tom Wolfe), or, in the title of Christopher Lasch's celebrated volume, the 'Culture of Narcissism'.[43]

But again, '70s cool seemed to have realism on its side – unlike the god-alternatives of the preceding decade. What the '60s had deified was now despised. David Bowie told *Newsweek*, 'I hated the whole togetherness, peace, love thing. It was conceited, flabby, suffocating – and didn't mean what it said'[44] – exactly what a beatnik might have said about the hollowness of an earlier humanism. Thus, if the dominant musical voice of the '60s was the Beatles' idealism, in the early '70s the keynote was contentlessness: the Europop of Abba or Boney M,[45] the self-indulgent triple-LP fantasias of 'art-rock', or the mindlessness of 'Get It On' – the result of Marc Bolan's profitable switch away from his earlier sub-Tolkien hippie anthems. (1960s hero John

Peel refused to play the new Bolan.) Hippie kaftans gave way to the poseur-flamboyance of glam-rock (Bowie and Iggy Pop, both heavily influenced by Velvet Underground nihilism), or the black, even satanically-oriented pessimism of heavy metal, which *NME*'s Phil McNeill described as '*the* sound of the '70s. It has underpinned the whole decade.' Lester Bangs listed

> a representative sampling of song titles from heavy metal albums by the genre's acknowledged punjabs: "Paranoid", "Killing Yourself to Live", "Children of the Grave", "Into the Void" (Black Sabbath); "Aimless Lady", "Winter and My Soul" (Grand Funk Railroad); "Dier not a Lover", "D.<ead> O.<n>A.<rrival>", "Hangman's Dances" (Bloodrock); "Into the Fire", "Living Wreck" (Deep Purple) ... Heavy metal music in its finest flower had one central, obvious message: *There is no hope.* Whatever you do, *you can't win.*[46]

Perhaps this collapse of values in white-dominated culture helps us understand the repeated importance of black music as a source for new life. It is striking how often fresh momentum comes from this direction – with its roots in gospel, in convictions that certain things are right, are wrong, are worth celebrating, worth singing about; that love is a reality, that people matter.

When such certainties have lost their grounding in white culture, there comes a desire for the conviction voiced by an Aretha Franklin, a Stevie Wonder, a Bob Marley; the sound of a reality for which our hearts are hungry. Don't we sense that, after the '60s, white popular culture oscillates between cynicism, irony or nihilism on the one hand, and romantic longings for something deeper, something with tradition and value? And, tragically, that these longings seldom encounter anything credible, no 'gods' with any substance; so as a result they grow purely commercial, economically-oriented, hollow at their heart?[47]

'I have nothing to say and I am saying it ...'

1950s humanism dead, '60s alternatives imploded; little left to believe in. But the story goes on. The main musical (and stylistic) movement of the late '70s amended that 'little' to 'nothing whatsoever'. In 1976, punk burst onto the scene.

Here indeed was a new burst of raw energy, but its motivating 'god' was a radical nihilism, expressed in posed violence and deliberate ugliness. Punk was the music of the 'blank generation' struggling with recession and unemployment, angrily in reaction against its predecessors. Sting told a *TV Times* interviewer, 'Supergroups like the Who and Led Zeppelin had things all their own way, releasing records of over-produced, over-rehearsed, hackneyed music' while a 'whole generation is being flushed down the drain. Many have no work, they feel unfulfilled, humiliated and abused. Punk groups articulate their frustrations.' In furious reaction to the previous generation's 'concept albums' (Mike Oldfield, Yes, Electric Light Orchestra), punks proudly declared their lack of musical skills, proclaiming themselves 'garage bands', 'three-chord wonders'.

But the nihilism went deeper. The Sex Pistols called for 'Anarchy in the UK'; 'No Future' was the slogan their followers painted on walls across Britain. If the 'fascist' establishment was rejected, from the monarchy downwards (as per the Pistols' 'God Save the Queen'), so, equally, were the gods of '60s idealism. 'Dosed out of their heads the whole time', sneered Johnny Rotten about the hippies. 'Yeah man! Peace and love!'[48]

But there was something profoundly pessimistic – to put it kindly: massively selfish, to be less generous – about the 'looking after number one' that resulted from this rejection of 'peace and love': 'I'm in love with ... my pretty little self, and nobody else', to quote the Pistols. Punk was consistent, but punk was hate: 'I Hate Pink Floyd' was Johnny Rotten's trademark T-shirt, and 'I hate them, I'd love to murder them' was his comment on his fellow-Pistols after the band broke up. The results were consistent too: the punk habit of bands spitting at their audience; the movement's self-image as exploitation, embodied when

Malcolm McLaren, the Pistols' creator, proudly presented his machinations in *The Great Rock'n'Roll Swindle*. ('Of course I exploited them', McLaren said of his next project Bow Wow Wow, 'and I'm proud of it!'[49]) Consistent, too, was the image of aggression cultivated at punk concerts – the girl blinded by a glass thrown at the stage at the 100 Club, and, finally, Pistols bassist Sid Vicious overdosing on heroin while facing a murder charge of killing his girlfriend after the Pistols' acrimonious break-up. In punk, the kids with nothing to lose from consistency had pushed '70s me-generation nihilism towards its limit.

But man cannot live by nihilism alone, any more than music can survive on three chords alone. (Though John Lydon – Johnny Rotten – did the best he could. When his next band, Public Image Limited, toured America, they deliberately recruited a novice bassist, band members might stop playing after half an hour, and once the whole band played from behind a screen. Lydon taunted the fans for having paid to hear them.) Thus what followed in the 'new wave' included a turning away from 'three chord wonders', and a willingness to concede the meaning of musical values. When ex-Pistol Glen Matlock formed his new band, Rich Kids, his change of direction was signalled in his announcement 'We're here to play music'. Sting said of the Police, 'We wanted to sing songs that people could remember and that were not necessarily anti-social.' Along with this, in contrast to punk's logically-consistent ugliness, came a rediscovery of style: Blitz Kids, New Romantics; Adam Ant, Culture Club, Ultravox, Duran Duran, Spandau Ballet. And, in place of the punks' hostility to their audience (spitting on their fans), came the audience-friendly approach of Bruce Springsteen or U2. ('I don't like music unless it has a healing effect', said Bono[50] – not very punk, but in those days most of the band were committed Christians, involved in a Dublin charismatic fellowship and influenced by Chinese Christian writer Watchman Nee.)

Outside U2, however, the swing away from nihilism didn't mean the nihilists' questions had found an answer. Culturally, as we've observed, emphasis on style tends to occur when there is not very much credible to be said. This was certainly the case with, say,

Boy George, who deliberately presented himself as a 'man without convictions'. ('I don't want people committed to an ideal', he told one interviewer, 'coz ideals go out of the window after a while. I could say something to you now and tomorrow something could happen that could make me change my mind.'[51]) Yet there was at least an opening for something positive. The change of climate was symbolized most strikingly by the Live Aid event of 1985, when most of rock's biggest names joined in a huge concert for the sake of the world's hungry. It would have been impossible to imagine the Sex Pistols, the Stranglers and the Damned arranging such an event in the heyday of punk; but now Santana, Sade, even Elvis Costello sang of brotherhood, love, togetherness. It was gut-reaction altruism, as its organizer Bob Geldof made clear in an interview the following year:

> I'm not this completely selfless individual ... I'd like to be as selfless as Mother Teresa, but I'm not ... I will never stop thinking about those people and wanting to help. But if I were to go on and do that I'd be bored and tired, and upset easily ... I don't care what people say or don't say, I just want to be a success.[52]

Altruism as this year's fashion choice, the cynic might say. Yet there was clearly in Geldof a serious desire for the ideals to make sense.

Perhaps this explains the curious resurgence of religious motifs in the next few years.[53] Steve Turner observes that several key figures in early '80s music, like Sting or Simple Minds' Jim Kerr, were

> lapsed Roman Catholics who, while not subscribing to the ethics and power structure of the church, nevertheless found themselves using the symbols ... These were people often deeply respectful of religious ritual, moved by the language and typology of the Bible but sceptical of church teachings.[54]

Springsteen does the same;[55] these musicians express a sense that there is power associated, somewhere and somehow, with what might be termed 'religion'. Even more fascinating is Madonna. The archetypal 'Material Girl' rode on a wave of religious symbolism ('Like a Virgin', 'Like a Prayer', 'The Immaculate Collection'), notching up en route the astonishing feat of hijacking one of humankind's great religious words and making it refer primarily to herself. Madonna embodied the '80s synthesis – on the one hand, unashamed materialism and quintessentially postmodern manipulation of image without content; yet drawing on the vestigial power of religious imagery, which (and here is the crucial paradox) she herself partly believed in. (Witness the bizarre fact of her prayer meetings with her dancers during a Canadian tour that was nearly cancelled for obscenity.)[56]

It is in these terms that we can understand the link between what was happening in youth culture and in politics in the '80s. A comparison between Madonna and Margaret Thatcher is oddly illuminating. Both were as far from the un-materialistic idealisms of the '60s as was Johnny Rotten; yet both were comfortable deploying religious symbolism as part of their packaging, and neither apparently lacked some genuine belief in it. But if the dark side of the rejection of '60s utopianism was the naked materialism embodied in punk and then in Madonna, that was the achilles heel of '80s Thatcherism, too. Its gods were at war with each other.

Style guru Peter York observed that '80s conservatism embodied a fundamental contradiction. There was an uneasy marriage between the religion-based values it professed, and the radical economic Darwinism it practised. On the one hand, there was a genuine desire to turn the clock back to traditional social values, including (as Thatcher said in 1988) a 'fundamental sense of fairness, integrity, honesty and courtesy for your neighbour'; Conservative government ministers appealed unashamedly (if selectively) to the churches to reintroduce morality to Britain. But their real devotion lay with the gods of market forces ('Let the market decide'); and in practice, the economic individualism outweighed the desire for moral renewal. This led logically to the exaltation of Darwinian competitiveness, rather than neighbourly collaboration, as the route to excellence; and then, equally logically, to the glorification of 'loadsamoney' individualism, with all the designer trappings, for the winners who came out on top.[57] Margaret Thatcher herself embodied this individualism in insisting that 'There is no such thing as society'; the climate she created was increasingly one where everybody had to compete for themselves,[58] whether the arena was health, schooling, or provision for old age. Whatever the quasi-Christian rhetoric, the results were close to the Darwinian law of the jungle.

> The point is, ladies and gentlemen, that greed, for want of a better word, is good. Greed is right. Greed works. Greed clarifies, cuts through and captures the essence of the evolutionary spirit. Greed in all its forms – greed for life, for money, for love, knowledge – has marked the upward surge of mankind.
>
> –Gordon Gekko, in *Wall Street*

The story of '80s conservatism might suggest that attempts to combine devotion to God and Money are as unsuccessful as Christ predicted they would be, two thousand years earlier. It also raises the issue we examined in Chapter 3: What is the underpinning necessary for effective moral values? Without a far clearer rediscovery – even 'vision' – of God, were not the conservatives' 'moral values' doomed to be swept aside by the economic forces they emphasized, and the self-orientation that that emphasis engendered? Neo-conservatism can sound religious; but outside the context of direct relationship with God, 'traditional values' become just another god-replacement. And an ill-defined and ineffective one;[59] we remember the '80s not as the 'moral decade' but as the 'designer decade', an era whose gods were money and style, one nearly as short of values as the '70s.

The dominance of that ethos can be illustrated by the completeness with which it took over the pop scene, formerly the bastion of counterculture ideals. Here, yuppie had comprehensively displaced hippie.[60] A 1985 *Radio Times* article wrote of star singer Paul Young,

Like most of his contemporaries he talks about his recordings as "product" and measures his sales in "units" ... Somehow, I can't imagine pop stars of the previous generation – Pete Townshend, say – slapping backs and giving handouts at the annual sales beano.

Young himself admitted, 'It's more to do with business than it is to do with music in some ways.' Michael Jackson's 1983 hit album *Thriller* was the biggest seller in the world; but as *Time*'s critic commented, it was

> not the kind of great album one has come to expect since the tumul-tuous days of *Sergeant Pepper's Lonely Hearts Club Band*: a record that provokes, challenges, raises questions. *Thriller* is not *Who's Next* or *The White Album* or *Blonde on Blonde* ... records that were argued over or championed like talismans that could change lives. It is like a piece of elegant sportswear; slip right into it, shrug it off.[61]

The change was mirrored in the music press; as William Leith remarked a year later, argumentative tabloids like *New Musical Express* had given way to 'a different type of magazine altogether. It is smaller, less serious, more lurid. It contains more photographs and fewer words. It is celebratory, rather than suspicious, of success, massive sales and media hype.' And the growing signifi-cance of video accelerated these trends: 'Nowadays, the product (the pop group) is tailored to suit the marketing device (the pop video), rather than vice versa.'[62]

Thus with the eclipse of the intellectual left in the west, and communism heading towards final collapse in the east, neo-con-servatism's gods had their chance. But the result was the triumph of naked economics – and widespread destruction in the health service, education system, and many other areas of culture as everything began to be controlled by the bottom line. (*Independent on Sunday* writer Michael Bywater defined 'what being British has become' as 'an unlovely struggle against the cost-accountants, who believe that money is the only motiva-tion, profit the only measure, and that an enlightened pianist would play all the notes of a Beethoven sonata in one cacophonous crash, in the name of efficiency.') The corollary of Thatcher's 'fondness for business and management', former Tory MP Sir Christopher Tugendhat remarked, was a 'lack of respect for most non-profitmaking activities. A certain harshness, even brutality, entered the picture.' That was true both at the affluent end of the social spectrum, with Gordon Gekko's gospel of greed in *Wall Street* – 'Greed is good. Greed is right. Greed works' – being worn proudly by City stock market traders on their softball jerseys; and at the opposite end, where 'in-your-face' self-glorification marked the lyrics of rap, heavy metal, and hardcore house. There was something quite Thatcherite about gangsta-rapper Dr Dre announcing bluntly on MTV, 'I'm just here to make money'; or the Wu Tang Clan's slogan C.R.E.A.M. – 'Cash Rules Everything Around Me'.

(One post-'80s trend whose effect we shouldn't underrate is the changing source of new impulses in black music. These now tend to come, not from musicians with roots in the black churches,[63] but rather from the violent and anarchic world of the ghettos. Rap pioneers Grandmaster Flash and the Furious Five focused on ugliness such as a teenage mother tipping her newborn child into the trash ('New York, New York');[64] respected African-American critic Armond White describes the high-selling gangsta rap as taking a 'capitalist approach to nihilism, finding it marketable … It fills up that moral hollow where Black pop's heart used to be', with its 'key subjects … sexual power and male competition' in an 'unabashed celebration of power and greed'.[65] 'Nobody cares about me so why should I care about anyone else', one gangsta rapper told an MTV special. But the music's deliberate violence and misogyny were not a joke; Snoop Doggy Dogg was acquitted on a murder charge after a shoot-out, but Tupac Shakur was convicted of real-life sexual abuse of a female fan and then gunned down, as was Notorious B.I.G., in what seemed a deadly feud between east and west coast rappers; hip-hop turning murderously inwards to consume itself. Meanwhile, the rappers' standard use of 'bitch' or 'ho' to describe women underlined again what logically happens to respect for women once the Christian base is gone; once it is every mutha for himself.)

In search of the 'vision thing'

Of course the '80s gods didn't last. The idolatry of economics exploded; first with the 1987 stock market crash, then in a series of court actions demonstrating the dishonesty of one key player after another in the economic free-for-all. In Britain, Robert Maxwell was revealed as a massive fraudster; in Australia, tycoon Alan Bond received a two-year sentence for dishonesty; in America, Michael Milken, once the most powerful player on Wall Street, ended up with a 22-month jail term. Suddenly, the bottom line and the economic imperative proved untrustworthy deities. As the shock worked through the system there came a sense of need for new vision – made doubly urgent by the desire for vigorous leadership in the deepening environmental crisis. 'One by one our gods fail us', an *Independent* editorial remarked. 'Paternalistic capitalism, corporatism, communism and, latterly, untrammelled individualism have been advocated, tried, and wholly or largely abandoned. The old isms are in disarray. Yet the Nineties are not characterised by a retreat into pragmatism and materialism. On the contrary, there is a search for meaning ...'

The question mark hung over the early '90s like a neon sign over a motorway motel. On one side of the Atlantic, George Bush hankered after a 'kindlier, gentler' America, even as he lamented his own lack of the 'vision thing' that could further that desire. On the other side, John Major was voted in as a leader who could temper the more destructive aspects of capitalism. But he too confessed to being 'uneasy with big ideas', and the only 'vision thing' he could muster was a wistful elegy for old maids cycling through the mist to communion as the true spirit of Britain.[66] Nor was much guidance to be found among the intelligentsia. Edward Said bemoaned the 'disappearance of the general secular intellectual'. The deaths of Sartre, Barthes, Foucault, Raymond Williams and others marked, he said,

> the passing of an old order: figures of learning and authority, whose general scope over numerous fields gave them much more than

professional competence ... As opposed to this there are technocrats, whose principal competence is ... to solve local problems, not to ask the big questions.

Thus both Bush's demise and Major's signalled a desire for some new framework. Soon after her husband's election, Hillary Clinton expressed her desire to find a 'unified field theory of life ... a way of looking at the world that would marry conservatism and liberalism, capitalism and statism and tie together practically everything'. In Britain, the Labour Party had set about a radical change of direction after its old-style leftism was discredited by the downfall of communism; it is interesting that its electoral breakthrough was grounded in a new ideology consciously constructed by John Smith, and then Tony Blair, on the principles of Christian Socialism.[67]

The same question marks appeared, thought-provokingly, elsewhere. In fashion, white briefly became the theme-colour – supposedly reflecting the new decade's more 'spiritual' mood. ('The 1980s was about materialism', said *Vogue* fashion booking editor Zoe Souter. 'The 1990s is all about individuality, personality and spirit. People are becoming spiritual.') A major feature of early '90s youth culture was the 'rave' scene, and here there were hints of a rediscovery of community not seen since the '60s. It had its roots in the legendary 'Summers of Love' – Ibiza, house music, smiley faces, Ecstasy, clubs like Shoom and Spectrum. These had been powerful experiences for those involved: 'Friendships became all-consuming. Suddenly all they could talk about was love, togetherness, sharing, the sheer joy of life ... Everyone had a story about spontaneous acts of kindness', writes Matthew Collin in his respected survey *Altered State*,[68] and many others have said the same. Likewise, when the 'raves' began, the 'sheer spontaneity was glorious; it felt like something wonderful could happen anywhere at any time'.[69]

But again, the 'vision thing' didn't last. By the time Collin wrote his book in 1997, the joy was long gone; indeed the 'Summer of Love' had proved, within a very few months, to be short on the ingredients needed for lasting community. Collin tells how the original participants couldn't handle the influx of newcomers wanting what they'd got, and soon 'began to close ranks' in an attempt to protect their community from interlopers.[70] But that community was already fracturing internally. 'I made deep friendships around that time', says Marc Almond of Soft Cell, 'friendships that I have to say didn't last. With all that group of us who first took Ecstasy, it all turned a bit sour in the end ... There was nothing really there to cement the friendship.'[71] The same story comes from a key player in the Manchester ('Madchester') scene, of the shift from 'I wish the whole world felt like this' to 'You were convinced that everybody was going to be your friend for life, and even that went sour.'[72] And it wasn't merely the Ecstasy-fuelled dreams of total consciousness change that proved unable to match reality. What is more painful is the story Collin tells of rave culture's powerlessness to resist infiltration by organized crime, resulting in its eventual suppression by the authorities. In the clubs, meanwhile, the scene splintered into consciously estranged subcultures; and the emergence of 'hardcore' and 'jungle' marked a deliberate rejection of acid house and all that went with it. ('That false high, that false hope. That false love.'[73])

'False love'? But Marc Almond's comment had already raised the question: acid house offered little to underpin the community that sprung up in the first golden idealism. Collin quotes remarks from the early participants that show how the exuberance felt 'religious' but lacked the underpinning any real-world religion needs to keep going: 'It was almost like a religious experience; a combination of taking Ecstasy and going to a warm, open-air club full of beautiful people'; 'We all had the same mentality, which was to have a really good time and try as far as possible not to think about anything else ... It felt like a religion.'[74] 'Have a good time and try not to think'; I remember watching John Lydon – *né* Johnny Rotten, Sex Pistol – blasting house music on MTV as a music of 'no content – "Don't worry, be happy, get on the floor and shut your mouth."' 'Saturday night fever, or a new way of life?', asks Collin, and the answer was obvious all too soon.[75] Ecstasy culture, he adds, 'was a culture with options in place of rules'; there was no robust base of convictions for the hoped-for sense of community, but rather a space for a pluralistic potpourri: 'Its definition was subject to individual interpretation.'[76] It looked back to the '60s, but history had moved on; it lacked ideologies – 'gods' – such as those that (despite their weaknesses) underpinned the '60s counter-culture and gave it the ability to reshape the face of the west. 'In some ways it was a throwback to the sixties but it was very much something else – it was totally non-political', says leading rave promoter Tony Colston-Hayter. 'It was the ultimate hedonistic leisure activity. It was about going out and having a good time.'[77]

To all this there were surely exceptions, most notably associated with groups like Spiral Tribe, drawing often on a serious commitment to 'New Age' spiritualities such as paganism, shamanism or witchcraft.[78] Unfortunately, all too much of what the New Agers verbalized would, in another climate, have been discarded instantly as crackpot. Their very success showed the hunger existing for some rediscovered framework of meaning; but too often there was no claim to any truth that could be discussed sensibly with an adherent of a different world-view. The gods were becoming tribal, closed-off; there was just a set of experiences to be shared, or not. Still, it was among these parts of the scene that the 'direct action' movements arose, most often with regard to 'green' issues, that had significant impact during the '90s. But the mainstream became increasingly hedonistic; it was often commented that club atmospheres had become much more sexualized, much more a matter of being 'on the pull'. Where the mainstream had any interest in social issues, it was largely selfish – 'You've got to fight for your right to party'.

('Club culture promotes a very hedonistic lifestyle, and its followers are often accused of being self-centred', said the *Independent* in a feature on club events sponsored by Amnesty International to focus on worldwide human rights issues. 'Yet, far from being apathetic, clubbers traditionally respond well to a wide range of charities.' The feature was titled 'Charity begins in clubland'. But in fact it showed all too clearly how apparent 'worldwide'-oriented altruism can actually be about rather more self-centred concerns. 'Alisha's

Attic's motivation for performing is typical of the artists on show. "This is a unique opportunity to reclaim our rights, to learn what they are and to tell the world's governments that we know our rights and will keep on shouting until they listen and respect them."' Another article featured Brixton-based rapper D Grim of Structure Rize. 'I have never heard of it', he said of Amnesty, 'but we are glad to be part of it if it's helping human rights, you know. Everybody wants to have the right to do what they wanna do.')

Collin observes that although acid house began as a rejection of the '80s style hierarchy and designer ethos, in fact it reflected the same issues: 'Ecstasy culture seemed to ghost the Thatcher narrative – echoing its ethos of choice and market freedom, yet expressing desires for a collective experience that Thatcherism rejected and consumerism could not provide.'[79] Ultimately it was an 'uneasy synthesis of individualistic [that is, self-oriented, hedonistic] and collective [that is, community-oriented] impulses'.[80] The failure of '90s rave culture, then, has been a very '90s failure. And by the mid-'90s, Collin argues, mainstream club culture was 'hedonism distilled to its purest essence', lacking 'any ideology bar the ceaseless pursuit of sheer pleasure'.[81] 'The dream was finally over'; the revolution had turned into style again, and rave culture into something formulaic and corporate.[82]

After the gods have gone

By 1996 Oliver Bennett could write in the *Independent on Sunday*, 'The Nineties were forecast to become a soft, warm era; a time for caring and sharing, nurturing and spiritual ... In the event, we work harder, have less faith and are more nihilistic, pessimistic and downright anxious than before.' One way or other the hopes of the early '90s had given way to something more depressing; a self-centred hedonism largely under the domination of contentless corporate commercialism; or, at best, alternative spiritualities whose truth could not be set out and debated in any really meaningful terms. And this collapse of confidence in the proclamation or discussion of truth is a discouraging hallmark of contemporary pluralism in general. There is no longer much faith that issues of value, belief or meaning can be settled by factual discussion.

This has a serious consequence. All we can then have is a plethora of competing lifestyles and world-views – competing, not on the grounds of truth, but on the grounds of power. And the '90s have indeed been distinguished by the steady balkanization of society, at least in America. Palestinian Edward Said has castigated the current fragmentation into a collection of competing ghettos, based on gender and ethnicity.[83] Postmodernism's disbelief in truth means that the liberal ideal of modernism – let our different beliefs be restricted to the private world, let's all work together for the common good – has increasingly been replaced by a 'tribal' climate[84] where different interest groups – gays, feminists, traditionalists, ethnic groups – compete in a naked struggle for influence. The process is even legitimated by contemporary gurus such as Foucault, who see the 'play of dominations' as the only fundamental reality.[85] But it runs counter to any hope of overall 'community';[86] and it often comes close to Fascism. 'Our own folk first', the slogan of the Dutch far right, might be a motto for many more politically correct but equally demanding groups. *Newsweek* viewed the '90s as the 'decade of anger: angry women, angry African-Americans, angry gays, angry taxpayers'. It's a recipe for an unattractive future. But isn't it made almost inevitable by the death of truth since the death of God?

These aspects of postmodernism have been mirrored in the development of pop. First, the fragmentation: 'The mainstream', wrote Andy Gill in 1994, 'as signified by the old Radio One/Top of the Pops consensus, all but dissolved a couple of years ago, leaving a plethora of sub-genres – rap, indie, metal, swingbeat, jungle, Britpop, and any number of house/techno variations.' More serious, however, is the issue of whether there is anything left to sing about. Music depends on a choice of what is worth singing, what is worthy of celebration; and postmodernism denies that anything is of absolute value or significance. There was an uneasy appropriateness when the early '90s saw music stores reducing their music displays to make room for computer and video games. (There were suggestions – maybe justified? – that these would take the place in the new generation's lives that music had had for their parents.)

Somehow the fire had gone out of pop; sales became dominated by 'back catalogue' (compilations of past artists), and the big events were the reunions of ancient groups – Velvet Underground, Sex Pistols, the Eagles, Television.[87] Subsequently the climate changed somewhat for the better. Yet even bands like Oasis were heavily 'retro', recreating old Beatles-style melodies in '90s terms.[88] 'People are now into old bands because the old bands are better than the new bands. It's just as simple as that', said Oasis' Noel Gallagher. 'Future historians may regard rock's first four post-Presley decades as its best', admitted the *Virgin Encyclopaedia of Rock* uneasily.[89] The nearest thing to a global superstar thrown up by early '90s rock was Kurt Cobain of Nirvana. And in his words – and suicide – the sense of self-destructive cul-de-sac, of the postmodern inaccessibility of meaning, became enormously tangible: 'I hate myself and want to die.'

But perhaps Cobain's life showed that our 'god-lessness', our lack of any 'vision thing', has its causes inside us, as well as in external factors. We are 'incredulous towards meta-narratives', say the postmodernists; the dialogue is over, there are no more 'god-substitutes' to believe in. But maybe we are the reason; maybe – even at a moment of deep environmental crisis – we've been losing the capacity for belief and for passion, even if there were things to believe and be passionate about.[90] Many observers sensed the shift in the '90s ethos. In America especially, grunge became the soundtrack of Generation X: a generation self-distrustful, marked by passivity, avoiding vulnerability, reluctant to step out or lead, staying within the 'comfort zones'. New York governor Mario Cuomo charged that America was producing unmotivated young adults averse to taking the risks required for endeavour. There are, of course, a high percentage of exceptions – but anyone in the student world has probably noticed something of what he meant.

Doesn't a sense of *déjà vu*, of exhaustion, hang over the whole contemporary scene? Underachievement seems a mark of postmodernity (with ironical appropriateness, given its rejection of the whole concept of greatness); Bart Simpson ('Underachiever and Proud of It') is its archetype. Baudrillard seems shallow beside Sartre or Camus, whatever the rights and wrongs of either; Eminem or Radiohead feel minor beside the Beatles or the Stones[91], Damien Hirst trivial beside Picasso, the succession of Booker winners transient compared to Lawrence, Joyce, Conrad. There are no new dreams to match the gigantic, even idolatrous, reach of Marxism or Freudianism. Of course such intuitions are subjective, and just three years could see them falsified. Yet there is a sense at present of something that is very *post-*. Modernity failed our deepest human needs, and comprehensively fouled our physical and spiritual environment in the process; yet the liberalism of modernity, and those other modernists who reacted against it, seem to have exhausted most of what can be said or achieved. There is a sense now of lack of vision, of aftermath, of epilogue.

Douglas Coupland's classic depiction in *Generation X* presented the 'slacker culture', opting out into 'McJobs'. 'Slackers' are the children of postmodernism, for whom there is simply nothing worth doing, hence little sense of vocation. ('Nobody believes in anything any more', reflected Neil Ascherson in a 1994 column on the death of activism.) Generation Xers and their successors are shaped by a postmodern culture dominated by the switchback of fashion, in which value judgements really don't apply. Long-term, nothing is much more important than anything else; today's hit will be in the garbage tomorrow. Andy Warhol, painter of soup cans and sculptor of Brillo pads, is our patron saint. To be concerned for value – to be concerned whether, say, *Citizen Kane* or *Casablanca* are among the ten greatest films of all time – is to reveal yourself as a 'cinema buff', something slightly abnormal. For the normal person, fashion, or the market, are the only determinants of value left; as Jeanette Winterson put it, 'Where there are no standards the market-place obtains', that is all.[92] 'Nothing really matters, anyone can see', sings the hero of Freddie Mercury's 'Bohemian Rhapsody' on his way to hell; 'Nothing really matters to me.'

Generation X: cool, ironical, unimpressed; detached (at least in the long-term) from achievement, commitment, idealism. But this fear of openness and involvement has its reasons; it is linked closely to the issues we considered in earlier chapters. First, one often notices in Xers and their successors a deep doubt of self-worth that seems connected to the issues of identity after the loss of God that we considered in Chapter 1.[93] Obviously, if you doubt your own value, you may well doubt the value of your commitments. Second, social psychologists might see a link between Xers' fears of risk, openness and commitment, and the collapse of (Christian) marriage as a lifelong loving commitment that we examined in Chapter 5. I recall an Atlanta youth worker saying of the teenagers he knew, 'These kids know nothing about commitment. How can they? They've never seen it at home: there's just been a succession of "uncles".' London church planter Roger Mitchell has invoked Jesus' story of the Lost Son in describing Generation X as the 'children of the prodigal ['60s] generation – the ones who no longer know there's any home left to come back to', and are deeply doubtful that they either are loved or can be. 'Papa was a rollin' stone', to quote the classic song, '... And when he died, all he left us was alone.'

And thirdly, Xers' detachment can express also a deep sense of fear – of commitments that may lead to date rape or AIDS; of risks that may lead to street violence; of a future shadowed by joblessness, nuclear terrorism or environmental breakdown. Again, we examined in our second chapter how this relates to our loss of God. Often beneath the X exterior (and picked up by

> My father's house shines hard and bright
> It stands like a beacon calling me in the night
> Calling and calling so cold and alone
> Shining 'cross this dark highway where our sins lie
> unatoned
>
> –Bruce Springsteen, 'My Father's House'

thriller-writers like John Grisham, and equally by *The X-Files*) is something of a nervy paranoia. The continuous need to perform in a management culture of audit and evaluation deepens that paranoia further. And all of this wearisome effort becomes doubly paradoxical when nothing is worth doing anyway.

'It doesn't matter whether there's a God or not.' But isn't the God-question fundamental to the 'understanding' of our time? Douglas Coupland, whose novel first defined Generation X, answered with a resounding 'Yes' when he published *Life After God*. 'YOU ARE THE FIRST GENERATION RAISED WITHOUT RELIGION', it said on the jacket; and two pages from the end came this:

> Now – here is my secret:
> I tell it to you with an openness of heart that I doubt I shall ever achieve again, so I pray that you are in a quiet room as you hear these words. My secret is that I need God – that I am sick and can no longer make it alone. I need God to help me give, because I no longer seem to be capable of giving; to help me be kind, as I no longer seem capable of kindness; to help me love, as I seem beyond being able to love.

Coupland's perceptions don't stand alone. 'It is countries where faith is weak and dwindling, like ours, that are full of fear and emptiness', remarked a 1994 editorial in the liberal *Independent*. Courtney Love, Kurt Cobain's widow, yelled at one New York audience, 'I'm really sick of this f***ing agnostic decade. Find something to believe in!' She added to an interviewer that she hoped by the time her daughter grew up 'drugs are not going to be chic any more. I pray religion, discipline, certain traditions will be cool.'[94] Possibly Coupland and Love point to the future; perhaps we are at the end of the secular century.[95]

Yet it is hard to believe today. The whole development of postmodernity – its denial of our identity and purpose, its doubts about love and truth and ethics – makes it psychologically difficult for us to think of commitments – to faiths, to relationships, to causes. 'Don't Worry, Be Happy'; postmodernism denies any real seriousness. There is no God now, so all that exists is image upon image, surface upon surface. There are no truths worth choosing, no passions uncorroded by irony, no causes worth stepping out of line for.[96]

Does it matter? It may; all this may turn out to be tragic beyond words. It may be catastrophic beyond words that this paralysis occurs just when a last effort needs to be made to turn the west away from collective selfishness, and into a seriously sacrificial concern for others and for the environment.[97]

But we seem unable to come up with any meaningful response. Are we now almost incapable of belief, purpose, commitment and self-sacrifice? Are we unable to believe anything intensely enough to make a difference, even as our McWorld slithers visibly towards disaster? Have we in the west made our fateful choice, one generation after another, during these successive decades?

Have our repeated choices against the biblical God, followed by the collapse of each of our god-substitutes, drawn us inexorably into the new dark ages?[98]

A good guide to the contemporary mood (depressing and entertaining in roughly equal quantities) is *Mostly Harmless*, the finale of Douglas Adams' *Hitchhiker's Guide* "trilogy". It's depressing because Adams uses it to re-enact for the worse the events of his first, much funnier book, and in the process to kill off all his main characters. It features the hippyish Ford Prefect finding that his hang-loose world has been taken over by faceless corporate bureaucrats – very much a '60s character's response to the postmodern dominance of the bottom line.

Prefect reflects on the collapse of the original dreams of the Guide's founders: 'All that had come when some of the original team had started to settle down and get greedy, while he and others had stayed out in the field, researching and hitch hiking, and gradually becoming more and more isolated from the corporate nightmare the Guide had inexorably turned into' (p.95). Meanwhile, Arthur Dent (who loses his lover suddenly and completely meaninglessly on p. 56) discovers he has arbitrarily acquired a daughter, named Random. Random is very much the passive, media-saturated Generation Xer coping with the results of the lifestyle of her parents' generation (pp. 126–34). Generally her conclusion is, 'Stupid! Stupid!'

Adams gives Random an enormous sense of homelessness. At the end she screams, "'I want a home! I want to fit somewhere!" "This is not your home," said Trillian (her mother), still keeping her voice calm. "You don't have one. We none of us have one. Hardly anybody has one anymore."' Random then completes a quite meaningless historical pattern, and precipitates the world's destruction, by accidentally shooting a bystander. As she collapses in guilt, Arthur 'wondered what he should do, but he only wondered it idly ... It was suddenly very clear to him that there was nothing to be done, not now or ever' (p. 218).

So the book ends, with everybody dead and the world destroyed. Its only hints of positives have to do with Elvis Presley and a casual concern for ecology (pp. 202, 206).

Notes

1. Cf. *In the Twilight of Western Thought*, pp. 35–36. I am not following Dooyeweerd's historical analysis here.
2. According to Dooyeweerd, 'Every idol gives rise to a counter-idol' (p. 166). We may restate that part of his argument like this: The principle that is absolutized or 'deified' is not broad enough to hold together all the other particulars; consequently it inevitably 'calls forth' its opposites, those other aspects or particulars that have been marginalized, which in turn then 'begin to claim an absoluteness opposite to that of the deified ones' (p. 36). Thus one 'god-substitute' succeeds another; ultimately, nothing but God is big enough to be God.

3. Obviously our history is an interplay of many types of processes – economic history, with the development of capitalism; political history, with the rise and fall of competing nation-states and political parties; and numerous others. But this approach has the merit of focusing on the things by which we ultimately live; and in practice it certainly offers a less soulless way of thinking about the past than, say, Marx's insistence that the key factor dominating any era is its 'means of production'.

4. There are constraints on this: what the artist perceives as acceptable or possible, and what patrons or audiences will tolerate or pay for. Also, to some extent what the artist is choosing to 'celebrate' is the act of artistic creation itself. But usually that is not all. (Or, if it is all – as has happened increasingly in modernity – then that itself becomes a statement about what (how little) is worth celebrating outside the work of art.)

5. Kenneth Clark observes that Rembrandt's mind 'was steeped in the Bible – he knew every story down to the minutest detail ... [His art] is an emotional response based on the truth of revealed religion' (*Civilisation*, pp. 143–44).

6. Cf. Rookmaaker, *Modern Art*, ch. 1.

7. Cf. Ian Watt, *The Rise of the Novel*.

8. See the Sermon on the Mount (e.g., Matthew 5:38–48).

9. Vinoth Ramachandra argues this point cogently in *Faiths in Conflict?*, pp. 149–51, which draws on William T. Cavanaugh, ' "A Fire Strong Enough to Consume the House": The Wars of Religion and the Rise of the State', *Modern Theology* 11.4 (1995).

10. There is still a God in the Enlightenment picture, but he tends to be pushed to the periphery – a distant divinity who created a perfect nature and perfect human reason, and then conveniently retired. Most expressions of Enlightenment thought tend towards deism.

11. An over-confidence that has been challenged by late-modernist thinkers. Docherty summarizes the position of Adorno and Horkheimer thus: 'Enlightenment itself is not the great demystifying force which will reveal and unmask ideology; rather, it is precisely the locus of ideology, thoroughly contaminated internally by the assumption that the world can match – indeed, can be encompassed by – our reasoning about it' (*Postmodernism*, p. 8).

12. The result was that 'progress' became central to the Enlightenment's ideology (or mythology). At the same time, the

Enlightenment looked back to the earlier triumphs of reason; there is a strong emphasis on the neo-classical in this period, often displacing the more relational, less abstract Judaeo-Christian vision.

13. As Karl Barth comments, in *Protestant Theology in the Nineteenth Century*, pp. 49–50.

14. At least until his more Christian *Amelia*.

15. In politics, too, perceptive observers recognized that 'Whatever is, is right' was not the whole story, that the apparently 'natural' political order was not the embodiment of reasonable perfection – insights leading in time to the French revolution and, in England, the great Reform Bills of the following century.

16. Of course there is no clean division between such periods as the 'Enlightenment' and 'Romanticism'; and any particular work contains a mixture of 'gods' that may or may not fit well together. Rousseau, for example, puts his faith in reason as he thinks about religion in a way that makes him clearly an Enlightenment figure, and is applauded as such by Kant. Yet in his championing of the unsullied child and of the individual over against the corruption of society, he is the first prophet of the gods of the Romantics. Thus to speak of, say, the Enlightenment, is to speak of the dominance of a particular synthesis of 'god-substitutes' that gradually gave way in influence, among more and more key figures, to a different synthesis.

17. Indeed, Edmund Burke remarked in 1790 that 'atheists and infidels' had now slipped into 'lasting oblivion' ('Who now reads Bolingbroke? Who ever read him through?'); while at the popular level, the blossoming of the evangelical wing of the church led to a considerable re-Christianizing of a great deal of British culture (and the abolition of slavery). Nineteenth-century evangelicalism owed a good deal to Romanticism, as is obvious from the passionate style of a C.T. Studd (see, for example, *Fool and Fanatic*); or, more destructively, in the attitude represented by Shaftesbury's bizarre comment that 'Satan reigns in the intellect, God in the heart of man.'

18. Although Wordsworth and Coleridge both moved back to Christian commitment in later life.

19. An example of how the change of 'god-substitutes' is embodied in general culture would be their effect on landscape gardening – from the rational, wide-open, geometrical arrangements of neo-classicism to the more unpredictable 'Romantic' arrangements popular a few decades later. Jane Austen (whose novels struggle

with the advent of the Romantic mindset – see *Sense and Sensibility* in particular) presents attitude to garden design as a key mark of personality in *Mansfield Park*.

20. The Romantic idolizing of the individual consciousness, as set over against society, is a key area in which it reacts against the Enlightenment synthesis. (This is a logical move onward from Kant's absolutizing of human autonomy: the Ego as God.) The figure of the Romantic Ego became embodied particularly in Napoleon. Dostoevski's *Crime and Punishment* questions how far this 'god-substitute' of the Napoleonic individual, free from all external constraints, can 'work', and how far it destroys those who put their trust in it.

21. There was also the 'satanist' end of Romanticism: Blake's *Marriage of Heaven and Hell*, Byron's *Lara*, de Sade, the teenage Marx's *Oulanem*.

22. And at greater length in the *Fall of Hyperion*, where Keats agonizes over the value of what the poet does as against those who make a tangible improvement to human existence – the choice he made in real life, as a former medical student. Imagination alone was not enough; what Keats lacked, compared to his Reformation predecessors, was a framework that could have underpinned the value of both, and a relationship with a 'nearby God' that could have made clear which of the two was his personal 'calling'.

23. Politically, the daydream-question arose with the disillusionment at the French Revolution (and its bloody aftermath), originally hymned with enthusiasm by Schiller, Beethoven (the Eroica Symphony dedicated originally to Napoleon) and Wordsworth.

24. Interestingly, this had far less impact in the USA, where many Christian thinkers adopted evolutionary theory into their world-view without obvious discomfort. B.B. Warfield would be an obvious example. But it is also clear that the broader world-view of evolution*ism* was a picture whose time had come. The Christian view of humanity as created perfect, then desperately marred, was already being challenged by a picture of our moving from primitive barbarism to ever-higher development. Lewis notes tellingly that the two key artistic embodiments of evolution*ism* (in Keats and Wagner) came before, not after, Darwin. Europe wanted to believe that we were automatically getting better and better, rather than needing supernatural redemption; now the scientific theory seemed to give an excuse (*Christian Reflections*, pp. 111–12).

25. Darwin was bad for the 'gods' of Romanticism too. The Nature that was so inspirational to Wordsworth becomes, for Tennyson, savage – 'red in tooth and claw'.

26. In Dickens' later work, his early optimism about the generosity of the human spirit slips into a far bleaker vision. Impersonal, dehumanizing forces are at work (reflecting the ongoing industrial revolution) against which Dickens' small 'alternative communities' (see, e.g., *Dombey and Son*) seem nonplussed, eccentric and powerless.

27. Quoted in Charles I. Glicksberg, *Literature and Religion*, pp. 221–22.

28. The great turn-of-the-century novelists James and Conrad can be read especially fruitfully in the light of this question; as Conrad puts it, 'how to be'. James (like Scott Fitzgerald) is very interested in what you can do with life if everything is possible; hence his interest in what the rich do (e.g. the wonderful *Portrait of a Lady*).

29. Space doesn't permit adequate exploration of where the aesthetic 'god' failed, but we may point to some further questions: the pervasive elitism, even hatred, directed against those who couldn't share the artist's intuitive values (extending often into crypto-fascism; see John Carey, *The Intellectuals and the Masses*); the egoism implicit in the wilful obscurity of the 'separate artistic universes' of, say, Pound's *Cantos* or Joyce's *Finnegan's Wake*; the sense of dilettantism, of failure to engage with the issues of the real world (if the 1920s saw the triumph of modernism, the '30s saw a reaction back to political (communist, Stalinist) commitment in writers like Auden); and the deep sense of horror and futility that recurs throughout much modernist writing – e.g. in most of early Eliot (before he became a Christian), or in Yeats' 'Why Should Not Old Men Be Mad?' or his end-point in the 'foul rag-and-bone shop of the heart' in 'The Circus Animals' Desertion'.

30. Quoted in Guinness, *Dust*, p. 10.

31. It should be added that in religion these years also saw an increasingly confident recovery of biblically-oriented faith after its interwar marginalization; for example in the rapid growth of the InterVarsity Fellowship (later UCCF). Sociologically, this can be seen as an example of new energies breaking through the logjam of humanistic complacency that is described in the following paragraph.

32. Quoted in Malcolm Doney, *Summer in the City*, p. 104.

33. Quoted in Doney, *Summer*, p. 66.
34. Quoted in Steve Turner's superb survey of rock and belief, *Hungry for Heaven*, p. 60. Turner's wide knowledge of the rock scene, and his personal acquaintance with a vast number of its key figures, make this book essential reading for anyone interested in music.
35. Quoted in Turner, *Hungry for Heaven*, p. 47.
36. Quoted in Tony Jasper, *Jesus and the Christian in a Pop Culture*, p. 34.
37. An outstanding assessment of the '60s, drawing out the underlying issues in a manner that is still deeply relevant, is Os Guinness' *The Dust of Death*. Guinness' work is crammed with perceptive insights and remains, I believe, one of the most brilliant pieces of culture criticism of recent decades.
38. Quoted in Turner, *Hungry for Heaven*, p. 61.
39. Quoted in Turner, *Hungry for Heaven*, p. 106.
40. Cf. the bitter opening of Julie Burchill and Tony Parsons, *The Boy Looked at Johnny: the obituary of rock and roll*.
41. Quoted in Dan Peters and Steve Peters, *Why Knock Rock?*, p. 180.
42. Quoted in Turner, *Hungry for Heaven*, pp. 107, 109.
43. 'After the political turmoil of the sixties, Americans have retreated to purely personal preoccupations. Having no hope of improving their lives in any of the ways that matter, people have convinced themselves that what matters is psychic self-improvement: getting in touch with their feelings, eating health food, taking lessons in ballet or belly-dancing ... overcoming the "fear of pleasure" ... Self-absorption defines the moral climate of contemporary society' (Lasch, *Narcissism*, pp. 29, 61).
44. Quoted in Peters and Peters, *Why Knock Rock?*, p. 30.
45. Also relevant here is a style, equally devoid of content, from later in the decade, disco – which was increasingly important from 1978 onwards. Unlike heavy metal, disco had a positive ambience, but a 1978 commentator (in *Newsweek* of all places) pointed out that it was equally meaningless, diluting the 'outlaw tradition' into 'outrageous chic'. 'Ten years ago, amidst war protests, Woodstock and the Democratic convention in Chicago, the Hollywood-rock connection would have been culturally unimaginable'; but now *Grease* and *Saturday Night Fever* offered a 'Dionysian celebration of middle-class values. The movies have a surface rebelliousness and danger, typified by Travolta's mesmerizing screen presence, that give way to a sweet, romantic heart.' It is perhaps significant that

disco culture arose in the context of the newly-emergent gay community. George Steiner has pointed out that an emphasis on self-referential style, devoid of other content, has tended to be a mark of European art where it has arisen within the homosexual context.

46. *New Musical Express*, 8 Oct. 1977.

47. The aftermath of the Beatles might offer a useful example: Lennon following his logic out onto the nihilistic frontier in tuneless material strongly influenced by John Cage (the creator of the *4'33"* piece of silent piano music), while McCartney declined into sugar-sweet commercialism?

48. Quoted in Turner, *Hungry for Heaven*, p.146.

49. Quoted in Peters and Peters, *Why Knock Rock?*, p. 104.

50. Quoted in *Virgin Encyclopaedia of Rock*, ed. Michael Heatley, p. 242.

51. Quoted in Peters and Peters, *Why Knock Rock?*, p. 105.

52. *TV Times*, 25 Oct. 1986.

53. One could cite other parallels. Looking back to Christian sources became a possible action again in the '80s. Julia Kristeva, one of the groundbreaking structuralist '60s radicals, now discovered a convergence between her concerns and those of 'St Bernard and St Thomas ... For me, in a very Christian fashion, ethics merges with love' (cf. *The Kristeva Reader*, pp. 8, 21). Or we might cite the 1983 *Standard* interview where John Cleese expressed a new interest to 'know if there is something going on' in religion: 'I feel some of the extraordinary achievements of the Victorians came out of a faith that sustained them through tough times, and so much has now been thrown out, particularly in the field of religion, because of the advance of science.' From a rather different perspective, the supernatural came back to life in the arts in a manner that would have seemed highly improper to '50s humanism, through the impact of 'magic realism': primarily from Latin American writers such as Gabriel Garcia Marquez, but finding echoes in Salman Rushdie or Ben Okri – or Britain's 'senior' poet, Ted Hughes, in his shamanistic or occultistic moods.

54. Turner, *Hungry for Heaven*, p. 154. Even in a secular society, the God-words – 'God', 'Christ', 'Jesus' – seem linked (along with sexual and scatological terms) to some awareness so fundamental that we are forced to turn to them when we need words to express deep anger, amazement or grief.

55. Turner, *Hungry for Heaven*, p. 159. The Beatles had done something similar in 'Let It Be'.

56. A similar bizarre combination was evident in Prince's mixing of flaunted sexuality with demands to his audience of 'Do you love God?'

57. A 1987 youth study by McCann Erickson showed that, compared with the generation ten years earlier, '80s youth were sceptical and hedonistic yet also conservative; doubting idealism and valuing health and money more highly than love – in striking contrast to their predecessors.

58. 'At no point', wrote Ian Aitken of star Conservative Chancellor Nigel Lawson's pamphlet *The New Conservatism*, 'does Mr Lawson touch upon those principles of compassion, charity or even "noblesse oblige" which once formed part of the Tory ethos' (*Guardian*, 6 Aug. 1980).

59. The weakness of 'traditional values' was demonstrated again in the early '90s by John Major's well-meaning challenge to the Conservative party conference to get 'back to basics'. It was unfortunate that the prurience of the tabloid media reduced his concerns immediately to sex ethics; and a series of Tory financial and sexual improprieties in the following months torpedoed the entire project. In themselves, 'traditional values' were shown to offer neither a robustly coherent programme, nor the internal power to live them out without double standards. The sad thing was that there was something good and significant about what Major was trying, in a well-intentioned if ultimately inadequate manner, to define and promote.

60. In the hippie '60s, it was said, students studied sociology in order to change the world; in the '70s, they studied psychology to change themselves; in the yuppie '80s they studied business administration to survive.

61. *Time*, 19 Mar. 1984.

62. *Guardian*, 3 Dec. 1984.

63. Marvin Gaye, Otis Redding, Ray Charles, Wilson Pickett, Curtis Mayfield, Randy Crawford, Gladys Knight, Dionne Warwick, Barry White, Aretha Franklin, Whitney Houston and Al Green all came from this background – and in many cases continued to seem proud of it.

64. Flash's lyricist commented 'I wanted to create my own image. It's a way of being anti-Christian' (quoted in Peters and Peters, *Why Knock Rock?*, p. 101).

65. Armond White, *Rebel for the Hell of It*, pp. 168, 161, 167.

66. The sense of disappointment was expressed by Hugo Young in the *Guardian*: 'At the end of 1991, this image of political leadership lies shattered. It is the most telling change not just of this year but of several ... What can now hardly be disputed is that wherever you look ... a generation of self-confident conviction politicians has been replaced by leaders hopelessly engulfed in events bigger than they are.'

67. Smith's Christian faith was 'central to what he was and stood for', says Blair in his book *New Britain*, p. 58. Blair's book contains a whole chapter titled 'Why I Am A Christian'. But although Christian Socialism supplied the original basis for a coherent 'New Labour' ideology, the party remains a slightly bizarre coalition of not very compatible elements.

68. Collin, *Altered State*, pp. 60, 62.

69. Collin, *Altered State*, p. 95.

70. Collin, *Altered State*, pp. 86, 82. 'All the early stuff you used to read about the London acid house scene was love and peace, but then they had the most strict door policy', complained a Manchester DJ (p. 146). 'We didn't want to go and mix with these people', says one of those involved from the beginning about her reaction to newcomers (p. 69).

71. Collin, *Altered State*, p. 38.

72. Collin, *Altered State*, pp. 159, 172.

73. Collin, *Altered State*, pp. 255–60.

74. Collin, *Altered State*, pp. 52, 53.

75. Collin, *Altered State*, p. 65.

76. Collin, *Altered State*, p. 5.

77. Collin, *Altered State*, p. 196. Collin quotes a comment that whereas the '60s counterculture gave rise to an articulate underground press, all the Ecstasy culture had was music magazines (p. 70).

78. Collin, *Altered State*, pp. 197–206. Note, too, the religious imagery used by DJs: 'the Shaman', 'the Prophet', 'the High Priest', 'Zen Inspired Pagan Professionals'. 'Along with the techno scene has come a lot of exploration in new spirituality', said Phil Hartnoll of Orbital: 'It seems as though everyone has got crystals hanging around their necks' (quoted in Turner, *Hungry for Heaven*, p. 228).

79. Collin, *Altered State*, p. 7. An interesting moment was when Colston Hayter presented his projects to the Tory conference (p. 111).

80. Collin, *Altered State*, p. 313. Collin argues that the same 'uneasy synthesis' has marked Blair's 'New Labour' ethos.
81. Collin, *Altered State*, p. 271.
82. Collin, *Altered State*, p. 275. This was the summary of a 1999 *Independent on Sunday* writer, Oliver Stanton: '"Peace, love and unity" may have been the constant Acid House refrain 10 years ago but, looking back now, we know it didn't mean much at all ... The "peace" mantra slowly became an advertising strapline at the bottom of increasingly glossy flyers for increasingly expensive raves. Then it was replaced by corporate sponsorship logos – beer, spirits, jeans, even cigarettes. No one noticed, no one cared.'
83. Noticeably, President Clinton's inauguration speech at the start of his second term took up this theme: 'Will we be one nation, one people with one common destiny? Will we come together or come apart?'
84. Postmodernists might defend this situation on the grounds that 'little, "local" narratives' do less damage than overarching 'master narratives'. But one only needs to think of the mass killings in the Balkan conflicts to see the horror that 'little, "local" narratives' can cause.
85. And again by the postmodern 'pragmatist' Rorty's argument (in *Objectivity, Relativism and Truth*) that 'There is ... this much truth in ethnocentrism: we cannot justify our beliefs ... to everybody, but only to those whose beliefs overlap ours to some appropriate extent ... The pragmatist ... can only be criticised for taking his own community *too* seriously. He can only be criticised for ethnocentrism, not relativism. To be ethnocentric is to divide the human race into the people to whom one must justify one's beliefs and the others. The first group – one's *ethnos* – comprises those who share enough of one's beliefs to make fruitful conversation possible.'
86. Kevin Ford asserts the distrust of America's Generation X for the structures of the broader business, political and religious worlds and their loyalty to more 'local' groupings, but then concludes, 'So they feel no connection, no loyalty, no responsibility toward the outside world ... The only world my generation feels any allegiance to or affection for is the closer, more intimate world of our friends. We desire friends who will be loyal to us. At the same time we're afraid of commitment. We're afraid of vulnerability. We want to communicate but we don't know how. So we

surround ourselves with other people just like us' (*Jesus for a New Generation*, p. 49).

87. 'Pop music in the Nineties will be remembered primarily for the reunions': Nicholas Barber, *Independent on Sunday*, 15 Nov. 1998.

88. 'The whole Beatles message was Be Here Now', said John Lennon on one occasion, and of course 'Be Here Now' became an Oasis album title. Even Oasis' name came from the club where the Beatles did their first gig.

89. *Virgin Encyclopaedia of Rock*, p. 7. Interestingly, as rock seemingly lost its way, various classical composers started to sell heavily – and these often drew strongly on the Christian framework in one way or another: John Tavener, Henryk Gorecki, Arvo Part, James MacMillan, Gavin Bryars' curiously cleansing 'Jesus' Blood Never Failed Me Yet', Gregorian chant.

90. Richard Hoggart has spoken of the rise of a generation of 'moral cretins' afraid to make judgements about anything. Ultimately, of course, relativism erodes passion.

91. Ian Macdonald's superb *Revolution in the Head* (hailed in *Q* as the 'most sustainedly brilliant piece of pop criticism for years') concludes that pop music is in 'catastrophic decline', and that anyone looking at '60s music must be 'aware that they are looking at something on a higher scale of achievement than today's ... That the same can be said of other musical forms – most obviously classical and jazz – confirms that something in the soul of Western culture began to die during the late Sixties' (p. 299). That may seem highly oversimplified, but the underlying question is an essential one.

92. The fact that amid the valuelessness of postmodernism only money is left to call the shots means that power moves to the class with the most disposable income. Hence single adults are now the key group at the core of cultural development whereas in, say, 1968, it was students.

93. As so often, Christopher Lasch's *The Culture of Narcissism* remains remarkably accurate in catching the postmodern mood (p. 174): 'Escape through irony and self-awareness is in any case itself an illusion; at best it provides only momentary relief. Distancing soon becomes a routine in its own right. Awareness commenting on awareness creates an escalating cycle of self-consciousness that inhibits spontaneity. It intensifies the feeling of inauthenticity ... We long for the suspension of self-consciousness, of the pseudo-analytic attitude that has become second nature; but

neither art nor religion, historically the great emancipators from the prison of the self, retain the power to discourage disbelief.'

94. I owe this quotation to Jock McGregor of L'Abri.

95. After all, Lyotard's classic description of the postmodern era as 'incredulous towards meta-narratives' referred not so much to Christianity as to the death of the liberal dream. It may be humanism that has crumpled most in the advent of postmodernism.

96. Rock critic Nicholas Barber, writing in the *Independent on Sunday* about nu-metal bands such as Limp Bizkit, Papa Roach and Slipknot, complains of their lack of any message except self-pity, and concludes that in most cases they merely 'greet everything … with a raised middle finger'. (Although that form of communication has some logic in a postmodernity which denies the feasibility of saying anything true?)

97. 'The global meltdown has begun', wrote George Monbiot (*Guardian*, 2 July 1999). 'The effects of climate change are arriving faster than even the gloomiest prophets expected. This week we learnt that the Arctic ecosystem is collapsing. Polar bear and seal populations appear to have halved. Three weeks ago, marine biologists reported that almost all the world's coral reefs could be dead by the end of the coming century … Climate change is perhaps the gravest calamity our species has ever encountered … One month ago, the Red Cross reported that natural disasters uprooted more people in 1998 than all the wars and conflicts on earth combined. Climate change, it warned, is about to precipitate a series of "super-disasters"'. These may in fact have begun; already the last year was the worst ever recorded for floods; plus it saw the western hemisphere's worst-ever hurricane, and three thousand dying as India was hit by the biggest heatwave in half a century. Almost all scientists expect the pace of these changes to accelerate. ('If you have some massive insight that the world is going to end, and end quickly, how on earth are you going to get this over to people?', asked Joseph Harman, discoverer of the ozone hole over Antarctica.) Meanwhile, the world has for the first time begun to eat more food than it grows; yet there are still 93 million more people being added to its population each year. The World Commission on Water reported that within 25 years we will need 56% more water than is currently available, leading perhaps to water wars. 'We are sawing through the branch that is holding us,' said a UN report on world population, 'and if we carry on as before, it

may break and bring us crashing down with it ... We are not talking about the interests of distant descendants. It is our own children.' (The maddening thing is that so many of these problems are directly traceable to our own, still-continuing, avarice – our own carelessness about the ozone layer, global warming, fossil-fuel overuse and rainforest destruction; our own demotivation to think beyond 'money sex and status'.)

98. I'm quoting this phrase from renowned culture critic George Steiner, who has written of the 'feeling of disarray, of a regress into violence, into moral obtuseness; our ready impression of a central failure of values in the arts, in the comeliness of personal and social modes; our fears of a "new dark age" in which civilization itself, as we have known it, may disappear' (*In Bluebeard's Castle*, p. 46). Robert Kaplan's controversial *Atlantic Monthly* article 'The Coming Anarchy' presented a similar view of post-postmodernity, where 'criminal anarchy' was 'the real "strategic" danger': 'Disease, overpopulation, unprovoked crime, scarcity of resources, refugee migrations ... and the empowerment of private armies, security firms and international drug cartels'. The horrendous brutality raging at that point in west Africa provided, he suggested, 'an appropriate introduction to the issues ... that will soon confront our civilization'. But then might not *Mad Max*-style external anarchy be matched by internal anarchy in a culture where the average person believes, 'post-God', that the individual has no value, life no meaning, right and wrong – and love – no reality; that it really is every man for himself, a Nietzschean world where the strong survive and the weak go to the wall? (Gangsta rap already presents music from such a world.) We recall how quickly (15 years?) Germany slid down the slope into killer-Nazism, once things went badly wrong economically. The generation now adult still believes, intuitively, in many things for which postmodernism, devoid of God, gives no foundation. But, as Os Guinness says, the real test of a cultural shift is not its effects on the first generation, but on the third. These will shape the world we grow old in; the world our children will have built on the disbeliefs we gave them.

roots

understanding the breaking-point

Postmodern culture is a stranger to profundity.

We've seen the 'modern/postmodern' story: generation succeeds generation, pursuing (at least till recently) one 'god-replacement' after another; and none of it quite meets our needs. Meanwhile, however, the fundamental value-structure of our whole 'civilization' is under very serious strain, and our physical environment still more so; but we seem incapable of dealing with, or even facing, the issues. Something is going badly wrong, but we seem unable to ask what it is. Postmodern culture is desperately shy of such seriousness.

Surface, immediacy, image: this is postmodernity. And it isn't enough. Yet to find 'profundity' you have to dig deep, beyond the surface – and to know where to dig. But we no longer know where to look; and one place in particular that we've closed off is the past. The postmodernist is sure of nothing about the past; history is a mass of conflicting interpretations. Sooner or later, it means nothing for us at all.

Yet we remain hungry. A mark of postmodern culture is the wistful yearning after tradition; we mix and match and come up with things bearing little relation to past reality. But we hunger for a story that gives us roots.

There is a contender. In previous sections, we've explored the pressure points we face in *identity* (who am I? what is my worth?); *purpose* (what am I living for?); *ethics* (how do we know what to do?); *truth* (why should we believe anything at all?); and *love* (why do our relationships fail? what could help make them work?). We've seen how many of these issues link in with the loss of God from our culture's heart.

Perhaps we need to listen again to the oldest story of all, because it unifies these themes, and suggests what's gone wrong.

Here it is, from the book of Genesis ...

Proud to be human

Genesis opens the Bible with a brief narrative depicting our world's origins and creation. (It's a good section to read with the question, 'What is God like?') But that's only the book's very first chapter. It then moves on to present the arrival of humankind.

And what it gives us here is an extremely important statement. It describes humanity, our identity and concerns, 'as we were meant to be', before everything went wrong. It offers a confident, attractive vision of fourteen aspects of what it means to be truly human – a confidence we badly need amid all the depersonalizing forces of postmodernity. Human beings, we can read, are:[1]

- part indeed of the animal creation; yet their coming also marks a radical break in our planet's story (see Genesis 1:24–26[2]). So, we're kin indeed to the animals; yet that's not all. We're not just 'naked apes', 'nothing but mammals'.
- created '*in the image of God*' (1:26–27). Now there is an astounding phrase. If we dare to believe it, it offers a highly significant element for our identity. So, *every* human being has absolute, intrinsic worth and dignity.
- responsible before God to steward and care for the environment (1:26–28).[3]
- called to 'be fruitful and increase in number' (until the earth is 'filled'; we must be close to that now? [1:28]). Family life and

growth, then, are basic to being human; they aren't just a biological drive that gets prettified by our sentiment.

- marked by an aesthetic sense – enjoying what is 'pleasing to
  the eye' or 'good for food' (2:9). So the love of artistic beauty
  (or good Chinese food!) isn't just an accidental by-product of
  the evolutionary process; it correlates to something deeply
  human.

- explorers and adventurers (look at the interests expressed in
  2:10–14).

- beings capable of making use of the earth's wealth for artistic
  and practical purposes (2:12).

- workers, whose nature is fulfilled in purposeful, creative
  labour (see 2:15). We recall again Brunner's remark: both
  Marxism and capitalism tend to see work as an unfortunate
  necessity, a means only to the acquisition of material goods.
  The Bible regards creative, caring work as an activity (and
  hence a need) intrinsically bound up with being human; even if
  its nature has been changed by the problems arising from the
  Fall. (Such a view has major implications for how we
  approach the urgency of the unemployment issue, of course.)

- in real relationship with God – God is not hidden from them
  (2:16).

- marked by genuine and responsible freedom. They know the
  commands of God and can obey or ignore them (2:16–17).

- built for friendship and companionship – lovers, sexual beings
  (2:18,22–24).

- scientists! (2:19) – called to discern and define the nature of
  each member of the animal creation.

- artists with words (2:19–20 again) – capable of taking language and using it to create something new, that will give
  expression to what is present in God's created reality.

- poets – watch how Adam bursts out in exuberant song as he
  encounters his lover (2:23)!

> This is such a relevant statement that it's tragic to find
> Genesis 'out of reach' for many people because of
> non-issues. 'Surely you can't think Genesis worth

reading?' Why not? 'Well, surely you don't believe in Adam and Eve?' But how does one go about 'believing in Adam and Eve'? The word 'Adam' is simply the Hebrew for 'Man', and 'Eve', as Genesis states, comes from 'Mother of all the living' (3:20). So 'believing in Adam and Eve' simply means believing that at some point there came a first-ever couple who could be described as human, which is obviously true. Logically, they're called 'The Man' and 'The Mother of All the Living'. What Genesis then offers is the idea that our history was shaped by a fundamental crisis occurring to this couple (rather than later on).

'But you really can't think Genesis worth reading? What about science?' Again, it's a tragedy to miss this profound narrative because of such a red herring – the whole question misses the point. Genesis isn't a scientific textbook, so it doesn't speak to questions we might find intriguing, like: To what extent did God make use of evolution in creation? And 'the Man' and 'the Mother': did other humanoids exist before their creation, similar yet lacking God's gift of that invisible 'spirit' which marks truly human life? Genesis simply doesn't tell us.[4]

'But doesn't it insist that the world was made in a week?' No, it certainly doesn't. It structures its story around six 'days' of creation, but it isn't concerned to spell out what it means by 'day' either. Indeed it puts a question mark over the matter; for the 'great light' of the sun, marking day and night, isn't part of the story till halfway through the process (the fourth 'day', 1:14–18). So we may read these 'days', if we choose, as 24-hour periods; or, as elsewhere in the Bible[5], far longer ones. In fact the Hebrew original, unlike our English Bibles, describes these days as 'day one', 'day two', etc; or, 'a first day', 'a second day'. So if this issue is getting in our way, we may recall that the text offers the option of five enormous gaps of millions of years of process, each of which follows and precedes 'a day' of God's intervening initiative, God's special creative action.

'But can you take Genesis seriously now we know about evolution?' In practice we evidently can, and do. Large numbers of practising scientists (e.g. members of Christians in Science in Britain, or of the American Scientific Affiliation) have no difficulty believing both in the Genesis accounts and in evolutionary theory. Clearly, learning from one doesn't rule out learning from the other.[6]

It would be tragic for such things to rob us of the real input from this profound, primal narrative ...

Here are things worth living for – things we were *made* for. And when we respond to the skilled craftsman, the Arctic explorer, the brilliant guitarist, the creative developer of natural resources, the campaigner for the environment, the loving parent, the innovative microbiologist, the imaginative novelist, the good cook or the exuberant lover – when we sense joy at seeing the glory of the human being expressed in these ways, we aren't just being sentimental. We're relating to reality.

Nor is this an idealism that should fade before hard sociobiological dogma, that insists we are machines sublimating in apparently 'human' acts our genetic drives and biochemical impulses. Rather, our gut reaction is an accurate perception of truth: of what it is to be authentically human as God made us.

It is good to be human! And that needs saying in our century. However, the story goes on. Something went wrong ...

The Fall

'Now the LORD God had planted a garden in the east, in Eden; and there he put the Man he had formed' (2:8). But into that garden[7] – this is Genesis 3 now – enters the serpent.

'The serpent' is an image we find in other biblical writers representing a spirit-power of conscious evil, utterly opposed to God.[8] As westerners we have a knee-jerk reaction against the notion of spirit-powers, but to a large extent this is a matter of packaging. Set the same notion in a context of Tibetan Buddhism, Latin American 'magic realism', or Native American or Australian Aboriginal belief, and many westerners find it easier to cope with.[9] Multiculturalism is eroding our easy assurance that we know how the universe works. But be that as it may, in the next verses the whole narrative comes right home. These are supposedly ancient myths; yet anyone with a code of right and wrong who has experienced temptation to depart from it will recognize the psychological realism of what follows in the primal catastrophe.

Temptation, step one: the serpent *'said to the woman, "Did God really say, "You must not eat from any tree in the garden?"'* It was the one command God had given these two first human beings – to prove, and enable them to express, their love and, especially, their trust. The attack is 'epistemological', challenging our grasp of truth: Did God *really* say? Do we have access to his words? Is it really so annoyingly clear what's right in the particular issue I'm facing?

How can we know what's right? This has been a prime question ever since the Enlightenment – but we've probably heard that voice whispering in our own moral lives too. But there's probably another issue here. Did God *really* say ... could his word to humankind *really* pivot on such a matter as food? Could so small an action really be important?[10] ('It's only a minor tax detail, and the taxman already takes enough.' 'It's only a white lie.' 'I'll only sleep with her once – it will do their marriage good.' 'Yes, we did fix the accounts, but it was for a good purpose.')

The point is immediately recognizable: temptation is powerful when it comes pretending to be so – extremely – minor. It's interesting that Jesus repeats this whole struggle (but in a desert, not a garden), at the start of his ministry; and again, the first temptation comes in these apparently 'minor' terms of food.[11] (His way of handling it also repeats Genesis: immediately he affirms the accessibility of God's commands with 'It is written ...'[12], confronting the truth-issue, the 'Did God really say ...?') Jesus' teaching was that ethics speaks directly to the detail of everyday existence, as well as to the major struggles: 'Whoever can be trusted with very little can also be trusted with much, and whoever is dishonest with very little will also be dishonest with much.'[13] The Genesis tempter urges the opposite: we can cheat on the small change and still hope to have the ethical muscle to do what is right when the major issues come (and perhaps our job is on the line).

Maybe there's a third issue here too. The tempter's 'You must not eat from any tree in the garden' caricatures the divine command as something stricter than it was. This, too, is a recognizable undermining of ethics – the lure of legalism, which triggers the reaction of abandoning restraint altogether. The woman makes the correction as the narrative continues: '*We may eat fruit from the trees in the garden, but God did say, "You must not eat fruit from the tree that is in the middle of the garden, and you must not touch it, or you will die."*' The first part of the serpent's reply – '*You will not surely die*' – again is so true to our experience of temptation. There will be no penalty; it's alright; nothing will go wrong (or, theologically, God won't judge us). And finally comes the most important sentence in the story: evil adds, '*God knows that when you eat of it your eyes will be opened, and you will be like God, knowing good and evil.*'

Here is the central decision from which everything will follow. To obey God, or not; to try to have your 'eyes opened' in apartness from God; to hope for autonomous self-fulfilment, to seek to 'know good and evil' in apartness from God; in the end, to attempt to be 'like God', determining and setting the rules for our own universe. 'Choose for yourself', 'dare to know' – the watchword of the 'modern' world, according to Kant. If autonomy was the hallmark of 'modern' western culture[14] – 'man come of age', functioning apart from God – then here is its image. If there is a God, that choice is the crucial issue for us, both as a race and as individuals.

The irony in the text is, of course, that they already knew what was good and evil: God had told them what, in his love, he wanted them to do. The issue was whether they trusted him. So to seek to 'know good and evil' was to deny that 'good and evil' were the same as 'what God desires or rules out'. It was to seek to be Nietzsche's Superman, fabricating your own ethics, deciding how your world should be run. As we have seen, dislodging God from the heart of our ethics has led in the long run to a moral vacuum. This fundamental question – Who is to run the world, to decide what is right and wrong? Who is to be the ultimate Lord: I or God? – finally determines life's direction for each of us, and for our culture.

The tragedy was that they lost the very thing they were reaching out to seize. The vital issue in life, says St Paul, is to 'live by faith'; so it's not surprising that faith, trust, is the question here. The first humans didn't trust God to love them totally; they thought there was something better to be grasped at than what he would give them. (Again, that choice, that untrusting temptation, is quite familiar for many of us.) The New Testament sets out the wonder of what God had in mind: he desires to share all his glory with us, to live within us and transform us from within, until ultimately, unimaginably, we actually grow transfigured into the 'image of his Son', Jesus. This is central to the radiant vision inspiring St Paul. Learning to know God means, eventually, that all that is his becomes ours: all that love, peace, joy, gentleness, glory and power for goodness can one day stream out through our personalities, as they did from Christ's.[15] The glory of the God of love is that he shares all he has with us.[16] But it is by entering into that loving process that we will 'be like God' – not (like the first humans) by snatching pitifully at control of our own universe. Yet we all do it: it's *my* life; this is *my* world; I'll 'do it *my* way'.

We know what happened next. The 'declaration of autonomy' tied in with a prioritizing of physical gratification (it often does). Man and woman rejected God's rule. And a total change of consciousness indeed followed. '*When the woman saw that the fruit of the tree was good for food and pleasing to the eye, and also* desirable for gaining wisdom, she took some and ate it. She also gave some to her husband, who was with her, and he ate it. Then the eyes of both of them were opened, and they realised that they were naked ...' And then come the tragic words: 'Then the man and his wife heard the sound of the LORD God as he was walking in the garden in the cool of the day, and they hid from the LORD God among the trees ...'

Immeasurable loss. Throughout the millennia that have followed, saints, sages, mystics and outright cranks have done almost everything imaginable in quest of recovered communion with the Eternal One. And here, in the dawn of human history, he had taken on human form and was walking in the evening coolness to meet the people he loved. They knew the relationship had irrevocably altered: they hid.

They hid among the trees; which were themselves God's gifts, 'pleasant to the eye and good for food' (2:9). Maybe we've been doing it ever since – hiding from the loss of ultimate transcendence among all kinds of inadequate, substitute, alternative desires. Hiding too from that disturbing voice among the gifts God has given us, among so many of the things we saw in Genesis 2 that are basic to our humanness; hiding from our sense of loss with the walkman, the packed schedule, the urge for power or achievement, acquisition, sexual ecstasy, the family unit.[17] Nonetheless, the voice comes to the man: 'Where are you?'

Not, of course, because God didn't know. A Being that a human writer could call God would not need to wonder where his people are. But for the humans, it was the key question that needed to be faced (so too, perhaps, today): Where are we? Why are we in this position?

'Have you eaten from the tree from which I commanded you not to eat?' The man is faced with another crucial choice. Confession and repentance were possible. Who knows what mercy might have followed? But no: what we read is again familiar and realistic, the rapid passing of the buck ...

'The man said, "The woman you put here with me"' (it is God's fault, my environment's, the woman's, anything but my own), '"she gave me some fruit from the tree, and I ate it."

'Then the LORD God said to the woman, "What is this you have done?"

'The woman said, "The serpent deceived me, and I ate."'

Paradise lost ... Yet at this point the utterly unforeseeable possibility of redemption enters the story. The judgement God pronounces on the demonic power that has contrived the whole catastrophe concludes, '*I will put enmity between you and the woman, and between your offspring and hers; he will crush your head, and you will strike his heel.*' Throughout the centuries that followed, expectation of this 'offspring' who would break the power of evil was a longing that haunted humankind. Christians believe it was when Christ himself was born to a woman, and then – in his death – was struck by the worst the Enemy could do, that evil was finally broken. In which case there could be no clearer picture of the unsearchably loving nature of the God we worship. Here, in the moment of treachery, he guarantees his own identification with this deceived and ruined rabble to the point where he himself, God in Christ, will hang on a cross to solve their problem, crying out in anguish and horror: '*My God! My God! Why have you forsaken me?*'[18]

... Now it begins

But now the wheels have begun to turn; the processes are underway that will lead to the world we know. The next verses record a spreading breakdown of relationships. The vertical, God/human relation is broken; the horizontal relationships begin to follow suit. It is as if we are disconnected from the power-source for love that would make them work; like a fire disconnected from the mains, still glowing now but slowly turning cold. We've already watched the man try to shift his guilt to the woman, instead of standing by her in mutual care and protection. A few verses later comes God's prophetic warning of the results in sexual relationship – '*Your desire will be for your husband, and he will rule over you*': desire and domination replace the liberty of love that God had planned.

And it spreads. The relationship between humankind and nature also now changes: '*Cursed is the ground because of you*' (meaningful enough words in today's environment); '*through painful toil you will eat of it all the days of your life. It will produce thorns and thistles for you.*' How different could it have been? We don't know; we are outside Eden. '*So the LORD God banished him from the Garden of Eden to work the ground from which he had been taken. After he drove the man out, he placed on the east side of the Garden of Eden cherubim and a flaming sword flashing back and forth, to guard the way to the tree of life.*' Banished from Eden; shut out from the heart of life.

Where does the break lie in our 'loss of God'? We sometimes view things (this book may have done so) as if our culture has somehow sent the Almighty packing. That would of course be a foolish thing to have done; and it might explain the difficulties we face. But the notion is arrogantly absurd. We sent the Almighty packing? The issue raised by Genesis is the same one raised at the end of the Bible, where the full, catastrophic consequences of our failed autonomy are repeatedly 'released'.[19] It is the issue expressed by French sociologist Jacques Ellul (better known for his acclaimed *The Technological Society*) in the title of his book *Hope in a Time of Abandonment*. Perhaps that is how we should think of our poisoned oceans, our repetitive but increasingly destructive conflicts, our ruined ozone layer; it may not be we who have abandoned God, it may be he who, provoked beyond endurance, has abandoned us to our self-destruction. (Or to quote the refrain of rock poet Steve Turner's catalogue of humanly-created evils in 'I Looked Down': 'And I'm turning my face from you.'[20])

But the breakdown of relations continues: the next verses introduce the first murder.

The Outsider

The fundamental human problem, according to Marx, can be defined in terms of alienation. Marx was right – though his diagnosis (and hence his solution) didn't go deep enough. Jesus insists that the most fundamental thing in our lives, determining our experience of alienation, is not our work (as Marx suggested). Rather, the ultimate focal point must logically be our relation with our Maker – if he exists. If he does, and if our relationship with him is broken, then the inevitable result must be alienation spreading into our other relationships in ever-widening circles: intra-familial crisis, marital crisis, class struggle, ethnic, racial, tribal and communal tension.

Something of this is what happens in Genesis 4. The realism is again striking.

Outside Eden, the issue that causes the first murder is worship. (Does that seem strange? If religion is where we seek to link into the universe's heart, then it's going to matter to us; and in our state of alienation, it will trigger major emotional storms as we find we 'can't make it work'.) Cain brings God a sacrifice of what grows naturally. Abel, the shepherd, sacrifices a sheep. Abel's offering is accepted; Cain's is not.

What is the point here? Is Abel to be seen as learning from what God did earlier (3:21); is he remembering that death was the inevitable consequence of our rebellion (2:17), and that somehow this must be taken into account – that (as the New Testament puts it, looking to Jesus' ultimate sacrifice[21]) 'without the shedding of blood there is no forgiveness'? Is the acceptance of Abel's offering over Cain's simply educational,[22] teaching both brothers the way to approach God, challenging them to reflect on the reasons? We don't know. What we do read is that Cain wasn't having it, and murdered Abel. So the breakdown of relationships moved a step further.

What happens then? God asks: *'Where is your brother Abel?' 'I don't know'*, replies Cain. *'Am I my brother's keeper?'* The answer, of course, is Yes; love involves each of us in unlimited responsibility for the well-being of one another ('Love your neighbour *as yourself*'). Cain denies that (just as we do, particularly when faced with global poverty); alienation is the inevitable result.

'The LORD said, "What have you done? Listen! Your brother's blood cries out to me from the ground. Now you are

under a curse and driven from the ground, which opened its mouth to receive your brother's blood from your hand. When you work the ground, it will no longer yield its crops for you. You will be a restless wanderer on the earth."

'Cain said to the LORD, "My punishment is more than I can bear. Today you are driving me from the land, and I will be hidden from your presence; I will be a restless wanderer on the earth ..."'

'The ground ... the ground ... the ground ... the earth ... the land ... the earth': the bond between ourselves and our environment is repeatedly stressed, strangely to western ears. But westerners aren't always right (and what have we done to the world from which we've separated ourselves?). It wouldn't be so strange to other cultures – 'First People', Australian Aboriginals, Native Americans – who sense much more intimate relationships binding us (and our right- or wrong-doing) to the land.[23] Still, Cain is alienated, egocentric man, and what he really worries about is not his loss of God's presence, nor 'the land', but his own physical safety ...

'"...I will be a restless wanderer on the earth, and whoever finds me will kill me."

'But the LORD said to him, "Not so ..." Then the LORD put a mark on Cain so that no one who found him would kill him. So Cain went out from the LORD's presence and lived in the land of Wandering, east of Eden.'

Homelessness, alienation. Cut off from the presence of God;[24] alienated from the land, and from his work; denying his brother; a 'restless wanderer on the earth', lost in the wasteland, a long way east of Eden. What does Cain do? (What do any of us do, struggling with our own sense of wandering?) Cain seeks shelter, in family and community; he 'lay with his wife, and she became pregnant and gave birth to Enoch. Cain was then building a city, and he named it after his son Enoch.' Putting down roots in his loneliness: seeking something he could rely on. But as many of us know too well, if you seek shelter by hastening into relationship, you may just bring your alienation into it ... And as for the city, alienation can await us there too.

Do the next verses offer us a final way of thinking about our own culture's wanderings? Cain's family are creative, and a mini-renaissance takes place. There are breakthroughs in agriculture (v. 20), music (v. 21), and metal-working (v. 22). Unfortunately, progress doesn't help if it's built on the wrong foundation;[25] the section draws to a close with Lamech (himself an innovator, the inventor of bigamy [v. 19] – relational breakdown carried a step further) boasting openly of the murder he has carried out. The dark deepens; technical progress built on bad foundations leads merely to greater violence. By 6:11 the earth is 'full of violence'. The eventual result is the obliteration of much of humanity in an ecological catastrophe (chs. 6–8).[26]

So the story goes. The central relationship breaks down through our declaration of autonomy and our determination to deify ourselves, run our own universe, determine our own 'good and evil'. The loss of God leads to ever-widening relational powerlessness and breakdown, then to increasing violence. Humans hide from alienation in sexual and familial relations and the flight to the city. Technical progress is built on bad foundations and so leads to yet more violence, and final environmental disaster.

And if the ancient narratives really were the Word of the living God, setting out a paradigm of what happens when a culture builds its life on exclusion of God; what 'way home', what possibility of healing and renewal, might they also offer?

Notes

1. Parts of what follows on Genesis 2–4 owe an enormous amount to the insights of David Gooding of Queen's University, Belfast, and John Lennox and Peter Elwood of Cardiff.
2. The creation of humankind is presented within the sixth section of Genesis 1 (that is, as part of the animal creation), but it is clear from v. 26 that it also marks a radical break in the story.
3. The word 'rule' in 1:26 obviously doesn't have the sense of egocentric exploitation, since that whole spirit of 'domination' is presented precisely as a consequence of the Fall in chapter 3, as we'll see. (In

fact, the right meaning of caring and fatherly 'rule' is a major theme in the early parts of the Old Testament; see, for example, Samuel's deep discomfort at Israel's move from 'judges' to more authoritarian 'kings' in 1 Samuel 8.)

4. This isn't to deny that it includes comments we can take as hints; but these aren't its main theme, and evidently, from the interpretative debates that take place among scientists who are Christians, they can be read in more than one way.

5. E.g., 2 Corinthians 6:2 or 2 Peter 3:8.

6. This writer, as a Christian, has assumed the correctness of evolutionary theory out of personal inability to assess the debates around it. But it should be added that our present construct of evolutionary theory isn't something complete and 'proven'. (Scientific theories never finally are, of course.) Some huge and fascinating problems do remain unsettled; see particularly Phillip Johnson, *Darwin on Trial*; Stephen Jay Gould's extended review in the July 1992 *Scientific American*; Johnson's response in his second edition of 1993; and Michael Behe's *Darwin's Black Box*. (As Berlinski remarked in *Commentary*, scepticism regarding Darwinian orthodoxy seems now to have erupted out of the ghetto.) It's evident that a number of theorists affirm Darwinian orthodoxy quite consciously because they are determined not to believe in God; but if you don't have a problem with God, then the turmoil generated by these challenges becomes intriguing. A particularly interesting issue is the possibility that evolutionary theory, to work, may even necessitate intelligent design underlying it.

As Johnson's and Behe's works are the current 'storm centre', it's worth noting how this whole design issue was raised earlier entirely outside the Christian context by the renowned cosmologists Fred Hoyle (the father of steady-state theory, described by the *Sunday Times* as 'Britain's best known astronomer') and Chandra Wickramasinghe. They asserted (in *Evolution from Space*) that the whole evolutionary process is so problematic, and the chance against random processes producing the complexity of life so high, that it becomes necessary to postulate a controlling intelligence watching over it. 'It is not hard', they say, 'to find writings in which the myth is stated that the Darwinian theory of evolution is well-proven by the fossil record. But one finds that the higher the technical quality of the writing the weaker the claims that are made' (p. 147). 'The evolutionary record leaks like a sieve'; yet 'nobody seems prepared to blow the whistle decisively on the theory. If Darwinism were not considered to be socially desirable ... it would of course be otherwise' (p. 148). The traditional theory, like pre-Copernican astronomy, survives because 'the issue is dominated more by sociology and religion than by science. More precisely, by anti-religion' (p. 2). Hoyle and Wickramasinghe are definitely not Christians, and are anxious to say that their 'clear-cut view' that 'there is a purpose' in the evolutionary process 'is not the old concept of special creation' (p. 147). They suggest the possibility of an extra-terrestrial 'non-carbonaceous intelligence' at work 'which by no means need be *God*, however', for instance 'an extremely complex silicon chip' (p. 139). But the intelligences postulated are to be responsible not merely for designing 'the biochemicals' and giving rise to carbonaceous life but also for creating at least some of the physical laws (p. 143). To say that mere physical laws (or 'Nature') necessitated the emergence of life on earth, they argue, is only a short step from saying that a God made the laws; so the 'obvious escape route' (an interesting phrase) 'is to look outside the earth ... The advantage of looking to the whole universe is rather that ... it offers the possibility of high intelligence within the universe that is not God' (p. 31). It's fascinating that the desire to avoid God should be such a motivating force behind their thinking. Of course their theories met with a chilly reception (the idea of cosmic intelligence 'sends shudders down the spine of orthodox scientists', commented the *Sunday Times*; 'It is rather like the arrival of an illegitimate child in a respectable Victorian family.') But it was significant to see internationally renowned, non-Christian cosmologists insisting that evolutionary theory, far from 'disproving creation', actually implied belief in a higher, guiding intelligence. Thus the idea that evolution rules out believing in a Creator – or learning from Genesis – is a total red herring.

7. This is an odd verse. In what sense can there be a 'garden' if the entire environment is a perfect creation? The Old Testament writers speak of other intelligences besides humankind in the universe, whose rebellion against God predates ours. Is the text hinting that there is already a problem in the world outside Eden? Is that why the word 'subdue' is used for the humans' task (1:28)? Is Eden envisaged as a special, divinely-created bridgehead from which a whole new order could flood out into the surrounding disharmony, bringing it to new life? Who knows?

8. E.g. Revelation 12:9 or 20:2. Serpent-worship was of course important for much ancient paganism.

9. *Star Trek* plots repeatedly present non-physical entities very similar to spirits, but call them 'sub-space beings', an image that circumvents the knee-jerk.

10. The best commentary on the issues at stake here and throughout the Fall narrative (for those who enjoy science fiction!) is arguably C.S. Lewis' novel *Perelandra*.

11. Matthew 4:3. Soon afterwards, he teaches his disciples a prayerful expression of faith where they consciously recognize that their dependence on God extends to the mundanities of food: 'Give us this day our daily bread' (Matthew 6:11).

12. Matthew 4:4,7,10.

13. Luke 16:10.

14. The link is often explicit. Erich Fromm titled one of his books *You Shall Be As Gods*, using the 1611 King James translation of this Genesis verse. Edmund Leach wrote, 'Men have become like gods. Isn't it about time that we understood our divinity? Science offers us total mastery over our environment and our destiny ... All of us need to understand that God, or Nature, or Chance, or Evolution, or the Course of History, or whatever you like to call it, can't be trusted any more. We simply must take charge of our own fate' (quoted in Chapman, *Christianity on Trial*, p. 233; note Leach's reference to the issue of trust here). And there is Sartre: 'If I have excluded God the Father, there must be somebody to invent values ...' (*Existentialism*, p. 54). New Age often makes the same move: 'Know that you are God', commands Shirley MacLaine in *Dancing*, p. 350.

15. See Romans 8:29, among many other passages: 1 John 3:1–2; Galatians 4:19; 2 Corinthians 3:18; 2 Thessalonians 2:14; Revelation 21:11, etc.

16. The end point is Revelation 3:21, that in our ultimate unity with God we will 'share his throne'.

17. Cf. St Paul on our attempts to 'suppress' the sense of God (Romans 1:18,28). He describes the result as a tendency to 'worship and serve created things rather than the Creator' (v. 25). We have seen that throughout this study.

18. Jesus' words on the cross in Matthew 27:46. In Kurosawa's cinematic epic *Ran*, there is a moment when the fool upbraids the gods: 'Are you so bored up there that you must crush us like ants? Is it

such fun to see men weep?' Another character responds: 'It is the gods who weep. They see us killing each other. Over and over since time began. They cannot save us from ourselves.' But the message of Genesis is different: God did step in, at enormous cost, to offer us the possibility of being 'saved from ourselves'.

19. The concept is repeated several times in the apocalyptic style of Revelation; for example, Revelation 9:1–2,13–16; 16:8; 20:7–8, and probably 6:1,3,5,7 and 7:1–3. We find the idea also in St Paul's more sober style, when he foresees the emergence of an ultimate evil dictatorial force but adds to his readers, 'Now you know what is holding him back so that he may be revealed at the proper time' (2 Thessalonians 2:3–7).

20. Steve Turner, *Up to Date*, p. 162.

21. Hebrews 9:22.

22. As perhaps 4:7 suggests.

23. Nor, indeed, to Old Testament Jews: see, for example, the effect of human wrongdoing on the land in Leviticus 26:34–35,42–43; Jeremiah 3:1; 12:4; 23:10; or at the close of 2 Chronicles. In this worldview, ecological collapse is directly linked to people's moral behaviour; 'the land' is very literally 'polluted' by bloodshed or sexual perversion, and 'vomits out its inhabitants' (Leviticus 18:24–28; Numbers 35:32–34). Cf. also Paul's linkage between the repentance of people and the transformation of the entire creation in Romans 8:19–23.

24. Even though it is still only by God's mercy (the 'mark') that Cain survives.

25. For example, in a totalitarian state matters become even worse if dictatorship can monitor its citizens continuously with highly advanced technology.

26. Jesus had an additional comment to make about this narrative, that that generation were so preoccupied with the everyday activities of 'eating and drinking, marrying and giving in marriage' that they ignored the crisis of their culture and were completely taken by surprise when catastrophe swept down upon them (Matthew 24:37–39). (Even the flood sounds less un-contemporary now that we have Greenpeace maps listing the cities and island-nations due to go underwater through global warming!)

8

transformations

What implications might emerge – how might we understand what's gone wrong around us – if we spent forty-five
minutes on a train meditating on the Bible's opening
sentence:

In the beginning God created the heavens and the earth ...?

Genesis' primal narratives offer a radical diagnosis of our alienation: that our conscious turn from God, our enthronement of
our autonomous ego in an unworkable independence, has led in
steady, logical progression towards cultural collapse.

'The ice that still supports people today has become very thin;
the wind that brings the thaw is blowing', wrote Nietzsche in
The Gay Science. We sense the foundations shifting beneath our
feet, and we know we haven't seen the end of the process yet.
Indeed, we feel an existential 'black hole' at the heart of the
west; an absence lies at the very centre of postmodernity. Who
am 'I'? Do 'I' still have value? Is there any real point to life? How
can 'I' know what's right and wrong, and what will it mean if
'I' can't? Is love a reality? Can we ever know truth? Is there any
reason for hope? We've reviewed these issues and others that
flow from them, and we've seen how often they seem triggered
by a common factor; that at the heart of the maelstrom of our
time there stands an Emptiness, a 'space in the shape of God'
(Pascal).

In short, the God-question matters, matters enormously. But how could we decide whether there really is a God who could make meaning in our world?

This book cannot give a full answer to that question. Firstly, because it hasn't set out (and doesn't have space) to survey adequately the evidence underlying historic Christian hope.[1] But secondly, because rediscovering God doesn't work that way. At least according to the Bible, rediscovering God isn't like discovering whether a particular subatomic particle exists. Rather, it is like learning to know, and love, a person. Above all it is *relational*.

Unlocking the skylight

To say that raises two immediate issues.

First, if knowing God is personal and relational, then the truth about him/her/it will be 'revealed' to us in a manner appropriate to – designed for – us, and not for anyone else.

Second, if we want to give real consideration to biblical-Christian faith, we must take seriously what it really says. This includes recognizing that we don't approach potential relationship with God from some ideal, objective starting-point. Rather, as we saw in the last chapter, if biblical faith is true, then we start from a condition of deep alienation from God. That could imply a major problem with our ever being able to learn the truth.

Let's consider this second issue first. 'You know I can't make it by myself', sang Bob Dylan in 'Precious Angel' on *Slow Train Coming*, the first album of his 'Christian' phase, 'I'm a little too blind to see'. Our entire 'modern', post-Enlightenment tradition revolts viscerally against that idea; progress-oriented western man has had enormous (and not unjustified) confidence in his investigative powers. We've been deeply committed to the faith that, in the end, we can observe and reason our way to the truth about anything whatsoever. As the last century drew to a close, however, we became less sure of ourselves. Postmodernism may be a little more humble; certainly it is somewhat less triumphalistic about the omnipotence of our (western) reason.

And according to Jesus, we do have a real problem.

'Why is my language not clear to you?', Jesus asked the Jews, and answered his own question immediately: 'Because you are unable to hear what I say.'[2] Just before this he had been even more blunt: nobody could know the truth about him, he declared, 'unless the Father who sent me draws him'.[3] St Paul was equally 'unmodern' (or maybe post-modern?): ordinarily, he declared, we human beings are 'blinded', so that we are simply unable to perceive the realities of the issues involved;[4] by nature we 'cannot understand them'.[5] There's a fundamental problem with our presuppositions, our paradigms, that goes deeper than the intellect. We 'deliberately forget' spiritual realities, says St Peter.[6] This possibility is hard on our pride. Unfortunately, we cannot rule it out: if God says he cannot be known by our unaided research, it might just be true.

To repeat: for Christian faith, knowing God is personal. The biblical hypothesis presents us as needing direct, individual revelation from God if we are to know the truth, on a par with the 'Word' that set the entire creative process in motion. This comparison is St Paul's: 'God, who said, "Let light shine out of darkness," made his light shine in our hearts to give us the light of the knowledge of the glory of God in the face of Christ.'[7] What's in view here is not an irrational or even (necessarily) mystical experience. Rather, Paul affirms that our hearts have a built-in prejudice, such that God's enabling power is indispensable if we are to see clearly the real, objective facts. It is in 'the face of Christ' that we can hope to see the glory of God, but we need God's light to grasp and evaluate aright what we are seeing.[8] But that very fact moves us from mere assessment of data to the challenge of relationship with a Person.

Two further points follow. First, the New Testament itself guarantees that the truly honest seeker will not be disappointed. Jesus' teaching presents a God who comes out like a shepherd looking for us as we are wandering in the dark: 'Seek and you will find; knock and the door will be opened to you'.[9] Second, however, we know that establishing a meaningful relationship with any person depends on our approaching them in a respectful and appropriate way. So it will be in this case. We are not now indulging in an intellectual game, or conducting a casual experiment in a test tube. Rather, we are exploring, opening ourselves to, the possibility that we have a Maker (even an Owner), a Father who we need to speak to us, to show us reality.

Perhaps no such being exists. But if he does, we approach him as members of a rebelled race, and as individuals who have chosen repeatedly to drive his presence to the periphery of our consciousness, to live as though he were unimportant. So as we come to him asking for 'grace', for his revelation of ultimate reality, we must be willing to face up (if he speaks) to his rights over us. And that's hard. Some thinkers suggest we live at 'the end of the secular century'; but while we may warm to the thought of a heavenly Santa Claus, or 'figure of light', to protect us and welcome us after death, we're often profoundly anxious that there should not be a God who we might need to obey; or still worse, who might assess what we've done with our (and his) environment, and to each other. Many of us have a built-in anxiety that such a God should not exist.

But we have to face the issue. In fact it is not necessary to believe that God exists before starting to treat him as God. Even the thoroughgoing agnostic can pray (if there is no God, it is only a minute lost): 'God, I do not know if you exist. Nor do I know if I can find out on my own. But I realize that, if you do, I may be entirely dependent on you showing your truth to me. Therefore, if you show me your truth and your ways, I vow that I will give myself to you, and start to follow you wherever you lead.'[10]

Does this not jeopardize our exploration by assuming its conclusion at the very start? Not really (though even if it did, we would only be following the rules of scientific method – presuppose the hypothesis and see if it matches up with what happens). Such a prayer says merely, 'God, *if* you are there, *if* you are all that Jesus taught, then I will follow you.' But it also offers us a step forward in self-knowledge. It's striking how many of us feel profound reluctance to pray in these terms – and our reaction reveals our hearts;[11] it helps us see whether our beliefs are controlled by deep-seated determination to preserve our independence. If that is so, there is not much point (yet) in looking at the evidence; we're maintaining a position from which, even if God is real, we will most probably never know (at least in this life). Rather, the question will be just why we feel so anxious to preserve our exile from God's presence.[12]

Such a prayer leads us beyond the safely cerebral. Logically, we would no more expect to meet the living God just through reading books than to meet a partner just through reading Mills and Boon. Sometime, something has to be done, the risk has to be taken. To pray such a prayer is to step outside what's been called the 'Cartesian madness of the West', the absurdity of thought in a bloodless vacuum. It is to set our total being as the stake of our gamble with the unknown. It is the only appropriate way to attempt an approach to the Creator who may perhaps be there. If there is no God, we shall ultimately prove to have wasted a little of our time: no great loss. If there is a God, we shall have opened the door for heaven to break in on our experience.[13]

Understanding faith

What, then, do we expect? We expect a journey: a journey into faith. And immediately that word presents a stumbling block. 'It's nice for those who "have" faith; I wouldn't even mind it myself; but you can't "work it up", can you?' Or: 'How can any intelligent person tolerate living on the basis of faith?'

But life is not so simple. In postmodernity it has become increasingly challenging to believe that we 'know the objective truth' about anything. How could one dare believe that one *knows*? 'The just live by faith', says the New Testament repeatedly, but there is a sense in which no one lives by anything else. It is absurd to say we refuse, or are unable, to live by faith. 'Absolute' proof never existed for anything – even our own existence. Descartes tried to prove the latter with his famous 'I think therefore I am'. But all that can be proven from 'There are thoughts' (not 'I think', which smuggles in the 'I' it is trying to prove), is precisely that and no more; 'There are thoughts', or, 'Thinking is happening'. What, if anything, is doing the thinking – whether it has any lasting identity, whether it is an octopus dreaming it is human – is in no way 'proven'. (Is our 'reality' any more than 'an illusion caused by lack of alcohol'? Probably, but the point cannot be proven!)

We live by reasonable faith. Every time I catch a bus home I make a whole series of acts of faith. Faith in my memory of the link between that bus' destination and where I live; faith in the driver's intention to go where his company promised; faith in my perception that he probably isn't drunk; faith that the bus is properly maintained. I cannot prove these absolutely, but there is enough real evidence to justify my steps of faith. When I pause at the corner shop to buy 'fresh' fruit, it is an act of faith in the shop-keeper. When I greet my wife, I am building confidently on faith in her – and thus faith in my judgement, faith indeed in my memories on which that judgement is based – that she is not secretly sleeping with the neighbour and plotting to poison me. Normal life depends on our willingness to take a thousand steps of faith each day – in our memory, our perceptions, our reason and the judgement and good intentions of others (to say nothing of our dress sense and our deodorant!) The world might be very different from the way we perceive it; we will have to live by faith in the evidence that it isn't. Only a paranoid would refuse to eat breakfast because of the impossibility of proving beyond all doubt that no burglar has poisoned his egg; but the possibility cannot rationally be ruled out, and faith is indispensable for breakfast.

There is no way of living except by faith: faith, not set against reason, but defined as stepping forward in a trust based on reasonably solid grounds, even though they amount to less than absolute proof.[14] And this, of course, is good scientific method:[15] to take a theory and then test it by its internal consistency and by how far, long-term, it integrates and matches the data we receive. In one sense such an approach (to life or science) remains a gamble of faith. But some hypotheses about the world come to make far more sense than others, and these we live by. So Christian faith, writes Colin Brown, is a 'hypothesis that ... makes sense as we go along living it'.[16] Jesus said something similar in

John 7:17, and his challenge to his first disciples also fits the need of a postmodern culture: 'Come and you will see.'[17]

Ways of seeing

Suppose, then, that we are willing to embark on this journey of personal exploration. We want to give consideration to the Christian hypothesis; and we've chosen (it is an act of our inmost, fundamental will) to let God be God in our lives if he should exist. What then?

For many people in the two-thirds world, these may seem stupid questions: anyone with a mind and heart knows there is a God. It is not easy to find atheists in, say, Iraq or Brazil or Nigeria. I remember a woman I deeply respected asking me – at a time when I very much doubted God's reality – 'But don't you just *know* he is there?' Such a condition is uncommon in the west. (Though not unknown: the great psychologist Carl Jung told a BBC interviewer shortly before his death, 'Suddenly I understood that God was, for me at least, one of the most certain and immediate experiences ... I do not believe; I know. I *know*.'[18]) I was willing to concede it might be a 'normal' condition for humanity, to which our western culture, its perceptions overwhelmed by the media dream-worlds it has created, has blinded and deafened itself. But I had to say to my friend: 'No, I don't "just know."'[19] Many others of us are the same. What do we do? Where might we explore (or be given) the basis for living by faith?

As we've noted, to Christian belief the knowledge of God is something deeply personal. There are many different areas which God may select to make us, as individuals, aware of his reality: the 'keys' to our particular 'lock'. For some it may be personal experience of God's presence, in the miraculous or in answered prayer – either in our own lives, or in the life of someone we know well enough to trust.[20] For others, it may be the experience of the meaningfulness of Christ helping someone we know to endure and even grow despite immersion in horrendous suffering. For many it may be the Bible: our experience of being 'spoken to' as we read it or hear it preached, our sense of its profundity, relevance and coherence[21] – our sense, as Peter said to Jesus, that these are 'the words of eternal life'.[22]

For yet others, what we love most may begin to 'turn the key'. The first 'intuition of God' may come through the long and moving process culminating in childbirth ('Searching for a little bit of God's mercy / I found living proof', wrote Bruce Springsteen after the birth of his first child). Jewish novelist Saul Bellow, writing about Mozart, said that 'At the heart of my confession, therefore, is the hunch that with beings such as Mozart we are forced to speculate about transcendence, and this makes us very uncomfortable.' George Steiner argues at length in *Real Presences* that the experience of great art only makes sense if it is underpinned by the reality of a God. Television naturalist David Bellamy wrote that his 'road to Damascus was the wonder of the natural world'.[23] To the Christian, such intuitions are actually the revelation of God, to be stewarded with care. 'Take heed how you hear', said Jesus; the intuition of grace may not return, and we are responsible for what we do with it.[24]

Or it may be other considerations that make us aware of God. It is hard to 'take God seriously' when the media don't; yet where does the majority opinion really lie? Don't our North Atlantic fashions of materialistic thought seem myopic when set in a wider context of history or geography?[25] The vast majority of the human race has always believed in a supernatural universe including a supreme God, so far as we can tell; and the majority certainly still does. 'The main issue is agreed among all men of all nations', said the Roman writer Cicero, 'inasmuch as all have engraved in their minds an innate belief that the gods exist.'[26] In the next generation, Seneca argued similarly that no race had departed so far from the laws and customs that it did not believe in some kind of gods.[27] Calvin concurred, fourteen hundred years later: 'There is, as the eminent pagan says, no nation so barbarous, no people so savage, that they have not a deep-seated conviction that there is a God.'[28] Without doubt, the Christian church has grown faster across the continents in the last century than in any previous one.[29] Of course we westerners tend to think of ourselves as 'humanity come of age', and we assume that, because we control the world's media and educational systems, our de-supernaturalized world-view must be the whole truth.[30] But humility might urge us to note the near-universality of belief elsewhere, and to wonder if the majority of humankind isn't sensing something we have grown deaf to. Shall I stake my life on the probability that they are right, or that they are wrong?

The universe we inhabit poses further questions. If there is no God, we must somehow conceive the cosmos as just 'sitting there', as it were, expanding and contracting perhaps, but in existence for no imaginable reason. Sartre's comment about the oddity of there being something rather than nothing has some force. And that 'something' includes the physical laws; the universe we live in is in many ways a stable place – we might say a curiously reasonable place. The pattern of laws and constants that enables its existence in so rational and unchanging a manner might seem suggestive of a Law-maker.[31] 'The mind refuses to look at this universe being what it is without being designed', said Darwin late in his life; Einstein remarked that the most incomprehensible thing about the universe was that it was comprehensible, and that he was glimpsing the handiwork of an 'illimitable superior spirit' in what he perceived of the universe.

> One fascinating recent development in science is the rise of Intelligent Design Theory. It argues that several branches of science now have well-defined procedures for distinguishing designed activity from chance phenomena. (For example, the study of artificial intelligence; forensic science; archaeology; and the search for extraterrestrial intelligence. All these fields need criteria for separating chance activity from what is intelligently designed.) By the criteria of these fields, various factors, particularly the issue of information-origin and the high level of 'irreducible complexity' in the universe, reveal clear signs of design.[32]

Such a notion is heresy, of course, running head on into prejudices built into at least a century of 'modern' culture (though by our philosophy rather than our science). Hence, these thinkers are seeking to avoid getting embroiled in the old debates about creationism. And the question of how, or by whom, these features were designed is being avoided, so that the central issue can be faced. But obviously if we come to see ourselves as the products of intelligent design, not chance, it will produce a radical change in our cultural consciousness. Inevitably, it raises questions about God.

More recently, the debates over the 'anthropic principle' have suggested that the ratios and constants of the fundamental forces in the universe – from the subatomic to the astronomical – are incredibly finely balanced. Indeed, they are balanced far too precisely to be the result of anything but intelligent design, since the margin of error was minimal (one part in a million in some cases) if a universe was to emerge that could contain intelligent life. 'It is hard to resist the impression that the present structure of the universe, apparently so sensitive to minor alterations in the numbers, has been rather carefully thought out', summarizes theoretical physicist Paul Davies in *God and the New Physics*. '... The seemingly miraculous concurrence of numerical values that nature has assigned to her fundamental constants must remain the most compelling evidence for an element of cosmic design.'[33] Cosmologist Fred Hoyle concurs: 'I do not believe that any scientist who examined the evidence would fail to draw the inference that the laws of nuclear physics have been deliberately designed.'[34] Do we not sense a Maker behind these astonishingly productive principles that have brought such complexities out of almost nothing in this strange, pulsating cosmos? Alongside this sense stand our intuitions of wonder: whether at the majesty of the galaxies, the glory and multitudinous living complexity of the natural world that has exploded out from the Big Bang, or the beauty of a sunset, a mountain-range, a stallion, a human baby.

Are those intuitions sentimentality, or apprehensions of a real Designer at work? As we gaze thankfully at our world, from the sparrow to the panther to the human eye, it can be hard to avoid seeing it as the work of a personal Creator.

Or there are the issues we have considered in earlier chapters. 'Two things fill the mind with ever new and increasing admiration and awe, the oftener and more steadily they are reflected on', wrote Kant; 'the starry heavens above me and the moral law within me.'[35] The singer of Psalm 19 reflects on the same combination: the 'heavens declare the glory of God', he says, and the internal 'law of the Lord' presents an equally life-giving stimulus, 'reviving the soul ... giving light to the eyes'. Culturally and individually, we too sense profound intuitions of that 'moral law' – intuitions of the reality of good and evil, the truth of love and beauty, the reality and value of the individual, the trustworthiness of reason. Yet, as we have seen, these intuitions have grown discredited as they lost their grounding in God.

So were they idealistic sentimentalities, or apprehensions of genuine truth? Is there indeed no intrinsic value for the individual, no reality in love beyond lust and tactical alliance, and ultimately no ethics beyond our personal preferences? Or maybe there is a God? 'Although man may say that he is no more than a machine, his whole life denies it', writes Francis Schaeffer. In our profound experiences of love, beauty or justice we touch, not God indeed, but objective realities that only make sense in terms of God.[36] The Triune God would be a 'meaning-maker' whose truth makes sense of our profoundest hopes and intuitions – that people do matter, that egoism and cruelty are wrong, that love is real. We're trained into world-views that negate these intuitions; yet still our hearts warn us that those atheistic world-views are dehumanized, arid, inadequate. Maybe we should listen; maybe our hearts were trustworthy all along.

> '... the face behind the universe, which now and then emerges through our subconscious mind ... Nietzsche described a "sea-sickness, as we go our troubled way without outside help through the world".

> Sartre wrote on the subject of man and called his book *Nausea*. But perhaps in such moments we might have a more profound intuition and call it, with Helmut Thielicke, "homesickness" ... that ache that occurs when we are alone on a mountain; or when the sun sets and we want to worship and don't know what to worship ... We know there is a Face behind the universe trying to get through again ... We have lost the Face that is behind everything, and so we too are becoming faceless ...'
> –Roger Forster[37]

Seeing Jesus

Yet these issues may be too impersonal. We need to explore what happened in Palestine two thousand years ago.

First, let's consider the issue of the resurrection, which the Bible presents as the final basis for our hope, the ultimate 'sign' of the supernatural's eruption into our world.[38] It's worth thinking about the body of the dead Christ. Everybody involved in the original events – friends or foes of Jesus – agreed that Christ was crucified, died and was buried. We have the arguments of some of Christ's opponents, and know the line they followed. That he genuinely died also seems clear from the details in the records that might not have been meaningful then but become proof of death to our more developed medical knowledge.[39]

That the body then vanished, and that this was not his enemies' doing, also seems definite. Then and later, Jews and Romans wanted to remove this threat to peace and orthodoxy. Religious factors aside, the authorities had good reason for fear, with thousands of Jews turning to Christ, either that they would be called to fatal account for 'this man's blood', or that the social instability would provoke a Roman takeover and the end of the Jewish nation.[40] If there was any way his enemies could have produced the body (or those who removed it) in the early days of the infant church's rapid growth, they would surely have silenced the teaching of the resurrection; but it never happened. Rather, the early church's enemies explained the body's absence by accusing the Christians of stealing it.[41] But it is noticeable, and remarkable, that the accusation never resulted in a trial. The disciples would have had nothing to gain by such an action. Yet with no motivation, they proceeded to centre their whole lives around their affirmation of the resurrection. Equally bizarre – as we expose ourselves to the ethical teaching of these earliest Christian leaders – is the notion that, underneath, they were some of the world's most effective conmen. Strangest of all is that as many of them (and their families) were beheaded, crucified upside down, whipped and otherwise tortured or executed, no one ever admitted the truth, that they had stolen the body. Nonetheless, if we would deny the resurrection, something like this is what we have to believe.

We can go further, however. Christ was seen after the resurrection. The careful historian Luke describes these appearances as 'many convincing proofs' (Acts 1:3). In the mid-50s AD, Paul writes to the people of the merchant port of Corinth, giving them a long list of living witnesses in Israel who had seen the risen Christ. This is very solid historical data.[42] We should consider James, Jesus' brother, who was a sceptic throughout Christ's lifetime; he encountered Christ after the resurrection, and was of sufficient moral stature to be accepted as leader by the thousands of believers in Jerusalem, finally being beheaded in AD 62. He, we must affirm, lied or was deceived. We should consider the meeting between the disciples and the risen Christ, recorded as the finale of both Luke's and John's Gospels (these documents for the contents of which so many Christians would soon die), and again at the beginning of Acts.

What are we to make of these appearances? We cannot think of legends arising in so short a time. Besides, as C.S. Lewis points out, they would be exceedingly odd legends by the standards of classical culture. There is no account of the resurrection itself (the later apocryphal gospels certainly make up for that), no appearance to his enemies, appearances first to women. Indeed, many people find the vivid realism of passages like John 20 and

21 and Luke 24 enough to authenticate them as definitive eye-witness accounts.

Are we to see the appearances as deliberate lies? When these men were engaged in giving the world some of its highest ethical teaching? Again, we are left with the spectacle of the disciples spending their lives building a new religion whose central practices focused on the resurrection (at the same time jeopardizing their eternal futures by abandoning their own religious background[43]), and finally dying unpleasantly, knowing it's all a lie. That seems highly improbable. But it is equally hard to believe these encounters were mere 'visions';[44] we note the authors' repeated emphasis on the disciples touching the risen Christ (Luke 24:38–39; Matthew 28:9; John 20:24–28), going for extended walks with him (Luke 24:13–32,50; John 21:20), and especially 'eating and drinking' with him (Luke 24:30,43; John 21:9–14; Acts 1:4; 10:41). Hallucinations don't eat fish, and they don't go with groups of people on long country walks.

So what transformed the twelve from a group of dispirited disciples who abandoned or betrayed their Lord (an account so detrimental to the church leadership that it's unlikely to have been fabricated), into men who turned the world upside down? What transformed Paul from persecutor to missionary? What, after Jesus' death, suddenly turned his own brother James into his follower, so that he too became a martyr? How much evidence, what kind of appearances, would we ourselves demand before staking our lives and deaths in that way? The disciples asserted that the key factor was their unmistakable encounter with the risen Christ. It is not easy to see any credible alternative.

The crux

But for myself, though there have been many other factors, the issues have finally centred on Jesus.[45] And logically, if we want to explore encounter with God-in-Christ, we will begin to read the Gospels – the four biographies of Jesus.

Here, as with the resurrection data, we don't need to begin by believing that the biblical texts are infallible.[46] To assess Christ's claims about himself, we need simply consider the records of his teaching as *generally* trustworthy documents. In taking this position, we are considering factors such as the wealth of documents (and the absence of radical divergences within them) that assures us we have a fairly reliable text.[47] There is the fact that these documents were written close to the events, in a culture marked by retentive memory and when many witnesses of the events would still be alive to challenge falsifications; and written by people, and in a community, whose moral rectitude seems a historically accepted fact – even among their enemies. There is the repeated stress on eye-witness testimony that we find in, say, John 19:35 and 21:24; 1 John 1:1–3; 2 Peter 1:16 or Acts 1:21–22 or 10:39–41. There is the careful historical approach displayed by the author of Luke ('Since I myself have carefully investigated everything from the beginning, it seemed good also to me to write an orderly account for you, most excellent Theophilus, so that you may know the certainty of the things you have been taught'[48]). Papias tells us that this characterized Mark's gospel-writing too ('He paid attention to this one thing, not to omit anything that he had heard, nor to include any false statement among them'). All this gives us good reason to believe that the documents will be generally reliable.

Other types of approach converge on the same conclusion. It was J.S. Mill, no friend of Christianity, who asked the crucial question about the Gospel material: if Jesus was not the source of the teaching attributed to him, who was? The 'community', some critics have answered. But Mill had more sense than that and saw in the Gospel sayings a grandeur that was the mark of a most unusual mind:

Who among his disciples or among their proselytes was capable of inventing the sayings of Jesus or imagining the life and character revealed in the Gospels? Certainly not the fishermen of Galilee; as certainly not St Paul, whose character and idiosyncrasies were of a totally different sort; still less the early Christian writers, in whom nothing is more evident than that the good which was in them was all derived, as they always professed that it was derived, from the higher source.[49]

Which suggests that most of that teaching goes right back to Christ himself.

Modern secular literary criticism provides another insight: it is incredibly hard to produce a convincing fictional saint-figure. (Consider Dickens, for instance; his evil characters are full of colour, but the good ones are such pale shadows that it is hard to believe in their triumph.[50] To Dostoevski, there was 'nothing more difficult' than 'to portray a positively good man' in a novel: 'All writers who have tried it have always failed.') Yet one generation after another has found the Christ of the Gospels an utterly compelling portrayal of goodness in all its robustness and complexity: striking in his teaching, devastating in debate, while at the same time earthy, gentle, and totally at ease with the women he knew; and (for example) so sensitive in his meeting with Peter after the betrayal (John 21). Where in the world's fiction do we find anything comparable? But if our best novelists have proved unable to produce such a figure, must not the Gospel writers have been copying theirs from a real original? In fact fictional prose marked by such realistic detail and seriousness of purpose simply didn't exist at that time (the novel as we know it emerged in the eighteenth century).[51] So if the Gospels, with their profound realism of style, are fictional prose, then their four writers (who were not artists but missionaries) somehow came up with a totally new type of prose writing; and, bizarrely, each of them also succeeded in constructing a fictional saint-figure no later novelist has been able to match! The idea seems absurd. Clearly, as Lewis concludes, their depiction of Jesus must be copied from reality, and at least 'pretty close up to the facts'.

But there is a final issue, which is often ignored to a quite astounding degree: the early Christians would have wanted as accurate as possible a record of what their Master did and taught.[52] Further, many of them came to very unpleasant ends for their beliefs, and had every reason to want to be certain of their authenticity. The recipients of the early Gospels weren't a flock of spaced-out hippies frolicking on a sunny hillside. One of the early Roman emperors took to using burning Christians as human torches for his garden. If we imagine ourselves in the position of someone who remains a Christian knowing this is how it might end, we can see that those early believers would want to be very sure of the historical basis for their horrendous gamble. People who were dying for the gospel story would want to be certain of its reliability. For all these reasons, then, we may well conclude that these colourful, earthy accounts are at least very close to what Jesus actually said and did.

But now comes the difficulty. On the one hand, we may be captivated by the shrewdness and sublimity of Christ's words and stories, and the glory of what he does: his identifying with the poor, the broken and marginalized, the untouchables and outcasts; his love for joyous celebrations, matched with his unflinching challenges to entrenched evil; his generosity in healing and forgiveness; the astonishingly moving incident when he washes his disciples' feet on the night of the betrayal. This, we so often feel, is the way to live: if ever life was lived the way it should be, this is that life. But then there is a serious problem. This Jesus who illuminates one moral complexity after another takes an extraordinary line on his own goodness, showing no awareness at all of any wrong in his own heart (in sharp contrast to his followers; cf. Luke 5:8; 1 Timothy 1:15). Indeed he even claims sinlessness. And John, the Gospel writer who knew Christ so well, doesn't flinch (he apparently has no debate to record in which Jesus fends off accusations; indeed, the effect of this claim on many of Christ's hearers is to convince them to follow him – John 8:29–30,46).

This is disturbing enough. But then come the astonishing claims Christ makes for his true identity, and the massive demands he makes of his disciples (to the point of their self-destruction, if he were not who he claimed to be). No other major religious teacher – Buddha, Muhammad, Lao Tzu,

Confucius, Socrates, Paul – ever made such claims. It is hard to think of Christ as 'a good man', when surely no 'good man' could be so hopelessly (arrogantly?) lacking in self-awareness. The more we grasp the Gospels, the more we find Christ's teaching centring absolutely, over and over again, on his hearers' response to himself. Repeatedly he demands, forces them, to a decision of total discipleship. If he is wrong here, he is a massive egoist and is wrong at the heart of his activity.

There are numerous examples. I must take absolute priority over your parents, your wife and children and everything else in your life, he insists in Luke (14:26); you must renounce everything for me (14:33); you must deny yourself, you must give up your life for me (note, not for the truths in my teaching, but for me; 9:23–24). I am in an utterly different class from all God's preceding messengers (20:9–14); greater than the greatest of Israel's kings (20:41–44); wiser than the wisest of the ancients (11:31); greater than God's own law (6:1–5). Everything has been given to me by God, and only I know what God is like (10:22); your public response to me (again, not the truths I teach, but to me) will decide your eternal fate (12:8). And there is more; we can try to imagine our reaction to a contemporary making such claims. It is fascinating – considering the uniqueness of these claims among the world religions – that the Gospel writers can cope. Indeed, Luke centres his book's entire structure on Peter's confession of Jesus as the Christ of God (9:20).

John's Gospel takes matters still further. Jesus states that he embodies the life of the resurrection, and anyone who believes in him will never die (11:25–26); he alone gives life to the dead, depending on whether or not they believed on him (5:25–26; 6:40). He, personally, is (not shows) the way, and the truth, and no one comes to God except through him (14:6); he always does what pleases God (8:29,46). Staggeringly, 'Anyone who has seen me has seen the Father' (God) (again, we should try to visualize a contemporary saying that; 14:9); 'I and the Father are one' (for that the Jews tried to stone him, 10:30–31,38–39). He, not the Father, will judge the world (5:22), 'that all may honour the Son' (himself) 'just as they honour the Father'. He is God's equal

(5:18), the eternal 'I AM', the very Creator who hung the stars in space (8:58–59). Perhaps most striking is 5:23: anyone who does not honour Jesus does not honour God; worship of God only has meaning if it is worship of Jesus. More could be cited. For Christ, the whole universe centres on a Person, and he is that Person. We find such claims in every stratum of the Gospel traditions;[53] and in sections too (e.g. throughout John 13–17) where the unbiased reader is compelled to sense teaching of a depth and stature that must surely come from Jesus himself. There are so many of these remarkable passages that, even if a couple had been invented by his disciples, the overall shape of Christ's self-image would be unmistakable.

As we have said, the purpose of this chapter is not to state con-clusively the basis for Christian hope. We cannot examine the data in isolation from the experience of exposure to the Gospels. This section seeks just to set out the question that demands our attention. And that question is: How can we deal honestly with the dilemma posed by these passages? Was Christ aware of the falsity of his enormous claims, for which his closest followers would die in agony – that is, was he a conscious deceiver? Or was he unaware – that is, was he a lunatic? Unless – the only other logical option – they were indeed true?

Let's postulate that Jesus was a fraudster, setting up his own bogus personality cult. How can we relate such a notion to our experience of, say, the profundity of the Sermon on the Mount? Can we think of him as a conscious deceiver, recalling how his 'image' had to be maintained through three years of travelling round an often-hostile Palestine with that handful of close disci-ples that would go on to die for him? If he was a conscious deceiver, how are we to understand the agony that his disciples witnessed in Gethsemane? And why ever did he go to the cross?[54]

> 'He expressed, as no other could, the spirit and will of God.'
> –Gandhi, on Jesus

> 'I know men; and I tell you that Jesus Christ is not a man ... Everything in Christ astonishes me. His spirit overawes me, and his will confounds me. Between him and whoever else in the world, there is no possible term of comparison ... The nearer I approach, the more carefully I examine, everything is above me – everything remains grand, of a grandeur which overpowers ...'
> –Napoleon[55]

> 'His penetrating humour, his iconoclastic challenge to the establishment, his devastating calmness in the midst of personal danger, his compassion and respect for prostitutes as sisters, his warm magnetism for children, his redemptive view of crooked politicians, his unorthodox social habits, his deep integrity in the face of full-blown dilemmas – all these characteristics should inspire us to ask, "Who then is this?" The deity of Jesus Christ awes me. So does his humanity.'
> –Chinese-American writer Ada Lum

It seems impossible. But the alternative of thinking of him as a lunatic is equally difficult – as the shrewdness, simplicity and sanity of his teaching speak into our lives; or as we watch the calm relational skills he demonstrates in so many varied situations. Claiming to be the very Creator (how could one imagine that?): how could he be so evidently wise, yet so enormously out of touch with his own psyche? And above all in Judaea – a culture shaped through and through by a sense of the utter uniqueness and otherness of God?

In the presence of the Gospels, the choice seems stark. To commit our lives to the stance that Christ was an egoistic trickster, consciously misleading (and so destroying) his closest friends, seems impossible. Therefore we must conceive of ourselves looking him in the face and saying that he was totally lunatic when it came to any perceptions about himself –

deliberately or not, Jesus was an utter megalomaniac. The only other option is to commit ourselves to him as the Lord – recognizing him as God truly incarnate, prophesied accurately for centuries beforehand[56] – that he claimed to be. For this writer, that seems the only reasonable alternative.

These are the basic issues. This book cannot handle all the data for the reasons indicated earlier. And it cannot replace experience of personal openness to God in the presence of what the historic Christian community has believed to be his 'living word'. If Christian faith is true at all, then we can only find out through placing ourselves in a position of humble (which does not mean believing) openness for encounter with God; by taking our Gospels and saying to God: 'If you are there, if you show me from these pages the truth about my life and about who Christ was, I will follow you wherever you lead.' To Christian belief, each of us stands in the presence of God with the possibility of choice; to take the whole issue off the periphery and expose ourselves to it realistically; to draw, and then live by, our conclusions.

What Jesus wanted

'Now there was a man of the Pharisees named Nicodemus, a member of the Jewish ruling council. He came to Jesus at night and said, "Rabbi, we know you are a teacher who has come from God. For no-one could perform the miraculous signs you are doing if God were not with him ..."'

(Is Nicodemus the prototypical western intellectual, preferring to pass approving comment but avoid the necessity of commitment? The liberal, it has been said, always prefers questions to answers ...)

Jesus looks him straight in the eye and informs him, 'You must be born again.'[57]

Transformation – as we shall see in a moment, this links in with issues crucial to contexts as diverse as Maoism, the feminist movement, the 'deep-green' movement and the griping of

Britain's own Prince Philip. The problem has been the trivialization of Jesus' phrase 'born again', after two thousand years. How are we to understand it?

'A voice says, "Cry out." And I said, "What shall I cry?" "All men are like grass, and all their glory is like the flowers of the field. The grass withers and the flowers fall, because the breath of the LORD *blows on them. Surely the people are grass! The grass withers and the flowers fall, but the word of our God stands for ever ..."*

'You who bring good tidings to Zion ... say to the towns of Judah, "Here is your God!" See, the Sovereign LORD *comes with power, and his arm rules for him ... Who has measured the waters in the hollow of his hand, or with the breadth of his hand marked off the heavens? Who has held the dust of the earth in a basket, or weighed the mountains on the scales and the hills in a balance? Who has understood the mind of the* LORD, *or instructed him as his counsellor? ... Surely the nations are like a drop in a bucket; they are regarded as dust on the scales ... Before him all the nations are as nothing; they are regarded by him as worthless, and less than nothing ...*

'Do you not know? Have you not heard? ... He sits enthroned above the circle of the earth, and its people are like grasshoppers. He stretches out the heavens like a canopy, and spreads them out like a tent to dwell in. He brings princes to naught, and reduces the rulers of this world to nothing. No sooner are they planted, no sooner are they sown, no sooner do they take root in the ground, than he blows on them and they wither, and a whirlwind sweeps them away like chaff.

' "To whom then will you compare me? Or who is my equal?" says the Holy One. Lift your eyes and look to the heavens: Who created all these? He brings out the stars one by one, and calls them each by name. Because of his great power and mighty strength, not one of them is missing.'[58]

Throughout the early Christians' proclamation, two basic issues recur, which combined lead to the joyous breakthrough of new birth. Paul summarizes his message in Acts 20:21: 'I have declared to both Jews and Greeks that they must *turn to God in repentance* and *have faith in our Lord Jesus.*' Jesus' own proclamation centred on the same two issues: 'The kingdom of God is near. *Repent*, and *believe the good news!*'[59]

Repentance is a word we don't much use. Its Greek original, *metanoia*, means a total turnaround of life. It means recognizing a deep-seated wrong direction in our existence, all the wrong thoughts and actions – the arrogance, anger, vindictiveness, greed, petulance, dishonesty we each sense within ourselves from time to time (e.g. as I relate to my children, parents, partner) – and determining to do very differently. But there is a deeper level. As we saw in Genesis, the fundamental issue is our attempt to dethrone and exclude God our Maker; our demand for autonomy, our rejection of his Fatherly love. We have chosen, generation on generation and year after year in our own lives, to live without him. It is this, above all, that *metanoia* confronts. It is the recognition of the One who sits on the circle of the earth; the acceptance of his claims on us; the realization that, hitherto, we have run our lives our own way, ignored him and often revolted against his purposes. *Metanoia* calls us to bring our lives back – to be his, for his glorious, loving, creative purposes, now and forever.

(This is hard for a culture that wants God to be, at most, a guide, not a judge – ironically, the same generation that, like none before it, is using up its planet's resources and bequeathing a poisoned planet to its successors. A friend told me recently: You've really understood Christianity when you've understood you need to be forgiven. Liberation is being able to admit that I am not OK, and that that problem has to be dealt with ...)

But to recognize the colossal glory of the living God is to realize the dangers in our own position. Once we begin to grasp the idea of a God of infinite majesty and joy, and of devastating purity, we may feel less surprised that we do not experience his presence the way we are! We may even feel relief; we know we aren't exactly 'pure in heart', and therefore (if Jesus is right) we cannot see God.[60] We know our nature is not his; we begin to grasp that to encounter his glory as we are – 'the King who alone is immortal and who lives in unapproachable light, whom no one has seen or can see'[61] – could be a disaster. (To walk into the blinding heat and light of a blast furnace is to meet with instant destruction. It's significant that the Old Testament's term for something 'devoted' to God sometimes carries with it connotations of destruction; to encounter God's presence, as things stand, outside Christ, might mean just that.[62]) The question Isaiah raises hangs over our situation too: 'Which of us can dwell with everlasting burning?'[63] We know there is the other, indeed more central side of God's nature, that he shows to us in metaphors of 'Father' and 'Lover' and 'Bridegroom'. But that is the God who came looking for Adam and Eve in Old Testament Eden, before everything had finally gone wrong. We are outside now, trapped in our abnormality on a dying globe, wandering as Cain wandered, shut out a long way from home.

(But to be shut out from the light would ultimately be to drift out into the darkness. We would be like an electric fire disconnected from the power of the mains; for now there is some warmth, some love, some joy, but it's cooling down, running out, dying. If indeed God is the true source of all these things, then to keep him on our lives' periphery, to choose to remain a long way outside Eden, would be to stay on course for a condition where finally (outside this life) there will be no love or joy or peace or hope at all: 'shut out from the presence of the Lord'[64] forever, with all the consequences that must logically follow. It certainly isn't what the Father-heart of God would want for us: we think of Jesus weeping broken-heartedly over Jerusalem: 'How often I have longed to gather your children together, as a hen gathers her chicks under her wings; but you were not willing!'[65] Logically, though, that is what the exercise of our freedom to stay alienated from God must ultimately involve.)

Nothing can survive in the white heat of a blast furnace that is not itself transformed into flame. (But what might it mean to be 'transformed into flame'?) So it's not surprising that such a transformation is precisely what God offers us; being filled with his glory, so that we can joyfully live in his presence ... First, however, there is a barrier to be overcome. For we are the generation that had it all and wanted still more; that used up the oceans, the ozone layer and the rainforests and wouldn't stop for our grandchildren's sake; that decimated species after species, watched poverty and genocide multiply, and nonetheless demanded our debts and our profits and grew rich from the arms trade. Racially and individually, we have broken his laws in the everyday issues of how we treat each other and our environment,[66] in our failure even remotely to 'love our neighbours as ourselves', and most fundamentally in the Eden issue (repeated at different levels in the western cultural process since the Enlightenment) – denying God's reign and centrality, insisting on running our own universe. We can see how we have followed in Adam's steps, day after day; thanklessly denying that God be God,[67] claiming that position in apartness for ourselves. The consequence of such alienation, says Paul, is death;[68] which is inevitable, if the Father is truly the source and heart of life. We know the physical laws don't change around from day to day; God is a God 'who does not change like shifting shadows'.[69] He is reliable – but that means he cannot deny his own law, cannot just change it for convenience. There is death in the system, and that penalty of death must be paid.

It is for this reason, says the Bible, that the cross happened, that God-in-Christ died; that God himself took our human place, to carry our penalty. When, therefore, we see the Man hanging on a cross and screaming 'My God, my God, *why* ... why have *you* forsaken *me?*', we know he has been to the uttermost, darkest limits of alienation – and paid our penalty, and opened the gates back (or onward) to Eden.[70] Here is the centre of history. It is because of the cross, the paying of the penalty and the shattering of the barriers, that the resurrection could occur, that the Father and we can be brought back together; Christ's resurrection was the proof of life's triumph over death, of God's passionate love available now to flood out and remake a lost world. It is after the cross that we can hear the Father challenging us to 'be reconciled to God' – just as he walked in Eden long ago, calling out to the frightened rebels: 'Where are you?'[71]

'You who bring good tidings to Jerusalem, lift up your voice with a shout; lift it up, do not be afraid! See, the Sovereign LORD comes with power ... He tends his flock like a Shepherd; he gathers the lambs in his arms, and carries them close to his heart; he gently leads those that have young ...

'Why do you say, oh Jacob, and complain, oh Israel, "My way is hidden from the LORD; my cause is disregarded by my God"? Do you not know? Have you not heard? The LORD is the everlasting God, the Creator of the ends of the earth. He will not grow tired or weary, and his understanding no one can fathom. He gives strength to the weary, and increases the power of the weak. Even youths grow tired and weary, and young men stumble and fall; but those who hope in the LORD will renew their strength. They will soar on wings like eagles; they will run and not grow weary, they will walk and not be faint.'

(Isaiah 40:9–11, 27–31)

And, explosively, it is after the cross that Pentecost can occur. What is Pentecost?

Pentecost, Acts 2 tells us, was when God the Holy Spirit swept down on God's people and filled them, began living in them. We could only survive in the presence of dazzling glory if we were being transformed into that same substance. So that, says the New Testament, is exactly what God does in us. We aren't invited just to 'get religious', to turn over a new leaf. This is nothing short of 'new birth' – the reintroduction of the presence of God turning us into radically different people. With the barriers gone, God comes to live in us. We share in what was gained when God-in-Christ died – which means we can share in his resurrection, 'in order that, just as Christ was raised from the dead by the glory of the Father, we too may live a new life'.[72] There is something deeply corrupt at the roots of our personality, and it cannot be reformed (hence the powerlessness of human religiosity); it simply has to be amputated. At that moment when we are 'born of the Spirit', our 'old self' actually dies, insists Paul, and its place is taken by a new identity shaped by the Spirit.[73] It will take many years of remoulding, reshaping and healing for that new identity to penetrate every area of our values and attitudes and emotions; indeed, the full process won't be completed this side of death. But at least now it can start; and only that in us which is transformed into the radical new nature from the Spirit will survive into God's eternal universe.

This is radical, original Christian faith. 'Repent and believe the good news', declared Jesus. On the day of Pentecost, 50 days after his resurrection, his followers preached the same basis for hope: 'Repent, and be baptized, every one of you, in the name of Jesus Christ' – the submergence of baptism[74] being the cathartic expression Christ had established of the absolute commitment of faith – 'for the forgiveness of your sins. And you will receive the gift of the Holy Spirit.' Paul's message was the same, as we have seen – 'I have declared to both Jews and Greeks that they must turn to God in repentance and have faith in our Lord Jesus.'[75]

Turning to God in *metanoia,* 'repentance': recognizing before him all I have done wrong, and above all my attempts at autonomy from God; turning to him, determined to abandon all wrongdoing, and make him central again, in a confession of Christ as absolute Lord of my whole being.[76] Believing the good news: that God has stepped in, that there is forgiveness and a new order through Christ's death, that the barrier is swept away; *'faith in our Lord Jesus'* – staking every aspect of my existence on my conviction that he will keep his promise to forgive, that he will indeed enter, forever, into my life by his transforming Spirit. Consciously inviting his genuine presence: 'If anyone hears my voice and opens the door', promises Christ, 'I will go in and eat with him, and he with me ... I am come that they may have life, and have it to the full.'[77] So, faith that Christ will henceforth be there forever, as father, brother, lover, king: identity, direction, relationship, truth, hope.

Real faith is relational, outward-directed. It is not mere 'self-realization', or finding some abstract 'integration point' for its own sake. Jesus actually said that 'Whoever finds his life will lose it'. The quest to 'find myself' and for abstract 'meaning in life' can be self-centred, inward-bound, a decoy away from relationship and transformation. It is, instead, the person who 'loses their life for my sake' that will 'find it', Jesus continued.[78] We live for God's glory, not he for our fulfilment – but that way lies joy. The Father ('undoubtedly the most joyous being in the universe'[79]) is real, and is the Lord at the heart of the cosmos; we are built for his presence, and any apparent substitute is, ultimately, a fatal narcotic rather than food. In the end, nothing else will be enough for us, and what we try to deify – to put in God's place – we merely destroy, as we have seen. Augustine had it right fifteen hundred years ago: 'Thou hast made us for thyself, and never will our hearts find rest until they find their rest in thee.'

The end of emptiness; this is what being 'born again of the Spirit' first meant, and it's vital to understand that if we're to grasp the Christian stance in the contemporary crisis. If radical Christianity has anything to offer, then Christ's challenge to Nicodemus is central to it. The intellectual pose that deigns merely to approve of Christ, and incorporate that approval into an analysis, will get us nowhere. What the new millennium demands is power that can offer some genuine transformation. The Christian asserts, with the French philosopher Pascal, that there is indeed a space in human beings in the shape of God, and that that space must be filled in very actuality if things are to begin to be put right. Jesus' challenge has to be taken seriously. It is only 'new birth', with the reintroduction of the presence of God, that can begin to produce radically 'new humanity'.

Which brings us, somewhat circuitously, to Prince Philip and Che Guevara.

The renewal deficit

The issue of power for transformation is a major one as the new millennium begins.

'It's inevitable that very grave damage is going to be done to this world in the next hundred years', Britain's Prince Philip told

Woman's Own a while ago. What could be done? 'Search me. I don't know. The older I get, the more cynical I get, in the sense that I just think things are going to get worse. I mean, there was a period in this country when you could leave your car unlocked, your front door open, when you could trust anybody across the social scale. Now you can't even trust your neighbour.' Or, as someone else has said: we've made it possible for a man to walk safely across the moon; we can't make it possible for a woman to walk safely across London (or Marseilles, or New York, or Berlin).

Crisis faces us on so many fronts. 'Green' issues have grown in importance in the last few years as we've realized what the hole in the ozone layer, global warming, and the death of the oceans will mean. With that awareness come fear and a deep sense of powerlessness: the sense that 'very grave damage' is indeed being done by structures far beyond our influence or control. Yet even the new environmental awareness might seem essentially self-centred; it seems we have reacted far more strongly to these issues than to the appalling realities we have known for years to be crippling the vast majority of the world. For example: 250,000 children will go permanently blind this year for lack of a daily vitamin A capsule worth a few pence, or a daily handful of green vegetables. Twelve million children die each year – over a thousand each hour – from common diseases or malnutrition, most of whom could be saved at very little cost; two million die from diarrhoea, for example, for whom a solution of eight parts sugar to one part salt in clean water is all that is needed. Over a thousand women each day die in childbirth (a process 150 times more dangerous in the two-thirds-world than in the west) for lack of nutrition or trained medical personnel.[80] The poorest nations have cut their health spending by a half and their education spending – for example on literacy, the key to so many fundamental life possibilities – by a quarter over recent years, to pay the interest on their huge debts to the west.[81] (Meanwhile, a high proportion of our own scientists and engineers expend their talents on the creation of ever more destructive weapons; and that's also how we spend the taxes that could genuinely transform African health systems.[82]) We might wonder how many women, widows especially, will take the step into prostitution this year because it is that or starvation for their families; or how many desperate parents will sell their children into slave labour or sexual exploitation in the brothels of cities like Bangkok for the same reason.[83]

'It's hopeless. That's my view. I believe there's no chance of the world coming to other than a very grisly end in twenty-five years at the outside. Unless God, as it were, finally speaks. Because reason is not going to do anything ... Finally it's hopeless. There's nothing one can achieve.'

–Harold Pinter

It cries out for change. It cries out for something that can actually take the people with the money and power and turn them into people who care for the poor (and the planet); equally, that will take the people with the skills and resources and send them to pour out what they have where the needs are greatest – both in the emergency zones and inside the crucial decision-making structures. But what power could do that in people's hearts today? How to turn me-generation yuppies inside out, into 'new people' who are genuinely serious about real self-giving, and will take at least the first steps towards some real transformation?

The question has been on the agenda in the best parts of the 'New Age', 'deep green', and feminist movements. And also on the left, though with a tragic record of failure;[84] 'If our revolution does not have the goal of changing men it doesn't interest me', Che Guevara remarked. But if (as the majority of the human race has always affirmed) there is a personal God, then logically it would be in that direction that we should look first for power for such fundamental surgery and re-creation. If (as we can consider for ourselves) there is solid, factual reason to believe that in Christ God actually broke the old order of defeat and entropy, and proved it by the tangible reality of the resurrection; then this is the kind of 'new birth' that must be available.

What kind of 'new life', based on the rediscovery of God's genuine presence, might we expect to follow?

Paths of transformation

One of the key issues dividing radically biblical Christians from nominal European religion has long been the radicals' insistence that faith's goal isn't merely to produce nicer people (nor, certainly, to 'give comfort in troubled times'). Rather, it is to bring to birth dramatically *new* people, whose life centres on the presence of God, and invest effort in an entirely 'new kingdom'.

Precisely this was the vision of Jesus' immediate followers. Paul defines the point of it all in a thought-provoking section of his most 'central' letter, Romans: 'Those God foreknew, he also predestined to be conformed to the image of his Son.'[85] Life isn't meaningless, he's saying; rather, God has lovingly 'foreknown' and orchestrated ('predestined') all the life-circumstances of each person who responds to the 'new birth', like a brilliant symphonist or dramatist. If we've given ourselves to his purposes, then the meaninglessness stops; every friendship, every anguish, every book or encounter or learning experience, is now growing together into a design of unimaginable, long-term transformation. (That doesn't mean believers are now 'better people' than not-yet-believers; but it does mean God is at work restoring broken people, and believers have stepped out into the restoration process.) And the Father's aim in this is to sculpture, in each of us, something unimaginably glorious: an identity so 'transformed into Christ' that eventually *all* the love, peace, joy, and power for goodness of Jesus start flowing out through us. (The apostle Peter talks about our 'participating in the divine nature'; John's vision is that 'when he appears, we shall be like him.'[86]) It's a tough thought for our intellects to seize; for most of us it will take an enormous amount of doing ... yet the power guaranteeing it is that which formed the universe out of nothing. Paul tells the Galatians he is 'in the pains of childbirth until Christ is formed in you'.[87] His goal echoes the vision we saw in Genesis, of man and woman created as a visible expression of God's nature – and now that begins to be consummated at last. Indeed, Paul goes further: the aim isn't just to make us 'like' Christ (until we've grasped what Jesus is like, that might sound a trifle dull), but actually to see 'Christ formed in you', to make us 'in' Christ, to unite us with the eternal glory, living in him and he living in us; what Paul gets really enthusiastic about is the 'glory that will be revealed *in* us'.[88]

Really knowing God, really being changed, really being unified with his glory. Following Jesus isn't just about being nicer, or having a series of 'moral values'; rather, it's about passion and worship, about reuniting with the purpose we were made for, a purpose extending far beyond our planet and its transient history. Nor is Paul inviting us merely to some private mystical ecstasy. In the same passage (Romans 8) he looks out across a whole cosmos groaning in futility, enslaved to laws of decay. And he knows, both from his own unique experiences[89] and from the proven fact of the resurrection, of the intrusion into this world's tragedy by an alternative order;[90] knows there is a different reality available. It is a new heaven and new earth, characterized not by the sad, deterministic cycles of entropy where everything winds down and falls apart, but by that alternative principle which Paul had spelled out three pages earlier: 'Grace reigns!' *Grace* – God's passionate love bringing something out of nothing; the God who once spoke creatively to bring light out of darkness, working actively, lovingly and creatively still.

Precisely this is what we see Jesus announcing and demonstrating, very practically, in one of the most famous and challenging parts of the New Testament. He began his public activity by declaring that a whole new order, the 'kingdom of heaven', was now within reach (Matthew 4:17). And he embodied it: 'Jesus went throughout Galilee teaching ... preaching the good news of the kingdom, and healing every disease and sickness among the people. News about him spread all over Syria, and people brought to him all who were ill with various diseases, those suffering severe pain, the demon-possessed, those having seizures, and the paralysed, and he healed them' (4:23–24). And then, just as 'large crowds' were turning out, thinking that God's reign 'on earth as it is in heaven' (6:10) might be quite a pleasant diversion, Jesus sat them down (5:1–2) and began to explain that joining that 'kingdom' involves following him (4:19–22) into deep transformation far beyond their own ability to achieve, a lifestyle based on radical overturning of all the old system's values.

Speed-reading the first five chapters of Mark's Gospel is a good way to grasp the nature of the 'kingdom' Jesus announces. Chapter 1 chronicles his first astonishing advance, where Jesus reveals his power to put things right in the face of ignorance, sickness and demons. Chapter 2 expresses the kingdom's joyous positiveness (2:19,22,23–28; 3:4–6), the way its love has strength to draw in the excluded (2:16–17). Then, after the kingdom's initial rejection in chapter 3 and its explanation in chapter 4, comes a further section revealing its power in action – triumphant over destructive nature, demonic evil, even death itself (4:35–5:43). We also watch Christ bringing purpose to individuals (1:16–20; 2:13–17), astonishing the villagers with huge new vistas of truth (1:27,38) and bringing joyous liberation ('new wine') from the constrictions of false religion ('old wineskins', 2:21–28). The 'good news' is firstly about forgiveness of sins (2:5), because dealing with that blockage is the gateway to everything else; but through this gateway a whole glorious new order floods in. Where Christ comes, the kingdom comes, and the kingdom reveals the heart of God: bringing truth where there was falsehood, love where there was hate, healing where there was pain, wholeness where there was brokenness.

Above all what Jesus brings is *goodness*. Reading how the new creation bursts into our world in these chapters, aren't we reminded of the repeated refrain describing God's handiwork in Genesis 1: 'And God saw that it was *good*'?

'Blessed are the poor in spirit', he said, those who realize they haven't 'got it sorted'. 'Blessed are those who mourn', who are deeply frustrated with the evil in themselves and in the world; 'Blessed are those who hunger and thirst for righteousness', because they will see the new kingdom, they 'will be filled' (Matthew 5:3–6). Jesus' alternative order centres on values about which the crumbling old system is utterly sceptical. He spells them out uncompromisingly: radical commitment to reconciliation, purity, total marital faithfulness, trustworthiness, generosity, refusal of revenge ('Love your enemies') (5:21–48). First, though, he simply declares, 'Blessed are the merciful ... blessed are the pure ... blessed are the peacemakers'. The 'pure' (the 'naïve'?) – those who miss out on all the fun? The 'peacemakers' (ditto the 'naïve'?) – who end up getting hated by both sides? Yes, said Jesus (who himself would end up crucified) – blessed, even, are those who get persecuted for the new order, 'for theirs *is* the kingdom of heaven'. Heaven's order is already here, embodied within all who commit themselves to its Lord – like grains of salt (5:13), tiny, yet flavouring, even preserving, what's around them; facing ridicule, opposition, even outright hatred, but nonetheless pursuing what is the only way to live, because it reflects the dynamic of the 'real', eternal world.

So the new universe of heaven doesn't stay (as Graham Greene once wrote) 'rigidly on the other side of death';[91] rather it begins to erupt into our world. To return to Paul in Romans 8:

> I consider that our present sufferings are not worth comparing with the glory that will be revealed in us. The creation waits in eager expectation for the sons of God to be revealed. For the creation was subject to frustration ... in hope that the creation itself will be liberated from its bondage to decay and brought into the glorious freedom of the children of God. We know that the whole creation has been groaning as in the pains of childbirth right up to the present time. Not only so, but we ourselves, who have the firstfruits of the Spirit, groan inwardly as we wait ...[92]

So from its human bridgehead ('firstfruits'), the freedom of the new resurrection order must flood out across a dying creation. As Jesus promised: '*Whoever* believes in me ... streams of living water will flow from within him' – that life-giving water being, as John immediately explains, the supernatural energy of the Holy Spirit.[93] If it isn't so, our faith isn't real.[94] True, our world's transformation will not even approach completion without the direct intervention of God himself (indeed the biblical material speaks of history closing in a final, nightmarish crisis, where the logic of our alienation from God culminates in domination by a dictator entirely given to evil[95]). But Christ's followers are called to be agents and footholds of the future transformation. The Spirit's energy that starts to flow within us, Paul affirms repeatedly, is a 'deposit, guaranteeing what is to come';[96] living, life-giving water flowing – trickling or gushing – out into a desert world; the point where God's new order breaks in right now.

Visionary stuff. But what does it all actually mean?

It means, first of all, that 'new birth' is not just a mental adjustment, to be reflected in a more accurate tax return, a tendency not to kick the dog and a newfound interest in attending church services. It means an absolute reversal of the loss of the presence of God that we have considered throughout this book. It means a new identity as a 'child of God', and a passionate commitment to express in practical action the love and truth of Christ. It means an all-consuming purpose, summed up in Paul's paean of longing:

> Whatever was to my profit I now consider loss for the sake of Christ. What is more, I consider everything as loss compared to the surpassing greatness of knowing Christ ... I want to know Christ and the power of his resurrection and the fellowship of his sufferings, becoming like him in his death, and so, somehow, to attain to the resurrection of the dead.[97]

Indeed, the Way of the crucified Christ in the west's disintegration may easily involve that 'fellowship of his suffering'; in apparent abnormality or real 'loss' (promotion, sexual fulfilment, status), in association with unpopular causes or minorities, we may be called to 'know' more deeply the Christ nailed up between heaven and earth. The cross was where Christ absorbed the evil from the world, as with a sponge; his people are called likewise to break the patterns of self-perpetuating evil by going the way he so radically taught – forgiving, refusing to retaliate, being truthful, outdoing evil with generosity.[98] (Hence the centrality of the celebratory meal of communion that refocuses us on the cross – bread symbolizing Christ's body broken for us, wine his blood poured out.) And, as they set out to do so, to experience more of his resurrection strength: 'Whoever loses his life for my sake will find it', promised Jesus uncompromisingly.[99] Transformation is grounded in the cross: 'We ... are always being given over to death for Jesus' sake', says Paul, 'so that his life' – Jesus' presence and reality – 'may be revealed in our mortal body'.[100] Heaven starts to break in – or break loose – now.

What is 'knowing Christ'? The New Testament points us to at least seven key aspects, involving thoroughly un-mystical, down-to-earth activity.[101] The first challenge is to learn a genuine, ever-deepening *relationship* with Christ: day by day to 'know' – absorb – more of his supernatural love for others, more of his energy and presence. It's not just about a sterner moral muscle or better attempts to be nice, but rather a directly personal power in place within us that enables us, choice by choice, to forgive and apologize and mend relationships, to care and to communicate, to work for radical change, to discipline our own egos. 'You will receive power when the Holy Spirit comes on you', said Jesus, because being 'born again ... of the Spirit' is the way we enter his family.[102] Obviously our availability to someone who can be called the '*Holy* Spirit' implies a life continually grounded on a hunger for holiness. But on that basis, we are told we can ask with assurance for more and more of his presence. 'Which of you fathers, if your son asks for a fish, will give him a snake instead?' asked Jesus. 'If you then, though you are evil, know how to give good gifts to your children, how much more will your Father in heaven give the Holy Spirit to those who ask him!'[103]

There is a vital link between this and our immersion in the *Bible*. Paul describes exactly the same things as marks of someone 'filled with the Spirit' and of someone who has 'let the word of Christ dwell in you richly'.[104] Jesus taught that the Scriptures had a unique status, unlike any other words: 'The words I have spoken to you are Spirit and they are life' – not just symbolic expressions for the presence of God, but that presence itself.[105] To read them in the presence of God is to meet God; as Chesterton said, a Jesus-follower is like someone who is 'always expecting to meet Plato or Shakespeare tomorrow at breakfast'.[106] What we read embodies the 'living and enduring' Word of God that is (as the apostle Peter puts it) God's 'imperishable' seed within us – the point where his new, undecaying order breaks through.[107] Paul makes clear that it is in the practical experience of in-depth Bible reading that we grow renewed, 'transformed into his likeness with ever-increasing glory, which comes from the Lord, who is the Spirit.'[108] Time in God's presence is, to borrow a phrase of Eliot's, the 'still point of the turning world': the gateway for the grace and the strength of God.

Such transformation takes place within relationship. So, as God speaks to us through his Word, we respond directly in *prayer* and in *worship*. A deepening vision of what God is like draws out a response in love and thanksgiving; a deepening perspective on the situations around us draws out a response in prayer, God's primary means whereby the transforming powers of heaven are released into this world.[109] And, unless we are just trying to play games with our faith, there will be many other results from this encounter, in terms of gradual but genuine changes in our own thought-patterns and lifestyle. Prayer involves learning to perceive situations as God does, and receiving the strength to respond as he would. 'Be transformed', says Paul, 'by the renewing of your mind.'[110]

> Recently I was in a moment where I did not want to trust God. Something others were doing seemed to have every potential to wreck some very good things and cause a great deal of pain to people who had

suffered enough already. And now the possibility arose of viewing things through faith – living by faith that the love of God was seeing and working – choosing, therefore, to forgive and to act accordingly, rather than manipulating and descending into grubby, egoistic machinations myself. Or, alternatively, to stay on the track I was on, my mind turning repeatedly to pointless frustration, resentment and fruitless bitterness. And isn't this the way the vital choice comes? There is a crucial moment of recognizing the possibility of response to the divine initiative, the moment when grace is, as it were, dangled in front of you. You see things, momentarily, as they are; and you have to welcome it, obey it, let it lift you up; to choose.

Central to all this is our participation in *community*. In Paul's letter to the Ephesians he prays that 'you, being rooted and established in love, may have power *with all the saints* to grasp how wide and long and high and deep is the love of Christ.'[111] Half a page later he emphasizes that, in '*each* one of us' in the believing community, the Spirit's presence is expressed in a unique 'gift', and that the whole body only 'grows and builds itself up in love' as '*each* part does its work' enabling all its fellow-members for 'works of service'.[112] We are all 'designed' to function within a local, diverse community of women, men and children with the same vision, passion and desire. Such communities can be found, if we look hard enough for places where ordinary people really are absorbed with Jesus – not perfect, and needing to grow in all kinds of ways, but real. And in such a community, nobody is ever dispensable; if God is present in each, then everybody has their unique and essential contribution.

By definition, a new community that lives for the purposes God has planned for humanity cannot exist for itself. Any community partly embodying the life of a God who 'so loved the world that he gave his one and only Son' must actively 'love the world' in its lostness, in a similar passion of self-giving. The monastic impulse is therefore a snare; the church isn't a fortress into which the faithful retreat from a darkening world, but rather a loving army on the road. Christ-followers are called to be spiritual guerrillas, planting time-bombs of joy, gentleness and truth, of 'senseless acts of random generosity'; spiritual microbes, tiny and negligible, yet collectively empowered to infect the egoistic cultures of this age with totally different life, as bridgeheads where the new order of heaven can unexpectedly break through. From 'new women and men' who are slowly being mended and reshaped, truth and love and power for goodness must flow, to use Jesus' image again, like living water into a desert. That is the purpose of the church in this world.

So two final ingredients we may list here are total commitment to *mission* – taking God's presence and 'good news' and practical love wherever on our planet there is darkness or hatred or pain; and *vocation* – the life-stance basing all its key decisions on a sense of God's calling. For the teacher, homemaker, pastor, foreman, vocation means consciously mobilizing all God has given – home, time, job choice, use or acquiring of possessions – for his purposes; for what increases the flow of respect, love, truth and justice that express him; for what enables others to be fed and housed and healed, and introduced themselves to the life of Christ's kingdom. If the loss of God really is a key to what is happening in our world, then we have an enormous amount to work on. Our own faith develops as we see how 'big' the 'good news' is, speaking across the range of humanity's challenges and touching their deepest roots; that it isn't shrivelled, colourless, small, powerless; that God is indeed the Sun holding each of us in our orbits, and his love alone brings everything else into place. Faith grows as we see that Jesus was right: if we seek first God's kingdom, everything else will follow[113] – for we've learnt that the alternative leads to insoluble problems. There can be answers, some genuine transformation that we can be involved in; a love and a hope that reward our confidence; the possibility of joy.

But this transformation must go far beyond the merely intellectual. For myself, I believe deeply that the contemporary crisis triggered by our alienation from God is such that – though our primary motive must always be God himself – still anything less than a passionate commitment to knowing God and making God and his kingdom known begins to constitute, at this time, a betrayal of humanity.

As we look at our world's situation, it seems that nothing short of a Jesus in every city is needed. Indeed, if the Bible is right, there are deep sicknesses in our situation that cannot be cured by anything less than God's direct intervention. In the meantime, however, 'proto-Christs' in every street is precisely the plan: God's people, with all their vices and weaknesses, slowly being remoulded and changed (God's church is a hospital where broken people get mended), so that, little by little, they can be footholds for his love and supernatural power, far more than their weaknesses would merit. (After all, we don't earn what God gives us. Rather, he is the creative one always offering, and able, to 'do more than all we ask or imagine'.[114]) All and each of us can choose to be a point where the transformation starts. God chooses the 'foolish things of the world to shame the wise', insists Paul; 'he chose the weak things of the world to shame the strong ... the lowly things of this world and the despised things ... to nullify the things that are.'[115] The one miracle-story told in all four Gospels is the 'feeding of the five thousand', maybe in part because it makes this point: if Christ is present, his love can take one kid with five loaves and two fishes, and divine power can surge through that bridgehead to feed an entire multitude.

An early signal of communism's fall was Mikhail Gorbachev's unexpected citation of that story. 'Only Jesus Christ knew all the answers to all the questions and could feed twenty thousand Jews with five loaves of bread', he remarked to an astonished audience, adding, 'We do not possess such miraculous power and have no ready-made answers.' It was true: Gorbachev's subsequent career made his lack of power for real transformation depressingly plain.[116] But it isn't only Russia that is dying now from that incapacity. In the west, too, we face issue after issue where the absence of that power is the cause. All of us, at the start of the new millennium, are a perilously long way from Eden.

The story goes ...

Jesus said: 'There was a man who had two sons. The younger one said to his father, "Father, give me my share of the estate." So he divided his property between them. Not long after that, the younger son got together all he had, set off for a distant country, and there squandered his wealth in wild living.

After he had spent everything, there was a severe famine in that whole country, and he began to be in need. So he went and hired himself out to a citizen of that country, who sent him to his fields to feed pigs. He longed to fill his stomach with the pods that the pigs were eating; but no-one gave him anything.

When he came to his senses, he said, "How many of my father's hired men have food to spare, and here I am starving to death! I will set out and go back to my father and say to him: Father, I have sinned against heaven and against you. I am no longer worthy to be called your son; make me like one of your hired men." So he got up and went to his father.

But while he was still a long way off, his father saw him and was filled with compassion for him; he ran to his son, threw his arms around him and kissed him. The son said to him, "Father, I have sinned against heaven and against you. I am no longer worthy to be called your son."

But the father said to his servants, "Quick! Bring the best robe and put it on him. Put a ring on his finger and sandals on his feet. Bring the fattened calf and kill it. Let's have a feast and celebrate. For this son of mine was dead and is alive again; he was lost, and is found." So they began to celebrate.[119]

Turning our back on the Father. Autonomy; exile; identity, from affluence; then loss. Comprehending the Father's absence: alienation, purposelessness, foolishness; a long way from home. Self-knowledge. Repentance, return. The Father running, almost bursting with joy. Unexpected welcome. The ring, with its seal of authority – acceptance, belonging, recommissioning, creative action. The party begins. Celebration. Life.

Christ's cross is now empty; the price has been paid for our forgiveness, the alienating barrier is gone. His burial-place is empty also; the concrete historical sign that the way back – the way forward – stands open to all of us. The absence is over; transformation is possible.

Anyone coming home?

Notes

1. Excellent starting points for exploring the reasons for faith include Norman Anderson's *Jesus Christ: The Witness of History* on the central historical issues; Roger Forster and Paul Marston's wide-ranging *Reason, Science and Faith*, or their popular-level *Christianity, Evidence and Truth*; or Moreland's more philosophical *Scaling the Secular City*.
2. John 8:43; cf. v. 47.
3. John 6:44.
4. 2 Corinthians 4:4.
5. 1 Corinthians 2:14.
6. 2 Peter 3:5. Cf. also Paul's comment about our choosing not to 'retain the knowledge of God' (Romans 1:28). In Jesus' story in Luke 16:31, Abraham tells the rich man in hell that his brothers' state of mind was such that they would not be convinced even if someone was to rise from the dead.
7. 2 Corinthians 4:6.
8. An additional point is made both by Jesus and the writer of Hebrews, that only a certain kind of being will ultimately be capable of 'seeing God', will have (as it were) the sensory ability necessary. This is implicit in the innocent statements 'Blessed are the pure in heart, for they will *see God*' (Matthew 5:8) and 'Without holiness no one will *see the Lord*' (Hebrews 12:14). There is no point in our complaining that if we saw God we would believe in him, if we are keeping ourselves incapable of such seeing. But who desires 'purity in heart' in our era?
9. Luke 15:3–7; Matthew 7:7.
10. Rebecca Manley Pippert offers what may be an even more logical experiment: 'Tell God (or the four walls if that is the one you think you are speaking to) that you want to find out if Jesus is truly God. And that if you could feel more certain you would follow him. Then begin to read the Gospels, every day. Each day as you read, something

will probably hit you and make sense. Whatever that is, do it as soon as you can.' And then see what happens. Again, this takes us out beyond the merely cerebral; so real relationship can begin (*Out of the Saltshaker*, p. 97; and see Jesus' promise in John 7:17).

11. As does our reaction to the related idea that we may have reason for deep gratitude to God. Again, St Paul points to the refusal of thankfulness as a fundamental element in human alienation (Romans 1:21), in our determination to maintain the illusion of our self-sufficiency. Lundin suggests that 'Ingratitude, and its attendant resentment, are distinguishing attributes of much of contemporary literary and cultural theory' (*The Culture of Interpretation*, p. 103). In this respect, the simple prayer 'Give us this day our daily bread' has real significance as a deliberate expression of grateful dependence.

12. Moreland remarks tentatively, 'Although I cannot prove it, I suspect that atheists fit a more tightly defined group than do theists, and it may be that other factors which help to define the class of atheists (for example, absent or passive fathers) may be key psychological causes for why people embrace atheism' (*Scaling the Secular City*, p. 229).

13. 'Opened the door' isn't quite the whole story; many Christians would add that even our praying in this way is a response (conscious or unconscious) to God beginning to speak into our thinking. But that is another matter.

14. Moreland observes that in most of our knowledge-assertions we do not supply full criteria for our claims. If we had to do that, then it would involve 'asserting that I know the criteria are true ones and before I could make *that* claim, I would need criteria for my first criteria, and so on to infinity. This would lead to a vicious infinite regress such that I could never know anything. But I *do* know some things (e.g., that I had breakfast this morning)' (*Scaling the Secular City*, p. 116, building on Roderick Chisholm, *The Problem of the Criterion*). Faith has to come in somewhere if we are to 'know' anything at all.

15. Science, too, involves an irreducible element of faith. Moreland observes a number of basic assumptions, including: 'Science must assume that the mind is rational and that the universe is rational in such a way that the mind can know it. Science must assume some uniformity of nature to justify induction (i.e., science must assume that one can legitimately infer from the past to the future and from

examined cases to unexamined ones of the same kind) ... Science also assumes that the laws of logic are true, that numbers exist ... that language has meaning, and that some terms refer to things in the world ... These and other presuppositions are necessary to ground science as a rational discipline which gives us approximate truth about the world. But these are philosophical assumptions or brute givens which cannot themselves be verified by science itself without begging the question' (*Scaling the Secular City*, pp. 198–99).

16. Colin Brown, *Philosophy and the Christian Faith*, p. 266.

17. John 1:39.

18. Quoted in Roger Hurding, *Roots and Shoots: A Guide to Counselling and Psychotherapy*, p. 80.

19. This deep uncertainty was despite the fact that a curious experience some years previously had shown a sense of God's reality to be rooted extraordinarily deeply in my own psyche. We lose touch with such intuitions at times of doubt.

20. This is more likely to be meaningful if it is first- or second-hand. However, ch. 9 of Forster and Marston's earlier book *Reason and Faith* offers some striking reflections on the miraculous in the life of the contemporary church. With regard to the specifically 'medical' dimension, Rex Gardner's *Healing Miracles* is an in-depth study by a Fellow of the Royal College of Obstetricians and Gynaecologists; see also *Healing* by anthropologist David Lewis.

21. Or its unique ability to foretell the future some centuries ahead – particularly the details of the life, death and resurrection of Jesus. See, e.g., the prophetic passages listed in ch. 9 of McDowell, *Evidence*.

22. John 6:66–68.

23. Even atheistic sociobiologist E.O. Wilson, in the opening section of *The Diversity of Life*, writes of the wonders of the Amazon rainforest in these terms: 'From such a place the pious naturalist would send long respectful letters to royal patrons about the wonders of the new world as testament to the glory of God. And I thought: there is still time to see this land in such a manner.'

24. A key aspect of C.S. Lewis' most complex narrative, *Till We Have Faces*, concerns the central figure Orual's rejection of the vision of the gods' palace, and the way that, having rejected it, she can only 'veil' her consciousness in busyness ('I did, and I did, and I did'), until the gods rip the veil away, and she again faces them 'bareface'.

25. Even to say 'North Atlantic' may be to overstate the prevalence of materialism. Elward Ellis, an African-American working for InterVarsity Christian Fellowship, wrote in *In Touch* that most African-Americans 'have a sort of ontological awareness of God, so apologetics for us needn't start with the existence of God. That God was always a given.' The issue in their context, he added, is where the saving power of that God is being encountered in practical reality: 'What did you confront that you could not contend with in your own resources? In what way did God bring you out?'

26. Quoted in Colin Brown, *Christianity and Western Thought*, p. 57.

27. Brown, *Christianity*, p. 352. It is striking that the 'apologetic' content of the *Qur'an* seems directed entirely at making clear the truth of monotheism as against polytheism. For Muhammad's culture, atheism was evidently almost inconceivable.

28. Brown, *Christianity*, p. 153. Even communism could not exclude the intuition of the supernatural. Throughout Russian culture, communism turned into a religion: whether we think of Mayakovsky's well-known slogan (parodying the New Testament) 'Lenin was, Lenin is, Lenin will be'; or the mausoleum in Red Square where Lenin's embalmed body was kept as close as Marxism could manage to resurrection; or the trinitarian, icon-like pictures of Marx, Engels and Lenin that adorned room after room of Soviet universities. Mao has 'become a god', a Chinese taxi man told an *International Herald Tribune* reporter, 'pointing to the Mao portrait that dangled like an amulet from his rear-view mirror … In some areas, a third or more of vehicles bear the portrait, and throughout China stories buzz of people surviving miraculously from terrible accidents because of their Mao photos … Mao may be the first atheist to have become a god.'

29. See, e.g., the massive statistical base in David B. Barrett, ed., *World Christian Encyclopaedia*.

30. In fact, our practically 'de-supernaturalized worldview' isn't the 'whole truth' even about our own perceptions. Even in the North Atlantic region, most people still 'believe' in God in some way. Various recent surveys have reported figures of around 70% in Britain, 90% in the USA, 85% among Canadian youth, 69% in France. (Obviously such surveys don't involve a high degree of definition of 'God', nor distinguish a purely abstract belief or intuition from a living and lived-out faith.) A particularly interesting study

of students in Leeds University, England, showed 55% believing in God – even though the respondents themselves expected such a belief to be very much a minority view.

31. This is one reason why modern science arose in a Protestant cultural context marked by faith in such a Law-maker – as against, say, the culture of ancient China, which was highly inventive but grounded in a very different world-view. This may also be why so many of the early scientific pioneers were Christians. Cf. R. Hooykaas, *Religion and the Rise of Modern Science*.

32. For a good introduction to Intelligent Design theory, see the symposium edited by William Dembski titled *Mere Creation*. Contributors include Michael Behe, David Berlinski, five-time Nobel Prize nominee Henry Schaefer III and others.

33. Paul Davies, *God and the New Physics*, p. 189, concluding a chapter on the topic. Moreland summarizes the evidence succinctly in pp. 52–53. The alternative seems to be a cosmos developing endlessly into multiple new universes (that is, everything that can happen does, along with every possible combination of physical laws, until the 'lottery' turns up a workable set) – an astonishingly prolific and unexplained generation of universes in a supposedly 'empty' cosmos that seems harder to believe in than a God. Daniel Dennett, in his militantly atheistic though very readable study *Darwin's Dangerous Idea*, brings his chapter on this topic to a lame conclusion: '*Why is there something rather than nothing?* Opinions differ on whether the question makes any intelligible demand at all. If it does, the answer "Because God exists" is probably as good an answer as any, but look at its competition: "Why not?"' (pp. 180–81).

34. Quoted by Dennett, *Darwin*, p. 164. Hoyle is well known as a father of 'steady-state' theory. As we noted in Ch. 7, he has argued (e.g. in *Evolution from Space*) that the evolutionary process is so problematic that it must have been supervised by higher intelligence – though he then opts for an extra-terrestrial intelligence rather than God. However, an intelligence capable of reworking the physical laws is not far short of divinity. If evolution is true, the idea that so much has come in such circumstances from so incredibly little might seem to demand God?

35. From the close of the *Dialectic of Pure and Practical Reason*.

36. Francis Schaeffer, *The God Who is There*, p. 110, cf. pp. 28–29.

37. Roger Forster, *Saturday Night ... Monday Morning*, pp. 16–17. Cf. also Alexander: 'Many years ago I was struggling with whether

God existed; I had heard and weighed all the rational arguments, and I was getting nowhere. Then one night walking alone in Switzerland, I saw the moon reflecting off the snow on the mountaintops, and I saw (or rather I felt) God in those works and in myself. It was an intuitive grasp of the invisible background of what I could see with my eyes' (*Secular Squeeze*, p. 86).

38. Romans 1:4, Matthew 12:38–40, John 2:18–22.
39. See Michael Green's remarks in *Man Alive*, p. 33.
40. Acts 5:28; cf. John 11:48, or the parallel problem when the new faith reached Ephesus in Acts 19:40.
41. This is the only hostile explanation the Gospels seem aware of (cf. Matthew 28:11–15), and is the one Justin Martyr has to face in his encounter with the sceptic Trypho a century later; Tertullian, in his apologetics a few decades later; and Origen in his debate with Celsus later still in the third century. It is also the explanation repeated in the medieval Jewish *Toledoth Jesu*.
42. 1 Corinthians 15:1–8. Anderson gives an excellent treatment of these issues.
43. Such 'forgers of the resurrection' would have faced massive internal struggles as well as external. The early church abandoned the Jewish Sabbath to begin holding its worship on a Sunday, because of the resurrection, which happened on the 'first day of the week'. But neglect of the Sabbath, in the Old Testament, was itself sufficient cause for God's judgement to fall. And they risked that judgement for what they knew was a lie?
44. The difference between the Gospel appearances and Revelation 1, when John really does have a vision of the risen Christ, will be obvious to any reader of the two.
45. Obviously we cannot review the truth-claims of the major world religions in any responsible manner here. This book has been concerned with the meaning of the loss of God in the west; this final chapter is therefore designed to explore the meaning of Christian faith in response to that loss. To assess the truth-claims of Islam, for example, one would examine the *Qur'an*, just as this chapter encourages the exploration of the New Testament. (Of course, if indeed Jesus is uniquely God the Creator incarnate, as he claimed, then that has implications for the completeness of all other religious truth-claims.)
46. If we become Christ's disciples ourselves, we may indeed conclude that that involves adopting his attitude to the Scriptures (cf. Wenham, *Christ and the Bible*); but this comes later.

47. A useful survey is Paul Barnett, *Is the New Testament History?* Barnett includes helpful treatments of issues such as the extensive quotation of the Gospels in other very early writers, and the massive quantity of manuscript evidence available compared with that for the transmission of other standard historical sources such as Josephus or Tacitus. See also his ch. 5 on the importance, in that culture, of not being a 'false witness'.

48. Luke 1:1–4. Luke had ample motivation to check the historical facts with care; he travelled with Paul, and saw first-hand the price – and pain – of serious discipleship to Christ.

49. Quoted in Anderson, *Jesus Christ*, p. 39.

50. Consider also the way the evil figure of JR completely dominated *Dallas*.

51. Cf. C.S. Lewis, *Fern-seed and Elephants*, p. 108. Lewis is building on Erich Auerbach's classic study of European fiction, *Mimesis*.

52. As Moreland observes (*Scaling the Secular City*, p. 143), there is in the New Testament a strong emphasis on the careful passing on of the Gospel tradition: e.g. 1 Corinthians 15:3–8; Galatians 2:1–21; Colossians 2:7; 1 Thessalonians 2:13. His whole chapter on New Testament historicity repays careful study.

53. Christ's claims can also be demonstrated even from the texts accepted by the most sceptical school of biblical scholars; cf. Moreland, *Scaling the Secular City*, p. 155.

54. A further, most un-contemporary, point would be Jesus' apparent ability to work miracles. This means little for us; but Quadratus, in one of the earliest apologias to the Roman Emperor, appealed to the fact that, of those healed or raised from the dead by Christ, some were still alive, and all were well known (Alfred Edersheim, *Life and Times of Jesus the Messiah*, iii.20).

55. Quoted in McDowell, *Evidence*, p. 111.

56. Forster and Marston have a thought-provoking chapter on how Christ fulfilled the prophetic expectations set out throughout the Old Testament: *Christianity, Evidence and Truth*, ch. 7.

57. John 3:1–2.

58. Isaiah 40.

59. Mark 1:15.

60. Matthew 5:8.

61. 1 Timothy 6:16.

62. This uncompromising recognition is another of the key insights marking authentic, radical Christian belief off from nominal European religiosity.

63. Isaiah 33:14. Chapters 1 to 5 of Paul's letter to the Romans are the classic New Testament expression of these issues – of our lostness and God's response – and they climax at the start of chapter 5: 'Therefore, since we have been justified by faith, we have peace with God ... and we rejoice in hope of the glory of God!' Only when we have grasped why peace with God was an issue will we comprehend why the cross was necessary. (Many people who wear crosses have no idea what it was for ...)

64. 2 Thessalonians 1:9.

65. Matthew 23:37.

66. Revelation 11:18 describes the last judgement as when God will 'destroy those who destroy the earth'.

67. Paul sees thanklessness as the root of our inability to think straight. 'For although they knew God, they neither glorified him as God nor gave thanks to him, but their thinking became futile' (Romans 1:21).

68. Romans 6:23.

69. James 1:17.

70. Cf. the quotations from the Eden narrative in the description of the final 'city' at the very end of the Bible: Revelation 22:1–3.

71. 2 Corinthians 5:18–20.

72. Romans 6:3–4.

73. Cf. Romans 6:3–6; 8:1–16; 2 Corinthians 5:17; Galatians 2:20; Colossians 3:1–4.

74. Acts 2:38. 'Baptism' derives from the Greek word for 'immerse', 'dip' or 'submerge'. In its original form, then, complete submergence in water, followed by re-emergence, expressed the believer's total self-identification with Jesus' death and resurrection. It was not merely a mental doctrinal assent, but a body-and-soul commitment to the cross and resurrection as the pattern for one's own life. As anyone who has experienced it can testify, it can be quite an emotional event – it was designed to be.

75. Acts 20:21.

76. Romans 10:9.

77. Revelation 3:20; John 10:10.

78. Matthew 10:39.

79. From a marvellous passage about God in Dallas Willard, *The Divine Conspiracy*, p. 72.

80. Poverty statistics obviously involve an element of uncertainty since they are sometimes drawn from countries with severely damaged

infrastructures. A good source of in-depth information is www.oneworld.net. Thanks too to Eric Miller of IFES Media.

81. Zambia, for example, by no means one of the worst cases, spends more on servicing its debts to the west than it does on health and education combined. Uganda has been spending £2 per person per year on health, and £11.50 on debt relief.

82. And less than 1% of what the world spends on weapons would be enough to put every child worldwide into school.

83. It's been estimated that up to a million children each year are sold as sex slaves in south-east Asia. Thailand alone has 800,000 child prostitutes, according to UNESCO.

84. Mao's rule in China saw an extended attempt to move from a culture where work was stimulated by material incentives – self-interested personal, financial gain – to one motivated by moral incentives, that is, the good of the people. 'At no time and in no circumstances should a Communist place his personal interests first: he should subordinate them to the interests of the masses', declared Mao's Little Red Book; real individual transformation was to follow from the communist restructuring of society. Mao's anti-rightist campaigns (especially the calamitous 'cultural revolution') were among other things assertions of the primacy of 'moral incentives'. But what history records is the self-interest, power-lust and failure of the radical-left 'Gang of Four' who were closest to the aging Mao. Russia has had the same experience; Solzhenitsyn's Shelub says, in *Cancer Ward*, 'We thought it was enough to change the mode of production and immediately people would change as well. But did they change? The hell they did!'

85. Romans 8:29. The whole chapter is an important one to grasp if we want to understand Christianity. It builds, of course, on the restoration of the broken relationship with God in chapters 1–5.

86. 2 Peter 1:4; 1 John 3:2.

87. Galatians 4:19.

88. Romans 8:18; see also 2 Thessalonians 1:10; 2:14; and Colossians 1:27, where Paul summarizes the heart of his entire message as 'Christ in you, the hope of glory'. Christ, the 'Bridegroom', and his community, the 'Bride', are so unified that when we finally see the ultimate expression of that community ('the holy city ... the Bride', Revelation 21) it actually 'shines with' (embodying, rather than viewing externally) 'the glory of God'. All of which, Paul adds

elsewhere, speaks to the meaning and centrality of love, marriage and sex to human experience; in them we catch, enact, a life-giving symbol of how utterly God loves and unites himself with the 'Bride' with whom he longs to share the experiences of eternity (Ephesians 5:25–32; 2:6–7). (A profound treatment of these themes is the Chinese writer Watchman Nee's *What Shall This Man Do?*)

89. Cf. 2 Corinthians 12:1–4.

90. Romans 8:11.

91. Graham Greene, *The Heart of the Matter*, p. 36.

92. Romans 8:18–23. Or, as the apostle Peter insists in a parallel passage (1 Peter 1:23–25): the possibility exists of us being 'born again, not of perishable seed, but of imperishable' – beyond the reach of the Fall, of decay – 'through the living and enduring word of God. For "All men are like grass, and all their glory is like the flowers of the field; the grass withers and the flowers fall, but the word of the Lord stands for ever." And this is the word that was preached to you' – something implanted in us that is a bridgehead of the 'imperishable' new universe.

93. John 7:38–39. Again, this emphasis on an active God, rather than a mere presupposition of belief, is a key feature distinguishing radical, original Christianity from secularized religiosity. Paul warns strongly against 'having a form of godliness but denying its power' (2 Timothy 3:5).

94. John, for example, emphasizes repeatedly in his first epistle that if we don't love others we aren't children of God at all; so does James 2:14–26. Jesus makes a similar point in Matthew 6:14–15 with regard to personal issues and 25:31–46 with regard to broader ones.

95. See, e.g., 2 Thessalonians 2, Matthew 24:21–22, and much of Revelation, e.g. 13:11–18.

96. 2 Corinthians 1:22, 5:5; Ephesians 1:14.

97. Philippians 3:7–11.

98. Cf. Jesus' teaching further on in the Sermon on the Mount on turning the other cheek and going the second mile (Matthew 5:38–48). Other key issues he focuses on (ch. 6) are freedom (through faith) from materialism, prayerfulness, seriousness, and consistency of life. The image of the cross absorbing evil is from the French sociologist Jacques Ellul.

99. Matthew 11:39.

100. 2 Corinthians 4:11. For both Paul and Peter, suffering and glory seem indivisible (e.g. Romans 8:17–18; 2 Corinthians 4: 7–18; 1 Peter 1:6–7,11; 4:13–14; 5:1,10). Christ, too, seems to use being 'glorified' as a description of his death (John 12:23–24,28,32–33; 13:31–32).

101. An ideal handbook for the new follower of Jesus wanting to grow in practical discipleship is John White's *The Fight*.

102. Acts 1:8; John 3:3–6. In Romans 8:9 Paul makes clear that everyone who belongs to Jesus receives the Holy Spirit.

103. Luke 11:13. The continual verb in Paul's exhortation 'Be filled with the Spirit' (Ephesians 5:18) makes clear this is a frequent (daily?) process of repentance and trusting request.

104. Cf. Ephesians 5:18–20 ('Speak to one another with psalms, hymns and spiritual songs. Sing and make music in your heart to the Lord, always giving thanks to God the Father for everything') with Colossians 3:15–17.

105. John 6:63. The explicatory comment is Anfin Skaaheim's.

106. Quoted in Pippert, *Saltshaker*, p. 101.

107. 1 Peter 1:23–25. Cf. Pete Lowman, *Gateways to God*.

108. Cf. 2 Corinthians 3:14–18.

109. In Romans 8:24–27, after the passage we cited earlier, Paul introduces prayer in terms of the difficulties of learning to be 'first-fruits' or bridgeheads of the new kingdom in a very broken world. In such a context, prayer becomes the channel opening the way for the powers of transformation, for heaven to come on earth, just a little bit more: 'Your kingdom come, your will be done on earth as it is in heaven.'

110. Romans 12:2.

111. Ephesians 3:17–18. By 'saints' Paul simply meant all the believers; the use of this word for some special elite was a later development, as the church lost its confidence in the possibility of direct access for every believer to God. Natural human religion prefers to keep God at a distance, to have someone special who will relate to him for us. But that's not what we were created for.

112. Ephesians 4:7,12,16; cf. 1 Corinthians 12:7,14–27.

113. Matthew 6:33.

114. Ephesians 3:20.

115. 1 Corinthians 1:27–28.

116. One of the striking realities about the coming of *glasnost* to Russia in the early '90s was that freedom is not enough. Without

power for internal transformation, freedom becomes a space for the gangster, the pimp, the pornographer and the hyper-capitalist profiteer to pursue their exploitation unhindered; a space where the weak are at the mercy of the exploitation of the powerful. That may increasingly be true of the ethically-bankrupt west as well.

117. Luke 15:11–24.

bibliography

Alexander, John F., *The Secular Squeeze* (Downers Grove: InterVarsity Press, 1992)

Anderson, Norman, *Jesus Christ: The Witness of History* (Leicester: Inter-Varsity Press, 1985)

Auerbach, Erich, *Mimesis* (Princeton: Princeton University Press, 1953 tr. edn.)

Barber, Lynn, *The Heyday of Natural History* (New York: Doubleday, 1980)

Barker, Paul (ed.), *Arts in Society* (London: Fontana, 1977)

Barnett, Paul, *Is the New Testament History?* (Carlisle: Paternoster, 1998 edn.)

Barrett, David B. (ed.), *World Christian Encyclopaedia* (Oxford: Oxford University Press, 1982)

Barrett, William, *Death of the Soul* (New York: Doubleday, 1986)

Barth, Karl, *Protestant Theology in the Nineteenth Century* (London: SCM Press, 1972)

Barthes, Roland, *Image – Music – Text* (London: Fontana, 1977 tr.edn.)

Baudrillard, Jean, *Simulations* (New York: Semiotext(e), 1983 tr.edn.)

—, *Symbolic Exchange and Death* (London: Sage, 1993 tr.edn.)

Behe, Michael, *Darwin's Black Box* (New York: Simon and Schuster, 1996)

Blackaby Henry, and King, Claude, *Experiencing God* (Nashville: Broadman, 1994)

Blair, Tony, *New Britain* (London: Fourth Estate, 1996)

Bloom, Allan, *Love and Friendship* (New York: Simon and Schuster, 1993)

—, *The Closing of the American Mind* (New York: Simon and Schuster, 1987)

Bloom, William (ed.), *The New Age: An Anthology of Essential Writings* (London: Rider, 1991)

Bloor, David, *Knowledge and Social Imagery* (Chicago: University of Chicago Press, 1976)

Bockmuehl, Klaus, *The Challenge of Marxism* (Leicester: Inter-Varsity Press, 1980)

Boulton, James T., and Andrew Robertson (eds.), *The Letters of D.H. Lawrence*, vol. III (Cambridge: Cambridge University Press, 1984)

Brazeau, Raymond, *An Outline of Contemporary French Literature* (Toronto: Forum, 1971)

Brown, Ann, *Apology to Women* (Leicester: Inter-Varsity Press, 1991)

Brown, Colin, *Christianity and Western Thought*, vol. I (Leicester: Inter-Varsity Press, 1990)

—, *Philosophy and the Christian Faith* (Leicester: Inter-Varsity Press, 1969)

Brzezinski, Zbigniew, *Out of Control* (New York: Scribner's, 1993)

Burke, Carl, *God is For Real, Man* (London: Fontana, 1967)

Cahoone, Lawrence (ed.), *From Modernism to Postmodernism* (Cambridge, MA: Blackwell, 1996)

Camus, Albert, *The Outsider* (London: Penguin, 1971, tr. edn.)

Capra, Fritjof, *The Turning Point* (Toronto: Bantam, 1982)

Carey, John, *The Intellectuals and the Masses* (London: Faber, 1992)

Carson, Don, *The Gagging of God* (Leicester: Apollos, 1996)

Catherwood, Fred, *It Can Be Done* (Cambridge: Lutterworth, 2000)

Chamberlain, Paul, *Can We be Good Without God?* (Downers Grove: InterVarsity Press, 1996)

Chandler, Russell, *Understanding the New Age* (Milton Keynes: Word, 1989 edn.)

Chapman, Colin, *Christianity on Trial* (Tring: Lion, 1981)

Chisholm, Roderick, *The Problem of the Criterion* (Milwaukee: Marquette University Press, 1973)

Clark, Kenneth, *Civilisation* (London: Penguin, 1982 edn.)

Clemo, Jack, *The Invading Gospel* (London: Lakeland, 1972 edn.)

—, *Wilding Graft* (London: Anthony Mott, 1948)

Cockett, Monica and John Tripp, *The Exeter Family Study: Family Breakdown and its Impact on Children* (Exeter: University of Exeter Press, 1994)

Cole, Michael, *What is the New Age?* (London: Hodder and Stoughton, 1990)

Collin, Matthew, *Altered State* (London: Serpent's Tail, 1998 edn.)

Cosgrove, Mark P., *Psychology Gone Awry* (Leicester: Inter-Varsity Press, 1982)

Coupland, Douglas, *Generation X* (New York: St. Martin's Press, 1991)

—, *Life After God* (London: Simon and Schuster, 1994)

Crabb, Lawrence, *Inside Out* (Aylesbury: NavPress, 1988)

—, *The Marriage Builder* (Grand Rapids: Zondervan, 1982)

Culler, Jonathan, *Barthes* (London: Fontana, 1983)

Cutsinger, James S., *Reclaiming the Great Tradition* (Downers Grove: InterVarsity Press, 1997)

Davies, Paul, *God and the New Physics* (London: Penguin, 1983)

Dembski, William (ed.), *Mere Creation* (Downers Grove: InterVarsity Press, 1998)

Dennett, Daniel, *Darwin's Dangerous Idea* (London: Penguin, 1995)

Derrida, Jacques, *Of Grammatology* (Baltimore: John Hopkins University Press, 1974 tr.edn.)

Dixon, Patrick, *The Rising Price of Love* (London: Hodder and Stoughton, 1995)

Docherty, Thomas, ed., *Postmodernism: A Reader* (Hemel Hempstead: Harvester Wheatsheaf, 1993)

Doney, Malcolm, *Summer in the City* (Tring: Lion, 1978)

Dooyeweerd, Herman, *In the Twilight of Western Thought* (Nutley, NJ: Craig Press, 1960)

Dostoevski, Fyodor, *The Possessed* (London: Penguin, 1953 tr.edn.)

Eco, Umberto, *Foucault's Pendulum* (London: Secker and Warburg, 1989 tr.edn.)

—, *The Name of the Rose* (London: Secker and Warburg, 1983 tr.edn.)

Edersheim, Alfred, *Life and Times of Jesus the Messiah* (London: Longmans, 1900)

Edwards, Michael, *Towards a Christian Poetics* (London: Macmillan, 1984)

Elkind, David, *The Hurried Child* (London: Addison-Wesley, 1989)

Ellul, Jacques, *Violence* (London: SCM Press, 1970)

Evans, C. Stephen, *Preserving the Person* (Leicester: InterVarsity Press, 1977)

Ferguson, Marilyn, *The Aquarian Conspiracy* (Los Angeles: J.P. Tarcher, 1980)

Fitzgerald, F. Scott, *The Great Gatsby* (London: Penguin, 1950 edn.)

Ford, Kevin, *Jesus for a New Generation* (Downers Grove: InterVarsity Press, 1995)

Forster, Roger, *Saturday Night ... Monday Morning* (Leicester: Inter-Varsity Press, 1980)

Forster, Roger and Paul Marston, *Reason, Science and Faith* (Crowborough: Monarch, 1999)

—, *Christianity, Evidence and Truth* (Crowborough: Monarch, 1995)

Foster, Richard, *Money, Sex and Power* (London: Hodder and Stoughton, 1985)

Fromm, Erich, *The Sane Society* (New York: Rinehart, 1956)

Gardner, Rex, *Healing Miracles* (London: Darton, Longman and Todd, 1986)

Glicksberg, Charles I., *Literature and Religion* (Dallas: Southern Methodist University Press, 1960)

Gooding, David, *According to Luke* (Leicester: Inter-Varsity Press, 1987)

Green, Michael, *Man Alive* (Leicester: Inter-Varsity Press, 1968)

Greene, Graham, *The Heart of the Matter* (London: Penguin, 1971 edn.)

Groothuis, Douglas, *Confronting the New Age* (Downers Grove: InterVarsity Press, 1988)

—, *Unmasking the New Age* (Downers Grove: InterVarsity Press, 1986)

Guinness, Os, *The Dust of Death* (Leicester: Inter-Varsity Press, 1973)

Hare, R.M., *Moral Thinking* (Oxford: Oxford University Press, 1981)

Hartland-Swan, John, *An Analysis of Morals* (London: George Allen and Unwin, 1960)

Hawkes, Terence, *Structuralism and Semiotics* (London: Methuen, 1977)

Hazard, Paul, *The European Mind, 1680–1715* (London: Penguin, 1964 edn.)

Hendin, Herbert, *The Age of Sensation* (New York: Norton, 1975)

Hitler, Adolf, *Mein Kampf* (London: Pimlico, 1992 tr.edn.)

Hoffman, Frederick J. (ed.), *The Great Gatsby: A Study* (New York: Scribner's, 1962)

Hooykaas, R., *Religion and the Rise of Modern Science* (Edinburgh: Scottish Academic Press, 1972)

Hoyle, Fred, and Wickramasinghe, Chandra, *Evolution from Space* (London: Dent, 1981)

Hurding, Roger, *Roots and Shoots: A Guide to Counselling and Psychotherapy* (London: Hodder and Stoughton, 1985)

Jameson, Fredric, *Postmodernism, or The Cultural Logic of Late Capitalism* (Durham: Duke University Press, 1991)

Jasper, Tony, *Jesus and the Christian in a Pop Culture* (London: Robert Royce, 1984)

Jencks, Charles, *What is Post-Modernism?* (London: Academy Editions, 1986)

Johnson, Phillip, *Darwin on Trial* (Downers Grove: InterVarsity Press, 1993 edn.)

Kafka, Franz, *The Trial* (London: Penguin, 1994 tr.ed.)

Kaufmann, Walter (ed. and tr.), *The Portable Nietzsche* (London: Penguin, 1959 edn.)

Keyes, Richard, *Beyond Identity* (Carlisle: Paternoster, 1998)

Kristeva, Julia, *The Kristeva Reader* (Cambridge, MA: Blackwell, 1986 tr.edn.)

LaHaye, Tim, *The Act of Marriage* (London: Marshall Pickering, 1984)

Lasch, Christopher, *The Culture of Narcissism* (New York: Warner, 1979)

Leach, Penelope, *Baby and Child* (London: Penguin, 1989 edn.)

Lewis, C.S., *Christian Reflections* (London: Fontana, 1981 edn.)

—, *Fern-seed and Elephants* (London: Fontana, 1975)

—, *Mere Christianity* (London: Fontana, 1972 edn.)

—, *God in the Dock: Essays in Theology and Ethics* (Grand Rapids: Eerdmans, 1970)

—, *The Four Loves* (London: Fontana, 1960 edn.)

—, *Surprised by Joy* (London: Fontana, 1959 edn.)

—, *Till We Have Faces* (London: Geoffrey Bles, 1956)

—, *The Great Divorce* (London: Geoffrey Bles, 1946)

Lewis, David, *Healing* (London: Hodder and Stoughton, 1989)

Lowman, Peter, *Gateways to God: Seeking Spiritual Depth in a Post-Modern World* (Fearn: Christian Focus, 2001)

—, 'Supernaturalistic Causality and Christian Theism in the Modern English Novel' (unpublished PhD thesis, University College, Cardiff, 1985)

Lundin, Roger, *The Culture of Interpretation* (Grand Rapids: Eerdmans, 1993)

Lyall, Leslie, *New Spring in China* (London: Hodder and Stoughton, 1979)

Lyon, David, *Karl Marx* (Tring: Lion, 1979)

Macaulay, Ranald and Jerram Barrs, *Being Human* (Carlisle: Solway, 1996)

MacDonald, Alan, *Films in Close-Up* (Leicester: Inter-Varsity Press, 1991)

Macdonald, Ian, *Revolution in the Head: the Beatles' Records and the Sixties* (London: Pimlico, 1995 edn.)

MacIntyre, Alasdair, *Whose Justice? Which Rationality?* (London: Duckworth, 1988)

—, *After Virtue* (London: Duckworth, 1985 edn.)

—, *A Short History of Ethics* (London: Routledge and Kegan Paul, 1967)

MacLaine, Shirley, *Dancing in the Light* (New York: Bantam, 1986)

—, *It's All In the Playing* (New York: Bantam, 1987)

Mangalwadi, Vishal, *India: the Grand Experiment* (Farnham: Pippa Rann, 1997)

Markham, Ian, *Truth and the Reality of God* (Edinburgh: T and T Clark, 1998)

Marquez, Gabriel Garcia, *One Hundred Years of Solitude* (London: Cape, 1970 tr.edn.)

Martin, Charles, *How Human Can You Get?* (Leicester: Inter-Varsity Press, 1973)

McClung, Floyd, *The Father Heart of God* (Eastbourne: Kingsway, 1985)

McDowell, Josh, *Evidence that Demands a Verdict* (Arrowhead Springs, CA: Campus Crusade for Christ, 1972)

McGrath, Alister, *Roots that Refresh: A Celebration of Reformation Spirituality* (London: Hodder and Stoughton, 1991)

Middleton, J. Richard and Brian Walsh, *Truth Is Stranger Than It Used to Be* (Downers Grove: InterVarsity Press, 1995)

Miller, Elliot, *A Crash Course on the New Age Movement* (Crowborough: Monarch, 1990)

Moreland, J.P., *Scaling the Secular City* (Grand Rapids: Baker, 1994)

Morrison, Wayne, *Jurisprudence: From the Greeks to Postmodernity* (London: Cavendish, 1997)

Nee, Watchman, *What Shall This Man Do?* (Eastbourne: Kingsway, 1961)

Noddings, Nell, *Caring: A Feminine Approach to Ethics and Moral Education* (Berkeley: University of California Press, 1984).

Nouwen, Henri, *Seeds of Hope* (London: Darton, Longman and Todd, 1998 edn.)

—, *Aging: The Fulfilment of Life* (New York: Doubleday, 1974)

Parfit, Derek, *Reasons and Persons* (Oxford: Oxford University Press, 1991 edn.)

Patterson, James and Kim, Peter, *The Day America Told the Truth* (New York: Dutton Plume, 1991)

Peters, Dan, and Peters, Steve, *Why Knock Rock?* (Minneapolis: Bethany, 1984)

Phillips, Melanie, *All Must Have Prizes* (London: Little, Brown, 1997 edn.)

Phillips, Timothy R., and Dennis L. Okholm (eds.), *Christian Apologetics in the Postmodern World* (Downers Grove: InterVarsity Press, 1995)

Pinter, Harold, *Plays: Two* (London: Faber, 1977)

Pippert, Rebecca Manley, *Out of the Saltshaker* (Downers Grove: InterVarsity Press, 1979)

Posterski, Don, *Friendship* (Scarborough: Project Teen Canada, 1985)

Postman, Neil, *Amusing Ourselves to Death* (London: Methuen, 1987 edn.)

Ramachandra, Vinoth, *Faiths in Conflict?* (Leicester: Inter-Varsity Press, 1999)

—, *Gods that Fail* (Carlisle: Paternoster, 1996)

Regis, Jr., E. (ed.), *Extraterrestrials* (Cambridge: Cambridge University Press, 1985)

Rookmaaker, H.R., *Modern Art and the Death of a Culture* (Leicester: Inter-Varsity Press, 1970)

Rorty, Richard, *Objectivity, Relativism and Truth* (New York: Cambridge University Press, 1991)

—, *Contingency, Irony and Solidarity* (New York: Cambridge University Press, 1989)

—, *Consequences of Pragmatism* (Brighton: Harvester, 1982)

Rose, Steven, *Life Lines* (London: Penguin, 1988 edn.)

Ruse, Michael, *The Darwinian Paradigm* (London: Routledge, 1989)

Sartre, Jean-Paul, *Existentialism and Humanism* (London: Methuen, 1968 tr.edn.)

—, *Nausea* (London: Penguin, 1965 tr.edn.)

Satin, Mark, *New Age Politics* (New York: Dell, 1978)

Schaeffer, Edith, *Affliction* (London: Hodder and Stoughton, 1978)

—, *Hidden Art* (London: Norfolk, 1971)

Schaeffer, Francis, *How Should We Then Live?* (London: Lakeland, 1980 edn.)

—, *True Spirituality* (London: STL, 1979)

—, *Back to Freedom and Dignity* (London: Hodder and Stoughton, 1973)

—, *Escape from Reason* (Leicester: Inter-Varsity Press, 1968)

—, *The God Who Is There* (London: Hodder and Stoughton,1968)

Schultze, Quentin, et al., *Dancing in the Dark: Youth, Popular Culture and the Electronic Media* (Grand Rapids: Eerdmans, 1991).

Sider, Ronald, *Completely Pro-Life* (Downers Grove: InterVarsity Press, 1987)

Singer, Peter, ed., *A Companion to Ethics* (Cambridge, MA: Blackwell, 1993 edn.)

Singer, Peter, ed., *Ethics* (Oxford: Oxford University Press, 1994)

Sire, James, *The Universe Next Door* (Downers Grove: InterVarsity Press, 1988 edn.)

Skinner, B.F., *Beyond Freedom and Dignity* (London: Penguin, 1972)

Smalley, Gary, *Love is a Decision* (Milton Keynes: Word, 1989)

Steiner, George, *Real Presences* (London: Faber, 1989)

—, *George Steiner: A Reader* (London: Penguin, 1984)

—, *In Bluebeard's Castle* (London: Faber, 1971)

—, *The Death of Tragedy* (London: Faber, 1961)

Stern, J.P., *Nietzsche* (London: Fontana, 1978)

Stoppard, Miriam, *The New Baby Care Book* (London: Dorling Kindersley, 1990 edn.)

Stott, John, *God's New Society: The Message of Ephesians* (Leicester: Inter-Varsity Press, 1979)

—, *Christ the Controversialist* (Leicester: Inter-Varsity Press, 1970)

Studd, C.T., *Fool and Fanatic*, ed. Jean Walker (Bulstrode: WEC, 1980)

Sturrock, John, *Structuralism and Since* (Oxford: Oxford University Press, 1979)

Tada, Joni Eareckson, *Joni* (London: Marshall Pickering, 1976)

Tawney, R.H., *Religion and the Rise of Capitalism* (London: John Murray, 1926)

Taylor, Charles, *Sources of the Self: The Making of the Modern Identity* (Cambridge: Cambridge University Press, 1989)

Taylor, Paul W., *Respect for Nature: A Theory of Environmental Ethics* (Princeton: Princeton University Press, 1986)

Tinker, Melvin (ed.), *The Anglican Evangelical Crisis* (Fearn: Christian Focus, 1995)

Tozer, A.W., *The Knowledge of the Holy* (Carlisle: OM Publishing, 1987 edn.)

Trobisch, Walter, *Love Yourself: Self-Acceptance and Depression* (Downers Grove: InterVarsity Press, 1976)

Turner, Steve, *Hungry for Heaven* (London: Hodder and Stoughton, 1995 edn.)

—, *Up to Date* (London: Hodder and Stoughton, 1983)

Vanhoozer, Kevin, *Is There a Meaning in This Text?* (Leicester: Apollos, 1998)

Vitz, Paul, *Psychology as Religion: The Cult of Self-Worship* (Carlisle: Paternoster, 1994 edn.)

Vonnegut, Kurt, *Cat's Cradle* (London: Penguin, 1963)

Watson, David, *Fear No Evil* (London: Hodder and Stoughton, 1984)

Watson, John B., *Behaviourism* (London: Kegan Paul, 1930)

Watt, Ian, *The Rise of the Novel* (London: Penguin, 1957)

Wellings, Kaye, et al., *Sexual Behaviour in Britain* (London: Penguin, 1994)

Wenham, D., and France, R.T. (eds.), *Gospel Perspectives,* vol III (Sheffield: JSOT Press, 1983)

Wenham, John, *Christ and the Bible* (London: Inter-Varsity Press, 1972)

White, Armond, *Rebel for the Hell of It: the Life of Tupac Shakur* (London: Quartet, 1997)

White, John, *The Fight* (Leicester: Inter-Varsity Press, 1976)

Willard, Dallas, *The Divine Conspiracy* (London: Fount, 1998)

Wilson, Colin, *The Outsider* (London: Pan, 1956)

Wilson, Edward O., *The Diversity of Life* (London: Penguin, 1994)

—, *On Human Nature* (Cambridge, MA: Harvard University Press, 1978)

—, *Sociobiology: The New Synthesis* (Cambridge, MA: Harvard University Press, 1975)

Wilson, James Q., *The Moral Sense* (New York: Free Press, 1993)

Wimsatt, W.K., and Beardsley, Monroe, *The Verbal Icon* (London: Methuen, 1954)

Zacharias, Ravi, *Can Man Live Without God?* (Milton Keynes: Word, 1994)

Zaehner, R.C., *Our Savage God* (New York: Sheed and Ward, 1974)

index